JOHN BELL
OF TENNESSEE

JOHN BELL OF TENNESSEE
From a photograph by Whitehurst Gallery, Washington, D.C.
(date unknown).

John Bell of Tennessee

By

JOSEPH HOWARD PARKS

Louisiana State University Press

BATON ROUGE

PRINTED IN THE UNITED STATES OF AMERICA
BY THE VAIL-BALLOU PRESS, INC., BINGHAMTON, N. Y.

To
My Father

PREFACE

John Bell was truly a Tennessean; he lived his entire life in that state. From 1817 to 1861 he was almost continuously in public life. After 1827 he was a party to most of those national controversies which seriously threatened the Union. His views were generally those of a conservative nationalist, but in the end, when there seemed no longer any ground upon which such a conservative could stand, he followed his state into the Confederacy. He became a rebel, but not a secessionist. A full-length study of Bell's contributions and influence has long been due. It is hoped that this biography will supply that need.

Those who do research are always indebted to the courteous staffs of the nation's major depositories of information. Most sincere thanks are herewith expressed to the staffs of the Library of Congress, Tennessee State Library, Lawson McGhee Library of Knoxville, Cossitt Library of Memphis, Tennessee Historical Society Collection, Buffalo Historical Society Collection, Peabody Institute of Baltimore, Nashville Public Library, and the Libraries of Duke University, University of North Carolina, University of Tennessee, and Vanderbilt University.

The author is also indebted to many individuals for their kind assistance in locating and securing copies of Bell letters and other useful items. In this connection thanks are due to G. E. Bell, Dallas, Texas; Charles Bell, Murfreesboro, Tennessee; J. G. deRoulhac Hamilton, University of North Carolina; Holman Hamilton, Fort Wayne, Indiana; Miss Martha Ellison, Knoxville; Glyndon G. Van Deusen and John R. Russell, University of Rochester; R. N. Williams, the Historical Society of Pennsylvania; Francis L. Berkeley, University of Virginia; Paul North Rice, New York Public Library; Mrs. Julia H. McLeod, Henry E. Huntington Library; Miss Dorothy Barck, New York Historical Society; Mrs. W. H. Knox, Nashville; and Mrs. Harry B. Howard, Harry B. Howard, Thomas R. Sills, and Robert F. Sexton, Dover, Tennessee. Special notes of appreciation are due Professor Henry T. Shanks, Birmingham Southern College, and Professor Robert D. Highfill, Mercer University, for their critical reading of the manuscript. Professors William C. Binkley, Vanderbilt University, Stanley J. Folmsbee, University of Tennessee, and Dan M. Robison, Vanderbilt University, gave valuable suggestions on select chapters. Professor T. Harry Williams, Louisiana State University, editor of the Southern Biography Series, and the general editorial staff of the Louisiana State University Press have been generous with their time and patience, contributing greatly to the improvement of this study.

Generous grants-in-aid from the Social Science Research Council, Birmingham Southern College, and the Committee on Carnegie Grants helped to finance the research connected with this study. For this assistance I am grateful.

JOSEPH H. PARKS

Birmingham, Alabama
March 25, 1949

CONTENTS

ILLUSTRATIONS

Chapter I

ON MILL CREEK

IN 1781 an invading British army was sweeping victoriously through South Carolina. At Eutaw Springs on September 8 an American force under General Nathanael Greene tried to halt the redcoats. With Greene was a company under the command of Captain Robert Bell. During the battle Bell was in effect the commander of a regiment since the French regimental commander, unable to speak effective English, relied heavily upon him. Following the engagement General Greene, in a letter to Governor Richard Caswell of North Carolina, made special mention of the meritorious service rendered by Captain Bell.[1]

A native of Caswell County, North Carolina, Robert Bell had moved to Guilford County prior to the Revolution and settled "about nine miles" from Guilford Courthouse. He had married Catherine Walker, probably in the early 1760's, and had become the father of six children [2] before his wife died early in the 1770's. He later married Mary Boyd and sired thirteen more children.[3] Following the Revolution he and his brother Samuel joined the throng of emigrants who moved into central Tennessee. Robert's first home in Tennessee is said to have been north of the Cumberland River in

[1] John Bell to ?, December 6, 1844, printed in Jonesborough (Tennessee) *Whig*, February 19, 1845; G. E. Bell to Tennessee Historical Commission, July 6, 1925, in Bell File, Tennessee State Library.

[2] Mary (1763–1827), Samuel (1766–1836), Ann (1768–1860), Robert, Jr. (1770–1853), Catherine (1770–1857), and an unnamed child who died in infancy.

[3] John, James, Hugh, Thomas, Francis, William, David, Nathaniel, Daniel, Abraham, Rebecca, Sarah, and Jane. Davidson County Wills and Inventories, Book 7, pp. 77–78; Genealogical Records, in possession of G. E. Bell, Dallas, Texas.

Sumner County.[4] Sometime during the 1790's he moved to Davidson County, settling on Mill Creek, a short distance southeast of Nashville, where he had previously located North Carolina grants for several hundred acres of land.[5]

The land in the Mill Creek area was fertile and well adapted to cotton culture. A small acreage was already in cultivation. And John Hague, an enterprising Englishman, was attempting to utilize the community's raw material by establishing a cotton factory at a point which he designated as Manchester. In an advertisement in the Knoxville *Gazette* on November 4, 1791, Hague stated that machinery had already been installed and weavers were urgently needed.[6] This experiment in frontier manufacturing failed, and the town of Manchester never materialized.[7] One cause for this failure was the Indian menace which kept the settlers in constant fear. During 1792–1793, Cherokee, Creeks, and Shawnee, hundreds strong, struck the central Tennessee settlements. The principal stations on Mill Creek were able to withstand the attack but the loss of life and property was considerable. The general plight of the settlers was such that Andrew Jackson, who had recently arrived in the Cumberland section, reported that the "Country is Declining fast." Unless Congress furnished better protection "this Country will have at length to break or seek a protection from some other Source than the present." [8] No substantial relief came until a band of enraged

---

[4] There seems to be no record of the place of his residence. In 1794 a Robert Bell and his wife Margaret purchased a tract of land on Drake's Creek. This could not have been the same Bell; his wife was named Mary. Sumner County Deeds, Book 1, p. 80.

[5] General John Bell to ? , n.d., in Richard Beard, *Brief Biographical Sketches of Early Ministers of the Cumberland Presbyterian Church* (Nashville, 1874), 114–17; see Index to Davidson County Deeds, 1784–1871.

[6] The 1791 volume of this early newspaper is in the possession of the Tennessee Historical Society.

[7] For interesting material on this experiment, see Samuel C. Williams, "The South's First Cotton Factory," in *Tennessee Historical Quarterly* (Nashville), V (1946), 212 ff.

[8] Andrew Jackson to John McKee, May 16, 1794, in John Spencer Bassett (ed.), *The Correspondence of Andrew Jackson* (Washington, 1926–1935), I, 12–13.

Chapter I

ON MILL CREEK

IN 1781 an invading British army was sweeping victoriously through South Carolina. At Eutaw Springs on September 8 an American force under General Nathanael Greene tried to halt the redcoats. With Greene was a company under the command of Captain Robert Bell. During the battle Bell was in effect the commander of a regiment since the French regimental commander, unable to speak effective English, relied heavily upon him. Following the engagement General Greene, in a letter to Governor Richard Caswell of North Carolina, made special mention of the meritorious service rendered by Captain Bell.[1]

A native of Caswell County, North Carolina, Robert Bell had moved to Guilford County prior to the Revolution and settled "about nine miles" from Guilford Courthouse. He had married Catherine Walker, probably in the early 1760's, and had become the father of six children [2] before his wife died early in the 1770's. He later married Mary Boyd and sired thirteen more children.[3] Following the Revolution he and his brother Samuel joined the throng of emigrants who moved into central Tennessee. Robert's first home in Tennessee is said to have been north of the Cumberland River in

[1] John Bell to ?, December 6, 1844, printed in Jonesborough (Tennessee) *Whig*, February 19, 1845; G. E. Bell to Tennessee Historical Commission, July 6, 1925, in Bell File, Tennessee State Library.

[2] Mary (1763–1827), Samuel (1766–1836), Ann (1768–1860), Robert, Jr. (1770–1853), Catherine (1770–1857), and an unnamed child who died in infancy.

[3] John, James, Hugh, Thomas, Francis, William, David, Nathaniel, Daniel, Abraham, Rebecca, Sarah, and Jane. Davidson County Wills and Inventories, Book 7, pp. 77–78; Genealogical Records, in possession of G. E. Bell, Dallas, Texas.

Sumner County.[4] Sometime during the 1790's he moved to Davidson County, settling on Mill Creek, a short distance southeast of Nashville, where he had previously located North Carolina grants for several hundred acres of land.[5]

The land in the Mill Creek area was fertile and well adapted to cotton culture. A small acreage was already in cultivation. And John Hague, an enterprising Englishman, was attempting to utilize the community's raw material by establishing a cotton factory at a point which he designated as Manchester. In an advertisement in the Knoxville *Gazette* on November 4, 1791, Hague stated that machinery had already been installed and weavers were urgently needed.[6] This experiment in frontier manufacturing failed, and the town of Manchester never materialized.[7] One cause for this failure was the Indian menace which kept the settlers in constant fear. During 1792–1793, Cherokee, Creeks, and Shawnee, hundreds strong, struck the central Tennessee settlements. The principal stations on Mill Creek were able to withstand the attack but the loss of life and property was considerable. The general plight of the settlers was such that Andrew Jackson, who had recently arrived in the Cumberland section, reported that the "Country is Declining fast." Unless Congress furnished better protection "this Country will have at length to break or seek a protection from some other Source than the present." [8] No substantial relief came until a band of enraged

---

[4] There seems to be no record of the place of his residence. In 1794 a Robert Bell and his wife Margaret purchased a tract of land on Drake's Creek. This could not have been the same Bell; his wife was named Mary. Sumner County Deeds, Book 1, p. 80.

[5] General John Bell to ? , n.d., in Richard Beard, *Brief Biographical Sketches of Early Ministers of the Cumberland Presbyterian Church* (Nashville, 1874), 114–17; see Index to Davidson County Deeds, 1784–1871.

[6] The 1791 volume of this early newspaper is in the possession of the Tennessee Historical Society.

[7] For interesting material on this experiment, see Samuel C. Williams, "The South's First Cotton Factory," in *Tennessee Historical Quarterly* (Nashville), V (1946), 212 ff.

[8] Andrew Jackson to John McKee, May 16, 1794, in John Spencer Bassett (ed.), *The Correspondence of Andrew Jackson* (Washington, 1926–1935), I, 12–13.

settlers destroyed the lower Cherokee towns of Nickojack and Running Water in September, 1794.[9] It is not known whether Robert Bell had moved to the Mill Creek community prior to these Indian attacks. But regardless of his place of residence, his family was apparently spared; the murder of ancestors by Indians is not a part of the Bell family stories.

In 1792 a Captain Robert Bell located on the Big Harpeth River west or southwest of Nashville a North Carolina military grant for 2,560 acres of land. Whether this was the Robert Bell who had acquired land on Mill Creek has not been established. It seems unlikely that two Revolutionary captains by the same name would locate land in the same general area. Yet there is an incongruity in the dates which makes this appear probable. The owner of the Harpeth tract sold one half of it to Garrett Goodlow in 1796, and the deed stated that Robert Bell was a resident of Franklin County, North Carolina. According to the family story Robert Bell of Mill Creek had migrated to Tennessee at least a decade prior to 1796. The reliability of this account is further strengthened by the fact that three of his children—Samuel, Catherine, and Robert, Jr.—married in the Tennessee Country in the early 1790's. The presence of older children in this area suggests, but does not prove, that the father had also arrived.[10]

Of one thing, however, there can be no doubt—the progeny of Robert Bell of Mill Creek was soon scattered over a wide portion of Tennessee and neighboring states.[11] He himself

[9] James Phelan, *History of Tennessee* (Boston, 1888), 160–62.

[10] Davidson County Deeds, Book E, 33, 77 con.; Manuscript Marriage Bonds, in Davidson County Court Clerk's Office.

[11] Robert, Jr., became a Cumberland Presbyterian preacher. In 1794 he married Grizzell McCutchan of Logan County, Kentucky, and moved to her home section. By 1806 he was back in Tennessee, residing in Franklin County and preaching at Goshen and Mt. Carmel. In 1820 he moved to Mississippi and became cofounder and superintendent of Charity Hall, a mission school in the Choctaw country near Aberdeen. When the school was discontinued following the removal of the Indians west of the Mississippi River, he settled in Pontotoc County, where he continued to reside until his death in 1853. Among his children was a son named John, who became Surveyor General of Mississippi. See General John Bell to ? , in Beard, *Biographical Sketches*, 114–17; Manuscript Marriage Bonds for 1794, in Davidson County Court Clerk's Office;

lived to the ripe old age of eighty-five, dying at his home "near Flat Rock on the Nolensville Road" in 1816.[12]

Samuel, the eldest son of Robert Bell and the father of "John Bell of Tennessee," was born in Caswell County, North Carolina, on February 11, 1766. He probably accompanied the family to Tennessee. On June 16, 1791, he married Margaret Edmiston, a daughter of John Edmiston.[13] Edmiston had the distinction of being probably the only man in the American Revolution to be shot with a ramrod. At King's Mountain a nervous British soldier, hard pressed for time, failed to remove the ramrod from his muzzle loader before firing into the ranks of Shelby's men. Edmiston received the missile and lived to relate the experience. Two of the other three Edmiston brothers who participated in this engagement were less

---

sketch of Robert Bell, Jr., by E. T. Winston, in Pontotoc *Sentinel* (clippings in Tennessee State Library); John V. Stephens, *Biographical Sketch of the Late Rev. Claiborn H. Bell* (Lebanon, Tenn., 1909), 7–11.

Catherine, a twin sister of Robert, Jr., married Samuel McCutchan, probably an uncle of Robert's wife. Ann married William Marshall and became the mother of John Marshall, a prominent Franklin lawyer and father of the late Park Marshall. Mary married Thomas Williamson. See Manuscript Marriage Bonds, in Davidson County Court Clerk's Office; R. H. Crockett to John Trotwood Moore, August 21, 1922, in Bell File, Tennessee State Library, Genealogical Records, in possession of G. E. Bell.

Little is known of the numerous children of Robert Bell, Sr., by his second wife. James married Mary Dean and moved to Wilson County, where he died in 1823, leaving nine children. He was the grandfather of G. E. Bell of Dallas, Texas. John married a cousin, Sarah (Sally) Bell, a daughter of his uncle Samuel. Thomas married Martha Edmiston, and Francis married Peggy Bails. Daniel and Rebecca never married. Nothing is known of the other seven. See Davidson County Wills and Inventories, Book 7, pp. 10, 79; Goodspeed Publishing Company, *History of Tennessee . . . Together with an Historical and a Biographical Sketch of Maury, Williamson, Rutherford, Wilson, Bedford and Marshall Counties . . .* (Nashville, 1886), 1080; Davidson County Marriage Records, Book 1, pp. 69, 116, 162; Genealogical Records, in possession of G. E. Bell.

12 Goodspeed, *History of Tennessee*, 1080; R. H. Crockett to John Trotwood Moore, August 21, 1922, in Bell File.

13 Margaret was born January 23, 1773. On the records her name is incorrectly spelled Edmondson. This fact is verified by the signature of John Edmiston on the marriage contract. Davidson County Marriage Records, Book 1, p. 30; Manuscript Marriage Bonds, in Davidson County Court Clerk's Office; Bell Family Bible, in possession of Mrs. W. H. Knox, Nashville. Mrs. Knox is a granddaughter of James and Martha Bell Crockett.

fortunate. One was killed and the other seriously wounded.[14] During the next few years following his marriage, Samuel Bell became owner of several tracts of land on Mill Creek and possibly on Stone's River.[15] He spent the remainder of his life as a "humble mechanic and farmer" in the Mill Creek community. In addition to regular farming, he operated a blacksmith shop. In 1824, conscious of his advanced years, he entered into a contract with his son Thomas whereby the latter was made manager of his father's farm and was to receive one third of the net income from its operation.[16]

Samuel Bell died intestate in 1836. Seven of his nine children survived him. The five daughters married into prominent local families. Martha became the wife of James Crockett of Williamson County. Catherine married Andrew Crockett, a nephew of James. Eliza Ann married Crymer McEwen. Mary married Littleton J. Dooley, and at the time of her father's death resided in Mississippi. Sarah, who had married William W. Gaines, died prior to 1836.[17]

As above noted, Thomas had been in charge of his father's

[14] John Bell to ? , December 6, 1844, in Jonesborough *Whig*, February 19, 1845.

[15] Davidson County Deeds, Book E, 241, 242, 243, 287, 289; Book K, 61, 254. Robert Bell's brother Samuel, who had married Jane Scott, also settled in Davidson County. The fact that uncle and nephew, by the same name, acquired extensive land holdings in this general area greatly complicates the problem of determining the possessions of each. And the additional fact that each Samuel had children named John, Thomas, James, Martha, and Sarah, makes a complete isolation of each family impossible.

A Samuel Bell acquired land on the main fork of Stone's River, lots in the projected town of Jefferson in Rutherford County and in Franklin, and land on the Harpeth rivers. The owner of the Franklin lots was probably the father of our subject; the owner of the Harpeth and at least one of the Stone's River tracts was the uncle, for this Samuel died in 1821, leaving his Harpeth estate to his son John. Previously he had transferred a portion of his Stone's River land to his son Samuel, Jr. Davidson County Wills and Inventories, Book 7, pp. 492–94; Rutherford County Deeds, Book O, 14; Williamson County Deeds, Book B, 16, 322, 630.

[16] Davidson County Register, Book Q, 871–72.

[17] *Ibid.*, Book 1, pp. 270–71; Bell Family Bible; Janie Preston Collop French and Zella Armstrong (comps.), *The Crockett Family and Connecting Lines* (Bristol, Tenn., 1928), 77–78. Andrew and Catherine Bell Crockett were the grandparents of the late Judge R. H. Crockett of Franklin.

farm since 1824. In the division of the estate, he received two hundred acres of land and two slaves, and apparently continued as a farmer.[18] He never married. James married Mary Dickinson, a daughter of the affluent David Dickinson of Rutherford County. He established a mercantile business in Nashville, and when it failed in 1834, moved to Carroll County, Mississippi. In 1841, while traveling on the *New Orleans,* he fell overboard and was drowned in the Mississippi River.[19] Robert, Samuel Bell's eldest son, born April 11, 1794, died in childhood.[20]

John was born on Mill Creek on February 18, 1796.[21] Nothing is known of his early life that distinguished him from other youths of his day. He worked on the farm and operated the bellows in his father's blacksmith shop. According to a family story, one day while young John was pumping the bellows his father suddenly asked him if he would like to go to college. John answered yes; and at the age of fourteen he entered Cumberland College, a struggling Nashville institution, the administration of which had recently passed into the capable hands of Dr. James Priestley, late of Salem Academy of Bardstown, Kentucky. This frontier college, with its limited faculty and equipment, had little to offer, but Bell's contem-

[18] Davidson County Register, Book 1, pp. 270–71; Davidson County Wills and Inventories, Book 11, p. 588.

[19] Davidson County Register, Book Z, 136; Book X, 174–81; Memphis *Enquirer,* quoted in Nashville *Republican Banner,* June 19, 1841.

James's son, David W. D. Bell, received from his grandfather Dickinson's estate 500 acres of land in Gibson County and slaves valued at $5,000. He apparently moved to West Tennessee. See David Dickinson's will, in Rutherford County Wills, Book 14, p. 411.

[20] Bell Family Bible.

[21] Some accounts give February 14, others February 15. The year 1797 is also frequently given. At the time of Bell's death a close friend made a public statement that Bell was born in 1796, not 1797. The date on his tomb is February 18, 1796. This is also the date given in the Bell Family Bible.

The house in which Bell was born was later known as the "Barnes House" and was located on Barnes Lane "two hundred yards on the left from where this lane intersects the Nolensville pike, 9½ miles from Nashville." This two-story structure, built of bricks made by Samuel Bell himself, burned several years ago and was replaced by a smaller house. John W. Gaines, "Where John Bell Was Born and Where He Died" (manuscript in possession of G. E. Bell).

poraries attested the fact that he took his scholastic work seriously and made the most of his opportunities.[22] Graduation from Cumberland in 1814 concluded his formal training. Neither at college nor later in life was he distinguished for his brilliance or his knowledge. A slow reasoner but a diligent searcher after needed information, he was more of a plodder than a scholar. Time, plenty of it, was required in reaching conclusions. Frequently, when his more brilliant associates had already taken their stand on an issue, Bell was still considering. Throughout his public career he showed ability as a formal speaker, a talent no doubt developed during his college days, but he always suffered when debate reached the point where quick decisions and immediate replies were necessary. Lacking in mental agility, he often became confused and then angry; at times he was not averse to using his fists when adequate words were not forthcoming.

No contemporary left an adequate description of Bell's physical appearance. This fact itself indicates that there was nothing about him that attracted special attention. Late in life he was inclined to obesity, and one gets the impression from his portraits that he was also large of frame. His hair was probably dark, for in 1854 an observer in the Senate gallery remarked that Bell was getting gray. Even as a young man his stiffness of bearing and his seriousness of demeanor gave him the appearance of a man of more advanced years. Usually solemn, often glum, he could smile but he had no hearty laugh. To him life, public and private, was a serious business.

The year following his graduation from Cumberland, Bell acquired 120 acres of his father's land on Mill Creek.[23] There is no evidence, however, that he intended returning to the life of a farmer, for he had already begun to read law in preparation for admission to the bar. In July, 1816, Ephraim H. Foster, a neighbor, assured the Davidson County court that

[22] Statement by Judge William B. Turley, in W. Woodford Clayton, *History of Davidson County, Tennessee* (Philadelphia, 1880), 112.
[23] Davidson County Deeds, Book K, 690.

Bell was a man of good moral character, and in October, he began the practice of law in Williamson County.[24] He immediately formed a partnership with J. J. White in the town of Franklin, where he already had numerous family connections. A portion of the equipment of his office consisted of a desk, a chair, and a few books, including a dictionary, which he had recently acquired at the sale of his grandfather's personal property.[25]

The following year, 1817, when he was slightly over twenty-one years of age, Bell was elected to represent Williamson County in the state senate. According to a friendly but unverified account, his election was a result of a rousing Fourth of July oration delivered after the campaign was already under way.[26] In spite of the brevity of his canvass, Bell won an impressive victory over "a gentleman of tried ability and high qualifications."

The legislature convened in Knoxville on September 15, 1817. Bell was active from the beginning of the session. The influx of settlers into the West following the War of 1812 made the land question one of prime importance. And to those who were interested in public education, the question was doubly important. Early in the session Bell called for an investigation of the situation which had almost completely tied up the income from school lands. According to an agreement of 1806 among Tennessee, North Carolina, and the United States, two 100,000-acre tracts of Tennessee lands were to be reserved for the support of a college in each of the two sections of the state and an academy in each county. These lands were to be sold at not less than two dollars per acre. Since the only adequate body of land in the state was the region south of the French Broad and Holston rivers, the school

24 Davidson County Court Minutes, 1814–1816, p. 619; Williamson County Court Minutes, 1816–1817, p. 179. The records fail to reveal the date on which Bell received his license to practice law.
25 Davidson County Wills and Inventories, Book 7, pp. 77–78.
26 Albert V. Goodpasture, "John Bell's Political Revolt and His Vauxhall Garden Speech," in Tennessee Historical Magazine (Nashville), II (1916), 254–55.

lands were located there. But another portion of the agreement of 1806 specified that the squatters south of the French Broad and Holston were to have pre-emption rights for 640 acres each at one dollar per acre.[27] Thus were the schools immediately deprived of one half of their anticipated income.

The squatters on the school lands had been slow in making their payments and the legislature had been generous with extensions of time. Bell's serious attention had first been attracted to the situation while he was a student at Cumberland College. He was greatly moved, he later related, by a public orator's pathetic description of poor settlers being evicted from cabins and fields so dear to them and upon which they had made a substantial payment in hardships and even blood, in order that "colleges and academies might be reared in the midst of a more fortunate and wealthy countryside." But some of Bell's sympathy was quickly dissipated when the orator referred to college students as the scions of the aristocracy, "wallowing in luxury and learning to say hic, haec, hoc." This remark young Bell considered as a "libel on the college." He knew quite well that he was "no bantling of the wealthy." [28]

Bell's remarks in favor of his senate resolution were not recorded, but years later, in a speech devoted to public education, he reviewed his attitude. He realized that the squatters on the school lands had settled there "at imminent peril of their lives," and he was willing to accord them due honor and gratitude for their meritorious achievements; yet the fact remained that they had failed to meet their legal obligations. But the loss of large funds was not the greatest damage which higher education had suffered from the attitude of occupants. Claiming that payments for their lands were beyond their

[27] For the principal points of the agreement, see Philip M. Hamer, *Tennessee: A History, 1673-1932* (New York, 1933), I, 57-58.

[28] John Bell, *An Address Delivered at Nashville, T., October 5th, 1830, Being the First Anniversary of the Alumni Society of the University of Nashville* (Nashville, 1830).

means, these squatters had easily persuaded themselves that "reason and equity" were on their side, regardless of what "public interests may be wounded by their success." Marshaling their full strength, the representatives from south of the French Broad and Holston became the "Swiss Corps" of the state legislature, "united and absorbed in a single interest, and prepared to make all others merely auxiliary and subordinate." It was his opinion, Bell asserted, that the great opposition to higher education in Tennessee had originated among the squatters on the school lands south of the French Broad and Holston rivers.[29]

Bell's resolution calling for an investigation was approved by the senate, and he was named a member of the committee; but for some reason, probably the lack of favorable house action, the committee never functioned.[30]

By a recent treaty the Cherokee had ceded most of their Tennessee lands. The governor proposed that the school lands might be marked off in this area west of the Little Tennessee River. When a memorial requesting congressional permission for this change came before the state senate, Bell voted in the negative. He gave the same vote on a new proposal for further postponement of payments due from squatters on the school lands, and then made an unsuccessful attempt to force the payment of all back interest by 1819.[31] It is not clear why Bell preferred to pursue the apparently hopeless task of forcing payments from squatters rather than joining in a movement which gave much more promise of success.

In the interest of a circulating medium adequate in amount to facilitate the growth of commerce, Bell supported the creation of ten additional state banks; but he opposed the efforts of the Nashville Bank and the Bank of the State of Tennessee at Knoxville to extend their financial power by doubling their capital stock. He also favored the protection of Tennessee

29 *Ibid.*
30 *Journal of the Senate* (Tennessee), 1817, p. 27. Cited hereafter as Tennessee *Senate Journal.*
31 *Ibid.*, 113–20, 161–62.

banking interests from outside competition. A group of business and professional men in Nashville were eager to secure
for their city a branch of the Bank of the United States. Hugh
Lawson White of Knoxville, the president of the Bank of the
State of Tennessee led a movement to block this proposed
establishment. Bell joined in support of a law levying an
annual tax of $50,000 on any bank doing business in Tennes-
see but not chartered by the state.[32] This expression of anti-
Bank sentiment was largely responsible for the further delay
in the establishment of a branch of the United States Bank in
Nashville.

Among other subjects on which Bell voiced his opinions
were the evils of the judicial system, the proposal to call a state
constitutional convention, and the selection of a new site for
the state capital. He introduced a bill vesting the judicial
powers of the county courts in committees of five members to
be chosen annually. He advocated the calling of a constitutional convention, and voted to move the state capital to
Murfreesboro, a town not far from his home town of
Franklin.[33]

There was nothing in Bell's brief legislative career that
marked him as exceptional. One interested, though critical,
observer thought only three members gave evidence of talents.
Bell was not among the three; therefore, he must have been
among those whom the same writer described as a "miserable
set." [34] Bell gave no evidence that he was especially impressed
with the life of a legislator; he refused to run for re-election in
1819, even though conditions resulting from the panic of that
year were certain to make the next session one of tremendous
importance. Probably the most valuable experience during
his stay in the state capital was his association with Hugh
Lawson White, a senator from Knox County. Years later the

[32] Tennessee *Public Acts,* 1817, p. 139; Tennessee *Senate Journal,* 1817, pp.
135, 169–70, 211–12; Phelan, *History of Tennessee,* 259.
[33] *Tennessee Senate Journal,* 1817, pp. 104, 105, 125 26, 130, 133, 204–205.
[34] James C. Campbell to David Campbell, October 21, 1817, in David Campbell Papers (Duke University Library).

two were to be leaders of the opposition to Andrew Jackson's attempt to control Tennessee politics.

Returning to Franklin and to the practice of his profession, Bell spent the next decade in acquiring "a high standing at the bar as a lawyer of great acuteness, research, and ability, and as a speaker of no ordinary merits." [35] There is no record of any participation in politics during this period or of any public statement on such exciting public controversies as relief legislation. In addition to his legal practice, he engaged in small-scale speculation in city property. He and William Banks opened up in Franklin a subdivision soon to be known as "Bell Town." [36] The expected boom was cut short by the depression of 1819, and little profit could have been realized from the adventure.

On December 10, 1818, Bell married Sally Dickinson of Rutherford County, the Reverend Robert Henderson officiating. Sally, a sister of James Bell's wife, was the daughter of David and Fanny Murfree Dickinson and a granddaughter of Colonel Hardy Murfree, a distinguished Revolutionary soldier.[37] Another of the Dickinson sisters, Fanny Priscilla, married William Law Murfree, a cousin. Their daughter, Mary Noailles Murfree, became the prominent writer known as Charles Egbert Craddock.[38] The Dickinson and Murfree families were people of wealth and culture. David Dickinson himself owned, or was soon to acquire, thousands of acres of land in Middle and West Tennessee and in Mississippi.[39] Sally was said to have been educated at the Moravian Female Academy at Salem, North Carolina, where she was a schoolmate of Sarah Childress, the future wife of James K. Polk. A

[35] Statement of Judge Henry Crabb, in Clayton, *History of Davidson County,* 112.
[36] Park Marshall, "Pertaining to Early History of Franklin and Williamson County," in *Williamson County News,* beginning January 4, 1917 (clippings in Tennessee State Library); Williamson County Deeds, Book F, 46, 47, 71.
[37] Nashville *Whig and Tennessee Advertiser,* December 19, 1818.
[38] Edd Winfield Parks, *Charles Egbert Craddock* (Chapel Hill, 1941), 7.
[39] See Dickinson's will, in Rutherford County Wills, Book 14, pp. 411–20.

family story also has it that she made the trip from Murfreesboro to Salem on horseback.[40]

Almost nothing is known of the home life of John and Sally
Bell, and what influence the cultured Mrs. Bell had upon her
husband must remain a matter for conjecture. The Bells
moved from Franklin to Murfreesboro late in 1820 or early
in 1821. In April of the latter year Bell bought a city lot there,
apparently with the intention of building a home thereon.[41]
His removal to Murfreesboro was undoubtedly prompted by
the prospects of greater opportunity in the new capital of the
state. Bell, however, did not remain long at his new place of
residence, for by January, 1822, he had moved to Nashville
where he formed a partnership with Colonel Henry Crabb
with offices on the public square, near the post office.[42] Crabb,
"a well-balanced, dignified, imperturbable, polished gentleman, of more than ordinary talents and of considerable learning," [43] proved a valuable legal mentor.

The Bells took up residence on the corner of Spring and
High streets in a house owned by Washington L. Hannum. In
1823 the Farmers and Mechanics Bank forced the sale of this
home to satisfy a mortgage, and Bell purchased it for $7,000.[44]

For the next few years Bell followed the routine life of a
small-town lawyer, profiting by his personal and professional
association with a host of distinguished members of the Nashville bar. By 1827, when Judge Crabb was made a justice of
the state supreme court, some rated Bell as second only to
William L. Brown as a legal expert.[45]

[40] Goodspeed, *History of Tennessee,* 735; Goodpasture, "John Bell's Revolt,"
loc. cit., 255.
[41] Rutherford County Deeds, Book O, 244.
[42] Nashville *Whig,* January 23, April 3, 1822.
[43] Goodspeed, *History of Tennessee,* 390.
[44] Davidson County Deeds, Book Q, 350.
[45] Archibald D. Murphey to Thomas Ruffin, November 27, 1827, in William
H. Hoyt (ed.), *The Papers of Archibald D. Murphey* (Raleigh, 1914), I, 367.

Chapter II

WINGING A WAR HAWK

"EXPIRED at Washington on the ninth of February, of poison administered by the assassin hands of John Quincy Adams, the usurper, and Henry Clay, the virtue, liberty, and independence of the United States." [1] Thus lamented the editor of a prominent newspaper when he announced the election of John Quincy Adams to the presidency in 1825. The failure of the electoral college to give the required majority to any presidential candidate in the election of 1824 had placed upon the House of Representatives the duty of selecting one from among the highest three candidates—Andrew Jackson, John Quincy Adams, and William H. Crawford. The alleged "bargain" between Adams and Clay, in which the latter was promised an appointment to the office of Secretary of State in return for his support of the former's candidacy, and the subsequent election of Adams by the House threw the Jackson followers into a fit of anger.

Bell was too inexperienced in politics to have a prominent part in the original movement to make Jackson President, although he was probably in sympathy with the plan. Older politicians, including William B. Lewis, John H. Eaton, John Overton, and Felix Grundy, were the original Jackson men, and the defeat of the Old General was a severe blow to their personal and state pride. When the "corrupt bargain" charge was made public, Jackson supporters, young and old, seized upon this "unholy alliance" as the cause of the defeat of their hero, and resolved to make it the chief issue in the next cam-

[1] Quoted in John B. McMaster, *History of the People of the United States* (New York, 1883–1924), V, 489.

paign. Thus the presidential campaign of 1828 actually began in 1825. And, during the intervening years, most Tennesseans who aspired to higher places in politics sensed a necessity for public avowal of their continued confidence in the "people's choice" the Hero of New Orleans.

As one of those aspiring politicians with an eye on a seat in Congress, Bell immediately realized the possibilities. On September 25, 1826, he addressed a circular to the voters of the Nashville congressional district.[2] Lawyers busily engaged in the practice of their profession, he explained, had little opportunity to meet their fellow countrymen in private social circles and exchange ideas on political topics of the day. For this reason he desired to make a formal declaration of his views on a topic which should be foremost in the minds of all public-spirited citizens. In the late presidential contest the people had expressed their choice "through a thousand channels and by the most infallible signs," yet their favorite had been ignored. By this action of the House "the first and best principle of the Constitution was violated and trodden under foot. . . . The noble fabric of American Liberty was endangered by the example, and the authors of it owe an *atonement.*" The price of this atonement must be their fall from power.

But even if there had been no violation of the spirit of the Constitution, Bell insisted, he would oppose any administration "brought about by the acts of political management and intrigue." Intrigue such as this belonged to only those countries where the thrones of princes were made secure by the "prostitution of public morals." Where conspiracy and management were masters, the people could not be free and the Republic must perish. Fortunately, however, the American people were still master, and he predicted that in the next presidential election they would "reject the services of those who win their way to office by practices that tend to general corruption and threaten the destruction of the government."

[2] He had announced his candidacy on August 26.

It was also the good fortune of the American people to have at their service a man like Andrew Jackson, "A man, whose purposes are admitted to be pure; whose mind seems formed for great emergencies, and whose splendid services place him, in deserving favor, at an immeasurable distance in advance of all others." Bell would deem it an honor, he humbly announced, to be instrumental in elevating such a man to the President's chair.[3] Although writing for public consumption, Bell was probably sincere in his eulogy of Jackson; as yet there was no sign of a rift between these two neighbors.

In announcing for Congress, Bell became the opponent of the old "War Hawk," Felix Grundy, who, craving anew the thrills of the political chase, had announced his candidacy early in August. A smooth politician, Grundy had distinguished himself as a member of that group of young congressmen who had pushed the United States into war with Great Britain in 1812. Resigning his seat in the House in 1814, he had returned to private law practice and had become probably the most effective criminal lawyer in the West. During the panic of 1819 he was elected to the Tennessee legislature, and as leader of the relief forces, gave an excellent demonstration of his mastery of political strategy, winning the support of the debtor class but losing the friendship of business and financial circles.

A few weeks after the appearance of Bell's circular, Grundy also issued a statement to the voters of the Nashville District.[4] Like Bell, he denounced the action taken by the House; furthermore, he accused the Adams congressmen of voting their own wishes rather than those of their constituents. The Constitution ought to be amended, he asserted, so as to "preserve to the states, respectively, their present relative weight and influence—and give, directly, to the people themselves the right of electing the president . . . —apart from the interfer-

---

[3] Nashville *Union*, June 19, 1839; *Tennessee Historical Magazine*, IX (1925–1926), 77–78.

[4] This district was composed of Davidson, Williamson, and Rutherford counties.

ence of the House." His support of Andrew Jackson had not diminished, he said half boastfully, since those eventful days when he drew up the resolutions for the nomination of the Old Hero for the presidency and also those resolutions directed against the power of the congressional caucus.[5] He disapproved of the extremes to which the Adams Administration had gone in pomp, ceremony, and dignity. What the country needed was simplicity and economy.[6]

This public statement was Grundy's finishing touch to an expert job of endearing himself to the Old General. The two had been close political friends in earlier years while Grundy was a "war hawk" congressman, but in 1820 a disagreement over legislation for the financial relief of debtors had resulted in a coolness. Nevertheless, Grundy did yeoman service as an original Jackson man, and the breach was apparently healed.

Both Grundy and Bell had been apprised of Congressman Sam Houston's intention to forgo re-election in order to make the race to succeed William Carroll as governor of Tennessee. Carroll could not succeed himself since he had already served the constitutional limit of three successive terms. Although he would be asking nothing for himself, his political supporters would play an important part in determining who should be elected governor and who should succeed Houston at Washington.

Jackson and Carroll had once been good friends. Each had appreciated the distinguished services of the other in the Creek War and the New Orleans campaign. In 1818 Carroll had given the name *General Jackson* to his steamboat, the first to reach Nashville.[7] But for some unknown reason there was a rift in this friendship by 1821, and in that year the breach was widened as a result of Jackson's support of the aristocratic Edward Ward against Carroll in their race for governor. The results of this campaign definitely established

[5] Nashville *Republican and State Gazette,* October 28, 1826; Joseph Howard Parks, *Felix Grundy, Champion of Democracy* (University, La., 1940), 168–71.
[6] Nashville *Republican and State Gazette,* October 28, 1826.
[7] Phelan, *History of Tennessee,* 254–55.

Carroll as a favorite of the common people. In spite of Jackson's opposition, a great wave of young democracy swept Carroll into office by a vote of almost four to one.[8] By 1827 he had lost little of this popularity.

At the time of his entrance into politics, Bell had attached himself to this young democracy. And when he announced as a candidate to succeed Houston in the House of Representatives, it was to this group that he looked for his principal support. Yet his proclamation of loyalty to the Jackson cause showed that he was not unmindful of the great influence of the General. Most Tennesseans, regardless of their local political affiliations, were supporters of Jackson for the presidency.

Grundy and Carroll had disagreed over the relief program in Tennessee during the years 1820 to 1823. Consequently, although not bitter enemies, they could not be considered as close friends; Grundy must look to Jackson for support. The campaign opened with enthusiasm and was "spirited and full of fire" to the end. Grundy, twenty years Bell's senior, had the advantage which comes from experience in public life and from a natural gift for popular oratory. Adopting the slogan "Jackson and Grundy," [9] he won the support of most of the General's close friends, especially the veterans of the War of 1812.

Bell issued a second appeal for votes in March, 1827. The Constitution should be amended, he explained, so that never again would the selection of a President devolve upon the House. Furthermore, the President should be limited to one term. He expressed a fear that, with the rapid growth of the West and the probable admission of many new states, the chief executive might become too powerful, should he avail himself of the "immense patronage for the inglorious purpose of securing his re-election." And as a further safeguard against

8 *Ibid.*, 257.
9 James C. Campbell to David Campbell, June 6, 1827, in David Campbell Papers.

too great a growth of executive influence, Bell would deny to the President the power to appoint to office any person who had served as a member of Congress during his Administration. He bitterly denounced the spoils system in general.

As soon as the national debt had been paid, Bell thought Federal money might be well spent in the construction of roads and canals and in the promotion of public education. He opposed the protective tariff on the ground that it might establish in America a factory system similar to that in England. Like Jefferson, he said, he was a great believer in the promotion of agriculture. He would not have the farmer's interests subordinated to the wishes of the industrialist.[10] There were few industrialists in the Nashville District.

Bell's most effective appeal was to the younger group which had come into its own since 1812. These young Republicans appreciated both his profession of loyalty to Jackson and his frank statement that, if elected, his course would always be *"open, direct and independent."* [11] The Grundy supporters, on the other hand, questioned Bell's friendship for Jackson and branded him a Clay-Adams man. This accusation was without justification, but the friends of Grundy knew that probably the most damaging stigma that could be attached to a Tennessee politician at that time was friendship for the Adams Administration. With the hope of nullifying this accusation, Bell took an active part in the Jackson celebration at Nashville's Vauxhall Gardens on July 4, 1827, and made himself conspicuous by the delivery of a well-directed toast: "The indignant murmurs which precede the distinct and full utterance of a free but insulted people's will—more terrible to the guilty statesman than the battle's din or tempest's roar." [12] At the same time that Jackson's supporters were honoring the Old Hero, another group of Nashvillians, about sixty-five in number, representing business and financial

10 Nashville *Republican and State Gazette,* March 31, 1827.
11 Circular to Seventh District Voters, September 25, 1826, in *Tennessee Historical Magazine,* IX (1925–1926), 78.
12 *National Banner and Nashville Whig,* July 7, 14, 1827.

circles and political conservatism, were dining at Decker and
Dyer's Reading Room.[13] Shortly their meeting would be related to Bell's campaign.

On the whole, the principal Nashville newspapers steered
a neutral course, but through the publication of communications supplied by partisans, they contributed to the intensity
of the campaign spirit. The *National Banner and Nashville
Whig*[14] pronounced both Grundy and Bell "able, efficient,
and distinguished men." Grundy, the editor explained, was
nationally known for his record in Congress and as a criminal
lawyer. He was "well suited, by his political experience and
great ability as a public speaker, to take a leading part in
the councils of the nation." As for Bell, he was a young man
of "the finest promise," a talented lawyer, orator, politician,
and statesman. The people of the Seventh Congressional
District were to be congratulated on having two such choices
before them.

Late in the campaign the *Republican and State Gazette*
published a communication from a Grundy supporter denouncing out-of-state reports that Jackson had considerable
opposition at home. "In all places," the writer argued, "there
are persons of narrow minds, who view with jaundiced eye,
those who by merit or good fortune are elevated to higher
promotions than themselves." Unfortunately, Nashville had
a few such persons. And there were also a few who as a result
of "wealth, connections, etc.," had been drawn into the opposition to Jackson. These were the gentlemen who had
dined at Decker and Dyer's while the patriotic people of
Nashville were honoring General Jackson at Vauxhall Gardens. "The friends of General Jackson . . . have brought
out for Congress, the distinguished and highly talented Felix
Grundy. His experience and qualifications render him the
decided choice of those who desire the elevation of that
worthy individual to the presidency. His opponent, Mr. Bell
. . . is espoused by the opposite party, and though he is

13 *Ibid.,* July 7, 1827.   14 *Ibid.,* July 28, 1827.

friendly to the election of the General, and a young man of much talents and promise, it is considered by his best friends that he has been premature." Editor Allen A. Hall replied to this communication in the same issue of his paper. The "real and disinterested" friends of Jackson, he declared, were the "great body of the people"; and these same people had brought out Bell as a candidate for Congress "because he is a man of vigorous intellect; of high attainment, and sterling integrity, and because it is known that he has been the undeviating friend of General Jackson from his youth." [15]

Had Jackson been a wise politician he would have steered clear of state politics, especially at this time. Regardless of the outcome of the congressional contest, a Jackson supporter would be elected. But, as was to be demonstrated many times in the future, the Old Hero could not refrain from expressing his wishes. Furthermore, he distrusted the Decker and Dyer "sixty-five" who were said to be supporting Bell. On the first day of voting he appeared at the polls, cast an open ballot for Grundy, and, according to some Bell supporters, electioneered in behalf of the "War Hawk." [16] Other Bell friends, however, were not so critical of Jackson's conduct. Allen A. Hall, editor of the *Republican* and friend of Bell, denied that Jackson did more than make "a simple expression of his preference" for Grundy and vote an open ballot for him. Even before Bell became a candidate, Hall explained, Jackson had resolved to support Grundy. And at no time did he express any doubt as to Bell's integrity.[17] At any rate, whatever efforts Jackson made were not well rewarded; Bell won the election by more than one thousand votes. And a future President had offended a congressman-elect.

An analysis of the election returns reveals that Bell's

---

[15] Nashville *Republican and State Gazette,* July 31, 1827.

[16] Goodpasture, "John Bell's Revolt," *loc. cit.,* 256; John Robb to Jackson, August 28, 1827, in Andrew Jackson Papers (Division of Manuscripts, Library of Congress); Baltimore *Patriot,* August 27, 1827; Nashville *Republican Banner,* August 11, 1838.

[17] Nashville *Republican and State Gazette,* August 23, 1827.

heaviest support came from Rutherford and Williamson counties. He had lived in the county seats of both of these counties and had many family connections in them. He also had numerous connections in Davidson County, but since this was also Grundy's home county he was able to carry it by fewer than 150 votes. Within Nashville, business circles in general supported Bell, not so much as a result of common interests, but rather from a dislike for Grundy who had sponsored stay laws and easy money while a member of the legislature. Mostly commercial rather than industrial, this group was not disturbed by Bell's position on the tariff. But even with business and financial support, Bell's majority within the city was only 163.[18] It is probable that Bell received the votes of most Clay-Adams men, but outside of Nashville this group was extremely small.

The Adams supporters outside Tennessee sought to make political capital of Bell's defeat of the Jackson-Grundy combination. This defeat, they insisted, was evidence of considerable opposition to Jackson's leadership within his home state. A few mutual friends of Jackson and Bell, fearing the effects such an assertion might have on the coming presidential election, requested Bell to speak out and again express, in no uncertain terms, his loyalty to the Jackson cause. Suppressing a desire for retaliation, Bell rose to the occasion, issued a severe denunciation of the party in power, and expressed the opinion that to continue this group in office "would be incompatible with the safety and well being of our political institutions." His earlier expression of loyalty, he insisted, had not been prompted by political expediency, for he believed General Jackson to possess "qualifications eminently calculated to impart to the administration of the government that character for simplicity and purity so necessary to be maintained, if we would cherish the republic." Having grown

---

[18] *Ibid.*, August 7, 1827. According to Charles Sumner and Horace Greeley Bell later stated that he also received the votes of the free Negroes. *The Works of Charles Sumner* (Boston, 1870–1883), X, 192; Horace Greeley, *The American Conflict* (Hartford, 1864–1866), I, 179.

up in the Hermitage neighborhood, Bell had observed in
Jackson's conduct "the impulses of a mighty intellect regulated by a spirit, ardent, patriotic and incorruptible; . . .
meeting great emergencies as though they had been created
but to distinguish him, defeating the expectations of his
enemies by evincing the greatest caution and deliberation in
moments when they had predicted rashness and precipita-
tion; and always preferring the public good to private considerations. . . . In the hands of such a man the honor and
interest of the nation may . . . repose in safety." [19] Such a
eulogy could scarcely have come from the depths of Bell's
heart. When he left for Washington he must have been at
least disgruntled, if not downright angry, with Jackson.

Among the other members of the Tennessee delegation
to the Twentieth Congress was James K. Polk, less than one
year Bell's senior, cultured, urbane, a graduate of the University of North Carolina, and a legal protégé and personal
friend of Felix Grundy. Then there was David Crockett,
Polk's antithesis in many respects, void of formal education,
a product of the raw West, who later lost his life in the Alamo
while battling for Texan independence. The other six members were run-of-the-mill congressmen, who never distinguished themselves in national affairs.

When the Twentieth Congress convened on December 3,
1827, political excitement ran high. The friends of both
Adams and Jackson were eager to increase the chances of
their candidate by detracting from the popularity of the
other. Early in the session Adams supporters revived the old
controversy over Jackson's execution of six Tennessee militia-
men during the War of 1812 and demanded a thorough investigation of the court-martial. Both Polk and Bell sprang
to Jackson's defense. He felt it his duty, Bell asserted, to
defend "the character of a distinguished citizen" and neighbor. He would give the same defense to any other "private

19 Baltimore *Patriot*, August 27, 1827; M. Barrow *et al.* to Bell, September
15, 1827; Bell to Barrow *et al.*, n.d., in Nashville *Republican and State Gazette*,
September 21, 1827.

citizen" of his district whose good reputation was being attacked and who had no opportunity to speak for himself. What General Jackson had done was in the line of duty. Why not investigate the conduct of his superiors—the President, the Secretary of War, and the Governor of Tennessee? If there had been neglect of duty in handling militia, Bell argued, it was among those who outranked General Jackson rather than on the part of the General himself. There was "little magnanimity in striking at the tail, instead of the head, of the offending series of public agents." [20]

Throughout the session Bell was consistent in his opposition to all measures designed to arouse party spirit. When certain supporters of Jackson proposed a resolution accusing the present Administration of extravagance and demanding investigation and retrenchment, Bell voted to table the measure. In defense of his vote, he explained that as a general rule he favored investigations. They were usually productive of good in quickening public sensibilities, if for no other reason. He also favored economy in government and did not doubt that the present Administration had been guilty of extravagance. But owing to the intensity of party feeling he doubted that there could be an inquiry sufficiently dispassionate to result in "judicious retrenchment." He did not wish the friends of General Jackson to take the offensive in partisan matters. "When we shall have carried this war of crimination and recrimination to the highest pitch to which party feeling can ascend, all we shall be able to accomplish will be, perhaps, to degrade the character of the Congress of the United States, consume ourselves in the heat of controversy, and vomit forth, through the channels of newspapers, upon the people of this Union, the poison of our own gall, to embitter and stir them up to a like useless rage." Congressmen should cease their party bickerings and get down to work. The floor of the House was not the place for electioneering, with one side warning against the dangers of a military dic-

[20] *Congressional Debates*, 20 Cong., 1 Sess., 1034–48.

tatorship and the other envisioning a country destroyed by the corruption of its own government.[21]

Bell's nonpartisan attitude toward public issues was also in evidence in his vote on the tariff of 1828. This political measure, designed by Jackson men for the purpose of embarrassing the Administration, was opposed by the entire Tennessee delegation. Bell, as he had stated during the late congressional campaign, was opposed to a protective system. He was doubly opposed to protection connected with politics.[22] Another point of interest, though the political implications are in doubt, was Bell's opposition to a proposal to sell the government's stock in the Bank of the United States and to apply the proceeds to the national debt.[23]

Bell's most extensive participation in debate during his first term in Congress was on the Tennessee land bill. North Carolina ceded the Tennessee country to the United States in 1790. Prior to the cession a military district had been set aside in north central Tennessee in which the land claims of North Carolina's Revolutionary soldiers were to be satisfied. This was the region into which Bell's grandfather had moved. According to the cession act all of these claims which had been authorized under previous laws and should be perfected by 1792 were to be satisfied in the Tennessee country. If the lands within the military reservation proved insufficient, then other unoccupied lands might be used.

Tennessee became a state in 1796, and the officials of the new state immediately took notice of the fact that North Carolina was still issuing land warrants to be satisfied in Tennessee. The triangular controversy among those two states and the United States resulted in the agreement of 1806: the United States was to have all lands south and west of a line drawn in an irregular manner from the intersection of the Tennessee River with the Kentucky line to a point on the Alabama line directly south of Columbia. After the satisfaction of North Carolina land claims, Tennessee was

[21] *Ibid.*, 1246–51.   [22] *Ibid.*, 2245, 2289 ff.   [23] *Ibid.*, 858.

to have such lands as remained north and east of that line, reserving for public education one section out of each thirty-six.[24]

The public lands were so mismanaged that no school lands were set aside. The same error was repeated when the Chickasaw lands in the western part of the state were opened for settlement.[25] Owners of land warrants used their influence in favor of good locations rather than public education. Soon there was nothing but poor lands left unappropriated. In 1823 a committee of the Tennessee house of representatives, headed by James K. Polk, reported that there was a deficit of 421,729 acres of school lands. In view of the great need for school funds, the committee proposed that Tennessee's congressmen "use their best exertions" to secure the cession of unappropriated lands for educational purposes.[26]

The matter was not pushed in Washington until Polk entered Congress in 1825. In 1826 and again in 1828 he introduced cession bills in the House. Speaking in behalf of the latter bill, he insisted that the cession of these lands to Tennessee would be no donation but an act in satisfaction of a just claim. It would merely be supplying a deficiency in the school lands which had been promised in the agreement of 1806 but had not been provided. These "vacant remnants" of land requested by Tennessee were extremely poor, he explained, since the better lands had been carved out through the division of large warrants into small ones. Although worthless to the Federal government, this residue, under careful management by the Tennessee land office, might yield some income for public education within the state.[27]

David Crockett, West Tennessee's representative in the House, argued that his people were asking for nothing more

24 Hamer, *Tennessee*, I, 256–57.

25 Henry D. Whitney (ed.), *The Land Laws of Tennessee* (Chattanooga, 1891), 200–20.

26 *Journal of the House of Representatives* (Tennessee), 1823, p. 325–29. Hereafter cited as Tennessee *House Journal*.

27 *Cong. Debates*, 20 Cong., 1 Sess., 2496–2500.

than their rights. During ten years' residence in that district he had familiarized himself with its lands. At least 200,000 acres were "mountainous and poor" and not worth one cent per acre; neither was the timber of any value. "For, sir, instead of wishing more timber on our lands, we should gladly avail ourselves of some invention, to wish a considerable quantity of it off, with less labor." The only value in timber lands was in furnishing mast for hogs and range for cattle. That portion of the area lying east of the Tennessee River was mostly "mountainous and rocky" with its few fertile valleys already thickly populated. West of the river the soil was comparatively free from rocks but was barren and undesirable. The lowlands along the streams would be of considerable value if they were not "usually inundated." He himself had "often rowed a canoe from hill to hill."

Crockett further explained that the hundreds of families squatting on West Tennessee lands had little and asked only for a place to call home. They could never acquire homes at the Federal minimum price of $1.25 per acre; therefore, the government's policy was unwise, for "to make of your citizen a landholder, you chain down his affections to your soil, and give him pride and elevation of character, which fires his heart with patriotism, and nerves his arm with strength."

Furthermore, Crockett wished to see a common-school education placed within reach of every youth of his district. His constituents had "but little to do with colleges," but as a plain farmer without the benefits of formal education, he realized the value of education and wished to see its advantages extended to all.[28]

This was a subject on which Bell had definite convictions. During his brief experience in Tennessee politics he had shown considerable impatience with those who treated lightly the obligations to public education. He now approached the subject from a different angle than that of his colleagues. He sought to show that Tennessee's claims went back to the

28 *Ibid.*, 2518–20.

Northwest Ordinance of 1787. That document had declared that " 'schools and the means of education should forever be encouraged,' " and the land act of 1785 also had provided that within the Northwest Territory one section out of each thirty-six should be reserved for schools. When North Carolina ceded the Tennessee country to the Federal government it was with the provision that the territory should " 'enjoy all the privileges, benefits, and advantages' " of the territory north of the Ohio River except in the case of slavery. By accepting this Southwest Territory under these conditions, the government had obligated itself to North Carolina and Tennessee. The proposed cession, therefore, would be nothing more than recognition of this obligation and would in no way involve the "power of Congress to make donations of public lands." Since the United States had assumed the obligation of providing means of education, Bell contended, then that obligation was binding until it could be definitely shown that sufficient provisions for education had been made. This he thought could scarcely be done since Tennessee was the only state carved from territory ceded by the original states which "had not had the full benefit of the usual provisions for the support of common schools."

Bell estimated that since 1806 at least half of Tennessee's legislation had been related to land claims. If all of the remaining lands should be ceded to the state their value would scarcely be adequate compensation for the expense of this legislation. "A million of dollars, paid directly from your treasury, would be but poor remuneration for having all the springs of improvement relaxed, and all the sources of her [Tennessee's] strength diminished and drained by the most expensive, dilatory and vexatious litigation, that ever visited its curses upon any people."

Should Congress refuse to cede these lands to Tennessee, Bell insisted that a Federal land office must be established in that section and the lands placed on the market. To do otherwise would be to "realize the fable of the dog, the ox,

and the hay." Yet, if placed on the market, probably four
fifths of the three or four million acres would bring not more
than one cent per acre. Therefore, the proper course would
be to cede the lands to Tennessee and allow the state to make
any possible use of them in the interest of public education.[29]

John Davis of Massachusetts challenged the arguments of
both Polk and Bell. He was unable to see that the Federal
government was obligated under either the agreement of
1806 or the earlier ordinance relative to the Southwest Territory. Why should the eastern states surrender their claims
to a portion of the public domain in order that a certain
western state might maintain common schools? If the arguments of the gentlemen from Tennessee should be pursued
to their conclusion, Davis explained, they would advocate
"forcing the rich man to divide with the poor; the man who
has fertile lands and large crops, to contribute to him who has
poor lands and small crops." Should the bill pass it would
constitute a "naked gift" to Tennessee.

Although Massachusetts had been the leader in the field of
public education and its people could appreciate Tennessee's
problem, Davis said he could not support a proposal to grant
land to one state unless similar grants were to be made to the
others. Besides, if these lands would be of such value to Tennessee, why would they not be of equal value to the Federal
government? It was unfortunate that Tennessee had made a
bad bargain and had been put to some expense, yet surely the
United States could not be expected to compensate for this
mistake. He considered that the western country had already
become the "petchild of this government, always asking, and
always receiving, as from an indulgent parent." [30]

Davis was joined by John Locke of the same state and by
William McCoy of Virginia. McCoy insisted that the Federal
government was not obligated to cede one foot of land to
Tennessee. Locke demanded a thorough investigation of the

[29] *Ibid.*, 2524–34.   [30] *Ibid.*, 2542–48.

amount and value of these lands before any action was taken.[31]

This was but a preliminary of a more extensive battle between eastern and western states over the disposition of the public domain. The Tennessee land bill was tabled for the remainder of the session but was called up again on January 5, 1829. By this time David Crockett had experienced a change of heart. He had lost some of his enthusiasm for common schools and become more interested in pre-emption rights for squatters.

Crockett's new idea was to substitute for the cession bill a pre-emption bill which would enable each of his squatter constituents to pre-empt the 160 acres on which he had settled. It was with regret, Crockett said, that he felt compelled to differ with his colleagues, and he was also cognizant of the instructions adopted by the Tennessee legislature. But he recognized a greater obligation to his constituents than to the legislature. He considered himself the representative of the "hardy sons of the soil" who had opened up the wilderness to make homes for their families. Many of those who were classed as squatters, he explained, had formerly settled on good lands to which they thought they had a legal claim. Then came strangers bringing warrants "of older date than theirs," and the occupants lost both their lands and improvements and were forced to move on to poor unoccupied lands still belonging to the Federal government.[32]

Polk replied that he, too, was friendly to the interests of the unfortunate squatters; yet he felt that such occupants could be cared for better by the state. In ceding the lands to Tennessee, Congress could specify that in disposing of them the state should give preference of entry to squatters.[33] Bell suggested that if preference was to be given to squatters a price of thirty-seven and a half cents per acre should be set for them. The residue should then be applied "to the con-

---

[31] *Ibid.*, 2514–15, 2523–24.　　[32] *Ibid.*, 20 Cong., 2 Sess., 161–63.
[33] *Ibid.*, 163.

struction of a road from Memphis to the Cumberland road at Zanesville." [34]

Whatever chance Tennessee had of securing these lands in her western district was ruined by the division within her congressional delegation. Furthermore, this discussion had important political results. Accused by his Tennessee colleagues of having been taken in by the most vindictive enemies of General Jackson, David Crockett, a "true frontiersman, with a small dash of civilization and a great deal of shrewdness," [35] became a permanent member of the opposition.

Concurrent with the discussion of the Tennessee land bill, the House was also debating a bill to repair and maintain the Cumberland Road. In 1803 Congress, in admitting Ohio into the Union, had agreed to spend five per cent of the proceeds from public land sales within that state in the construction of public roads, including one "leading from the navigable waters emptying into the Atlantic to the Ohio." Congress later authorized the expenditure of two per cent of this income on the building of a road from Cumberland, Maryland, to the Ohio River. The amount of money appropriated was inadequate, and construction was spread over a period of years. Before the heavy work was completed, much of the older part of the road was in such bad repair as to render it almost impassable.

Even though internal improvements at Federal expense were an important part of the "American System" which was being advocated by the nationalists in the period immediately following the War of 1812, many Republicans chose to remain loyal to the original principle of strict construction of the Constitution. During their presidencies, both Madison and Monroe frowned upon the expenditure of Federal money on internal improvement projects within the states. In 1817

34 *Ibid.*, 100.
35 Ben Perley Poore, *Perley's Reminiscences of Sixty Years in the National Metropolis* (Philadelphia, 1886), I, 152.

Madison vetoed the "Bonus Bill," and in 1822 Monroe rejected a proposal to appropriate money for the construction of toll gates along the Cumberland Road. John Quincy Adams, on the other hand, being an advocate of the "American System," was more liberal in his interpretation of the Constitution.

On January 15, 1829, the House began discussion on a bill to appropriate $100,000 for the purpose of constructing toll gates, at intervals of not less than ten miles, along a seventy-one-mile stretch of the Cumberland Road. Advocates of the bill claimed that the tolls would be adequate to defray all future expense of upkeep on the road.[36] But since the tolls were to be collected and spent by the Federal government, the old argument over state-Federal relations was revived.

Bell thought that if Congress possessed the power to construct roads, then it also had power to erect toll gates and to keep the roads in repair. The real error, he contended, had been made by those who had assumed that Congress possessed the power to construct roads. The exercise of such a power by Congress placed the property of every citizen at its mercy, should that property happen to lie within the path of a projected road or canal. Bell denied that roads could be constructed under the constitutional power to establish post offices and post roads, for that power must be interpreted in the light of the English meaning. During the colonial period the king's postmaster general was authorized to establish posts on the roads but not to establish roads. There was no justification, then, for the claim that a "mere transit right or right of way over the roads of the State, given for the purpose of carrying the mail, conferred upon Congress the right to legislate upon, or in any manner to interfere with, the construction of roads." Bell had reached the conclusion that should Congress assume supervision of a system of internal improvements the result would be disastrous to the liberty and prosperity of the people.

[36] *Cong. Debates,* 20 Cong., 2 Sess., 215.

There was still another point of objection, Bell argued. It was common knowledge that the sponsors of one internal improvement project could secure a majority vote in the House "only by making appropriations, or holding out expectation of early appropriations" for projects advocated by other members. Owing to this fact, the system resolved itself into "downright pillage and plunder, carried on in the regular forms of legislation, by one portion of the Union, against their fellow-citizens of other sections." The continuation of such a practice would cause the states to look upon the Federal government as a dispenser of "gratuities and bounties." Then, Bell reasoned, the Federal government would become all important and the states sink into insignificance. Congressmen would become mere seekers after appropriations for their home districts, and a congressman's worth would be measured by the appropriations he secured.[37]

During his first term in Congress, Bell had distinguished himself by his unobtrusive yet active course. One correspondent thought his argument was the ablest made on the Cumberland Road bill. Another admired the Congressman's "forcible and animated eloquence." [38] And, most important of all to a freshman congressman, his course was enthusiastically approved by his constituents.[39] To Bell himself the most challenging issue before the Twentieth Congress had been the proposed cession of lands to Tennessee for educational purposes. Several months later, in a speech to the alumni of the University of Nashville (the successor to Cumberland College), he explained fully his views on public responsibility for education. Deploring the fact that Tennessee ranked very low educationally, he pointed to the correspondingly "low ebb" of science. It was true, he said, that the earlier settlers had been forced to spend their time fighting

---

[37] Ibid., 339–50.
[38] Baltimore Republican and New York Statesman, quoted in National Banner and Nashville Whig, March 10, 1829.
[39] National Banner and Nashville Whig, March 10, 1829.

the forest and savages. They had won this fight. But, like the lands they occupy, the minds of every new people are in a forest state. "The incumbrances of both must be cleared away before the fruits and flowers of mature society spring up under the hand of cultivator, physical or moral. Fields, the dwelling, the farm-house and shop, precede the temples of science and the more costly monuments of art." The savages were now gone and much of the forest had been cleared. The remaining task was to provide "the staff of mental life to our children." In performing this duty it was necessary to "roll back the waves" of hostile public opinion. But he had confidence that the people had reason enough "to lay hold of this pillar of their safety" before it was too late.

What had been responsible for the neglect of education in Tennessee? How had it happened that school funds had not been provided and the colleges and academies had been "compelled to drag on a doubtful existence?" Why had no champion of the cause of education assumed the lead and aroused the people from "this extraordinary apathy?" The reasons, Bell thought, were quite logical. Educational funds had been dependent upon collections from the sale of school lands, and both in the location of these lands and in collections from their sale there had been a conflict with owners of land warrants and with the squatters. These two groups had proved adept at convincing legislators that the existing method of raising school funds was inimical to the welfare of the common man. Indeed, whole regions in each division of the state had become "standing and zealous declaimers against colleges and academies." Such institutions, it was being said, were solely for "the rich, the aristocracy of the land," and the common man would contribute to his own welfare by pulling them down. Thus had public opinion become so badly tainted that, in some sections, institutions of higher learning were "regarded not only with disfavor, but with positive odium." And politicians, sensing this public attitude, had in their quest for popularity and votes, "disregarded the rules of honor, propriety and justice in the discharge of a public trust."

Sectional jealousy, Bell asserted, had also helped to check educational growth. Those sections in which no colleges had been established were using this fact as an excuse for non-support. But certainly learning was not local. "It distributes itself, and seeks a theatre for its usefulness, in every quarter of the country." No town nor city had a monopoly on science, but the scarcity of funds made concentration necessary. The "object of human science, is the happiness of the human family." All acquisitions of knowledge by individuals must be "held in trust for the benefit of the whole society in which they live." What the people must be made to realize, Bell insisted, was that their efforts would be handsomely rewarded if the colleges turned out even a few scholars to lead their "countrymen into new paths of innocent pleasure, or open new sources of wealth and comfort."

Bell wished to connect the cause of common schools to that of higher learning. It was a mark of progress, he said, when the "schoolmaster is abroad in the land." Yet the schoolmaster must be a well-trained scholarly man; therefore, colleges must precede the extensive development of common schools. Bell did not advocate higher education for the masses; all could not become scholars. Common schools should provide for the needs of the masses; the colleges should give further development to the exceptional. "Besides," Bell thought, "practical husbandry, the first and noblest of the useful arts, and the mechanic trades can never be so successfully taught, whatever theories may exist to the contrary, as in the field and workshop."

An educational system adequate to the needs of Tennessee, Bell estimated, would cost from $120,000 to $200,000 annually. This amount could be provided either from a permanent fund or from taxation. There was no longer any need to look to the lands of West Tennessee as a possible source for school funds. Should Congress ever cede them to Tennessee they were "already pledged to the occupants, at a price which would not yield a twentieth part of the amount required." But there was another source—the 200,000,000 acre Federal domain in the western states and in the territories. He thought it quite likely that Congress might be persuaded to divide among the states the proceeds from the sale of these lands. From such a division Tennessee should get a total of about $5,000,000. Such a disposition of surplus Federal funds would be more beneficial than voting them away "in splendid bribes to particular states and sections of the Union, to answer political views, without regard to the general good." [40]

[40] Bell, *An Address Delivered at Nashville.*

Chapter III

RIDING WITH THE GENERAL

WHEN Jackson became President in March, 1829, no one gave clearer evidence of support of the new Administration than did Bell. During his first term in Congress he had consistently opposed legislative interference in presidential politics. The sensitive Old General must have observed with satisfaction Bell's vigorous opposition to the proposed investigation of the Mobile court-martial. Obviously, the exigencies of politics had registered a victory over human emotions. The new President needed support; the young Congressman needed prestige. Yet this was the extent of their friendship, for Jackson never invited Bell into the inner council of friends; and, as far as records reveal, never asked his advice or opinion in the formation of Administration policies or in matters of patronage.

When the Twenty-first Congress assembled in December, 1829, Bell was made chairman of the House Committee on Indian Affairs, a position he continued to hold until his retirement in 1841, except for the years 1833–1835 when he was chairman of the Judiciary Committee. Owing to the friction between Georgia and the Cherokee Nation and the simultaneous demand for removal of all Indians to territory west of the Mississippi, the Committee on Indian Affairs now occupied a position of more than ordinary importance. And since the administration of Indian affairs was among the duties of the Secretary of War, Bell was to be placed in close contact with an old friend and neighbor, John H. Eaton of Franklin, whom Jackson had recently appointed to the War Office.

In his first annual message to Congress Jackson invited attention to the condition of the Indian tribes, explaining that although the government's policy had been "to introduce among them the arts of civilization, in the hope of gradually reclaiming them from a wandering life," these unhappy people had been pushed farther and farther into the wilderness and had in general "retained their savage habits." In recent years the more civilized southern tribes had attempted to establish independent governments within the states of Georgia and Alabama. Such action could not be countenanced by the Federal government; therefore, these tribes had been notified either "to emigrate beyond the Mississippi or submit to the laws of those States."

Past experience, Jackson explained, had conclusively demonstrated that the subjection of Indians to white civilization tended to destroy their vigor. Then in the interest of "humanity and national honor," such a calamity ought to be averted whenever possible. In order "to preserve this much-injured race," the President suggested that a district be designated west of the Mississippi and "guaranteed to the Indian tribes as long as they should occupy it." Migration to this promised land should be voluntary, but those Indians who chose to remain in their present location were to be "distinctly informed" that they would be subject to the laws of the state in which they resided.[1]

Bell did not share Jackson's inveterate hostility to Indians; yet he did not believe that they possessed abstract rights. This portion of the President's message was referred to the Committee on Indian Affairs, and a lengthy report from that committee was presented by Bell on February 24, 1830. The British crown, the committee stated, had never recognized that North American Indians had any sovereign rights which must be respected by whites; neither had the English colonial governments recognized such rights. The treaty-making

---

[1] James D. Richardson (ed.), *A Compilation of the Messages and Papers of the Presidents* (New York, 1917), III, 1020–21.

policy which had long been followed had been prompted
by a desire for peace and economic advantage rather than
recognition of sovereign rights. The so-called relinquishment
treaties, in which Indians surrendered claims to certain lands,
were necessary only because of recognition of temporary
boundaries.

The Cherokee, in particular, the report explained, had
recognized the sovereignty of Great Britain in 1730, and in
more recent years, they had agreed to become wards of the
United States. The treaty guarantees granted these Indians
during Washington's administration were "more for the intimidation of the whites, than for the effect . . . on the Indians." Furthermore, the Federal government had never
possessed power to regulate Indian boundaries within a state.

It was not the pure-blooded Indians who opposed migration, Bell's committee contended, but a few whites and half-
breeds who dominated the tribes, disregarding the welfare of
the thousands of purebloods who were becoming more
miserable and would, if not relieved, eventually perish. Only
through migration to a region where there was opportunity
for physical and moral improvement could extinction be
averted.[2]

The House report and removal bill, both of which were
written by Bell, were vigorously denounced by eastern and
some northwestern congressmen. The demand for Indian removal, they charged, was purely an Administration measure,
a product of the greed of white men rather than a desire to
promote the interests of the red men. As passed by the two
houses of Congress, the bill authorized the President to arrange for the exchange of trans-Mississippi lands for those
claimed by tribes east of the river. The use of force in effecting the removal of the Indians was not authorized.[3]

[2] *Cong. Debates,* 21 Cong., 1 Sess., 580–81; *House Reports,* 21 Cong., 1 Sess.,
No. 227.

[3] *Cong. Debates,* 21 Cong., 1 Sess., 1135–36. For a full discussion of Indian
removals, see Grant Foreman, *Indian Removal, The Emigration of the Five
Civilized Tribes of Indians* (Norman, 1932).

The miserable plight of the southern Indians was a topic of frequent discussion during the period of removal and after, but the red man found few capable defenders in the section from which he was being removed. Not being given to nostalgia himself, Bell was among those who did not appreciate the Indian's love for his native soil. Furthermore, in view of his future speculation in lands ceded by the Indians, one suspects him of being one of those white men possessing some greed. The information collected by his committee must have been of considerable value to him in locating good lands. And members of the Bell family already residing in the Choctaw country no doubt furnished further data.

During the year following the passage of the removal bill, Edward Everett of Massachusetts made an unsuccessful attempt to convince Congress of the desirability of repealing the measure. Bell had not changed his mind. In reply to Everett, he insisted that the Cherokee were in a "most squalid and miserable condition; no further advanced in civilization, or in the arts of social life, than their ancestors of a century ago." The red man himself was receiving no benefits from the existing system. It was the few whites and half-breeds, "who had insinuated themselves into the confidence of the Indians," that were acquiring "wealth at the expense of those for whose welfare so many philanthropic wishes were expressed." The people of Georgia, he insisted, would never recede from their expressed stand; the laws of the state would be executed. Those who were pressing the repeal legislation were doing so "at the awful risk of producing a civil war." [4]

Owing to exhaustion from illness, Bell did not extend his remarks to great length. But his vigorous defense of the removal policy and the President's motives was described by a correspondent of the Boston *Statesman* as "a fine business-like, energetic speech, not one of your speeches for the ladies, rehearsed a dozen times before a glass." [5] Bell "is an ac-

[4] *Cong. Debates,* 21 Cong., 2 Sess., 774–75.
[5] Quoted in Nashville *Republican and State Gazette,* April 14, 1831.

complished and powerful orator," commented a reporter to the New York *Observer*. "I love to hear him." He was "probably as good an advocate for Georgia as was likely to stand up." [6] Bell himself was a bit disappointed over the failure of the Washington press to give more space to his speeches on Indian affairs. When a New Jersey admirer requested a copy of his latest speech, he replied that none had been printed. "The journals at Washington have never thought my efforts worth preserving & therefore, the public has never been able to pass of [*sic*] them. I am not ambitious enough to submit my pretentions in the usual way of speech makers at Washington." [7]

During the discussion on the Indian question Congress was also debating whether the government should invest $150,000 in the Maysville, Washington, Paris, and Lexington Turnpike Road Company. The real question was not the advisability of the construction of a turnpike from Maysville to Lexington, Kentucky, but whether the Constitution permitted such an expenditure of Federal money. The advocates of the proposal were uncertain of Jackson's attitude. Even though, during his short term as senator, he had supported measures of internal improvement, his first annual message to Congress had been indefinite on this point. He had called attention to the great value of improvements; but at the same time, he had raised a constitutional question and warned against "encroachment upon the legitimate sphere of State sovereignty." [8]

In spite of misgivings on the part of some political associates,[9] Jackson vetoed the Maysville Road Bill on the ground that it was local rather than national in character. Lavish expenditures on internal improvements, even of a national

6 Quoted in *National Banner and Nashville Whig,* March 23, 1831.

7 Bell to Isaac Lyon, May 12, 1831, in collection of Lincoln National Life Foundation.

8 Richardson (ed.), *Messages and Papers,* III, 1014–15.

9 John C. Fitzpatrick (ed.), *The Autobiography of Martin Van Buren,* in American Historical Association, *Annual Report,* 1918, II (Washington, 1920), 325–26.

character, he further explained, must necessarily depend upon a continual surplus in the Treasury. Should there be such a surplus, its reduction could be better accomplished through a reduction in taxes. But if the people wished to have Federal money appropriated for minor improvement projects, then they should so amend the Constitution as to give Congress that power.[10]

Bell gave unreserved support to Jackson's veto; it was in harmony with his recently expressed opinions on internal improvements. If the people disapproved of the President's action, Bell said, they could make the fact known at the next election. He did not consider that Jackson had expressed opposition to all improvements. It was only "the present unequal and distracting mode of appropriating the public treasure" that the President opposed. Bell felt certain that the Chief Executive would approve all expenditures which would cement the Union, if the power of Congress to make them was embodied in an amendment to the Constitution.[11]

An attempt on the part of the House to override the President's veto revived the controversy over Indian removal. This veto, declared William Stanbery of Ohio, was more the voice of the "chief minister" than that of the President himself. This document was "artfully contrived" to place internal improvements in disrepute and to deceive the public. It could not have been the work of the President, for it was "not characterized by that frankness which marks his character." In fact it had "every appearance of a low, electioneering document." The whole affair was reminiscent of the recent pressure which the cabinet had applied in favor of the Indian bill.

As soon as Stanbery had concluded, Bell tried to get the floor. Three were ahead of him. One of the three was Polk. This attack upon the President, Polk charged, "was gratuitous, and wholly unjustified, not sustained in a single par-

10 Richardson (ed.), *Messages and Papers*, III, 1046 ff.
11 *Cong. Debates*, 21 Cong., 1 Sess., 1145–47.

ticular by the truth, and wholly unfounded in fact." He was
glad to see Stanbery come out in the open, however, for, although that gentleman had been elected by the friends of
Jackson, he had not supported the Administration on a single
important measure.

When Bell finally got the floor, he had cooled down somewhat but was still excited. He called the House to witness
whether such an attack upon the so-called ministry "had not
assumed the manner of a blackguard." The Chair called him
to order. Continuing in a bit more cautious manner, he
denied that the House had been "dragooned into the passage
of the Indian bill by the heads of the departments." The
President, in taking his stand, had been aware of the prejudices on the Indian question, "yet he dared take the course
he did, because he loved his country." And those who had supported the Indian bill had not done so for political reasons.
Addressing themselves "to higher and nobler feelings," they
had placed the "welfare of the Indians" and the "honor of
the country" above all other considerations. As for the President, "He threw himself on the side of the weak, and braved
the opposition of the strong; and in that measure, as well as in
the one under consideration, he had indicated the destiny to
which he was born—to rescue his country from the midst of
dangers which threatened to overwhelm it." [12]

During these early tests of Administration strength the
close friends of the President had no cause to find fault with
Bell's actions. Even Jackson himself looked with favor upon
the Nashville Congressman. When the Peggy Eaton affair
rocked the Administration and eventually wrecked the
cabinet in 1831, Bell, making no recorded statement, conducted himself with circumspection; he had no desire to become needlessly involved in an affair which was dividing his
friends. His sympathy was probably with the Eatons, yet he
had friends on the other side. Jackson, in recasting his cabinet, offered Hugh L. White of Tennessee the War Office

12 *Ibid.,* 1140–47.

vacated by John H. Eaton. White, in declining the offer, recommended Bell for the position.[13] Even William B. Lewis, a confidant of the President and a resident of the White House, thought it likely that Bell would be brought into the cabinet, probably as Attorney General.[14]

A cabinet post might have been offered Bell had it not been for the breach between Lewis and Andrew Jackson Donelson, the President's nephew and private secretary. Both were Bell's friends and, working together, could have influenced Jackson. But the Eaton affair, added to the jealousy which had already developed, removed all possibility of cooperation between Lewis and Donelson. The latter felt that Lewis' residence at the White House had inflated his ego and that he was even desirous of seeing the Donelsons, A. J. and Emily, leave so that his own daughter might become mistress of the White House.[15] Furthermore, Emily Donelson refused to associate with the notorious Peggy Eaton as a social equal and was sustained by her husband. The irate Jackson gave the Donelsons their choice of accepting Mrs. Eaton or returning to Tennessee. They chose Tennessee, and the Old General's feelings were badly hurt. Unburdening himself to John Coffee, he told of the great humiliation he had suffered as a result of "the course taken by Andrew and Emily." Except for Bell, he said, all of Donelson's recent associates were enemies of the Administration.[16]

Back in Nashville during the summer of 1831, Bell, John C. McLemore, who had married a niece of Rachel Jackson, and Alfred Balch, a planter friend and neighbor of Jackson, attempted to reconcile Donelson and his uncle. After discussing the matter with Donelson, Bell and McLemore advised him to return to Washington just as if nothing had happened.

[13] Hugh L. White to William Vaulx *et al.*, August 22, 1836, in Nashville *Republican and State Gazette*, September 6, 1836.
[14] William B. Lewis to Amos Kendall, May 25, 1831, in James Parton, *Life of Andrew Jackson* (Boston, 1866), III, 383.
[15] Marquis James, *The Life of Andrew Jackson* (Indianapolis, 1938), 513–15.
[16] Jackson to John Coffee, May 13, 1831, in Bassett (ed.), *Correspondence*, IV, 280–84.

McLemore then wrote Jackson [17] of the advice to Donelson, which had been given after conference with "our much esteemed friend Colo. John Bell who on all occasions has shewn himself the true friend of your administration and an honest desire to keep your friends and particularly your connections United and in whose judgement [sic] I have great confidence." It was hoped, McLemore continued, that should the Donelsons return, there would be "no necessity for the specification of terms on one side or the other." [18] In September, 1831, the Eatons left Washington for Tennessee, and during the same month the Donelsons returned to the White House.

Peggy Eaton was well received in her husband's home state. According to John Overton's report to Jackson, Mrs. Boyd McNairy was the only prominent Tennessee lady who refused to be sociable.[19] Dr. Boyd McNairy, sometime president of the Nashville Bank, had long been one of Jackson's most vigorous enemies. During the presidential campaign of 1828, he had revived and placed again in circulation the old charge of Jackson's complicity in the Burr "conspiracy," publishing two alleged Jackson letters to prove his charge.[20] Overton was not exactly correct in his statement as to Mrs. Eaton's reception; McLemore told Donelson that, in deference to Emily's feelings, his wife had also refrained from calling on Mrs. Eaton, although Bell had insisted that a call would be quite proper. Both McLemore and Bell were friendly to Eaton and attended the public functions given in his honor.[21]

While Jackson's Nashville friends were entertaining the

[17] John C. McLemore to Jackson, July 29, 1831, *ibid.*, 323. Bell also signed this letter.

[18] At an earlier date Jackson had insisted that should Emily return to the White House she must change her attitude toward Peggy.

[19] Jackson to Martin Van Buren, November 14, 1831, in Bassett (ed.), *Correspondence*, IV, 374–75.

[20] *Id.* to Richard Call, August 16, 1828; *id.* to Lewis, August 19, 1828, *ibid.*, III, 426–28.

[21] McLemore to Andrew Jackson Donelson, November 9, 1831, in Andrew Jackson Donelson Papers (Division of Manuscripts, Library of Congress).

Eatons, John Branch and family arrived in the city. Branch, recently Secretary of the Navy in Jackson's cabinet, was among those who had unwillingly retired from office as a result of the Eaton controversy. Shortly before his retirement, his daughter Margaret had married Daniel Donelson, a brother of the President's secretary. After his resignation from the cabinet, Branch had retained his close friendship with the Donelsons and Bell. He was now returning to Washington as a member of the House, and a number of Jackson's friends were interested in healing the breach between the two men. Donelson's return to Washington prior to Branch's arrival in Nashville left the responsibility upon Mc-Lemore and Bell. In addition to discussing with Branch his recent relations with Jackson, they also attempted to make his visit "as suthing [sic] to his feelings as possible." He was a guest at several dinners in Nashville and in Franklin, Eaton's home town. He was also honored with an elaborate dinner at the home of Dr. Boyd McNairy. McLemore was not present but Bell and several other "thorough going Jackson men" attended. Bell also took Branch to a session of the state legislature and the two were honored with seats within the bar. "Bell done [sic] every thing he cou'd to render Branches [sic] situation as agreeable as possible," reported McLemore, "—he is a noble fellow. Jackson and Branch never had a better friend than he is." [22]

Bell's effort at reconciliation was a failure; Branch was in the opposition ranks in the election of 1832. Jackson left no record of his reaction to Bell's attempts to restore harmony, but the Congressman's friendly gestures dispersed all opposition to his own re-election to Congress. When he returned to Washington for the opening session of the Twenty-second Congress, he was in a loyal mood toward Jackson. The introduction of the Bank recharter bill soon put this loyalty to a test.

On January 9, 1832, Nicholas Biddle, president of the Bank

22 *Ibid.*

COURTHOUSE AT NASHVILLE, 1832
Nashville Inn is at the left, City Hotel at the right.

of the United States, petitioned Congress for a new charter
for his institution. The Bank, which had been granted a
twenty-year charter in 1816, had four more years of privileged
existence; [23] but Biddle, after months of serious consideration,
had decided to push the issue in 1832. He had been in close
touch with Thomas Cadwalader, his representative at Washington, who was seeking to ascertain the attitude of the President and a number of doubtful congressmen. On two
occasions Cadwalader mentioned Bell in his reports. On
December 21, 1831, he wrote Biddle that Bell was for recharter "but not if *now tested.*" Four days later he reported
that Bell "will vote with us *if he can.*" [24] Cadwalader might
have known something of the earlier coolness between Bell
and Jackson. On the other hand, he certainly knew that Bell's
position back home was such that he could not afford an open
break with the President at that time.

Jackson's avowed opposition to the Bank in its existing
form, the advice of caution from the President's friends, the
urging by the National Republicans, and Cadwalader's intimate reports had all been carefully weighed before Biddle
made his request for a new charter. Bank opponents met this
request with a determination that no action should be taken
until the institution and its activities had been investigated.
Accordingly, on February 23, 1832, Augustin S. Clayton of
Georgia introduced in the House a resolution calling for the
appointment of a select committee to carry on the investigation. In support of his resolution, Clayton called attention to
seven alleged violations of the Bank's charter which should
lead to forfeiture and to fifteen alleged abuses which, if true,
should prevent a recharter.[25]

[23] The charter provided that the Federal government should own one fifth
of the stock, appoint one fifth of the directors, and keep its surplus funds on
deposit with the Bank, unless the Secretary of the Treasury should see fit to
do otherwise.

[24] Thomas Cadwalader to Nicholas Biddle, December 21, 25, 1831, in Reginald C. McGrane (ed.), *The Correspondence of Nicholas Biddle Dealing with
National Affairs, 1807–1844* (Boston, 1919), 150, 156.

[25] *Cong. Debates,* 22 Cong., 1 Sess., 1846.

Clayton's resolution and points of indictment drew from Bell his first public discussion of the Bank question. He pronounced the proposed investigation both "proper and desirable" since it would satisfy the public as to the true condition of the institution. Furthermore, such an investigation should precede any action on the recharter proposal. If the Bank had abused the privileges conferred upon it by its charter then those abuses should be publicly known. Their repetition could be prevented by the provisions of any new charter. For, in Bell's opinion, if all of Clayton's charges "should be established, they would still not be conclusive against the recharter of the same bank, or of a new one." Such a revelation would merely indicate the need for greater "circumspection and vigilance" in determining the provisions of the new charter. He, for one, would not favor an investigation for the purpose of destroying the Bank. He thought it was unfortunate that the question of recharter had been brought at that time and expressed a desire to see the whole matter postponed until the next session of Congress. At the same time, he said that he concurred in the opinion that "questions of great public interest should not yield or be postponed on the ground of any probable effect their decision may have upon the elevation of one man or another to mere place of power." Still he was unable to see how the public interests could suffer from the postponement of this bill. "As to the propriety of rechartering the bank, I will say that I am friendly to the policy of giving to, or of maintaining the exercise of the power of this Government, of administering a corrective to a vitiated, excessive, or fluctuating currency; and I hope that the proposition to recharter the present bank will assume such a shape, that I can give my vote in favor of it."

Bell said he had observed that speakers on both sides of the question had attempted to interpret the views of the President as expressed in his messages to Congress. On the one side, it had been declared that the President was definitely hostile to the Bank and would be unalterably opposed to its recharter in any form. On the other, the opinion had been expressed that the President would sanction any recharter bill which Congress might see fit to pass. Bell could find no justification for either of these opinions; President Jackson had not expressed his intentions, but had reserved the privilege of exercising his own judgment. Should a recharter bill eventually be sent to the President, Bell had no doubt but that he would act "under a full and solemn sense of his responsibility to the country—upon a deliberate consideration of all the great interests connected with the question, and in perfect consistency with his own character."

Bell challenged the assumption that there was necessarily a connection between the Bank question and political parties. The Jackson Administration, he contended, had ardent supporters in all sections of the country, and they included both friends and foes of the Bank. If those in charge of the affairs of that institution were seeking to make it a political issue, then this was the most serious charge that could be brought against the Bank. Those who were responsible for such a situation must be held strictly accountable for this most fatal of all injuries.

Owing to his failure to make a bold statement of his position, Jackson was being accused of shunning his responsibility. Bell saw no justice in such an accusation. Both Congress and the President had their own duties; neither was responsible to the other. When the proper time should come it would then be seen whether the Old Hero would shirk his responsibility. Never, Bell exclaimed, would political considerations influence Andrew Jackson in making a decision. Regardless of whether or not the public approved of whatever stand he felt compelled to take on the Bank question, the people would "still sustain him, upon the ground of their confidence in his integrity, and in the wisdom of his course in relation to other great interests of the country." Bell prophesied that the Bank question would have little influence in the coming presidential campaign.

Biddle's desire to secure a new charter well in advance of 1836 was understandable, Bell admitted, but he doubted the wisdom of granting such a charter in 1832. The remainder of the public debt would soon be retired, and he thought it advisable to wait and observe the effects this action might have on the economic and financial conditions of the country. Congress would then be better prepared to say just what provisions should be incorporated in the new charter. The purpose of the time limit in the existing charter was to cause those who managed the Bank to be regardful of their behavior. The continuation of the institution was to depend on how well it served its purpose. To recharter in 1832 would be to relieve the Bank of four years of responsibility.

Before any action should be taken on this important subject, Bell concluded, he, for one, would like "to hear the voice of the people uttered through the next Congress." The representation of the people should never forestall public opinion by "precipitate and premature action." Since there was no proof of a settled public opinion on the Bank question, Bell did not believe the friends of the President could conscientiously advise him to sign a recharter bill in 1832.[26]

Not having definitely made up his mind on the recharter proposal, Bell needed more time. He had no desire to see the Bank become a political question, though he professed not to fear its influence; neither did he wish to see the institution destroyed. He was certain of only one thing—he wished the recharter proposal postponed. Increasingly Bell was being drawn into closer relations with Nashville business circles. These business men liked the services rendered by the Nashville branch of the Bank which furnished a considerable portion of the state's circulating medium and had been liberal in its loan policy. Further, Bell's brother James, a Nashville business man and a heavy borrower from the Bank, was a member of the board of directors of the Nashville branch.[27]

[26] *Cong. Debates*, 22 Cong., 1 Sess., 2076–87.
[27] Nashville *National Banner and Daily Advertiser*, April 9, 1833.

It was later revealed that in 1832 John Bell himself was obligated to the Bank as borrower and endorser to the extent of $53,000. That he hoped for further accommodation is quite likely, for during the following year his obligation was increased by another $7,000. Against this financial pressure, however, Bell must weigh the probable political reaction of westerners who were opposed to banks in general and to the United States Bank in particular. Truly the Congressman was astride the fence, faced with the necessity of walking with bankers and not losing touch with the common man. The Old General in the White House must have raised his eyebrows when he read Bell's speech, for here was the first indication that the Nashville Congressman might not go all the way with the Administration.

Although the Clayton committee uncovered nothing for which the Bank could properly be condemned, Jackson appeared confirmed in his opposition. Whatever chance Biddle previously had had for an understanding with the President vanished. To continue to push the recharter bill meant to break completely with Jackson, but to fail to do so would result in losing the support of Clay and the National Republicans. Biddle chose to push the bill. It passed each house of Congress by a small margin, and was vetoed by the President. The Executive Department had no desire for the continuation of the Bank, Jackson recorded in his veto message. He considered such a privileged institution both unconstitutional and dangerous. Its recharter would place in jeopardy the liberties of the people.[28]

At the same time that Clay and his friends were pushing the Bank issue they were also eager to make some adjustment in the tariff schedule. In its existing form, the tariff could scarcely be defended by even the most rabid protectionist. Preparatory to a solution of this problem and as a test of Senate opinion on the tariff question, Clay introduced a resolution calling for the abolition of duties on all non-

28 Richardson (ed.), *Messages and Papers*, III, 1139 ff.

competitive goods except wines and silks.[29] A heated and lengthy debate began immediately.

A similar debate opened in the House when John Quincy Adams introduced a bill which eventually became the tariff act of 1832. High duties were to be levied on such items as came into competition with American-produced goods; noncompetitive articles were either to be exempt or subjected to a very low rate.

Bell, expressing fear for the safety of the Union, registered a vigorous opposition to the proposal. The price of cotton and wool and the profits from manufactured goods, he asserted, were secondary in comparison with "domestic peace, of free Government, of liberty itself." Already, in those sections which were adversely affected by the protective tariff, a probable dissolution of the Union was being widely discussed. Only a short time ago such a suggestion would have been considered as "downright blasphemy." But now the freedom and happiness of a prosperous country were being threatened by "the thirst for accumulation, and the desire of personal distinction, avarice and ambition."

Bell pointed out that from the beginning of the Federal government there had always been two political extremes. One group had feared the concentration of too much power in the hands of the Federal government. The other wished to see state powers diminished in favor of the national government. Some feared "the forms and arbitrary powers of a monarchy"; others feared the insecurity and disorder of "uncontrolled anarchy." In recent years the extremists of these two groups had acquired new vigor as a result of their selfishness and mercenary desires. One extreme now avowed the "doctrine of infallibility of the Supreme Court" in matters involving constitutional interpretation. The other proclaimed the doctrine of nullification. Both groups were advocates of union—a union "upon their own terms."

Bell professed to see only one ray of hope. In past political

[29] *Cong. Debates,* 22 Cong., 1 Sess., 55.

struggles there had always been a group of moderates sufficient in strength to give to the government a "spirit of moderation and compromise." As one of those moderates, he now felt compelled to insist that the existing tariff be modified. In his opinion, Bell said, the so-called "American System" was nothing more than a "European system transferred to America," a transfer made "without the slightest regard to the peculiar and distinguishing circumstances in the condition of American States." This European system was designed to protect thrones and perpetuate inequality among subjects. If the United States intended adopting this "system of monopolies, then, we must proceed upon the idea that it is proper to assimilate the condition of our population to that of the States of Europe, in respect to the inequality of rank and fortune; and, further, to concentrate the wealth of the country in the pockets of the few, that it may be always most accessible to the wants of the Government." Bell could not conceive of a system more directly in violation of the interests and principles of America. He considered all monopolies and trade restrictions which were "not essential to the preservation of the order and morals of society" to be "directly at war with every end and aim of all our political institutions." A truly American policy, he explained, must be one that encouraged equality in rank and discouraged the concentration of wealth in the hands of a few; this was the fundamental principle upon which the American government was founded. The "accumulation of overgrown individual fortunes" was nothing short of a "positive national evil." Only with the assistance of unwise or faulty laws, he asserted, could one accumulate a fortune out of proportion to the amount of capital and labor involved. Such laws were destructive of both equality and liberty; they enabled a few, through "cunning, imposition, and fraud," to gather the fruits of the labor of others.

Bell reasoned that all wealth was the product of mental or corporeal toil; therefore, a nation's aggregate wealth in any given year was "the result of the labor of the whole population during that year, and of the employment of the capital accumulated by the labor of preceding years." True increase in national wealth was measured by the general increase in comforts among the masses of the people.

Tracing the development of protectionist demands, Bell pictured manufacturers in the late postwar period as humble petitioners for moderate protection. Then came the depression of 1819, with its attendant suffering among the masses, which, combined with the "impatience and avarice of the wealthy," was used to produce a general impression that a further increase in the tariff was necessary. It was a "disastrous day" for America when Congress became a party to this effort to relieve the oppressed by means of government regulation. Since the passage of the protective act of 1824, Bell charged, the industry of one section had profited "at the expense of the labor and capital of others." Instead of promoting the common good, the policy of government had inaugurated a "mercenary war of sections." In this war the North and East had been the winner, and their cities were rivaling those of Europe in luxury. Meanwhile, the fertile soil of the Southwest had enabled that section to hold its own fairly well; but exhausted soil, low prices for farm produce, and high prices for the products of industry were having a disastrous effect upon the Southeast. Certainly those who were boasting of the growth of national prosperity could not be including the South or Southeast as a part of the nation! "Rome is substituted for Italy, or, rather Italy is substituted for the whole empire."

Bell said he was unable to see that the South and Southwest had derived any benefits from the protective tariff either in the form of increased wages or additional dividends on invested capital. Yet, at the same time, there was "not a Yankee notion vended in the South" but which was more expensive on account of the tariff. Bell also refused to accept the claim that the protective system stimulated the growth of factory towns which in turn furnished additional markets for farm produce. The only farmers to benefit, he contended, were those in the immediate vicinity of the towns.

Some persons, both in and out of Congress, had insisted that if the South was not prosperous then it should abandon cotton culture in favor of a more lucrative pursuit. Bell denounced this suggestion as the result of either pure ignorance or "a disposition to spoil with the misfortunes of the South." The cotton capitalist could no more afford to abandon his investment in slaves than the industrial capitalist could his investment in buildings and machinery. Besides, Bell exclaimed, there were legal and moral codes which demanded that slaves be supported regardless of profits. Concluding his attack on the protective system, he declared:

> I assert that the effect of this system, even in the States most benefited by it, is to degrade and depress the mass of the people, which must always consist of laborers and operative mechanics. I reaffirm that its inevitable tendency is to depress the present poor below the condition to which, from the advantage of soil, climate, and a Government free in form, they might aspire. By this system the poor are made poorer and the rich richer. It is a false theory, a fatally false theory, which maintains that the tax imposed by the protective policy falls equally upon the capital and labor of the country.[30]

Although Bell opposed the protective system, he aided in the passage of the bill before the House; it gave some relief even though it did no serious damage to the protective principle.[31] His constituents found no special fault with his action. The populace applauded his tirade against the concentration of wealth; and his business friends, most of whom were merely well-to-do, not wealthy, saw no threat to their prosperity.

The proximity of Bell's tariff views to those of closer friends of the President was evidenced by the remarks in the Washington *Globe*, the official Jackson organ. Bell's views, the

---

[30] *Ibid.*, 3348–86.   [31] *Ibid.*, 3830.

editor wrote, were "enlarged and statesman-like" and not the type that were "engendered in the brain of the visionary and theoretical political economist." His speech was "distinguished for the eloquence and judgment which pervaded it, [and] *the temper* by which it was characterized." [32]

Among the interested spectators in the House during the heated debates in the spring of 1832 was the eccentric Mrs. Anne Royall whose caustic words were as a scourge to those who fell under her displeasure. Through the columns of her small newspaper, *Paul Pry,* she was fond of scrutinizing the motives and actions of public men. And woe be unto those who treated her with disdain or advocated measures of which she disapproved. Bell was among the more fortunate:

> He [Bell] is one of the great champions of the people's rights, nor does he lack the talents or the independence to stand up for them in debate. He is all powerful, and though not a flowery speaker, his arguments are convincing, and his reasoning clear and strong. His gestures are graceful and pertinent, and his language flows with great fluency and ease. If he is not already, the time is near at hand when Mr. Bell will have few equals in the House. He improves every session. His fine appearance and his dignified manner command great respect.[33]

The first session of the Twenty-second Congress adjourned on July 16, 1832, and Bell hurried home to the bedside of his sick wife, who died on September 28, leaving five children.[34] There is no indication that Bell's family had ever accompanied him to Washington. Who now assumed the responsibility of caring for the five motherless children is not revealed. It is probable that they went to Murfreesboro to live in the home of their grandfather Dickinson. When Dickinson died in 1848 these grandchildren were well provided for in his

[32] Washington *Globe,* June 11, 1832.
[33] *Paul Pry* (Washington), August 4, 1832.
[34] Nashville *Republican and State Gazette,* October 3, 1832. The children were Mary, who married David Maney; John, Jr., who married Fanny Maney; David Dickinson, who married Kate Gibbs; Fanny, who married Thomas Maney, a brother to Mary's husband; and Sally, who married Edwin A. Keeble.

will.[35] No letters between Bell and his children exist to furnish knowledge of his family relations. Nothing is known of the education or training of the children. Neither of the two sons became active in politics. Years later John, Jr. was in some undetermined way connected with his father's mining business, although he continued to reside in or near Murfreesboro. The three daughters likewise established homes in that locality. David Dickinson moved to West Tennessee in the vicinity of Union City.

[35] Rutherford County Wills, Book 14, pp. 411–20.

Chapter IV

TOWARD THE OPPOSITION

THE dire punishment promised Jackson by the National Republicans for his veto of the Maysville Road Bill and the bill to recharter the United States Bank failed to materialize in the presidential election of 1832. Jackson was overwhelmingly re-elected, and he considered his victory over Clay a mandate from the people to remain firm in his views and carry to completion the tasks he had begun.

Shortly after the election, a South Carolina convention issued an Ordinance of Nullification, declaring the tariff acts of 1828 and 1832 null and void within the limits of that state. This action brought to a climax a growing grievance in the state against the protective system. During the 1820's South Carolina had become restive under the high tariff; in 1828 John C. Calhoun had written his momentous *Exposition and Protest,* which set forth the theory that a state convention could nullify a Federal law which was believed to be unconstitutional. In 1830, Robert Y. Hayne presented this doctrine to the Senate during the course of the debate on the Foot Resolution, and it was well received by many friends of the President. Jackson made no public statement as to his position on the subject until the Jefferson Birthday Dinner at which time he offered his well-known toast: "Our Federal Union: it must be preserved." This stand on the part of the Chief chilled the enthusiasm of some of his followers who had sanctioned nullification in the abstract, but the doctrine remained a threat, especially in South Carolina.

Following the passage of the tariff of 1832, a majority of

South Carolina's congressional delegation, despairing of any relief from either Congress or the President, advised their constituents to take matters into their own hands. The passage of the Ordinance of Nullification soon followed. Jackson replied with his Nullification Proclamation, in which he urged South Carolinians to abandon the leadership of those designing disunionists who had led them into the error of attempted nullification. Peaceable nullification, he said, was impossible; the use of force was treason. Since the chief executive of the Union was pledged to its preservation, he must and would enforce Federal law in every state.[1]

The President's proclamation was a blow to state rights; and many Southerners, still loyal to original Jeffersonian principles, considered it an ominous sign. Nowhere was the division on nullification along strict party lines; neither was it the same as the division on the tariff. Many Jackson supporters, Bell among them, were opposed to high protection and at the same time opposed to nullification. On the other hand, most anti-Jackson men, although reluctant to support the Administration in any matter whatsoever, were likewise opposed to nullification. Both major political groups were eager to receive credit for a satisfactory solution of the problem.

Late in December, 1832, Gulian C. Verplanck of New York, a Jackson supporter, introduced in the House a bill providing for a 50 per cent reduction in the tariff within the next two years. This bill made little progress. High tariff men of both parties considered the reduction too drastic; anti-Jackson men were lukewarm because the bill came from Administration sources; and the nullifiers remained silent. On January 12, 1833, Bell confided to John Overton of Tennessee that he doubted the passage of the Verplanck bill in its existing form. In fact, he doubted the passage of any tariff bill during the session. He had noted that, even though most of the opposition applauded the President's proclamation, their bitterness

[1] Richardson (ed.), *Messages and Papers*, III, 1203 ff.

toward the Administration had not subsided. In Washington, Bell concluded, "Political consideration and personal hate growing out of political contests supersede patriotic feelings." [2]

Bell had friends among the South Carolina delegates, and his sympathy for them was noticeable enough to cause John Quincy Adams erroneously to suspect him as a nullifier.[3] Bell later explained that he thought Jackson, in breaking with Calhoun, committed a blunder. It was both unstatesmanlike and bad political judgment for the President to drive from "his confidence" this influential Southern leader and take "under his patronage and training for the succession . . . a gentleman of the North, but of very different character and pretensions." [4]

Apparently in an attempt to relieve the tension produced by the tariff-nullification controversy, Bell privately suggested to Edward Everett of Massachusetts that a bill for the distribution of the proceeds from the sale of public lands be substituted "as an equivalent for the Tariff bill." When the protectionists showed no enthusiasm for this proposal, he then suggested that the Verplanck bill be made less severe by postponing the date on which some of its provisions were to become effective. This suggestion also found few supporters, and Adams, one of the protectionists, thought Bell appeared "in no small perplexity." [5]

In the meantime, Jackson, aroused by the defiant attitude of the nullifiers, had decided to take action. On January 16, 1833, he sent to Congress a special message requesting permission to use the army and navy in the enforcement of the revenue laws.[6] The Judiciary Committee of each house took the request under consideration, and in less than a week the

2 Bell to John Overton, January 12, 1833, in John Overton Papers (Tennessee Historical Society).

3 Charles Francis Adams (ed.), *Memoirs of John Quincy Adams* (Philadelphia, 1874–1877), VIII, 522.

4 *Cong. Debates*, 31 Cong., 1 Sess., Appendix, 1103.

5 Adams (ed.), *Memoirs of John Quincy Adams*, VIII, 522, 526.

6 Richardson (ed.), *Messages and Papers*, III, 1173 ff.

Senate committee had reported a revenue collection bill, commonly known as the Force Bill. The House committee, of which Bell was chairman, showed some reluctance to approve so drastic a procedure. In presenting his committee's report on February 8, Bell explained that it represented a majority rather than a unanimous opinion.[7] The minority group, of which he was a member, subscribed to some but not all of the sentiments expressed and was contemplating the preparation of a separate report. What portion of the majority opinion he himself approved Bell did not say. The separate report was never made.

The majority report expressed opposition to the use of force except as a last resort. The very seriousness of South Carolina's attitude, it maintained, was evidence of a just complaint. Rather than devise means of enforcing an "obnoxious law," why not modify it? The passage of the Verplanck bill would "tend more effectually to allay the excited feeling of the south, to avert the crisis with which we are threatened, and to restore harmony to our once happy Union, than any provision which can be adopted for the removal of custom houses, clothing the courts with additional powers, or invasion by fleets and armies." The report further called attention to the fact that the power of the Federal government to coerce a state by military force had been discussed by the framers of the Constitution, but had not been conferred.[8]

The Senate rushed its Force Bill through on February 20. On the following day Bell attempted to call up this measure in the House by requesting a suspension of the special order of the day so as to clear the way for a proposal to have the Senate bill printed. Richard Wilde of Georgia objected, and the suspension motion failed for lack of a two-thirds majority.

---

[7] *Cong. Debates*, 22 Cong., 2 Sess., 1654. William W. Ellsworth of Connecticut and Samuel Beardsley of New York stated in the House that they were with Bell in the minority. This left the majority composed of Thomas F. Foster of Georgia, William F. Gordon of Virginia, Henry Daniel of Kentucky, and Richard Coulter of Pennsylvania.

[8] *House Reports,* 22 Cong., 2 Sess., No. 85.

Bell then asked unanimous consent of the House for the printing of the Senate measure. There was objection. Charles Wickliffe of Kentucky charged that the sole purpose back of the effort to get the Senate bill before the House was "to give quietus to the tariff bill for the residue of the session." He had no objection to the proposed printing, he explained, but he was impressed by the evidence that the Administration majority intended "to give the tariff bill the go-by." He was convinced that should the tariff bill be sidetracked for the Force Bill, there would be no return to the tariff.[9]

There was truth in Wickliffe's charge. He represented those who, although opposed to nullification, preferred a conciliatory tariff to the proposed use of force. A few days earlier this same viewpoint had been manifested in the Senate and had greatly irritated the Old General. Exhibiting both sternness and impatience, he wrote to Senator Grundy on February 13: "Surely you and all my friends will push that bill through the Senate—this is due to the country—it is due to me, and to the safety of this Union. . . . I have confidence you will push the bill, the whole bill and nothing but the bill." [10]

On February 25 an effort was again made to call up the Force Bill. Wickliffe renewed his previous charge that the friends of the Administration were trying to get a vote on this drastic measure in preference to a proposal designed "to give peace to the country." Bell denied that he wished to cut off debate. But as for the bill itself, he could not see that it was "fraught with the mischief which some gentlemen apprehended." He considered it to be "comparatively peaceable in its nature, and calculated to prevent bloodshed." If there was a disposition to pass the measure, said Bell, action should be taken immediately. Delay would mean death. Following

[9] *Cong. Debates,* 22 Cong., 2 Sess., 1755–61.

[10] Original in possession of Mrs. Whiteford Cole, Sr., Louisville. A copy, with slightly modified wording, is in the *American Historical Magazine* (Nashville), V (1900), 137. For some of the maneuvering in the Senate, see Parks, *Felix Grundy,* 196 ff.

quick action on the Force Bill, there would still be ample time to take up the proposed change in the tariff. Therefore, he insisted that the Force Bill be made the special order for the following day.

The report from the Judiciary Committee had been sent to the committee of the whole, observed Thomas Foster. Why not send the Senate bill to the same place? Bell's proposal to grant tariff relief *after* the passage of the Force Bill reminded Augustin Clayton of the anecdote of the fox's suggestion to his "importunate creditors" that collection of debts be postponed to the day following judgment day. The passage of the Force Bill, Clayton remarked, would create considerable sympathy for South Carolina, but the passage of the tariff measure would settle the controversy.

Warren R. Davis of South Carolina was most vehement in his opposition to Bell's apparent effort to give precedence to the Force Bill. South Carolina had not been responsible for the lack of progress made by the tariff measure, he exclaimed. Although the members from his state had been tortured by the "false, malicious, and defamatory libels on the State and people," they had refrained from discussing the tariff bill, which "had been creeping, loitering, drivelling, and dragging itself through six weeks of the session," lest they "shake too rudely the leaves of its olive branch." But now, Davis observed, the tariff bill was to be set aside and this "firebrand" given precedence because the President wished it. The sword was to be substituted for the olive branch! He desired to ask the chairman of the Judiciary Committee a direct question: Was it the intention of the Administration to give precedence to the revenue collection bill? Bell made a candid reply: "it was desired to have the measure passed as soon as practicable, and, for that purpose, to give it precedence." However, instead of holding South Carolina responsible for the lack of progress of the tariff bill, Bell added, he approved of the delegation's course "on the occasion." [11] A motion to postpone

[11] *Cong. Debates,* 22 Cong., 2 Sess., 1766–72.

for another week failed, and Bell succeeded in getting his bill made special order for February 26.

Before calling up the Force Bill on the twenty-sixth, the House passed a compromise tariff measure, sponsored by Henry Clay, which had been substituted for the Verplanck bill. All duties above 20 per cent were to be reduced gradually until by the close of 1842 there would be no rate above that figure. The feeling of certainty that South Carolina would accept this compromise and rescind her ordinance of nullification caused the opponents of the Force Bill to fight even harder to prevent what they considered unnecessary humiliation. But Bell and his associates were adamant. The Force Bill must pass. Motions to postpone, to table, to adjourn were voted down. There was considerable confusion in the House. Henry Dearborn of Massachusetts was calling for the previous question. The Chair was seeking a second to this motion. Midst cries for "order" and "count," George McDuffie of South Carolina cried out for "fair discussion." If forty members would stand by him, he yelled, he would "continue to move adjournments, and call for yeas and nays until the end of the session." Bell tried to speak but was drowned out. McDuffie began his motions to adjourn and was declared out of order by the Speaker. Bell finally made himself heard. If the opponents of the bill wanted discussion, he said, they could have it. He would not support the move for the previous question. McDuffie again called for adjournment and was again declared out of order. Bell attempted to continue his remarks, but could not be heard. Finally a semblance of order was restored, and the House agreed to a two-hour cooling-off period.[12]

The Force Bill was not discussed at the evening session, but was again taken up on February 27. No further postponement should be permitted, Bell contended. "It was due to the country, it was due to the friends and the opponents of the bill, that it should be disposed of."[13] The striking similarity

[12] *Ibid.*, 1811–12.   [13] *Ibid.*, 1817.

between these words and those written by Jackson to Grundy causes one to suspect that Bell had also had a communication from the White House. It is certain that the Chairman of the Judiciary Committee, although already somewhat on the fence as a result of the Bank discussion, was not yet ready to break with the Administration, especially when the Tennessee press was so outspoken in its support of Jackson.

The Force Bill finally passed a second reading on March 1. Bell demanded an immediate third reading, and the measure passed by a vote of 111 to 40.[14] The clock had just struck 1:00 A.M. Bell could now breathe freely; he had sustained the Administration, even though he was a bit uncertain about the advisability of its course; and he had pleased the people back home who had shifted from cheers for the advocates of the doctrine of nullification in 1830 to jeers for those who attempted to apply it in 1832. The great majority of Tennesseans were still under the charm of Old Hickory.

Two days after signing the tariff and Force bills, Jackson was inaugurated for a second term. The most important piece of unfinished business carried over into the new term was the Bank issue. The determination of the pro-Bank group not to give up the fight and the President's unwillingness to allow the institution to die a natural death three years later made a revival of the issue inevitable. Already, during the recent short session of Congress, Jackson had suggested further investigation of the Bank, questioned the safety of deposits, and recommended the sale of the government's one-fifth stock in the corporation.[15] Polk, carrying out instructions, introduced a bill authorizing the sale of the stock, but it was rejected. The House Ways and Means Committee conducted an extensive investigation and made both majority and minority reports. The majority report, favorable to the Bank, was adopted by the House; so was a resolution affirming the safety of the de-

[14] *Ibid.*, 1898.
[15] Richardson (ed.), *Messages and Papers*, III, 1162–63; Jackson to James K. Polk, December 16, 1832, in James K. Polk Papers (Division of Manuscripts, Library of Congress).

posits. Owing to extremely cold weather, Bell and three other Tennessee congressmen were absent when the resolution was called up for vote![16]

The minority report, submitted by Polk, accused the Bank officials of engaging in numerous irregular practices, and, in general, placed the institution in an unfavorable light. Although this report had no chance of acceptance by the House, it created considerable stir among Bank supporters both in and out of Congress. Bell, still hesitating to take a definite stand, kept quiet; but a number of Nashville business men, including several of his friends, held a protest meeting and denounced Polk's report as destructive of the economic welfare of the state and the people.[17]

Jackson gave little consideration to the majority report or to the House resolution expressing confidence in the safety of deposits; Polk's report was more to his liking. Spurred on by evidence of popular support and professing to believe the Federal deposits unsafe, Jackson resolved to have them gradually withdrawn. During the congressional recess of 1833, speaking through a new Secretary of the Treasury, Roger B. Taney, he ordered that no further Federal deposits be placed in the United States Bank. Owing to attendant financial derangement, a minor depression was probably inevitable, but Nicholas Biddle, through a drastic curtailment of Bank business, increased the severity of the panic. Who was responsible for the depression? Jackson and Biddle accused each other.

Jackson's many other activities during 1832–1833 did not preclude his meddling in Tennessee politics. The term of Senator Felix Grundy was to expire on March 3, 1833. Even though Grundy had been a loyal supporter of Administration measures, Jackson preferred to see John H. Eaton returned to the Senate in compensation for the treatment he had received

[16] Adams (ed.), *Memoirs of John Quincy Adams,* VIII, 533; *Cong. Debates,* 22 Cong., 2 Sess., 1936.

[17] Nashville *National Banner and Daily Advertiser,* March 29, April 3, 30, 1833.

at the hands of the President's enemies.[18] A third aspirant was Ephraim H. Foster, a boyhood neighbor and friend of Bell. Eaton was reluctant to run against Grundy but decided to do so upon being assured by Foster men that after casting a few votes for their candidate they would shift to Eaton.[19]

The Tennessee legislature convened on October 5, 1832, for the purpose of selecting a senator. Thirty ballots were cast and still no candidate received a majority, and the legislature adjourned without making a selection. The Foster men had failed to shift to Eaton. Bell opposed the re-election of Grundy and took some part in an attempt to brand the Senator as a nullifier,[20] but it is not clear whether he preferred Foster or Eaton. The Nashville *Union* later maintained that Bell had urged Foster to enter the contest and then deserted him, even going so far as to attempt to persuade him to retire in favor of Eaton. Failing in this, the *Union* charged, Bell "was absent when the 'tug of war' came, engaged in the intellectual and noble occupation of shooting ducks!" [21]

A year later the legislature returned to the task of selecting a senator. For some obscure reason Bell's name was added to the list of candidates. His apparent friendship for both Foster and Eaton gave him some strength as a possible compromise candidate to defeat Grundy. Eaton's voluntary withdrawal of his own name tended to indicate as much. But a few of Eaton's friends stood by him to the end, and although Bell received 23 votes on the forty-seventh ballot, he was still short of a majority. Grundy was elected on the fifty-fifth ballot.[22]

By the time Congress reconvened in December, 1833, an

[18] Jackson to A Committee, September ? , 1832, in Bassett (ed.), *Correspondence*, IV, 478.

[19] William Carroll to Jackson, December 3, 1833, in Samuel G. Heiskell, *Andrew Jackson and Early Tennessee History* (Nashville, 1921), III, 528; William A. Wade to William B. Campbell, October 10, 1833, in David Campbell Papers.

[20] John W. Childress to Polk, December 30, 1832, in Polk Papers. Grundy had openly proclaimed the doctrine of nullification in 1830.

[21] Nashville *Union*, October 28, 1837.

[22] Tennessee *House Journal*, 1833, pp. 77–94; Nashville *Republican and State Gazette*, October 8, 10, 1833.

aroused public was expressing its reaction to the removal of the deposits from the United States Bank. Some praised the courage and foresight of Old Hickory; others denounced him as the enemy of business. In the Senate, Clay and his associates unleashed a bitter attack which netted them nothing more than the adoption of a resolution censuring the President for his action. The House spent months debating the legality of the removal of the deposits and the advisability of ordering their restoration. Polk, as chairman of the Ways and Means Committee, bore the burden of defense and proved himself the master of the situation. Finally, on April 4, 1834, the debate was terminated; the deposits were not restored; and Polk induced the House to authorize a further investigation of the Bank by a select committee chosen by the Speaker.

While Polk fought Administration battles, Bell was conspicuously silent; but with the authorization of a Bank investigation, his silence changed to near panic. Seeking out John G. Watmough, a representative from Pennsylvania and a confidant of Biddle, Bell dragged him into a committee room, locked the door, and began "to unburden his soul." According to Watmough, he gave signs of great distress and was so excited as to render himself incoherent. Finally, he came to the point: he had recently written Biddle two letters concerning a possible loan for his brother. And in these letters he had fully expressed his sentiments "in relation to the Bank and *to the Party*," from which, Watmough surmised, Bell did not have "courage enough to disenthrall himself." These letters, Bell explained, were "*purely* confidential" and had been addressed to Biddle as a private individual, not as president of the Bank.

Bell's excitement had resulted from a hint, dropped by a member of the investigating committee, that all correspondence between congressmen and Bank officials was to be made public. Therefore, Bell asked Watmough to write Biddle, urging him not to surrender the correspondence if demanded by the committee. In reporting to Biddle this conversation with Bell, Watmough added: "He [Bell] is only held to the Party by the Will of his Constituents . . . [and] he looks forward to the time when he will be of use, when Public Sentiment will sustain him." [23] Bell's silence had already become noticeable, and anti-Bank men correctly suspected that his relations with Biddle were closer than was generally known.

On May 1 the investigating committee, sitting in Philadelphia, asked Biddle to submit copies of all correspondence between Bank officials and members of Congress, including unanswered letters, which had taken place since July 1, 1832, touching the subject of recharter or the removal or restoration of the deposits. Biddle refused to comply with the request, but not knowing what legal action might be taken by the committee and wishing to preserve the friendship of his correspondents, he assured Bell that there was no cause for alarm. Since he suspected a plan to injure the Tennessee Congressman, he was returning the two letters Bell had written. No person other than himself had read them or ever would unless Bell permitted it. He hoped the Tennessee Congressman would "perceive in this proceeding . . . evidence of deep respect." [24] The Banker saw future need for the support of the Congressman! No doubt Bell destroyed these letters. The historian can only wonder how far he had gone in his criticism of the Administration. It was certainly far enough to assure Biddle of his friendship and to secure further financial accommodation. It was too far to turn back, and he was now at the point where the opposition could use him as an entering wedge into the ranks of the Administration party. Biddle's refusal to submit either books or correspondence nullified the efforts of the investigating committee and its work came to nought. Nevertheless the final sentence had already been pronounced on the Bank: it must die in 1836.

During the hectic fight over the removal of the deposits,

[23] John G. Watmough to Biddle, April 19, 1834, in Nicholas Biddle Papers (Division of Manuscripts, Library of Congress).

[24] Biddle to Bell, May 2, 1834, *ibid.*

there was a rumor afloat that Speaker Andrew Stevenson might resign and accept a diplomatic post. Among those who had given circulation to this report were the close friends of James K. Polk. As early as August, 1833, Polk and Cave Johnson, a congressman from Clarksville, Tennessee, were sounding out members of the House on their attitude toward a possible elevation of Polk to the speakership.[25] There appears to be no evidence that President Jackson was the instigator of this movement; neither is it certain that he was especially interested in Polk's future. In fact, he had been looking with some favor upon James M. Wayne of Georgia, whom he pronounced "true and faithful." Stevenson had confided his intention to Wayne some months earlier and insisted that the Georgian become a candidate for the speakership. Wayne consulted Jackson and assured him that he would do nothing that would "split the party." Jackson expressed doubt as to whether Wayne could be elected but noted that Wayne himself thought so. The friends of the Administration "ought to have an understanding on this subject," Jackson informed Francis P. Blair.[26]

James Walker told Old Hickory about the plan to elevate Polk to the speakership, and Jackson was reported to have endorsed it *"decidedly and frankly."* [27] But Walker, a brother-in-law of Polk, did not say that Jackson was enthusiastic, and he got the impression that William B. Lewis, the President's close friend and adviser, preferred Bell for Speaker. Nevertheless, the news got around that Jackson favored Polk and the latter would be the party's candidate. It developed, however, that some twenty to thirty members of the party refused to respect the alleged wish of the President and resolved to support Bell. A number of anti-Jackson men, sensing division

[25] C. C. Clay to Polk, August 19, 1833; *id.* to Cave Johnson, August 19, 1833, in Polk Papers; Polk to *id.*, September 26, 1833, in *Tennessee Historical Magazine*, I (1915), 212–13.

[26] Jackson to Francis P. Blair, November 30, 1833, in Bassett (ed.), *Correspondence*, V, 230.

[27] James Walker to Polk, October 22, 1833, in Polk Papers.

within Administration ranks and regarding Bell as "no friend of Jackson, further than his present interest requires," determined to give him their support.[28]

Stevenson's resignation was finally submitted on June 2, 1834, and the election of his successor began a political controversy which grew in intensity during the following months and eventually rocked the foundation of the Democratic party. On the first ballot Polk received 42 votes to Bell's 30, with 64 going to Richard H. Wilde of Georgia. Following the casting of a few ballots, Wilde's friends lost hope and shifted to Wayne. Prior to the voting, some Whig newspapers had prophesied that Wayne would get more Whig support than any other Democrat.[29] When Wayne failed to command the required majority, a major portion of the Wilde-Wayne supporters, plus most of the eighteen who originally voted for Jesse Speight of North Carolina, shifted to Bell. The only other serious contender—Joel B. Sutherland of Pennsylvania —never received more than 34 votes and his friends eventually shifted to Polk. On the tenth ballot Bell received 114 votes to Polk's 78, and was escorted to the Chair by John Quincy Adams and Richard M. Johnson.[30]

An analysis of the vote reveals that Polk's support came entirely from Jackson–Van Buren men, although it does not appear that the President applied any pressure in Polk's behalf. Even after the election, Jackson still considered Bell his personal friend.[31] Bell held the vote of a minority within the Jackson party but was elected by opposition votes. That he was conscious of Bank support is evidenced by his immediate promise to Watmough to do all he could to assist that institution.[32] This friendship for Biddle and the Bank con-

[28] James Love to John J. Crittenden, May 27, 1834, in John J. Crittenden Papers (Division of Manuscripts, Library of Congress).

[29] Alexander A. Lawrence, *James Moore Wayne, Southern Unionist* (Chapel Hill, 1943), 70.

[30] *Cong. Debates*, 23 Cong., 1 Sess., 4371–73.

[31] Jackson to Van Buren, August 16, 1834, in Bassett (ed.), *Correspondence*, V, 282.

[32] Watmough to Biddle, June 17, 1834, in Biddle Papers.

tinued even after the Federal charter had expired.[33] Throughout the contest for the speakership, Bell kept his trail well covered, and what he did to secure election is not a matter of record. Of special interest is the unanswered question of what promises and assurances he was required to give the opposition party in return for votes.

Polk and his friends, seeking an excuse for defeat and sensing the political capital that might be made from the circumstances of the election, declared Bell had gone over to the opposition and began collecting evidence to prove their contentions. Jackson was not seriously concerned until the Polk group raised the cry. On the day following the election of Bell, Jackson's Washington organ, the *Globe,* informed its readers that the new Speaker had "given uniform, able, and consistent support" to Administration measures and was "a man of fine genius, high attainments, and distinguished for his eloquence." [34] But Duff Green of the *United States Telegraph,* who had been hostile to Jackson since the break with Calhoun, added salt to the opening wound when he commented that although the *Globe* seemed highly pleased with the selection of Bell, it was known that the new Speaker had received the vote of the opposition and had indirectly affirmed the fact that he was an anti–Van Buren candidate. Green pronounced Bell's election a sore defeat for the Administration, especially the "Kitchen Cabinet," the members of which had made themselves conspicuous in the House lobby. The very presence of Amos Kendall and William B. Lewis on Capitol Hill, Green contended, had lost votes for Polk.[35] Blair of the *Globe* denied "Kitchen Cabinet" interference; Lewis was a Bell man and Kendall had remained silent.[36]

As a part of the plan to expose Bell as an ally of the opposition, James Walker, Polk's brother-in-law and a resident of

---

[33] Bell to *id.,* July 14, 1835, January 3, 1839, in manuscript collection of the Historical Society of Pennsylvania.

[34] Washington *Globe,* June 3, 1834.

[35] Washington *United States Telegraph,* June 4, 1834.

[36] Washington *Globe,* June 5, 1834.

Columbia, hastened to Nashville with some editorials for publication in the newspapers there, but was astounded at the small amount of co-operation accorded him. He and James Grundy, the son of Senator Grundy, finally persuaded W. Hassell Hunt, proprietor of the *National Banner and Daily Advertiser,* to publish some "communications" from Washington. Allen A. Hall of the *Republican and State Gazette* refused to do even that much. Walker reported to Polk that Bell had "many warm and powerful friends" in Nashville, especially within the Bank group, and that the people of that city were "a most wretchedly Bank ridden population." Walker still believed, however, that Bell's popularity could be destroyed if the Speaker could be completely unmasked. He was attempting, he said, to show the people that Polk was defeated because he occupied higher ground than did Bell.[37]

Walker was not at all pleased with the *Banner*'s mild treatment of Bell. He maintained that the "communications" were not anything like what Hunt had promised James Grundy. "I suppose," he lamented, "that the Nashville editors cannot be induced to publish anything that they believe will affect Mr. Bell." [38] Failing in his effort to secure support from the Nashville papers, Walker was forced to use the columns of the Columbia *Observer* and give that paper wide circulation throughout Middle Tennessee.

Some of Bell's friends, especially Balie Peyton of Gallatin, replied that Polk's defeat was a result of his being too closely associated with the nullifiers.[39] Although vigorously denied by Polk, this charge was at least partially substantiated by Senator Willie P. Mangum of North Carolina. According to Mangum, the majority of the state rights group was not only opposed to Bell's election but actually had strong prejudices against him. The state rights men were particularly eager to

[37] Walker to Polk, June 24, 30, 1834, in Polk Papers.

[38] *Id,* to *id.,* June 30, 1894, *ibid.*

[39] Cave Johnson to *id.,* July 1, 1834; William C. Dunlap to *id.,* July 26, 1834, *ibid.*

defeat any and all friends of Van Buren; so they decided to support Richard H. Wilde as long as he had a chance and then shift to Polk. This decision to support Polk had come after Senator Felix Grundy, a kinsman of Calhoun and at one time a nullifier, had assured state rights men that Polk could be depended upon to oppose Van Buren and the "Kitchen Cabinet." It was further agreed, Mangum related, that Warren R. Davis of South Carolina was to take command of the state rights forces and give the signal if and when a shift was to be made from Wilde to Polk.

When balloting got under way in the House, business in the Senate chamber came to a standstill as members congregated in groups to discuss possibilities. Mangum observed that each time an increase in Polk's vote was announced Vice-President Van Buren appeared highly pleased, and Mangum concluded that the state rights men had been duped and cheated. Rushing across to the House chamber, he informed Davis of his suspicions and asked him to "withhold his fire." While crossing the lobby, Mangum met Polk and the latter remarked that if his state rights friends intended to assist him now was the critical moment. Mangum, however, had already made up his mind. At lunch that day, Balie Peyton had remarked in his presence that even though Bell was an Administration candidate, he would, if elected, feel it his duty to respect the parliamentary rights of all parties. It was this assurance, plus the feeling that they had been duped by Polk's friends, that resulted in the shift of state rights support to Bell. As far as Mangum knew, neither Bell nor his friends made any overtures to state rights men as a group.[40] Peyton's account of this affair would be most enlightening, but such papers as were preserved by him have been destroyed. He was a shrewd and elusive politician, and his friendship for Bell was no small factor in the latter's political advancement. Bell frequently used him as a front and Peyton enjoyed it thor-

[40] Willie P. Mangum to Bell, June 15, 1835, in *Tennessee Historical Magazine,* III (1917), 198–200.

oughly. His wit, sarcasm, and cleverness complemented the caution and stolidity of Bell.

Polk, apparently feeling a necessity for public explanation of his defeat, set about collecting statements from friendly members of Congress. Those who replied to his request for their version of the election were agreed on the principal points. Prior to the selection of a Speaker, they testified, the friends of the Administration, fearing defeat if too many candidates were put forth, had proposed a caucus for the purpose of nominating the strongest man. Henry Hubbard of New Hampshire and John McKinley of Alabama talked with Bell, but he rejected the caucus idea, stating that he did not expect more than twenty or thirty Administration votes anyway. On the other hand, Polk's friends stated, Polk agreed to accept a caucus decision, and although no caucus was held, he was generally considered the Administration candidate and Bell the candidate of the opposition. John M. Felder of South Carolina, they asserted, was the only state rights man to vote for Polk.[41] Regardless of the testimony of Polk's friends, it is clear that Bell received more than twenty Administration votes. The total vote of his opponents on the final ballot was 104. Certainly the friends of the Administration numbered more than 124.

Congress adjourned on June 30, and Bell was in Nashville by July 26. A number of his friends, eager that he take the fight to the people, offered him a public dinner. Out of deference to the approaching dinner in honor of President Jackson, Bell declined,[42] but he publicly defended himself in a speech at Murfreesboro on October 6, 1834. Two months previous to this date Felix Grundy had spoken in this same town, calling upon the people to remain firm in their battle to destroy that "unshorn Sampson," the Bank, and making

41 Cave Johnson to Polk, September 12, 1834; C. C. Clay to *id.,* September 13, 23, 1834; John McKinley to *id.,* August 13, 1834; Dunlap to *id.,* September 28, 1834; James Standifer to *id.,* September 29, 1834, in Polk Papers.
42 Bell to Samuel Hogg *et al.,* July 30, 1834, in Nashville *Republican and State Gazette,* July 31, 1834.

veiled allusions to its support by a certain Tennessee congressman.[43] Bell's speech, therefore, was considered as a reply to Grundy. Bell had gone to Murfreesboro to visit his children; but since his visit was timed so as to be concurrent with a session of the local court, it seems quite probable that he had planned to deliver a public address.

According to an unfriendly report by the editor of the Murfreesboro *Central Monitor,* Bell was on the defensive from the beginning to the end of his speech. He denounced those designing men who had made efforts to extract from President Jackson an expression of opinion hostile to him and denied that the President had expressed any preference in the contest for the speakership. He claimed to have supported Administration measures when he could have influenced enough votes to defeat them. He supported these measures, although some were in opposition to his own principles, rather than go with the opposition. As for his election to the speakership, it could have been accomplished with less difficulty before the Bank controversy than after. This his opponents knew; consequently, they had prevailed upon Speaker Stevenson to retain the Chair for several months. During this period, Bell charged, his enemies had hoped to "weaken and beat him down." He did not say that Jackson was a party to this plot; he thought the President had merely been deceived. Certainly he received opposition votes in the Speaker's election, Bell admitted; it was but the natural result of his courteous treatment of men of all parties.

As for the Bank and the monetary question, Bell was quoted as saying that he would not vote for a bank until the President's experiment had been given a fair trial. If that experiment should fail, then Bell felt certain of popular support of a bank. He thought there was no question as to the power of Congress to establish a bank, although he did believe the consent of the states was necessary to the establish-

[43] Murfreesboro *Central Monitor,* August 23, 1834, quoted in Nashville *National Banner and Daily Advertiser,* August 29, 1834.

ment of branches. In any event, gold and silver could not be established exclusively as the currency of the country; they could only serve as the basis for a circulating medium.[44]

This version of Bell's Murfreesboro speech was substantiated by John W. Childress and William R. Rucker, brothers-in-law of Polk, and by William Brady. They considered the speech "most vehement and flaming," a "most intemperate and ill advised defence," and they asserted that during its delivery Bell's countenance was "bitter & revengeful." According to Brady, he "evidenced the most consummate arrogance at one moment and cringing servility at another." All agreed that no direct reference was made to Polk; innuendo was the principal weapon used by the Speaker. Brady, however, thought the speech so anti-Jackson that he considered it his duty to address the General a letter, relating its high lights.[45] Polk's relatives and enthusiastic friends no doubt misquoted and misrepresented portions of Bell's address, but their excitement was evidence of its importance. Even though not yet ready to break with the Administration, the Speaker had resolved to defend his position. Furthermore, having become aroused by his own oratory, he probably went further than he had intended.

Polk was highly pleased with these reports of Bell's speech; he now considered the Speaker "unequivocally at issue with the policy of the administration." The speech must be given full publicity and the Murfreesboro people must take the lead. Polk declined to go to Murfreesboro to speak, fearing such a course would appear as a follow-up of Bell's speech. He even preferred not to take public notice of the Speaker's indirect reference to him until the proper time should arrive. Then he would be "prepared, fully prepared." [46]

Meanwhile, Bell was quietly getting control of the principal Nashville newspapers. On September 22, 1834, W. Has-

[44] Murfreesboro *Central Monitor*, October 11, 1834.

[45] John W. Childress to Polk, October 7, 1834; William R. Rucker to *id.*, October 12, 1834; William Brady to *id.*, October 14, 1834, in Polk Papers.

[46] Polk to Rucker, October 16, 1834, *ibid.*

sell Hunt dismissed Samuel H. Laughlin from the editorship of the *Banner*. For some weeks Laughlin had been a
Polk spy in the camp, receiving suggestions from him and
promising to keep him informed concerning developments
in the Bell stronghold. Laughlin charged that he was dismissed because of Hunt's opposition to his support of Jackson measures, but John W. Childress confided to Polk that
Laughlin had been drunk for a week just prior to his dismissal. However, Childress did learn from an employee in
the *Banner* office that Hunt and Bell were very intimate and
that "the whole concern" would soon take the field in support of the Speaker.[47] Laughlin had reported to Polk as early
as September 6 that the *Banner* had long espoused the mercantile interests "of this blessed town of Nashville" and that
those same interests supported Bell.[48]

Following his dismissal, Laughlin gave vent to his feelings, exposing both real and imaginary grievances. Hunt
hated Jackson and his policies, Laughlin told Polk, and he
hated Van Buren even more. George C. Childress, the new
editor of the *Banner,* had been hand-picked by Bell. Childress was chosen because he classed himself as a Jackson man
and because he was a brother-in-law of John Catron, the chief
justice of the state supreme court.[49] Laughlin completely
despaired of the *Banner* under its new management, for that
paper, he said, was "now a prostitute, open to the embraces
of all politicians of all parties, but is the peculiar mistress of
the Bank and Bank men."

Laughlin was interested in setting up a strong Jackson-
Polk paper in Nashville and suggested to Polk that, if money
could be made available, he himself and Medicus A. Long,
a former editor of the Sparta *Law Journal,* would buy the
Republican from Allen A. Hall. Should such an acquisition
be made, Laughlin promised to devote to the management of

[47] Childress to Polk, September 16, 1834, *ibid.*
[48] Samuel H. Laughlin to *id.,* September 6, 1834, *ibid.*
[49] Laughlin erroneously considered Catron an anti-Jackson man.

the paper all the talents which God had given him, regardless of pay. As the situation stood, he considered that both the *Banner* and the *Republican* virtually belonged to Bell. And unless a vigorous paper could be developed in Nashville, Van Buren would have little chance in Tennessee in 1836, since the existing papers held the whip over local politicians and politics. All Laughlin wished, he said, was an opportunity to swing into "full operation against all plotters, U.S. Bankites —state juntas—and corruption in all high places." [50]

Laughlin was correct in his prophecy that the Nashville press would rally to Bell's support. Both Hunt's *Banner* and Hall's *Republican* took up the fight. The latter denounced the *Central Monitor* for its extreme hostility to Bell and declared its report of his Murfreesboro speech a "gross caricature" of the original.[51] This remark prompted Polk's Murfreesboro friends to begin a movement to republish the *Monitor* report, accompanied by statements from many who heard the speech.[52] The editor of the *Monitor,* however, his paper having become defunct, was reluctant to consent to a republication. As explained by John W. Childress, the editor had expected substantial support when he opened the attack upon Bell, but had been disappointed by the attitude of the press in other places. Nevertheless, still hopeful of republication, William Brady had assigned himself the task of collecting statements from Polk men who had heard Bell's speech.[53]

Unable to get a hold on the Nashville press, Polk and his active supporters were forced to rely on small-town papers which could be fed through the columns of the Columbia *Observer.* Bell's silence on the Bank question and his elevation to the speakership by opposition votes were the chief points of attack. The Nashville press was vigorous in reply, and in the eyes of Bell men, completely refuted the charges.

The President's continued silence on the speakership con-

[50] Laughlin to Polk, October 20, 1834, in Polk Papers.
[51] Nashville *Republican and State Gazette,* November 11, 1834.
[52] Brady to Polk, November 29, 1834, in Polk Papers.
[53] Childress to *id.,* December 20, 1834, *ibid.*

troversy and the attitude of the Washington *Globe* gave Bell's friends an opportunity to deny that there was hostility between the President and the Speaker. The whole controversy, they charged, had been brought on by a disgruntled, defeated candidate. So effectively was this argument being used that John W. Childress warned Polk that unless "some evidence to the contrary" came from headquarters immediately, the people would accept "that notion." [54]

During this period of silence, Jackson's private correspondence revealed a greater interest in the complete destruction of the Bank and in the establishment of a metallic currency than in the controversy over the speakership. Early in August he arrived for his summer vacation at the Hermitage and was pleased with what he thought to be the attitude of the home folk. "Our friend Bell has found what I told him in Washington to be true that his silence had injured him at home," he reported to Van Buren. And unless Bell came out "boldly against a Bank as well as the Bank" he would be politically destroyed. For this reason, according to rumor received at the Hermitage, Bell's friends would probably compel him to oppose the Bank and support Van Buren for the presidency.[55]

On August 13, at Vauxhall Gardens, Nashville's most celebrated entertainment center, no fewer than fifteen hundred persons sat down to a sumptuous dinner in honor of the President of the United States. H. R. W. Hill toasted the health of the Old General and Jackson replied: "*The true constitutional currency—gold and silver coin—* It can cover and protect the labor of our country without the aid of a National Bank, an institution which can never be otherwise than hostile to the liberties of the people, because its tendency is to associate wealth with an undue power over the public interests." [56] The friendly audience cheered lustily and the Old Hero felt very much gratified.

[54] *Ibid.*

[55] Jackson to Van Buren, August 8, 1834, in Bassett (ed.), *Correspondence,* V, 281–82.

[56] Nashville *National Banner and Daily Advertiser,* August 14, 1834.

Comparing the dinner to the Jefferson Birthday Dinner of 1830, at which his toast had chilled the nullifiers, Jackson reported to Van Buren that his toast pleased all of those present except the friends of Bell, who, he understood, considered it "a death blow to *the Bank*," but were attempting to convince the people that it was intended as a "death blow to Mr. Bell." Nevertheless, as for Bell himself, Jackson added, "I am Bells [*sic*] personal friend, he is mine, I believe; I am also his political, if he will adopt what I believe the true policy for the safety and interest of the country." Since Bell's silence on the Bank question had already destroyed most of his popularity, Jackson concluded that there was but one sensible course for the Speaker to follow—to denounce openly all banks. "I fear the Bank influence will destroy Bell—his constituents are fearful of him from his silence last congress and unless he comes out against *all national Banks* he will have opposition of the strongest kind, and I fear the bank influence will prevail over him; all his Nashville friends are in favour of a *Bank*. . . . The Bank junto will endeavour to keep him with them. I hope he will have more sense than to be destroyed by them." [57]

Obviously Jackson was reluctant to strike Bell from his list of friends. Yet the determined Old General had made up his mind on the Bank question; those who professed friendship must either fall in line or become political outcasts. Few men ever had even an honest disagreement with Jackson and retained his friendship.

Bell was approaching a fateful parting of the ways. He must follow the path well marked by Jackson or the uncertain one which led toward the camp of the opposition. And Polk and his friends would allow the Speaker no leisure in reaching his decision. As Bell returned to Washington to preside over the House during the second session of the Twenty-third Congress, he was indeed in a quandary. Plagued by promises to

57 Jackson to Van Buren, August 16, 1834, in Bassett (ed.), *Correspondence,* V, 282–83.

opposition men, goaded by those who would destroy him politically, fearful of the attitude of his constituents, and devoid of much courage in time of crisis, he was a marked man, standing with a foot in each camp. It was fortunate for him that he was Speaker rather than active participant; he could preside impartially and observe and reflect without the necessity of action.

As Speaker, Bell gave evidence of a sincere desire to be fair. In arranging the House committees, he gave the chairmanship of each to a Jackson man, even though he might have wished to do otherwise. Polk was not removed from the chairmanship of the Ways and Means Committee. Bell undoubtedly reasoned that since the Jackson party was in the majority, it should have power to carry through its program and then be held strictly accountable for the exercise of this power. On one occasion when the chairman of a committee resigned to take a place on the Supreme Court Bench, Bell refused to sanction the promotion of an opposition man who was next in line.[58] And during the tumultuous days of debate on the alleged corruption in the Post Office Department the Speaker went so far as to order an opposition speaker who had "wandered a little from the direct line" to take his seat, but later rescinded his order.[59]

Probably the most important topics of the short session were the questions of the French spoliation claims and the proposed $3,000,000 appropriation for national defense. The vigorous discussion of the latter ran on into the night of March 3, making it one of wild disorder. Finally, well after midnight and after the quorum had been intentionally broken, Bell made a short speech of appreciation, received a unanimous vote of thanks for his services, and declared the House adjourned.[60]

A newspaper reporter who had been present during a considerable portion of the session wrote in the Baltimore

[58] Cong. Debates, 23 Cong., 2 Sess., 1025-39.
[59] Ibid., 1489.   [60] Ibid., 328.

Gazette: "I have closely watched Mr. Bell's manner throughout the session, and a more courteous, prompt and decisive Speaker could not be chosen from the House. His enunciation of the forms is perfect, and the tone and manner in which they are given, are more eloquent to my ear than a greater part of the magnificent flourishes pronounced upon the floor." [61] John Quincy Adams thought that "on the whole" Bell had been "a good Speaker, and impartial as far as he dares, though occasionally subservient from timidity." [62] Acid old John Quincy's summary well characterized Bell's entire political course at this time.

[61] Quoted in Nashville *Republican and State Gazette,* March 19, 1835.
[62] Adams (ed.), *Memoirs of John Quincy Adams,* IX, 214.

Chapter V

REVOLT

ON the evening of December 23, 1834, a number of Tennessee congressmen were seated around the fire in Balie Peyton's Washington residence, discussing the propriety of proposing Senator Hugh Lawson White of Tennessee as a candidate for the presidency. The subject was not a new one; for several months White's candidacy had been openly advocated by a number of Tennessee newspapers. Sedate, reticent, and laborious, a symbol of virtue and efficiency in public life, White was not an ambitious politician; the interest manifested by his friends was apparently unsolicited. Long years of service as judge, senator, and, more recently, president pro tem of the Senate had marked him as a man of courage and conviction, conscientiously correct and precise to the point of sternness. A true Scotch-Irishman of the Southern highlands, the son of the founder of Knoxville, White's independence of spirit rebelled against all forms of autocracy.

Early in his public career, Andrew Jackson had recognized these qualities in his fellow Tennessean, and after becoming President, had made two unsuccessful attempts to persuade White to enter his cabinet.[1] Although the Senator refused to assume cabinet responsibility, Jackson had been able to depend upon him for the type of support that comes from a

[1] There is some question as to Jackson's sincerity in offering the cabinet post to White. Writing to a West Tennessee relative, Jackson expressed hope that White would accept, but devoted most of his letter to plans for having "my faithful Eaton" elected to White's seat in the Senate. Jackson to Samuel Jackson Hays, April 13, 1831, in Emma Inman Williams, *Historic Madison* (Jackson, Tenn., 1946), 403. The original of this letter is in the possession of Mrs. Walker Hays, Memphis.

sense of duty rather than a hope for gain. Beyond that point White would not go; consequently, it was inevitable that at times he had been found in opposition to Administration measures. In recent years his desire for public life had been greatly diminished by grief almost beyond human endurance. Between 1825 and 1831 death had taken from his home eight grown children and their mother.

The plan for the caucus of Tennessee congressmen appears to have originated with James Standifer. In conversation with individual members of the delegation, he had received the impression that most of them were desirous of seeing White succeed Jackson. Some had told him, however, that Polk and Grundy were opposed to such a succession. When Standifer broached the subject to them, both, according to Standifer, professed friendship and admiration for White, but promptly inquired as to Bell's attitude. When informed that Bell was believed to be favorable to White, both Polk and Grundy accused him of playing a double game. They claimed to have evidence that he had been courting the friends of Martin Van Buren.[2] Standifer, according to his own statement, then resolved to call a meeting of the Tennessee delegation for the purpose of talking matters over, and, if possible, ascertaining "who was playing the double game."

On the day preceding the scheduled date of the meeting, while Bell and Standifer were walking together along Pennsylvania Avenue on their way to the Capitol, Standifer mentioned the proposed meeting and insisted that the Speaker attend. Bell appeared hesitant, Standifer later related, and "spoke with caution, and seemed to measure his words," but finally stated that he could not very well refuse to confer with his colleagues. Soon after arriving at the Capitol, Standifer

[2] Twenty-five years later Bell's opponents published a letter purported to have been written to Congressman Campbell P. White of New York in 1834, stating that "as yet Tennessee has taken no active decided course on this question [presidency], but the sagacious politicians among us are going for Mr. Van Buren." Printed in *John Bell: His Past History Connected with the Public Service* (Nashville, 1860), 5.

found Polk in the Ways and Means Committee room and told him of the proposed meeting. Polk immediately inquired whether Bell would be present and, upon receiving an affirmative reply, declined to attend on the ground that he and the Speaker were not on friendly terms.[3]

Polk and Grundy were absent from the meeting. Standifer and Luke Lea reported that the two had been notified and that, although they refused to attend, they expressed themselves in favor of White. Cave Johnson, a close friend of the absent gentlemen, testified to the correctness of this report and added that Polk and Grundy wished to be considered as original White men.[4] Polk subsequently disclaimed any such expression of sentiment on his part. He had merely informed Lea that self-respect forbade his going into consultation with Peyton, Bell, and Bell's brother-in-law, David W. Dickinson, since they had demonstrated hostility toward him. Besides, his constituents had not instructed him to speak for them in the nomination of a presidential candidate.[5]

Polk confided to his brother-in-law, James Walker, that although he believed the East Tennessee members of the delegation to be sincere in their desire to elect White, he was suspicious of the motives of Bell, Peyton, and Dickinson. He was convinced that those three were prompted by an inveterate hostility toward him. Through co-operation with the opposition, they hoped to enable Bell to retain the speakership in the next Congress. What could be more embarrassing to his own friends, Polk queried, than for him to suffer a second defeat in his competition with Bell? The very best that the advocates of White's candidacy could hope for was to divide the Democratic party and send the election to the House where Bank money might influence sufficient votes to defeat the party's nominee. As to his own attitude toward White, Polk assured Walker that he would be pleased to sup-

[3] Standifer's statement, dated August 15, 1853, in Nancy Scott, *A Memoir of Hugh Lawson White* (Philadelphia, 1856), 260–62.
[4] Standifer *et al.* to Cave Johnson, January 1, 1835, *ibid.*, 259–60.
[5] Polk to Walker, December 24, 1834, in Polk Papers.

port the Senator if he should be run by the Democratic party, but he was not in favor of nominating White without first consulting members of the party in other states.[6]

The Tennessee congressmen who attended the caucus decided to address a letter to Senator White, requesting his permission to use his name as a candidate for the presidency in 1836. Cave Johnson immediately notified both Polk and Grundy of the decision, and apparently one of the three conferred with Jackson. There is still a question whether Johnson had attended the caucus as a friend of White or as a spy for Polk. At any rate, Johnson denied that he had pledged Grundy and Polk in support of White. As for himself, Johnson now informed the other members of the caucus that he would not support White if he should be run by "opposition Nationals and Nullifiers—aided by a small portion of the Jackson party."[7] The other seven participants in the caucus addressed to Johnson a letter, giving their version of his participation in the meeting.[8] It was the testimony of seven against one; Johnson's reputation for veracity had at least been damaged. Still, what Johnson did or did not say was of little consequence. The important question was what did he, Polk, Grundy, and Jackson propose to do.

When the proposed letter to White was ready for signatures, Luke Lea took it to Polk and suggested that he be the first to sign. Polk declined. He had no ill feeling toward White,[9] he said, but he was unwilling to act in concert with a mere faction of the party. In spite of proof to the contrary, Polk charged Bell with the responsibility for the White movement, and began collecting evidence to prove that destruc-

[6] *Ibid.*   [7] *Id* to *id.*, December 25, 1834, *ibid.*

[8] James Standifer *et al.* to Johnson, January 1, 1835, in Scott, *Memoir of Hugh L. White*, 259.

[9] White had taken no part in the Polk-Bell controversy over the speakership. To a friend he confided: "I fear a want of kind feeling between them may grow out of the canvass and be the means of dividing, at home, those who now pass for friends. Both are to me like children; therefore I took no part in the contest." White to Editor of Knoxville *Register*, n.d., in Scott, *Memoir of Hugh L. White*, 253.

tion of the Democratic party was Bell's ultimate aim. From one congressman he heard a rumor that Bell wished to form a new party; from another that Bell had no scruples against sacrificing principles for votes; and from a third source he heard that Bell's friend, Duff Green, was attempting to get a White newspaper established in Washington. All of this and more Polk recorded in a letter addressed to J.B. & Co. (John Bell and Company), which he apparently never made public.[10]

Polk's supporters, especially his three brothers-in-law, kept him informed about rumors and speculations current in Tennessee. Although Bell was a "dissembling Hypocrite," he had been detected, wrote William R. Rucker, and every one now knew that he was Jackson's bitter enemy. Even the Speaker's relatives around Murfreesboro, it was said, had turned against him. Further, it was rumored that, in Nashville, a junto was being formed for the purpose of electing White, keeping Bell in the Speaker's chair, and controlling all of the more important national and state offices.[11] Rucker also confidentially reported that Samuel H. Laughlin was on his way to Washington to purchase type for the establishment of an anti-Bell newspaper in Nashville.[12]

John W. Childress sensed a serious threat to Polk and Johnson in their home districts. Since it would probably be the plan of the Bell group to have White elected by the House of Representatives, Johnson and Polk would certainly be marked for defeat in their campaign for re-election to Congress.[13] Daniel Graham, a former secretary of state in Tennessee and a stanch Jackson man, believed Bell had several objects in mind. In the first place, if the Speaker could persuade enough Jackson men to join with the opposition to elect White, that would "sanctify the ploughing with the

---

[10] Polk Papers under date of January 28, 1835. Other material was added later and the letter apparently turned into one to Johnson instead of Bell.

[11] John Catron and William Carroll were erroneously listed as a part of the White group. Neither supported him.

[12] Rucker to Polk, January 5, 1835, in Polk Papers.

[13] Childress to *id.*, January 23, 1835, *ibid.*

enemies' heifer, of which the Speaker was guilty in attaining the chair." Graham further suspected that Bell had long wished to see the hand of death snatch Jackson from the scene. If that should happen and the union of some Jackson men with the opposition could be cemented, then Bell would eventually be the leader of this united force; for White's advanced years and poor health would not permit his being the chief for any lengthy period.

Graham was not too optimistic about the proposed establishment of an anti-Bell newspaper in Nashville. Although he recognized Laughlin's capabilities, he thought that, on the whole, the proposed editor was "a weak vessel." Laughlin was too likely to get drunk during a crisis and "let the cup pass." Still if the proposed paper could be the means of giving proper circulation to Bell's Murfreesboro tirade, then Graham believed it ought to be patronized by the party.[14]

Martin Van Buren, writing later when his version was probably colored by the happenings of the intervening twenty years,[15] stated that Bell, fearing Polk's influence, originally hoped to use White's candidacy for bargaining purposes. Van Buren related that, prior to White's nomination, he received several hints of Bell's desire for a conference. On one occasion, when the two were dinner guests in the home of a mutual friend, Van Buren, suspecting that the presidency was to become the topic of conversation, developed a toothache and departed immediately after dinner. At a later date, after the Tennessee delegation had secured White's permission to use his name, the Speaker and the Vice-President met again. The occasion was a joint meeting of the two houses of Congress for the purpose of hearing John Quincy Adams deliver an address on Lafayette. According to Van Buren, Bell expressed concern over the probable split in the party that would result from White's candidacy and added that if

14 Graham to id., January 29, 1835, ibid.
15 Fitzpatrick (ed.), Autobiography of Van Buren, 226 n. Van Buren did not begin writing his autobiography until 1854.

anything was to be done it must be done immediately. Van Buren, suspecting an attempt to extract from him some promises in return for a possible withdrawal of White's name, dismissed the subject with a few remarks about the debt White's friends owed to the party.[16] This was indeed a rare event; the "Little Magician" was not accustomed to evading political discussion with those who could be of service to him.

In view of his feud with Polk, Bell's political position in 1834–1835 was not an enviable one; nevertheless, it is difficult to see how he could have hoped to profit by a conference with Van Buren. Faced with the necessity of either surrendering to Jackson's demands or being driven into the ranks of the opposition, Bell saw in the White candidacy an opportunity to hold his popularity while in transition. He was gliding into the anti-Jackson–Van Buren camp and was conscious of the fact; personal pride and regard for the future bade him carry with him as many Democrats as possible. He definitely wished to continue as Speaker, but he probably had no immediate ambition to head a new party. He was not the originator of the White movement, but undoubtedly he, Peyton, and Dickinson had discussed fully its political possibilities. Although proof is lacking, one suspects that Polk's friends were correct in branding the Speaker the key man behind the action of the Tennessee delegation. To allow others to appear to take the lead when public reaction is uncertain is characteristic of cautious politicians. When the White movement gave evidence of popularity, Bell stepped to the fore and became its most effective leader.

Jackson approved of the attitude taken by Polk and Grundy toward the caucus of the Tennessee delegation, even though it does not appear that they consulted him in advance. It was public knowledge, however, that Jackson had chosen Van Buren as his successor; all who gave support to White must have known from the beginning that they were opposing the wishes of the Old Hero. According to Polk,

16 *Ibid.*

Jackson's immediate reaction to the proposal to nominate White was that if the Senator should be brought out by *the party* then he should be supported by the party. But should professing friends ignore the party and persist in White's nomination, they would eventually destroy both him and themselves.[17] Jackson and Polk felt themselves safe in such promises and prophesies; no one knew so well as they that the power of the Administration would be sufficient to nullify any Democratic opposition to Van Buren's nomination by the party. Perhaps on no other subject during his public life was Jackson's intolerance more evident than in his determination to make Van Buren President. To him it was unbelievable that a good Democrat could oppose this succession.

After a few weeks of meditation, Jackson concluded that Bell was neither his personal nor political friend. "From his [Bell's] course the last three years, and his late duplicity," he confided to a Tennessee friend, "it is now clear that he has been working against the administration, *secretly,* and that to promote his own interest." Jackson further charged that "Mr. Bell and Co. are more intimate with Duff Green [18] and the nullifiers than with the friends of the administration." It was not White but Clay that Bell hoped to elect; therefore, his plan was to throw the election into the House where the Bank could use its influence. Speaker Bell knew that White could not be elected, Jackson insisted, yet he was willing to sacrifice the Senator in order to destroy the accomplishments of the present Administration. "Mr. Bell may say what he will but he is a bank man at heart, and would tomorrow vote

[17] Polk to Walker, December 25, 1834, in Polk Papers. David Crockett, who was absent from the caucus of the Tennessee delegation but who had previously declared that he did not intend being a "little puppy Dog to yelp after a party," rather shrewdly said: "The truth is the poor Superanuated [*sic*] old man's vanity has prompted him to think that his popularity could stand anything." Crockett to T. J. Dobyns, May 27, 1834, in Samuel Gordon Heiskell, *Andrew Jackson and Early Tennessee History* (Nashville, 1921), III, 18.

[18] Green had once been a close friend and adviser of Jackson, but the two had parted company at the time of the break between Calhoun and the President. Green's *United States Telegraph* was replaced by Francis P. Blair's *Globe* as the Administration organ.

for its recharter." If Bell's constituents did not "give him trouble in his next election," wishfully prophesied the Old General, "then I have been allways [*sic*] deceived in the virtue and sterling republican principles and integrity of my neighbours in Davidson and Wilson counties."[19]

When, on February 7, 1835, a new White newspaper, the *Appeal*, made its appearance in Washington, Jackson immediately pronounced it the work of John Bell and Duff Green. According to Jackson, William A. Rind, Jr., the editor, was from Green's office, and the first issue, which called for united opposition against the Baltimore convention of Jackson's friends, was from Bell's pen.[20] The first issue was said to have been secretly taken to Georgetown and then sent off to be circulated in Tennessee, Alabama, and Mississippi. Even the secrecy observed in circulating the paper, growled Jackson, was in keeping with Bell's "usual mode of carrying on intrigues."[21]

Jackson refused to believe that any appreciable number of people could be deceived by a mischievous plan the purpose of which was so obvious. Certainly all unbiased persons should be able to see that "Messrs Bell & Co." had allied themselves with "blue light federalists," "modern Whiggs," and nullifiers. Surely Republican Tennessee would not abandon the old party and its principles.[22]

Although threatening to make him odious to society if he continued in the race for President, Jackson expressed for White more sympathy than anger. He professed to believe that the veteran Senator had been seduced by the artful management of Bell. He fervently hoped, however, that the scales would fall from White's eyes and that he would free himself from this disgraceful entanglement and false posi-

[19] Jackson to Alfred Balch, February 16, 1835, in Bassett (ed.), *Correspondence*, V, 327–28.

[20] The *Appeal* was absorbed by the *Sun*, the successor to the *North American* and another White paper, in April, 1835.

[21] Jackson to Balch, February 16, 1835, in Bassett (ed.), *Correspondence*, V, 328.

[22] *Id.* to Polk, May 3, 1835, in Polk Papers.

tion in which he had been placed. This alone could save him from utter ruin.[23]

Thomas Hart Benton of Missouri, a strong Jackson–Van Buren supporter, declared that there was another side to White's candidacy. In 1899 the Tennessee Senator had married Ann Peyton, a daughter of Colonel Craven Peyton of Loudoun County, Virginia. For a number of years she had been hostess of a Washington boardinghouse in which White had lived. Benton thought the new Mrs. White very ambitious. He later wrote that Mrs. White "having made an immense stride from the head of a boarding-house table to the head of a senator's table, could see no reason why she should not take one step more . . . and arrive at the head of the presidential table." [24]

In spite of Jackson's expressed belief in the loyalty of Tennesseans, the news from the home state was mostly bad. Bell controlled both Nashville newspapers, and the Bell-White forces were winning over practically all of those in the smaller towns. Even Polk's home town paper, the Columbia *Observer*, had deserted to the White ranks. White was reported to be gaining strength daily, and even James Walker felt compelled to admit that the Tennessee Senator would carry his home state.[25] Indeed, it was rumored that Tennessee Democrats would not even send delegates to the Administration-sponsored convention scheduled to meet at Baltimore.

Jackson received this news with a mixture of sadness, contempt, and anger, and resolved to apply Administration pressure through a public statement. In a letter intended for publication, he told James Gwin:

You are at liberty to say, on all occasions, that regarding the people as the true source of political power, I am always ready to bow to

[23] *Id.* to Josephus C. Guild, April 24, 1835, in Bassett (ed.), *Correspondence,* V, 338–41; *id.* to William Blount, May 10, 1835, in *Cong. Globe,* 25 Cong., 2 Sess., Appendix, 559.

[24] Thomas Hart Benton, *Thirty Years in the United States Senate* (New York, 1866), II, 185.

[25] Walker to Polk, February 28, 1835, in Polk Papers.

their will and to their judgment: that, discarding all personal preferences, I consider the true policy of the friends of republican principles to send delegates, fresh from the people, to a general convention, for the purpose of selecting candidates for the presidency and
vice presidency; and, that to impeach that selection before it is
made, or to resist it when it is fairly made, as an emanation of executive power, is to assail the virtue of the people, and, in effect,
to oppose their right to govern.[26]

Jackson could not have been unmindful of the fact that his
appeal for support of the convention's nominee was veiled
electioneering for Van Buren. The reins of control over a
Democratic convention were firmly in the hands of the President.

Jackson's greatest concern was over the persistent reports
that White would probably carry Tennessee regardless of
what the Democratic convention should do. To Polk he
wrote:

How is it that there is no man in the Republican ranks to take the
stump, and relieve Tennessee from her degraded attitude of abandoning principle to sustain men who have apostatised from the republican fold for the sake of office? . . . What, Tennessee, the once
Democratic Tennessee apostate from the republican fold, and the
only state in the Union unrepresented at the national republican
convention at Baltimore by members fresh from the people and left
as the only associate of the nullees in So. Carolina headed by that
arch apostate Calhoun, and seperated [sic] from all her republican
brethren? How strange; how humiliating to every real friend to the
democracy of our beloved country. if [sic] my hands were free, if I
was a mere citizen of Tennessee again and wanted everlasting
fame, I would ask no other theatre to obtain it than before the
people of Tennessee. I would bring to their view what Tennessee
once was, her present degraded attitude, and then enquire the
cause—by whom she was placed in this dilemma and then apply
the remedy, and Tennessee in six weeks would be . . . erect upon
her republican legs again, and Mr. Bell, Davy Crockett and Co.,
hurled, as they ought, from the confidence of the people.[27]

[26] Jackson to James Gwin, February 23, 1835, in *Niles' Weekly Register*
(Baltimore), XLVIII (1835), 80–81.
[27] *Id.* to Polk, May 12, 1835, in Bassett (ed.), *Correspondence,* V, 345–46.

The Chief had spoken. Polk, Grundy, and Johnson must save Tennessee from disgrace!

Neither threats nor appeals could daunt the White supporters; they knew their cause was popular in Tennessee. Bell himself, however, was concerned over the charge that he had intrigued with nullifiers in order to secure the speakership and was continuing that intrigue with the hope of destroying the Democratic party. A letter was dispatched to Senator Willie P. Mangum. Would he state "fully and frankly" whether it was Bell or Polk who had been closely identified with the state rights group? Mangum was out of town and did not receive Bell's letter. A second request followed three weeks later. Mangum obligingly supplied the information. It was Polk, not Bell, who had intrigued with the state rights group, declared the Carolinian. The shift to Bell had come only after the friends of state rights had suspected that they had been duped and were about to support a friend of Van Buren.[28]

Through the eyes of Jackson supporters, White's long years of public service sank into insignificance when he allowed himself to become the tool of a group of political tricksters led by Bell. By permitting the use of his name, White had arrayed himself in opposition to the Jackson Administration and all that it had accomplished. The task was to convince the people of Bell's duplicity and White's mistake. Since Bell controlled all of the important newspapers in Middle Tennessee, Polk and his associates found it necessary to establish the Nashville *Union* under the editorship of Samuel H. Laughlin.

The Washington *Globe* had already entered the battle to stem the tide. "The public ought to know," it exclaimed, "that there has been a great selling out, and buying up of the Tennessee press, since Messrs. the Bank, Bell, and Co. have

[28] Bell to Mangum, February 25, March 19, 1835, in Willie P. Mangum Papers (Division of Manuscripts, Library of Congress); Mangum to Bell, June 15, 1835, in *Tennessee Historical Magazine,* III (1917), 198–200.

entered upon the scheme of playing a new game for the Presidency—the Speakership—and a recharter." A new set of editors had been installed in the offices of those Bell-Bank
papers and had been given instructions on the salient points.
Although they professed the highest regards for President
Jackson, their actions belied their words.[29]

The nomination of White, the *Globe* charged, was a part
of a scheme to divide the party and the country by stressing
the personal popularity of favorite sons. Chief among those
ambitious politicians who were promoting that scheme were
Calhoun and Bell. It was not a personal preference for White
that had prompted Bell's action, the *Globe* further insisted,
for he had tried to persuade Richard M. Johnson of Kentucky
to make the race. When Johnson declined, then Bell and
Calhoun decided to make White their *"stool pigeon."* If
the White movement gathered momentum in the South and
Southwest, the managers planned to further their political
intrigues by bargaining with the opposition in the North. But
should this bargaining fail, they might even go so far as to
divide the Union and take control of the southern part.[30]

Not only were the instigators of the White movement
friendly with nullifiers, continued the *Globe,* they were working in co-operation with the Bank men. The editor alleged
that in November, 1834, just prior to the opening of the session of Congress, Senator White journeyed to Philadelphia
to visit Samuel Jaudon, his son-in-law, who was cashier of
the Bank. Speaker Bell soon joined them, and plans were
made for "future operations." White was to run for the presidency; Bell was to pull the necessary strings to get him nominated; and the Bank would support the movement, receiving
a new charter for its efforts.[31]

Bell categorically denied all of the *Globe*'s charges except
one. He admitted having been connected with the effort to

29 Washington *Globe,* May 22, 1835.   30 *Ibid.,* May 5, 1835.
31 *Ibid.,* April 13, 1835.

get White's name before the people. However, in holding him responsible for this act, he regretted to say that the *Globe* did him too much honor. Bell explained that as early as December, 1833, he had noted strong White sentiment in Tennessee; nevertheless, he had resolved to have no part in the nomination unless there was a reasonable prospect of doing more than splitting the party. Furthermore, Bell said that at the time he was being denounced as a Bank man, a number of Van Buren's friends had urged him to come out in favor of the New Yorker. As a reward for such support, he was to have no opposition in his district in the race for re-election to the House. He had stated then and had often reiterated that he would support White in case the contest should be between Van Buren and the Tennessee Senator. Bell denied that he had had any knowledge of the proposed caucus of the Tennessee delegation until the day it was held. He was not the author of the letter which the delegation sent to White although he approved the action. The coming campaign, he insisted, would be a test between White and Van Buren, not White and Jackson. He was opposed to Van Buren, not Jackson.

Bell admitted having written a letter to Richard M. Johnson, but he stated that he had no recollection of its contents. Although the letter was not written for the public and might even have been "carelessly written," he had no objection to its publication if the public wished to know its contents.

The charge of co-operation with the Bank was particularly irritating to Bell; this was his most vulnerable point. Undoubtedly he was a Bank man, although he emphatically denied making any agreement with Jaudon or receiving any special favors from the Bank. Indeed, he had not met Jaudon until months after the alleged bargain was supposed to have been consummated, and at no time had he ever talked Bank matters with Jaudon; neither had he and White ever discussed the subject. And as for special favors, Bell insisted that he had never been indebted to the Bank beyond his "ability to discharge at any time." [32]

Jackson carefully read Bell's defense, pronounced it pregnable at all points, and sent a marked copy of the Nashville *Republican* to the office of the *Globe*. ". . . you must answer it soon," he instructed Editor Blair; "he [Bell] has opened a field for your reply to settle all matters with and prostrate him." [33] Blair again took up his pen. Bell had conspired with New England Whigs in order to secure the speakership, he averred. Bell had assured Speaker Stevenson that if he would resign, the Webster group in the Senate would vote to ratify his nomination as minister to Great Britain. That this was a trick, the editor explained, was evidenced by the vote to reject the nomination. And the necessity of protecting the secrecy of this Bell-Webster conspiracy explained the Whig support of Wilde before shifting to Bell.[34]

Returning to the Bank question, Blair asserted that Bell had conspired with Secretary of the Treasury Louis McLane to prevent the Bank from becoming a subject of public discussion in the campaign of 1832, and had delivered an "elaborate speech" against bringing up a recharter bill at that time. Even Bell's support of Clayton's resolution calling for an investigation of the Bank was given in the interest of postponement. And the vote which he finally cast against recharter was not prompted by a desire to kill the Bank but to avert a presidential veto which would give to the people the privilege of choosing between Jackson and Biddle. Moreover, Blair continued, when Bank men were mincing no words in their abuse of the President, the Congressman from his home district uttered not one sentence in his defense. But apostasy had its temporary rewards; the Bank forces made Bell Speaker of the House. Nor was that all, Blair charged; the Bell family

[32] Bell to Editor, May 4, 1835, in Nashville *Republican and State Gazette,* May 9, 1835.
[33] Jackson to Blair, May 19, 1835, in Bassett (ed.), *Correspondence,* V, 349.
[34] Washington *Globe,* May 28, 1835.

had been doing some heavy land speculating on money furnished by the Bank. Bell's debt to the Bank, which was $53,-
000 in 1832, was increased to $60,000 in 1833, and that dur-
ing the period when Biddle was supposedly curtailing his
loans. Furthermore, David W. Dickinson, Bell's brother-in-
law, had increased his debt from $5,000 to $15,000.[35] Bell denied that he had ever owed the Bank even a major portion of
this sum; he had been endorser only on more than $40,000 of
this amount. This was true. Following his failure in business in
1834, James Bell signed over to his brother John his interest
in the estate of his late father as repayment of the money
John had already paid out, or was bound to pay as endorser,
to the United States Bank at Nashville and "certain bills of
Exchange on Merchants of New Orleans."[36] In the meantime, James had left Nashville and taken up residence in Carroll County, Mississippi, probably locating on lands owned
by the Bells and Dickinsons.

The Bell brothers and the Dickinsons, father and son, had
been speculating in Mississippi lands. There is no proof, however, of a statement in the *Globe* that they had deposited huge
sums of money in Baltimore for the purpose of purchasing
slaves in Maryland and Virginia and sending them to Mississippi. It appears that eventually the financial burden was
shifted to the elder Dickinson. John Bell was hard pressed
for cash; in 1848 he still owed his former father-in-law more
than $28,000, a portion of which had been owed since 1827.
James was drowned in the Mississippi River in 1841, and
David Dickinson, Jr. died insolvent in the early 1840's. In
1845 the elder Dickinson owned plantations in Bolivar
County and near Grenada, Mississippi. In his will, written
in that year, he specified that David, Jr.'s debts were to be
paid from the portion he would have received from his
father's estate. Debts owed to the Bank of Tennessee were
specifically mentioned.[37]

[35] *Ibid.*, June 2, 3, 1835.   [36] Davidson County Register, Book Z, 136.
[37] See will of David Dickinson, Sr. in Rutherford County Wills, Book 14, pp.
411–20.

Chapter VI

WITH THE OPPOSITION

WHILE the Administration organ in Washington and the newborn Nashville *Union* sniped at Bell with increasing fire, his friends were planning to honor him with a dinner at Nashville's Vauxhall Gardens on May 23, 1835. The Gardens, a fashionable resort in the southern outskirts of the city, was said to have been modeled after the London resort of the same name. Its spacious quarters and formal gardens provided welcome relief from the drabness of the city.[1]

In spite of a heavy spring rain, about two hundred people came out to applaud their Congressman. The fluent and forceful Balie Peyton was unable to attend, but the toast prepared by him sounded the keynote: "Our distinguished guest the Hon. John Bell—A native of Tennessee and a noble specimen of her firmness, independence and republican principles—he has proudly sustained her character in his political course, and the slanders of his enemies cannot take from him the confidence and approbation of his countrymen." Bell, spirited and eager for battle, responded, paying compliment to the people, calling for a national press free from "intrigue and defamation," and denouncing the Baltimore convention as a "genuine son of its deceased progenitor, 'old King Caucus.' " Tennessee's attorney general, George S. Yerger, added a tribute to "The 'Bell' of Democracy" which was pealing the "death knell of personal slander at home, and political vituperation abroad." [2] Bell then addressed the group.

He said that on most points he agreed with the principles

[1] Easton Morris, *The Tennessee Gazeteer* (Nashville, 1834), 122.
[2] *National Banner and Nashville Whig*, May 25, 1835.

of the Democratic party and had given his faithful and devoted support to the Jackson Administration. And, assuming a spirit of humility, he added that although he had always tried to make himself useful he had never attempted to set himself up as a party leader. Deprecating party excesses, he confessed fear of the truth of the old maxim " 'when politics run highest, public morals are lowest.' " Likening the party in power to the Jesuit Order, he expressed a fear that "implicit obedience to the mandate of the General or Chief in all things" would eventually obliterate "every trace of its original policy." Just as the Order proscribed, persecuted, and sent to the stake those who questioned the supremacy of the Pope, so was the party in power threatening with political oblivion those members who dared show independence. Those who aspired to places of distinction within the Jackson party must renounce all individualism and become absolutely subservient. If this policy of proscribing the independent and promoting the subservient continued, the "influence of executive patronage" would soon take complete control of elections.

Those who were maligning him, Bell charged, were attempting to produce an open break between the President and himself. He contended that he had always respected General Jackson and had given him all the support that "could consistently and reasonably be expected." It seemed, however, that past services meant nothing to those who were filling the President's ears with lies; they knew that the defeat of John Bell would require the open assistance of Andrew Jackson. Some of those traducers, Bell said, had told the President that he was responsible for the meeting of the caucus of the Tennessee delegation. Some had pronounced the meeting a nullification assembly; others had professed to see behind it the sinister influence of the Bank. All were wrong. To have failed to support White, Bell explained, would have required on his part the sacrifice of "both my feelings and principles." Certainly no one who knew Hugh Lawson White could believe him capable of improper connections with any group.

The friends of White, Bell announced, had no desire to "disturb the tranquility" of the Jackson Administration nor to detract from any glory to which it was entitled. No differences in principles were involved. The crux of the whole matter was that some professed to believe that Jackson, if permitted to choose his successor, could exercise the "wonderful faculty of transmitting . . . [to him] his own stern principles, and his power over public opinion." The friends of White did not share that belief. They considered Martin Van Buren void of the requisites of a President. "It is no puny arm that can wield the truncheon of Jackson!"

As to his future policy, Bell announced: "While I am resolved to support General Jackson and his administration, upon the same principles I have heretofore done, I am equally determined to expose the hollowness of the professions, and the worthlessness of the principles of those who are in the habit of denouncing every man who dares to support Judge White, as anti-republican in his principles." And with a flare of oratory, he concluded: "When *Party* is the watchword, and the ensign of those who fight for the spoils, the warning voice of patriotism says to every freeman, to every White man, inscribe your country upon your banner, and *'in hoc vince.'* " [3]

From the standpoint of oratory, Bell's contemporaries were pretty well agreed that his Vauxhall speech was the best effort of his political career. In later years he himself confided to a friend that more labor had been put on the preparation of that speech than any other. [4]

The friends of Van Buren denounced Bell's speech as an attack upon the Old Hero and his policies, and resolved to reveal the Speaker's apostasy in a still clearer light. For

[3] *Ibid.,* June 15, 1835.
[4] Henry S. Foote, *Bench and Bar of the South and Southwest* (St. Louis, 1876), 179.

months they had been seeking more information concerning his correspondence with Richard M. Johnson, and they thought they had something. At the time of the Vauxhall Gardens dinner, Francis P. Blair, editor of the *Globe,* had in his possession a letter from T. J. Pew, editor of the Lexington *Kentucky Gazette.* Pew reported that he had seen a letter from Bell to Johnson in which the latter was urged to come out in favor of a bank. Pew could not recall whether in this letter Bell had insisted that Johnson run for President, but he knew that at other times Bell had pressed him.[5]

Grundy was called into conference, and he immediately sent a copy of Pew's letter to Editor Laughlin of the Nashville *Union.*[6] Jackson was kept informed and apparently approved the publication of the document.[7] It appeared in the *Globe* on June 2.

While the Pew statement was still a topic of public discussion, Polk and his associates exposed what they considered a much more important correspondence. Early in May, Charles Cassedy of Bedford County, Tennessee, apparently an honest seeker of information, wrote Bell, inquiring as to White's position relative to the recharter of the Bank. In the same letter he also stated that friends were making the election of a Speaker an important point in the congressional campaign.[8]

Bell replied:

You will receive enclosed, the manifesto of the White cause and party. I think it contains our *principles* and the *arguments* upon which they may be sustained briefly set forth.

You will see by my letter all I know of Judge White's views about

[5] T. J. Pew to Blair, May 15, 1835, in Washington *Globe,* June 2, 1835. One friend of Jackson had advanced the existence of this correspondence as a reason why the Baltimore convention should not nominate Johnson for the vice-presidency. Should the Democrats name him "it will be *from the fear* he goes over to Mr. Bell's side." John Catron to Jackson, March 21, 1835, in Bassett (ed.), *Correspondence,* V, 330–32.

[6] Laughlin to Polk, May 30, 1835, in Polk Papers.

[7] Grundy to Jackson, June 6, 1835, in Andrew Jackson Papers.

[8] Charles Cassedy to Bell, July 20, 1835, in Nashville *Republican and State Gazette,* July 30, 1835. This letter states the substance of the earlier one.

the Bank. He doubtless never will swerve from them, but it would be most unprecendented, and do him, and very justly too, a great injury, to be declared before hand, that he would put his veto upon any measure whatever.—It would be said to be an electioneering declaration, and besides Mr. V. Buren has given no such pledges. To defeat me for the Speaker's chair, is the *main interest* which Mr. Polk and Johnson have in this whole contest, as I believe.

It would not do to ask Polk to vote for me against himself, but he might be made to pledge himself to go for me against any other candidate. My course in appointing him chairman of the Committee of Ways and Means, could be used to show that I have not been influenced by personal consideration against him, when the country is concerned.[9]

According to Cassedy, soon after receiving Bell's letter, he left home on a trip to Ohio and Pennsylvania, leaving his private letters with Henry Wineow of Giles County. Wineow was given permission to show Bell's letter to a few confidential friends. James Osborn, a neighbor whose friendship for Polk was well known, had already been denied the privilege of seeing Bell's letter. However, after Cassedy's departure, Wineow not only allowed Osborn to see the letter but also to make a copy of it. That copy was immediately sent to Polk.[10]

By the time Osborn's copy reached Polk, the existence of the Cassedy letter was already known in Nashville, and the exaggerated rumor of its contents made it appear as a document of prime importance. Laughlin hurriedly dispatched a note to Polk, requesting that a trustworthy person be sent to secure a copy from Osborn. It should then be mailed to Laughlin from Shelbyville or Cornersville, "not Columbia," Polk's home town.[11]

A copy was received and Laughlin published it in the *Union* on June 26. Although Osborn had originally given

[9] Bell to Cassedy, May 11, 1835, Washington *Globe*, July 8, 1835; Nashville *Union*, June 26, 1835. The italics are probably the editor's.

[10] Cassedy to Laughlin, July 10, 1835, in Nashville *Republican and State Gazette*, July 30, 1835. The Osborn copy is in the Polk Papers under the date of the original Cassedy letter.

[11] Laughlin to Polk, June 17, 1835, in Polk Papers.

his consent, on the day following publication, Laughlin received a letter from him stating that he doubted if he had authority to authorize publication. Laughlin laughingly remarked to Polk: "The note came too late." [12] Cassedy wrote immediately to Laughlin giving the details of the whole matter and denying that publication had been properly authorized.[13] This letter was suppressed by Laughlin and was not made public until Cassedy sent a copy to Bell.

Jackson–Van Buren men professed to see in Bell's Cassedy letter a veiled promise that White would not veto a Bank recharter bill. To their way of thinking this promise definitely branded Bell as a Bank man. To Polk's friends, however, the letter contained a still more important section. They charged that the Speaker was trying to meddle in Polk's district. According to their interpretation, Bell was recommending that Polk be defeated if possible. But should he be re-elected, he must be instructed to support Bell for Speaker. Indeed, this proved to their satisfaction what they had long suspected: Bell had been sending confidential men into Polk's district to sound sentiment and, if feasible, arrange to bring out an opponent.[14]

The Old Hero, vacationing at Rip Raps, was highly pleased with the news of the Cassedy letter, and was soon engaged in more wishful thinking. The Cassedy letter was the "finishing stroke" to Bell's intrigues, he wrote Polk, and had so completely disrobed the Speaker as to leave him an object of scorn "by all honest men of all parties." From what the Old General could hear, he also dared prophesy that Bell's "political sun has set in Congress." [15]

Grundy, the master politician, although equally desirous of witnessing Bell's political destruction, did not share Jackson's optimism. He observed considerable excitement as a

[12] Id. to id., July 5, 1835, ibid.
[13] Cassedy to Laughlin, July 10, 1835, in Nashville Republican and State Gazette, July 30, 1835.
[14] Polk to id., April 28, May 18, 1835, in Polk Papers.
[15] Jackson to Polk, August 3, 1835, in Bassett (ed.), Correspondence, V, 357.

result of the letter, and believed it would be the means of electing Polk Speaker of the next House; but he saw no chance of defeating Bell in his home district. Grundy thought the letter could be used with greater advantage in the congressional districts represented by Polk and Cave Johnson. Accordingly, he called upon each of the two to furnish the names of one hundred prominent men in their districts to whom might be mailed copies of the *Union* containing the Cassedy letter.[16] Bell sensed the uneasiness on the part of his adversaries and was pleased. Tennessee was ten to one for White, he wrote Samuel McKean, and Grundy, Polk, and Johnson were at the mercy of the White men.[17]

In refusing to commit White to any special course relative to the Bank, Bell was acting with prudence. The claim that he gave assurance of White's approval of a recharter bill could not have found lodging in the mind of any unbiased Tennessean; the biased could not be changed anyway. It is possible, though, that the exaggerated importance which the Jackson press outside Tennessee attached to this letter might have contributed to Bell's loss of the speakership.

As to the charge of political interference in Polk's district, Bell was undoubtedly guilty. Nothing would have pleased him quite so much as for Polk's constituents to instruct their Congressman to vote for Bell for Speaker. It is reasonable to assume that he intended for Cassedy to pass the word around among a few close friends. Still, Polk, on the other hand, was equally guilty of trying to exert influence in Bell's district. For weeks his friends had been vainly seeking an opponent for the Nashville Congressman. Early in May they began sending up kites to test the political breeze. "Correspondents" of the *Union* demanded that Andrew Hays, Dr. Felix Robertson, or Robert M. Burton announce against Bell. To these suggestions, the *Banner* replied: "We suppose that the

---

[16] Felix Grundy to *id.*, June 25, 26, 1835, in Polk Papers.
[17] Bell to Samuel McKean, April 22, 1835, in Miscellaneous Collection of the Historical Society of Pennsylvania.

reason that *those* gentlemen are called upon is, that they are among the *very few* who are known to be in favor of Mr. Van Buren for the Presidency." [18] The *"knowing ones,"* as Jackson later called them, decided that Burton was the man. He resided in Wilson County, which, together with Davidson, composed Bell's district. Polk's friends planned to have Burton come to Nashville for a conference, but he failed to make his appearance. Sickness in his family was assigned as the reason. The managers grew impatient. "Burton's failure to come down . . . paralises every thing here," wrote Grundy to Jackson.[19] A lieutenant was sent to confer with the missing politician and returned with the bad news that Burton refused to run.[20] His friends, although dissatisfied with his lack of co-operation, decided not to apply additional pressure.[21]

The discovery of the Cassedy letter had revived hope of defeating Bell for re-election. There was even talk of again approaching Burton. Then came the news that he had disgraced himself by engaging in a fist fight at Lebanon. Had it not been for this affair, Grundy assured Polk, Burton could have defeated Bell. Since the fight, however, he would run at a distinct disadvantage.[22]

At Rip Raps, Old Hickory spent much of his summer vacation pondering the results of Bell's unopposed re-election. The Nashville Congressman would certainly interpret the indifference of his constituents as tacit consent to a recharter of the Bank! [23] Jackson was unable to understand the lethargy of the people when it was clear that "the great object of Mr. Bell and Co. were [*sic*] to destroy me, and all the effects of my administration, and hand me down to posterity as an old dotard, ruled by corrupt office holders and corrupt office seekers whilst he was sacrificing all principle, for the sake of

---

18 *National Banner and Nashville Whig,* May 13, 1835.
19 Grundy to Jackson, June 6, 1835, in Jackson Papers.
20 *Id.* to Polk, June 7, 1835, in Polk Papers.
21 *Id.* to Jackson, June 17, 1835, in Jackson Papers.
22 *Id.* to Polk, June 26, 1835, in Polk Papers.
23 Jackson to *id.,* August 3, 1835, in Bassett (ed.), *Correspondence,* V, 357–59.

the speakers [sic] chair and his private facilities from the
U. States Bank." [24]

In the meantime, three days prior to the Bell celebration at
Vauxhall Gardens, the Jackson–Van Buren delegates, "fresh
from the people," assembled in convention at Baltimore.
Tennessee sent no delegates; but, determined that the President's home state should not go unrepresented, the convention
seated one Edward Rucker, a Tennessean who happened to
be in Baltimore, and permitted him to cast the state's fifteen
votes for Van Buren. As expected, Van Buren was nominated
unanimously.[25] The White-Bell group roared with laughter
over the "Ruckerized" convention, while many friends of
Van Buren expressed mortification over such silly conduct.[26]

Throughout the summer and fall of 1835, the Washington
Globe, Jackson's official organ, continued to keep Bell's alleged apostasy before its readers. The fact that there was
nothing new to reveal and but little evidence to substantiate
what had already been said never daunted the editor. Day after
day the same charges were repeated with increasing monotony.
At times, as if angered by the dearth of news, Blair would burst
forth in severe condemnation. Bell was "jealous-hearted, cold,
selfish, and suspicious," he exclaimed, and the White-Bell
supporters were the President's enemies.[27] And when the
Washington *National Intelligencer* persisted in its support of
the White cause, Blair denounced the editor, Joseph Gales,
and Bell as the "Siamese assailants of the Republican party."
Indeed, the *Intelligencer* had done nothing more than adopt
Bell's views as its own.[28]

As summer passed into autumn and President Jackson returned to the White House, he was grimly determined to
break the strength of the White movement and destroy the

[24] *Id.* to Andrew J. Hutchings, June 30, 1835, in John Coffee Papers (Collection of the Tennessee Historical Society). A copy was published in Bassett
(ed.), *Correspondence,* V, 554–55, but the date is erroneously given as 1838.
[25] Edward Stanwood, *A History of the Presidency* (Boston, 1928), I, 182.
[26] Grundy to Jackson, June 6, 1835, in Jackson Papers.
[27] Washington *Globe,* July 18, August 24, 1835.   [28] *Ibid.,* July 2, 1835.

political future of those who had sponsored it. He was sorely disappointed in the results of the state elections in Tennessee; Peyton, Bell, and Standifer had been re-elected to Congress. The defeat of David Crockett was small comfort, for his following was not large. Moreover, not even the re-election of Polk and Johnson was assurance that their constituents preferred Van Buren to White. In fact, in no congressional district within the state was the election a test of strength between presidential aspirants.

Next to the defeat of Bell, Jackson's greatest interest was in the attitude of the new legislature. Senator White's term had expired and his successor would be chosen by the next general assembly. There was no chance of defeating White; so Jackson's only hope lay in legislative instruction. If the legislators could be persuaded to instruct the senators to support Administration bills and resolutions, White, too independent to conform, would probably resign and pass into political oblivion. Neither would Bell be immune to such an expression of public opinion; he too would be forced to conform or eventually follow White into retirement. In either case, the victory of the Jackson forces would be complete.

This plan had already taken form in Old Hickory's mind before the results of the Tennessee elections were known. Writing to Polk on August 3, he suggested that instructing resolutions be prepared and presented to the legislature before nominations for senator were made. Such a course, Jackson thought, would forestall the cry of persecution should the name of either White or Bell be placed in nomination.[29] Suspecting that "Bell and Co. would like to have a bare vote against the bank," Jackson advised his friends that the stand should be made on Benton's expunging resolution.

Following Jackson's order to Secretary Roger B. Taney to cease depositing Federal money in the Bank of the United States, Clay had proposed and the Senate adopted a resolution

[29] Jackson to Polk, August 3, 1835, in Bassett (ed.), *Correspondence*, V, 357–59.

censuring the President for "the exercise of a power . . . not granted to him by the constitution and laws, and dangerous to the liberties of the people." [30] Jackson vehemently denounced the Senate for violating both the word and the spirit of the Constitution. Thomas Hart Benton immediately assumed the leadership of a movement to have the objectionable resolution expunged from the Senate journal. White objected to the word "expunge" and suggested the substitution of "rescind, reverse, and make null and void." To expunge, he explained, would be to deface the journal which the Constitution commanded the Senate to "keep." [31] Jackson's friends considered White's attitude definitely unsympathetic.

To Jackson, expunging was a very personal matter, for the resolution of censure had cast a shadow across his Administration. He was unable to see how his friends, especially Tennesseans, could fail to lift their voices in loud protest against the injustice which had been done him. Surely Tennesseans would not join the friends of Clay in condemning his upholding the Constitution and destroying the Bank. Clinging to hope for vindication and determined to destroy those who refused to grant it, Jackson sent to Governor William Carroll a draft resolution instructing Tennessee's senators to vote to expunge. Carroll was to see that the resolution was presented to the legislature for adoption. "If Whites [sic] conduct in the Senate on Bentons [sic] expunging resolution is only *well explained and commented on in debate*," Jackson wrote Grundy, "it will kill him and Bell politically." He wished to see the yeas and nays recorded so that those who failed to support the resolution could be called to answer for their conduct.[32] In adopting such a course, Jackson was lending a strong hand to those who were seeking to make the presidential campaign a contest between White and Jackson rather than White and Van Buren.

30 *Cong. Debates,* 23 Cong., 1 Sess., 58.
31 Benton, *Thirty Years in the Senate,* I, 549-50.
32 Jackson to Grundy, September 24, 1835, in Bassett (ed.), *Correspondence,* V, 367; *id.* to Polk, October 20, 1835, in Polk Papers.

On October 5, as the Tennessee legislature was organizing
for business, the impatient Old Hero sat in the White House
wondering if there was "an honest and virtuous man in the
Legislature that has the energy and firmness to rise in his place
. . . and unrobe these hypocritical apostates [Bell, Crockett,
and White] . . . [who] had carried dismay throughout Tennessee that had paralised truth and patriotism." [33] Though
tormented by doubts,[34] Jackson should have received some
consolation from the fact that he had done his best to prepare
the legislators for the task ahead. In addition to furnishing
the instructing resolution, he had caused each member to
receive a copy of the *Extra Globe* containing Benton's expunging speech.[35]

On the second day of the session, the legislature unani-
mously re-elected White to his seat in the United States
Senate. On the same day Josephus C. Guild, an ardent Jackson
supporter, introduced in the House the instructing resolutions, which were promptly sent to the table.[36] The White-
Bell forces were expecting them and thoroughly understood
the purpose. Someone very close to Jackson had been keeping
Bell informed concerning what was going on in the White
House. Polk and Andrew J. Donelson suspected William B.
Lewis; they were probably correct. Still, neither possessed
sufficient courage to bring the matter to Jackson's attention.
They did nothing more than denounce Bell as one "damned
with treachery and intrigue." [37]

Ten days after the senatorial election, the White-Bell legislators adopted resolutions reaffirming their loyalty to the

[33] *Id.* to Grundy, October 5, 1835, in Bassett (ed.), *Correspondence,* V,
371–72.

[34] On July 19, 1835, Jackson had written Amos Kendall that "since the
apostacy of White and Bell I am becoming doubtful of many that before I
had full confidence [in]." *Ibid.,* 356–57.

[35] William B. Campbell to David Campbell, October 6, 1835, in David
Campbell Papers.

[36] Tennessee *House Journal,* 1835, pp. 13–14; Josephus C. Guild, *Old Times
in Tennessee* (Nashville, 1878), 145–56.

[37] Donelson to Polk, September 24, 1835; Polk to Laughlin, September 6,
1835, in Polk Papers.

original principles upon which Jackson had been elected and expressing general approval of the policies of his Administration. At the same time they perceived in the Baltimore convention the same tendency toward evil for which they had so vigorously denounced the congressional caucus in 1823. Without mentioning the name of Van Buren, they announced that since no acceptable person had been nominated for the presidency, they wished to present Hugh Lawson White as the man who could be trusted to carry out the original principles of Jacksonian democracy.[38]

White immediately accepted the nomination, and Jackson read him and Bell out of the party, denouncing them and their friends as nullifiers, Federalists, Bank men, and new Whigs. They had dared to defy the Old Hero; henceforth, they would be classed as his avowed enemies. Already Jackson had threatened to make White odious in case he became a candidate. Now the President announced, half boastfully: "Judge White will not get a vote except in Tennessee . . . and Mr. Bell will not reach the speakers [sic] chair. . . ." The White supporters were crying out against a caucus, Jackson observed, and were charging that he had been brought out by the people. Was there ever such a "miserable *little* caucus" as the eleven-man body that just nominated White?[39]

The President's effort to block White's nomination and force the acceptance of Van Buren reacted unfavorably upon him and his Administration; eventually it made many recruits for the Whig party. William B. Campbell, a member of the Tennessee house of representatives and a future Whig governor of the state, expressed the attitude of many when he confided that he would vote for White (if for no other reason) because of the "direct & palpable attempt on the part of Jackson, to force this state to vote for Van." In Tennessee, Campbell added, Van Buren had "no weight, merit or importance

[38] Tennessee *House Journal,* 1835, pp. 68–73.
[39] Jackson to Hutchings, October 31, 1835, in Bassett (ed.), *Correspondence,* V, 373–74.

of his own—like the moon, his fame & glory are borrowed from an illustrious orb." [40] Campbell's uncle, David Campbell of Virginia, disagreed with the opinion expressed by his nephew; he thought Van Buren a man of considerable merits. As for Bell, David Campbell sarcastically remarked, he was still a friend of the Jackson Administration—"Such a friend as the devil is to religion." [41]

While Bell was sponsoring White's nomination, Polk and his friends, in addition to opposing the nomination, were quietly lining up support for Polk's candidacy for the speakership of the national House of Representatives. As soon as the congressional elections were over, Samuel H. Laughlin began contacting congressmen in other states. The defeat of Bell and the elevation of Polk to the Speaker's chair, he told the Jackson–Van Buren men, would destroy the Bell-White cause in Tennessee by revealing how the Speaker stood outside the state. Since Polk had remained loyal when others had faltered and since a part of Bell's treachery had been against Polk, Laughlin argued, he ought to be the instrument by which Bell should be defeated.[42]

Polk encouraged his friends to be active in his behalf, but refrained from writing political letters himself. As he explained to Laughlin, he did not intend "to write any *Cassedy letters.*" Polk feared intrigue even within the ranks of avowed Van Buren men. Some of Bell's friends, especially Ephraim H. Foster, the speaker of the Tennessee house of representatives, circulated the rumor that, although Bell would probably not be re-elected Speaker, the successful candidate would be John Y. Mason of Virginia, not Polk. To this the Bell press of Nashville added the claim that Blair, editor of the *Globe,* had, at the Baltimore convention, promised the speakership to Virginia. These rumors aroused in Polk a suspicion that William B. Lewis, whom he referred to as Bell's "confidential-

40 William B. Campbell to David Campbell, October 6, 1835, in David Campbell Papers.
41 David Campbell to William B. Campbell, October 15, 1835, *ibid.*
42 Laughlin to Polk, August 30, 1835, in Polk Papers.

man," was the prime mover in an intrigue to prevent his being run as the Administration candidate for Speaker. "Lewis is a *White* & a *Bell man*," fumed Polk, "[and] is in every way wrong in his politics, but he takes special care to conceal this at Head Quarters." Owing to the fact that Lewis was a resident of the White House and a confidential adviser of the President, Polk recognized his "ability to do mischief." Lewis' friendship with Blair gave Polk additional reason to fear that the rumor was true.[43]

On the question of the speakership, Polk was sensitive, even to the point of engaging in self-pity. He felt that he had borne the brunt of the battle and had suffered at the hands of the Bell group. He confided to Laughlin that should he be passed up by the Administration group he would consider himself "very badly treated." Both his pride and future standing were at stake; nothing short of victory could erase the humiliation of recent defeat. In order to break up the alleged intrigue against him, Polk urged Laughlin to write Blair a strong letter. Laughlin was also to have other friends write to Silas Wright of New York and Richard M. Johnson of Kentucky.[44]

While Polk was campaigning for the speakership, Bell was devoting his attention to a wealthy Nashville widow. Among those who had heard him deliver his Vauxhall Gardens speech was the socially prominent Mrs. Jane Erwin Yeatman, daughter of Andrew Erwin of Bedford County and widow of Thomas Yeatman. The late Thomas Yeatman and his partners, Joseph and Robert Woods, had made a fortune as commission merchants, dealing principally in cotton and tobacco. While on a business trip to Philadelphia, Yeatman had learned of a great increase in the price of cotton in Europe. Securing a horse, he rode full speed to Nashville, arriving ahead of the mails, and bought up large quantities of cotton which he sold at 100 per cent profit. Yeatman, Woods and Company later went into the banking business and also spent large sums in developing iron works in Stewart County. At

[43] Polk to Laughlin, September 6, 1835, *ibid.*   [44] *Ibid.*

the time of his death, on June 11, 1833, while en route to Louisville by boat, Yeatman was reputed to have been worth $500,000.[45]

According to Mrs. Yeatman's own statement, made many years later, she had never seen Bell prior to the Vauxhall celebration. Throughout his address she listened with great admiration, and when he had concluded remarked that, although she had given little thought to a second marriage, she doubted her ability "to refuse a nuptial offer" from such a man as Bell.[46] As was probably intended, the remark reached Bell, and Mrs. Yeatman soon had an opportunity to demonstrate her inability to refuse.

Tall and stout of stature, dark of complexion, oval of face, and open in countenance, the new Mrs. Bell appeared as a lady of distinction rather than beauty. Dark gray eyes, a rather large mouth, and beautiful teeth, which were ever exposed by a continual smile, gave her a natural charm. These personal characteristics plus "sound sense and judgment" [47] made her an ideal companion for the more sedate and dignified Bell. For the next twenty-five years her charm, wealth, and family connections contributed greatly to Bell's political advancement. In Washington she soon became "part & parcel" of Congress, and in the words of John J. Crittenden, there was "no getting along without her." [48]

Immediately prior to their marriage, Bell and Mrs. Yeat-

45 Clayton, *History of Davidson County,* 203. At the time of Yeatman's death, Yeatman, Woods and Company's holdings included 18,000 acres of land in Stewart County, on which iron mines were located, two blast furnaces, one forge, a rolling mill, and 200 slaves. It was estimated that the company spent at least $100,000 annually on labor and supplies. See Nashville *National Banner and Daily Advertiser,* November 29, 1833.

Yeatman had five children—Thomas, Henry C., Emma, James, and William. In a division of their father's estate made in May, 1835, each received about $58,000. There were probably subsequent divisions. Davidson County Wills and Inventories, Book 10, pp. 321, 506–11; Stewart County Deeds, Books 7–12.

46 Foote, *Bench and Bar of the South and Southwest,* 179. In later years Foote was a close friend of the Bells.

47 Mrs. Ann Royall, in *The Huntress* (Washington), February 23, 1839.

48 Crittenden to Mrs. Ann Mary (Crittenden) Coleman, October 9, 1837, in Crittenden Papers (Duke University Library).

man signed a property agreement. The partnership arrangement which she had made with Joseph and Robert Woods
following the death of her husband was to continue for ten
years. The banking firm of Yeatman, Woods and Company,
in which she had a half interest, was placed under the management of the Woods brothers, and the iron works, under the
title of Woods, Stacker and Company, in which she had a one-
fourth interest, was placed under the supervision of Samuel
Stacker.[49] During the ten-year period Mrs. Yeatman's interests
were to be looked after by her father, Andrew Erwin, and
Bell was to have "no right or power" to interfere. After ten
years the future Mrs. Bell was to retain for her sole use one
third of her above mentioned property plus the real estate
left her by Yeatman. The other two thirds of her banking and
iron interests were to be "vested in the said John Bell" for his
sole use and control.[50]

    There is a family story that immediately following their
marriage, Mrs. Bell, in order to relieve her husband of worry
and embarrassment, used $40,000 of her own money to liqui-
date his debts.[51] Regardless of the truth of this story, it is
certain that the Yeatmen wealth brought welcomed relief to
the Bell household. Since the failure of James Bell's Nashville
business in the spring of 1834, John had been financially
embarrassed. It is probable that he had an interest in the business, and it is certain that he had endorsed James's notes for
considerable sums borrowed from the United States Bank. In
1833 he had mortgaged his Nashville home to John H. Eaton
for $5,000.[52]

[49] See agreement of partnership in Davidson County Register, Book Y,
237–41. Other interests in the iron works were: Joseph and Robert Woods
$5/16$, James Woods $2/16$, Samuel and John Stacker $4/16$, and William Yeatman $1/16$.
William Yeatman had purchased his $1/16$ share from his mother for $22,081.
See Stewart County Deeds, Book 12, p. 88.
[50] See Davidson County Register, Book Y, 221–23.
[51] Octavia Z. Bond, in Nashville *Banner*, March 19, 1910.
[52] W. G. Childress to Polk, June 21, 1834, in Polk Papers; Bell to President
of the United States Bank at Washington, July 5, 1834, in Collection of Historical Society of Pennsylvania; Davidson County Register, Book Z, 136,
Book X, 195.

But even his wife's wealth did not give him complete relief from financial troubles. He was a poor business manager. In later years he acquired extensive holdings in lands and coal mines; yet he constantly complained that they yielded him little profit.[53] During the depression which broke upon the country in 1837, he was forced to beg the United States Bank of Pennsylvania not to compel him to sacrifice his property in order to meet his obligations. Apparently for the purpose of raising some needed cash, he sold his Nashville home to his brother-in-law, James Erwin, for $24,000.[54]

On November 7, 1835, Mr. and Mrs. Bell left Nashville for Washington. As the newlyweds' boat floated down the Cumberland River, Polk's ever-active brothers-in-law were pondering the probable effect this marriage would have on Bell's political future. Mrs. Bell's brother, James Erwin, had married Anne Clay, the second daughter of Henry Clay, in 1823. Another point of some importance that the brothers-in-law did not know was that Mrs. Bell was a close friend of Ann Mary Crittenden, the daughter of John J. Crittenden.[55]

53 Bell to Lewis Coryell, June 27, July 3, 1848, January 15, 1853, in Collection of Historical Society of Pennsylvania; James Lee, Jr. to Bell, April 20, 1857, in Polk-Yeatman Papers (Southern Historical Collection, University of North Carolina Library).

54 Bell to J. Cowperthwait, February 29, 1838, in Bell Papers; Davidson County Register, Book 1, p. 580.

55 Rucker to Polk, November 20, 1835, in Polk Papers; Glyndon G. Van Deusen, *The Life of Henry Clay* (Boston, 1937), 151; Mrs. Ann Mary Coleman to Crittenden, December 20, 1835, in Crittenden Papers (Duke University Library).

The Erwin family had long been anti-Jackson. Andrew Erwin was a supporter of William H. Crawford for the presidency in the days when there was bitter enmity between the Secretary of the Treasury and the General. In 1819, in an effort to block the possible appointment of Erwin as marshall for western Tennessee, Jackson had described him to President Monroe as "a Bankrupt both in property and charactor [sic]." A land litigation increased the hostility between the two, and, in 1828, Erwin joined Dr. Boyd McNairy in publishing letters revealing the close association between Jackson and Aaron Burr. Erwin further charged that Jackson had told him in 1811 that he was engaged in the Negro business. See Bassett (ed.), *Correspondence*, I, 149, 152 n., 181 n., 217 n.; Jackson to James Monroe, September 28, 1819, in *ibid.*, II, 433-37; Jackson to Coffee, June 20, 1828, *id.* to Lewis, July 10, 1828, in *ibid.*, III, 409-10, 412-13; Thomas P. Abernethy, *From Frontier to Plantation in Tennessee; A Study in Frontier Democracy* (Chapel Hill, 1932), 263 ff.

Chapter VII

DICTATION FAILS

POLK'S fears failed to materialize; neither Bell nor Mason proved to be a serious competitor for the speakership. When the Twenty-fourth Congress assembled early in December, 1835, Polk was elected Speaker on the first ballot by a vote of 132 to Bell's 84.[1] The Jackson–Van Buren men were in complete control of the House.

Polk's friends were overjoyed. "*Big Bell* has lost the clapper shure [*sic*] enough," gleefully exclaimed one loyal constituent. "You can tell a White Whig any where in Maury [County]," wrote another, "by the *unusual longitudinal attenuation* of his phiz." Bell's friends "about Nashville are truly mortified," added a third. "They attribute Mr. Bells [*sic*] defeat to the influence of the President." From New York State an enthusiast declared that Polk's victory over that "apostate, John Bell," had produced as much rejoicing as had the proclamation of the Declaration of Independence. In Nashville the loyal Jackson-Polk men repaired themselves to Vauxhall, the scene of the Bell celebration, and "screwed the neck off a few dozen Champagne, under the roar of 48 rounds of cannon." [2]

It was inevitable that a political controversy of such intensity should extend to the floor of Congress and greatly influence legislation. And the malignant spirit with which the Jackson press greeted Bell's defeat further intensified the

[1] *Congressional Globe*, 24 Cong., 1 Sess., 2–3; James C. Campbell to David Campbell, February 1, 1836, in David Campbell Papers.

[2] James McKisick to Polk, December 23, 1835; H. B. Kelsey to *id.*, December 23, 1835; H. M. Watterson to *id.*, December 21, 1835; John P. Burgett to *id.*, December 23, 1835; A. O. P. Nicholson to *id.*, December 20, 1835, in Polk Papers.

friction. The House had performed its duty "with the most scrupulous fidelity," boastfully announced the *Globe*, and John Bell had been marked "with the reprobation of an indignant country." [3]

From the beginning until the close of the session, the floor of the House was the scene of considerable disorder. Charges and countercharges filled the air as both factions sparred for political advantage or vented partisan spleen. Speaker Polk, considered by the opposition as the mere tool of the Administration, was frequently attacked as a result of his parliamentary rulings, although he appears to have been competent and as fair as his partisanship would permit. Henry A. Wise of Virginia, a former member of the Nashville bar and a close friend of Bell, and Balie Peyton, White's nephew, led the Bell supporters in baiting the Speaker. In questioning many of his decisions and making frequent use of insinuations as well as direct attacks upon the President and his friends, they became so personal as to cause some of Polk's friends to believe a duel was desired. Peyton explained to a friend:

We have struck when and where we could but have been trammeled & bound by damnable shackles of 'the party.' We have been unable to get up any great question of general interest. Bell has been prepared since the first of the Session on several great leading questions, such as Executive patronage, Election of Pres. & Vice Pres. &c &c. He has been hailing, & struggling for opportunities to hold forth; but he has been denied the floor when he was plainly entitled to it, & prevented from speeking [sic] by caucus arrangement. They dread, they fear Bell, & hence the difficulty for him to catch the Speaker's eye—hence the impossibility to submit any proposition which may ellicit [sic] general debate.[4]

Wise was Bell's "man Friday," declared the Nashville *Union*,[5] and James Walker warned Polk that it was Bell's plan to disgrace the Speaker by drawing him into a duel with

[3] Washington *Globe,* January 4, 1836.
[4] Balie Peyton to William B. Campbell, March 9, 1836, in David Campbell Papers.
[5] Nashville *Union,* March 17, 1836.

Wise or Peyton.[6] The *Globe* complained that, although Bell pushed Wise and Peyton into the lead in bringing up points of order, the former Speaker "manifested a peculiar ardor" in debating the points. He criticized the decisions of the Speaker, the precedents of the House, and even the rules. Some of Polk's friends thought Bell was attempting "to show off his knowledge"; others sarcastically remarked that he wished to make the House realize what a "great loss it sustained, in the removal of such a prodigious expounder of rules from the Chair." [7] Editor Blair, on the other hand, claimed that Bell's motive was to block legislation on important matters and then blame the majority for "a session of words and not of acts." [8] None of these accusers were correct. Since marrying into an anti-Jackson family and becoming personally interested in banking and commercial enterprises, Bell had definitely joined the opposition. To have led the attack on Polk, however, would have given the appearance of vindictiveness; so he sat back, for the most part, and enjoyed seeing Wise and Peyton keep the Speaker uncomfortable. At the same time, he must have known that regardless of his words or actions, the Jackson–Polk–Van Buren men would hold him responsible for the conduct of Wise and Peyton.

Bell did not definitely throw down the gauntlet until March 16, 1836, at which time the House was debating the naval appropriation bill. He first proposed that the amount be cut in half, but later withdrew this proposal and suggested that the appropriation for the improvement of the Portsmouth, New Hampshire, navy yard be stricken out. The United States had more navy yards than were needed, he explained; this additional appropriation was nothing more than a political payoff for New Hampshire's loyalty to the Administration party.[9] Bell wished to see the war spirit of the Administration put to the test, for he did not believe any war with France was

---

[6] Walker to Polk, March 14, 1836, in Polk Papers.
[7] Washington *Globe*, March 16, 1836.   [8] *Ibid.*
[9] *Cong. Globe*, 24 Cong., 1 Sess., 238–39.

intended. Since the close of the Napoleonic wars the United States had been attempting to induce France to pay for the damages inflicted upon American commerce. The king's government had finally agreed to settle for $5,000,000, but the Chamber of Deputies refused to appropriate the money. Jackson then assumed a bellicose attitude. Bell insisted that the Administration party, like the Federalists in 1798, merely wished to increase its strength. If there was a real danger of war, he charged, then the Administration and the chairman of the Ways and Means Committee had "paltered with the honor and safety of the country" during the last session of Congress. Not a hand had been raised to relieve the defenseless condition of the nation. This, Bell said, was a sample of the incompetence and negligence prevalent in all departments. Administration officials, from the highest to the lowest, had used Jackson's name and popularity as a "shield and buckler" behind which to conceal their acts.

Bell denied that he was hostile to Jackson; he only opposed the President's "illegitimate desire" to elevate a favorite to the presidency. Indeed, it seemed that the one thought which pervaded all officialdom was the promotion of Van Buren. In order to accomplish this purpose, Bell continued, the will of the people had been disregarded and "absolute acquiescence" demanded. The purity of the press had been destroyed by political subsidies, and freedom of elections within the states had been reduced to mockery.[10]

Bell continued active throughout the running debate which lasted for several weeks. The Administration press charged that he was "continually devising petty expedients" for the purpose of foiling the business of the House. Bell fought back, declaring that his sole purpose was to test the sincerity of those who had stirred up a war panic. If war was imminent, why had not the majority party terminated debate and recorded its vote? At any rate, voting appropriations, Bell growled, was not the only duty of the House. "A much greater

[10] *Ibid.*, 251–52.

and more important duty is to watch over and guard the executive administration of the country."[11]

While both factions in Congress displayed their pettiness, the political caldron was boiling vigorously outside. Both Polk and Bell were reassured of the loyalty of their supporters. Polk's correspondents complimented him on the dignified manner in which he handled the troublesome opposition and assured him that the actions of the White-Bell group were "perfectly understood" by the people. These same correspondents, however, were somewhat concerned over the huge amount of anti-Administration material that was being franked into Tennessee by White and Bell. Almost every mail brought additional copies of the speeches of Wise and Ben Hardin.[12]

The White press reproachfully suggested that the Jackson papers were passing judgment on Bell's speeches without giving their readers the privilege of reading them. "They know full well," taunted the Randolph *Recorder*, "that . . . the startling and astounding facts which he [Bell] develops would blow their consolidated unit into ten thousand vulgar factions, and emancipate their readers from the chains attempted to be forged upon them by the Rucker Convention."[13] Another complaint came from Lebanon, where the *Mirror* sponsored a protest meeting which adopted resolutions accusing Speaker Polk of denying to Bell ample opportunity to express his views and those of his constituents. Polk's every action, they stated, was "influenced by a zeal and partiality for his party." "We consider his conduct subversive of sound constitutional right of free and untrammelled discussion."[14]

---

[11] Washington *Globe*, April 8, 12, 14, 1836; *Cong. Globe*, 24 Cong., 1 Sess., Appendix, 555. According to the editor of the *Globe*, when Bell's proposal finally came to a vote, he "hung his head, and declined to vote."

[12] Walker to Polk, March 14, April 11, 20, June 7, 1836; A. C. Hays to *id.*, April 26, 1836; Moses Lynch to *id.*, May 19, 1836; George Gammon to *id.*, May 25, 1836; Nicholson to *id.*, May 30, 1836; George W. Jones to *id.*, June 7, 1836; Laughlin to *id.*, April 12, 1836, in Polk Papers.

[13] Randolph (Tenn.) *Recorder*, May 20, 1836.

[14] Nashville *Republican and State Gazette*, April 9, 1836.

Bell was not long in availing himself of another opportunity to arraign the Administration. The occasion was the debate on a proposal to appropriate approximately $700,000 for the improvement of harbors during the year 1836. In the beginning, Bell labeled the bill as a part of a deliberate system of extravagance—of a plan for increasing the wants of the Government, and of exhausting the Treasury." What a Ways and Means Committee Speaker Polk had appointed! Its very composition, Bell asserted, was a "palpable desertion of the principle of representation." Seven of the nine members were from the commercial cities of the coastal states; their sections stood to benefit most in such an unequal distribution of public money. The bill before the House, Bell said, had none of the merits of the recently enacted distribution bill; [15] that Act would allot to each state "its due proportion" of the surplus. Indeed, he thought that an equitable distribution of surplus money was advantageous; it would produce a desire for a government strong enough to raise considerable revenue from customs and the sale of lands. It would also result in a constant public inquiry into abuses and extravagance. On the contrary, such bills as the one before the House, by allotting to New York $200,000 and giving nothing to several inland states, would destroy all community of interest. In Bell's opinion, the greatest calamity that could result from a Treasury surplus was in evidence—"an increased number of public offices—increased naval and military establishments— an undue increase of Government patronage—and a profuse and profligate waste of the public treasure."

Departing completely from the topic under discussion, Bell next launched a defense of his present course and past record, interspersing his remarks with direct thrusts at the President and his Administration. In spite of what the Administration press had reported, Bell denied ever having abused President

[15] Congress had recently passed a bill providing for the distribution of the Treasury surplus among the states in the form of a loan. Distribution was to be on the basis of representation in Congress.

Jackson. Never, he insisted, had he referred to the President as a "tyrant, a usurper, a crouching sycophant, or a degraded slave." Jackson "may be the master of *slaves* and *menials,*" he exclaimed, "but nature has disqualified him from becoming one himself." Despite the President's greatness, rank, and popularity, Andrew Jackson was "still but a man." Although he venerated the Old Hero and recognized his public services, Bell made it clear that he would never prostrate himself before any man or eulogize him in order to secure favor. He said that he had neither sought nor received any advancement at the hands of the Chief Executive. On the contrary, on every occasion when Bell was candidate for office, whether before the House or the people, the President had been his "most powerful opponent."

Bell told the House that, although he did not propose the impeachment of the President, he did wish to see that body, "the constitutional supervisors and overseers of the conduct of the Executive," keep a close check on him. General Jackson was interfering in both state and national elections! Bell said he realized that, in the eyes of some, to criticize the Old Hero was to tread upon "holy ground"; "but this, thank God," he exclaimed, "is not a part of my superstition." He had supported most Administration measures and would continue to do so; still he was determined to oppose vigorously the President's attempt to select his successor. And "neither ignorance nor prejudice . . . nor artifice, nor falsehood" could deter him from performing this duty. In order to destroy those who would not do his bidding, General Jackson, Bell averred, had resorted to extensive letter writing and had filled the mails with materials "containing the most virulent and inflammatory attacks upon the character and conduct of particular candidates." Bell pronounced this a radical departure from the President's promise (in his inaugural address) to correct all abuses which brought patronage " 'into conflict with the freedom of elections.' " Should this Executive interference continue, Bell prophesied the formation of a new officeholder's party with an estimated 200,000 working members who would henceforth "constitute the Praetorian guards of America, to ratify the appointment of a successor by the Executive." Then the President's power to select his successor would be complete.

But that was not all. Bell charged that already the influence of the Executive was being felt not only in the election of congressmen but also in the deliberation of both houses. The next step would be to make the speakership of the House "an appendage of Executive patronage." When these things should come to pass, the United States would be an elective monarchy; but the method of election would make the monarch absolute, and his power to select his successor would, in effect, make the office hereditary.[16]

Following the adjournment of Congress on July 4, the presidential campaign increased in intensity. The recently organized Whig party made no official nomination. Instead, local conventions and state legislatures were encouraged to bring out their "favorite sons." The strategy was so to divide the electoral vote as to throw the election into the House. Daniel Webster and William H. Harrison were the most prominent Whig candidates. The Whigs made no nomination in Tennessee, leaving the field open to White. Jackson was not entirely in error when he prophesied that "when Judge White has been *used to distract and divide the republican ranks* and Van Buren abused until, as far as the abuse of the opposition can make him odious, the nullifiers in the south, and the Whiggs [sic] will unite upon Clay and abandon the judge." [17]

By 1836 leaders of the White movement could not have been ignorant of the hopelessness of his candidacy, yet there is no evidence that it cooled their enthusiasm. They had defied presidential dictation and gained sectional, if not na-

16 *Cong. Globe*, 24 Cong., 1 Sess., Appendix, 651 ff
17 Jackson to Polk, August 3, 1835, in Bassett (ed.), *Correspondence*, V, 357–58.

tional, popularity by the act; local pride and White's sterling qualities were challenging the personal rule of the Old Hero. Political and personal enemies, increasing in number through years of action and intolerance, were eager to contribute to the termination of the reign of Andrew Jackson. In the heat of the campaign, the editor of the Memphis *Enquirer* exclaimed: "The power of Andrew Jackson in Tennessee is consigned to 'the tomb of the Capulets.' " [18]

Most of the newspapers in Tennessee were opposed to Jackson. The Memphis *Enquirer,* Nashville *Republican, National Banner,* Knoxville *Register,* Randolph *Recorder,* Lebanon *Mirror,* Columbia *Observer,* Jackson *Truth Teller,* Paris *West Tennessean* all carried the White-Bell banner. The best the Jackson–Van Buren–Polk forces could offer in opposition was the recently established Nashville *Union* reinforced by the weak Memphis *Intelligencer* and an unimpressive list of small-town papers; local pride forced many an editor to desert the ranks of Old Hickory and join in the support of Hugh Lawson White. The *Union* was in constant financial and editorial difficulties. Editor Laughlin's weakness for drink sometimes made it necessary for outsiders, such as Alfred O. P. Nicholson, to take over the editorial duties. And in the midst of the campaign, M. A. Long, Laughlin's associate, left for East Tennessee to edit incognito the Athens *Republican* which was to be *"peddled* about in every nook and corner" of White's home section.[19]

Never before had Tennessee seen so many political dinners and barbecues as in the summer and autumn of 1836. Polk, Grundy, and Cave Johnson bore the burden of the Van Buren campaign, while Bell, Peyton, and Ephraim H. Foster led the White forces in Middle and West Tennessee. Bell's first important appearance after returning from Washington was at

18 Memphis *Enquirer,* September 8, 1836.
19 Nicholson to Polk, February 7, 1836; M. A. Long to *id.,* August 21, 1836, in Polk Papers.

a dinner at Pleasant Grove, on the Murfreesboro road, about six miles out of Nashville. The *Republican* observed that this was "the largest company ever assembled in this state, to welcome home a faithful public servant." [20] A procession a mile and a half long, composed of eleven hundred horsemen and fifty-six carriages, formed on Nashville's Broad Street, proceeded up College, then around the public square and out the Murfreesboro turnpike.[21]

Other celebrations in the Nashville vicinity were held at Mill Creek, White's Creek, and Love's Spring. In accepting an invitation to the latter, Bell deplored the existence of a "servile, acquiescing spirit" among certain citizens; some people so greatly undervalued self-government as to submit to domination by a few political managers. Some individuals "in the shape of men" wished nothing more than to know the desires of Andrew Jackson. But he, for one, Bell explained, had seen enough during the past eighteen months to convince him that unless the spoils principle "which cements that combination of office holders and office seekers, who, with the most profound cunning and by hypocrisy arrogate the name of the Republican Party, can be sooner or later, successfully resisted, our government will become the most degraded among nations." [22]

At Mill Creek, Bell's old home community, Peyton and Bell created a sensation when they produced a letter from Richard M. Johnson, denying the accuracy of the Pew letter which had been published in the *Globe* and other anti-Bell papers during the preceding year. Never, Johnson said, had Bell requested him either to become a candidate for the presidency or to support the Bank.[23] Laughlin, much disturbed, rushed a letter to Polk. "There is some fraud in this matter," he complained, "or else Johnson is a dupe or dishonest man. I fear Bell may have cheated him out of some kind of certificate in

[20] Nashville *Republican and State Gazette,* September 3, 1836.
[21] *Ibid.,* August 30, 1836.　　[22] *Ibid.*　　[23] *Ibid.,* September 15, 1836.

the form of a letter last winter." Polk and Cave Johnson must see Johnson.[24] Nothing more was heard about the matter.

At Lebanon a dinner was spread for more than four thousand persons, and Bell delivered a three-hour speech.[25] Other celebrations were held at Carthage and at least two places in Polk's congressional district before the White campaigners moved west of the Tennessee River. Congressman William C. Dunlap, a friend of Polk, resented Bell's and Peyton's invasion of his district. Dunlap feared that his own loyalty to Jackson and Van Buren might prove embarrassing should the White movement become too popular in West Tennessee. Besides, Bell and Peyton were aggressive politicians, and might attempt to dictate to the people of the Bolivar District as to what person to send to Congress.[26]

The White press in West Tennessee hailed with great delight the coming of Peyton and Bell. Go over to Somerville, the Memphis *Enquirer* advised its readers, and "listen to the high-toned eloquence of John Bell" and to "the pungent wit, scorching sarcasm, irresistible humor and powerful pathos of Balie Peyton." [27]

Apparently Congressmen Polk and Johnson had not intended campaigning outside their home districts, but Senator Grundy, after a swing through the western section of the state, advised more action.[28] Polk-Grundy-Johnson dinners were organized throughout Middle Tennessee, but, for the most part, Van Buren's name was kept in the background. Big celebrations were held in Nashville and Gallatin, the home towns of Bell and Peyton. Polk followed Bell into West Tennessee, and at Somerville, delivered a two-and-a-half-hour speech, which a correspondent of the Memphis *Enquirer* crudely characterized as "slangwang balderdash of the *Globe*,

[24] Laughlin to Polk, September 8, 1836, in Polk Papers.
[25] Benjamin R. Owen to William B. Campbell, September 13, 1836, in David Campbell Papers.
[26] Dunlap to Polk, September 17, 1836, in Polk Papers.
[27] Memphis *Enquirer*, September 15, 1836.
[28] Grundy to Polk, October 4, 1836, in Polk Papers.

stale from use and age. . . . All borrowed from the *Globe;* not an original idea . . . stuff, mere stuff." [29]

Jackson, unable to keep out of the active campaign, left Washington for Tennessee, traveling a circuitous route so as to visit several East Tennessee towns. Later he extended his tour into West Tennessee and northern Alabama. On more than one occasion he denounced White as a "red hot Federalist." At Nashville the President was guest of honor at a political barbecue, and, in response to a rousing welcome, offered a toast: "Republican Tennessee: Her motto, 'principles, not men'—She will never abandon her good old Jeffersonian democratic republican principles which she has so long maintained and practiced, to throw herself (on any occasion) into the embraces of the federalists, the nullifiers or the new born whigs." [30]

In reply to Jackson, White, speaking at a public dinner in Knoxville on August 31, reasserted his faith in and adherence to the original principles upon which Andrew Jackson had been selected as chief magistrate. He had been a stanch supporter of the Administration, he said, in every case where those principles had been respected. If, as Jackson had said, he and the President were as far apart as the poles, then it was because the President himself had departed from the old principles of Jeffersonian Republicanism. "I have no controversy with the Chief Magistrate," White explained. "I aspire to nothing which he wants." If Jackson had any quarrel it was with those Tennesseans who had chosen to honor another Tennessean by nominating him for the succession. The truth was, White insisted, that Jackson thought it a part of his Administration to select a successor and had determined "to use all his influence and patronage" in the interest of his choice, at the same time denouncing as Federalists and enemies of the Administration all men who refused to vote as the President directed. In answer to Jackson's toast, White proposed:

[29] Memphis *Enquirer,* November 1, 1836.
[30] *Niles' Weekly Register,* LI (1836), 17.

"Practices, not professions:—The Republicans of Tennessee are now what they were in 1828, *Jacksonians, following the creed of that Apostle of Liberty, Thomas Jefferson.* Should this entitle them to a 'New-born' name, they care not; provided they are left in the *full enjoyment* of their inalienable right of suffrage. They would rather have even a *bad* name with good principles, than bad principles *concealed under a good name."* [31] Undoubtedly White had expressed the sentiments of the majority of Tennesseans; they had no quarrel with Andrew Jackson other than his determination to force the selection of an unpopular northern man in preference to a favorite son.

While Tennessee was being thoroughly aroused to the support of White, and Jackson's loyal few, shouldering the burden of the unpopular Van Buren, fought back with more vigor than hope, the Washington *Globe* neglected the election in other states in order to empty vials of wrath upon John Bell. The stories of conspiracy and intrigue were again paraded before the reader. Then, as if sensing the hopelessness of his cause, Editor Blair lashed out against Bell as the alleged perpetrator of a movement to destroy the fame and influence of the Old General. Here was "a man educated as a pettifogger, and improved into a political Machiavel [*sic*] by persevering study of the arts of deception in a seven year's apprenticeship in Congress. John Bell has arrived at a point which entitles him to a diploma as a political impostor." [32]

Polk made an eleventh-hour attempt to clinch the accusation of duplicity which Van Buren men had hurled at Bell. Churchill C. Cambreleng of New York had told him, he wrote Francis Thomas of Maryland, that prior to the election of a Speaker, Bell had assured Thomas of his support of the party's nominee for President. Polk wished to use Thomas' name in making this story public. The reply was disappointing; Cambreleng had misunderstood, and Thomas, although a Van

[31] *Ibid.,* 59–61; Scott, *A Memoir of Hugh L. White,* 346 ff.
[32] Washington *Globe,* September 30, October 7, 1836.

Buren man, would not permit the use of his name in an effort to injure Bell.[33]

As late as October, Jackson still had hope of defeating the Bell-White forces even in Middle Tennessee, which he admitted was their stronghold. The General was indignant at the tactics of some rowdies who, he supposed, were friends of Bell. Robert M. Burton had reported that, while speaking against White and Bell in the latter's district, he had been set upon by "hired bullies" who "attempted to silence him." Jackson rejoiced over Burton's assurance that he gave "two of them broken heads." Although not on the scene of action, Jackson believed the Van Buren ball had really begun to roll in Tennessee. One thing was certain, he wrote, "in four months from now, Bell White & Co, will be politically destroyed." [34]

The outcome of the election in Tennessee was the reverse of what Jackson had prophesied. White swept the state by a majority of more than 10,000 votes, carrying 44 counties to Van Buren's 19. Even the Hermitage precinct went to White by a vote of 43 to 18.[35] The fact that White carried only one other state—Georgia—was no disappointment to "Bell & Co.," for after the nomination of Van Buren, no well-informed White supporter expected the Tennessean to win. From the beginning, the only hope lay in the remote possibility that Jackson, seeing the citizens of his home state rallying to their esteemed Senator, might give him the support of the Administration. White made the race "against his wish"; [36] he had no real desire to be President. He yielded to the admiration of a local public and to a determination to assert his independence of the dictations of Andrew Jackson. Perchance he also al-

[33] Polk to Francis Thomas, September 28, 1836; Thomas to Polk, October 14, 1836, in Polk Papers.

[34] Jackson to Van Buren, October 2, 1836, in Martin Van Buren Papers (Division of Manuscripts, Library of Congress).

[35] Phelan, *History of Tennessee*, 374; Powell Moore, "The Revolt Against Jackson in Tennessee, 1835–1836," in *Journal of Southern History* (Baton Rouge and Nashville), II (1936), 356.

[36] Henry A. Wise, *Seven Decades of the Union* (Philadelphia, 1881), 161.

lowed himself to become the tool of ambitious politicians. Van Buren, for one, thought Bell controlled White's action "by force of superior capacity and knowledge." [37] Bell's superiority lay only in his capacity for political maneuvering.

Nevertheless, whatever the causes for White's candidacy, the results of the campaign in Tennessee were conclusive— Tennessee had become a Whig state in all but name, and the name was soon to be assumed. Bell, Peyton, Foster, and their associates had accomplished their purpose. Jackson had overestimated his political influence. "Men here are more independent than in the old States," wrote a Maury County schoolmaster who had recently arrived from North Carolina, "and I thought President Jackson knew Tennesseans better than to dictate to them." [38] The Old Hero never lived to see Tennessee go Democratic again in a national election.

Jackson's reaction to the loss of Tennessee was a mixture of humiliation, disappointment, and rage. Should he live long enough to become a private citizen again, he vowed his determination to destroy the fabrication of falsehoods which, he declared, had been the only weapon of the White Whigs. It was a duty he owed "to truth & the morals of society," he said, to expose White, Bell, and Peyton, so that those who loved the truth might have an opportunity to learn it.[39] Jackson, still unable to grasp the significance of this political upheaval, gave no sign of a change in tactics. Political punishment for John Bell for his desertion had become an obsession with the Old General.

[37] Fitzpatrick (ed.), *Autobiography of Van Buren*, 226 n.
[38] William Ransom to Mangum, February 10, 1836, in Mangum Papers.
[39] Jackson to H. R. Cryer, November 13, 1836, in *American Historical Magazine,* IV (1899), 242–43.

Chapter VIII

DIRECTING THE ONSLAUGHT

F{LUSHED} with local victory and realizing that they could expect nothing from the Van Buren Administration, Peyton and Bell no longer felt a necessity for a semblance of loyalty to Andrew Jackson or the Democratic party. They had "bearded the lion in his den" and their constituents had applauded. Returning to Washington early in December, 1836, Wise, "the incarnation of effective eloquence," and Peyton, brilliant and bellicose, reopened their onslaught on the Administration. These "political pimps . . . speak slander in duet" at the bidding of their master, growled the Nashville *Union*.[1] But in this session Bell was not long in coming into the open. On January 10, 1837, while reports from the standing committees were being received, he interrupted and requested leave to bring in a bill to ensure the freedom of elections. Speaker Polk declared the request out of order, and Bell chose to make an issue of the decision. On a previous day, he explained, he had served notice of his intention to offer a resolution, but he later decided to substitute a bill for a report. Polk stood firm; Bell then appealed from the decision of the Chair. In explanation of his course, Bell said that he could see no essential difference between a request for leave to report a bill and any other report. Polk replied that the rules provided an order of business; therefore, Bell's request must await the conclusion of the committee reports. Bell then withdrew his request.[2]

---

[1] Nashville *Union*, January 7, 1837.
[2] *Cong. Globe*, 24 Cong., 2 Sess., Appendix, 111–13.

Two weeks later the request was renewed and a bill presented. The preamble of the bill called attention to the great number of removals from office which had been made "upon political grounds, or for opinion's sake." Consequently, Federal officeholders, in order to gain favor and retain their jobs, were intermeddling in state elections. Indeed, the Federal patronage was now being distributed in compensation for influence in elections. A continuation of this practice, it was asserted, would "speedily destroy the purity and freedom of the elective franchise."

The bill itself provided that, after March 4, 1837, no person holding a Federal office of profit or trust should contribute to campaign funds; use the franking privilege in distributing literature for or against any candidate; threaten, menace, or coerce other officials or citizens; or in any other way meddle in state or Federal elections. Violators were to be fined not more than $1,000 and, except in the case of the President, Vice-President, or judges, be removed from office. This act, however, was not to prevent the President or the department heads from removing those officials who had been interfering in elections.

The bill further provided that no official possessing nominating or appointing power should give or promise office to any person in return for election activities. The penalty for the violation of this provision was not to exceed $5,000 for the giver and $1,000 for the receiver. Guilty officials, except the President, Vice-President, or judges, were also to be removed from office.[3]

In support of his bill, Bell charged that a "malignant distemper has seized upon, and now deeply affects, our political system." Autocratic power was being wielded in the name of the people. There was a time when the people asked their friends what the representatives of the people would likely do about a certain matter; now the question was what would Andrew Jackson do. Whatever course Jackson took, it was

[3] *Ibid.,* 24 Cong., 2 Sess., 124.

generally understood that Congress would conform. This fact alone, Bell cried, was "sufficient to stamp the present as the period of transition from popular representative Government to the Government of an *elective Presidency*—of a *political chief.*

During the past two years, Bell argued, the House had made but one show of independence—the passage of the deposit bill—and even that was accomplished "only by opposing patronage to patronage, money to money, and arraying corruption against corruption." Seeing that the party in power would use the public treasury to corrupt individuals and sections in an attempt to win or retain their political allegiance, the people had demanded a better distribution of the spoils.

Already the Senate, the body which was supposed to advise and counsel the President, had been "reduced to a state of absolute submission; given over to the guidance of every popular gale, blown up by the artifices of as unprincipled and reckless a class of men as ever made their appearance in any age or country." Every time the puffings of the *Globe,* "that great political bellows," threw the "sea of public sentiment" into commotion, the "unhappy Senate must tack and change its course . . . or be denounced as contumacious." The President had used his veto power to an excess, while the Senate's veto on appointments had been "abrogated, rescinded, *expunged,* practically, from the Constitution and trampled under foot."

The press of the country, Bell asserted, had become so polluted that it no longer performed its important duty of improving the morals of society. Taking their cue from the *Globe,* that "pensioned engine of falsehood and calumny," Democratic editors had thrown decency and truth to the winds and had stooped to the lowest type of invective and slander. The chief purpose of the party in power—self propagation—had apparently been accomplished, but the sun of liberty had suffered an eclipse.

Yet in spite of multiplied evils and abuses, Bell conceded that the Administration remained popular. On the other hand, he would not agree that popularity was a true test of either merit or propriety. There were too many ways of creating artificial popularity. Too often popularity was but the homage of those who had been purchased or of the deluded ignorant. Apparent popularity, Bell insisted, was just one of the results of the competition for office which had become so fierce as to threaten the structure of American society. Misuse of the patronage, he exclaimed, was the Pandora's box from which had come the other evils of the times.

By wholesale removals for political reasons, Bell contended, Jackson had degraded American elections to mere contests for executive favor, making public officeholders subservient tools who supported the Administration right or wrong. And the President's " 'wanton removal of meritorious officers,' " Bell declared in words ascribed to James Madison, constituted an act of maladministration. In short, Andrew Jackson was guilty of a misdemeanor, an impeachable offense.

In Bell's opinion, it was the death struggle of desperate officeholders that won the recent election for Martin Van Buren. Andrew Jackson's interference in that election deserved the severest denunciation:

When, sir, the practice of official interference has arrived at this height; when rewards are openly bestowed for open apostacy and treachery to party engagements; when corruption walks abroad through the land in her own nakedness, without a veil or a mantle to cover her native deformity; when neither regard for principle nor the honor of the country can restrain such practices, so far, at least as to preserve the semblance of purity; when disguises are rejected as unnecessary; is it not time to sound the alarm to the sleeping sentinels, and call every patriot to his post.[4]

No one expected Bell's bill to pass or even to come to a vote. It died with the expiration of the Twenty-fourth Con-

4 *Ibid.*, Appendix, 291 ff.

gress on March 3, 1837, but it had served its purpose. Bell had used it as a means of exposing alleged administrative abuses, arousing thoroughly the wrath of those who felt his sting. Of all the ingenious tricks ever used by the crafty John Bell, that master of intrigues and subtle devises," shouted the Nashville *Union,* this so-called freedom of elections bill was the most ridiculous and despicable. The sole purpose of such a proposal, Editor Laughlin averred, was to deceive the public. The former Speaker was as a drowning man catching at a straw; he hoped to make freedom of elections the subject of his stump speeches in an effort to gull and beguile his constituents into re-electing him to Congress in 1837.[5]

Bell had no need for any issue with which to deceive his constituents. His loyalty to White and, apparently, his open break with Jackson had pleased the majority of the voters in Davidson and Wilson counties. Even the *"knowing ones"* among the Democrats at Nashville conceded his re-election; no arrangement was made for a candidate to oppose him. John Hall, an unimportant would-be politician from Lebanon, announced his candidacy but received no special support from the party. In retirement at the Hermitage, Old Hickory, still smarting over his recent defeat in Tennessee, could not understand the "Whys, and the Wherefores" of the failure to run Burton against Bell. He thought Burton could have won with ease. Perchance, Jackson reasoned, certain members of the party were too concerned over the condition of banks to desire to see a strong candidate expose the deception and fraud practiced by such institutions.[6]

Indeed, many Tennesseans were greatly concerned over the banking situation. Owing to the severity of the depression which had settled upon the nation, Yeatman, Woods and Company and a number of other banking houses had suspended specie payment. Nashville business men were critical

[5] Nashville *Union,* February 23, 1837.
[6] Jackson to Blair, July 9, 1837; *id.* to Van Buren, June 6, 1837, in Bassett (ed.), *Correspondence,* V, 486–89, 495–97.

of the Democratic Administration for its alleged responsibility for the financial distress and the general stagnation of business. In view of these facts, it is quite understandable why Nashville Democrats did not choose to make the congressional election a test of party strength.

Hall withdrew before the campaign was well under way, leaving Bell unopposed. This was very irritating to Speaker Polk who, living some distance from Nashville, did not fully appreciate the difficulties under which his Davidson County friends were laboring. Bell must have opposition, he insisted. Andrew J. Donelson replied that Polk need not expect the defeat of Bell in that election.[7]

Bell's re-election was but one of the causes for rejoicing among the anti–Van Buren men in Tennessee. William C. Dunlap was decisively defeated by Christopher H. Williams of Lexington, and Cave Johnson was nosed out by Richard Cheatham of Springfield, who, according to Johnson, was as "bitter and malignant" as Bell. Johnson attributed his own defeat to the activities of the mercantile class and the iron-workers.[8] It is strange that Bell was not blamed for this since the Bells owned an interest in the Cumberland Iron Works. Peyton was not a candidate for re-election, having decided to move to New Orleans; nevertheless, his successor, William B. Campbell of Carthage, was a strong White Whig and a friend of Bell.

Throughout 1837 the depression increased in severity. Overexpansion of the volume of state bank notes, extensive land speculation, an unfavorable balance of trade with Europe, two years of bad harvests, and general extravagance had contributed to the creation of a situation that made a nationwide panic almost inevitable. Jackson's Specie Circular, decreeing that specie only was to be receivable in payment for public lands, pricked this bubble of speculation.

[7] Polk to Donelson, June 21, 1837; Donelson to Polk, June 23, 1837, in Donelson Papers.

[8] Dunlap to Polk, August 7, 1837; Johnson to *id.*, August 7, 1837, in Polk Papers.

Withdrawal of government deposits for the purpose of distribution among the states, in accordance with an act of June, 1836, further increased the woes of the banks and of their debtors. Business progress was seriously halted as hundreds of individuals and corporations went into bankruptcy. Public confidence was shaken; optimism gave way to pessimism. To avoid having their insufficient specie reserves depleted, banks began to suspend specie payment on their paper money. The New York banks suspended on May 10, and hundreds of others, including Yeatman, Woods and Company, probably the strongest banking house in Tennessee, followed immediately. The Nashville *Union* hastened to inform its readers that, although Yeatman, Woods and Company had ceased paying out specie, Joseph and Robert Woods were high-class gentlemen. In spite of Mrs. Bell's interest in their firm, these gentlemen had no special interest in John Bell's political welfare.[9]

Friends of the United States Bank pronounced the panic a logical consequence of Jackson's destruction of that institution. Conversely, Jackson charged the Clay-Biddle group with the responsibility for the depression. Biddle's purpose, Jackson wrote Van Buren, was to destroy the deposit banks and then try for a recharter of the old Bank. That was the reason, Jackson insisted, that Bell and Peyton, acting through their Nashville newspapers, were trying to persuade all banks to suspend specie payment.[10]

During the summer of 1837, Administration men in Tennessee were watching every move made by Bell. Justice John Catron reported that Bell was carrying on an extensive correspondence with Henry Clay and had definitely lined up with the Bank and high tariff group. At the same time, Catron insisted that Bell would not dare assist in the re-establishment of the United States Bank, since revival of the old Bank would seriously affect such firms as Yeatman, Woods and Company. Mrs. Bell knew the power of such an institution, Catron explained, "and her pennyless husband, dare have no will, other than her's in money matters. . . . In *her* affairs, he is only allowed the privilege of being dry-nurse, to her younger boy." Catron was convinced that Bell's policy would be to create confusion, while he secretly hoped for a continuation of monetary derangement. Bell would make use of Wise and others to keep up the clamor, while he himself remained silent. "Keep his associates out of his house," Catron concluded, "& they will not have the wit to catch him." [11]

With the hope of alleviating the depression and of providing a more adequate depository for Government funds, President Van Buren called the new Congress into special session on September 4, 1837. It was immediately evident that the economic plight of the nation had not diminished political animosities. Polk and Bell were again opposing candidates for the speakership of the House; Polk won by a vote of 116 to 103. In view of the fact that Polk's majority in the recent Congress had been 48, this was not such a comforting victory. Furthermore, much to the humiliation of Jackson men in general and Francis P. Blair in particular, Thomas Allen, editor of the *Madisonian,* was designated as public printer, a position Blair had held for several years. The Lion of the Hermitage was very much aroused. "I suppose I may say that you are really *Bellised,*" he wrote Blair. From the day of its first edition, he said he had considered the *Madisonian* a Trojan horse capable of playing a Bell game, further dividing the party by making common cause with the opposition. Jackson notified Van Buren to be on his guard lest he too be "Bellised" in the next election.[12]

In his message to the special session of Congress, Van

[11] Catron to Polk, July 7, September 2, 1837, in Polk Papers.
[12] Jackson to Blair, September 15, 1837, in Bassett (ed.), *Correspondence,* V, 511–12.

Buren attributed the panic to "overaction in all the departments of business . . . stimulated to its destructive consequences by excessive issues of bank paper and by other facilities for the acquisition and enlargement of credit." He made it quite clear that although the "pet bank" system had its weaknesses, he would not countenance the chartering of another national bank. Instead, he proposed that the Government divorce itself from banks, construct its own vaults, and be the custodian of its own funds. Further, in view of the pecuniary embarrassment resulting from an unbalanced national budget, he suggested that the payment of the fourth installment [13] under the Deposit Act of June 23, 1836, be withheld. Until Federal funds could be collected from the deposit banks, he thought Treasury notes might be temporarily issued.[14]

Bell's immediate reaction to Van Buren's message was a demand for retrenchment in public expenditures. He presented to the House a resolution calling upon the Secretary of the Treasury for a report on the unexpended portions of the existing appropriations. The Secretary was also requested to state which proposed expenditures could be dispensed with and which others might be substantially reduced.[15] Secretary Levi Woodbury submitted the report three days later.[16]

In the meantime, Churchill C. Cambreleng, from the House Ways and Means Committee, proposed the postponement of the payment of the fourth installment under the Deposit Act.[17] Bell objected to indefinite postponement. This scheme was the child of those who had originally opposed distribution, he argued, and was designed to defeat the execution of the law. Where Secretary Woodbury had, in his report, pictured a probable deficit by the end of the current

[13] $9,367,214.
[14] Richardson (ed.), *Messages and Papers*, IV, 1541 ff.
[15] Cong. Globe, 25 Cong., 1 Sess., 19.
[16] *Ibid.*, 34.
[17] *Ibid.*, 21.

year, Bell juggled the figures, and changed them to a probable surplus of more than $9,000,000. In arriving at these
figures, he proposed curtailment of current expenditures for
roads, the armed forces, and national defense. He explained
that while the President was advocating economy and the
Secretary predicting a deficit, neither had recommended retrenchment in public expenditures. This, Bell charged, was
a result of the Administration's plan to keep patronage at a
maximum, for to reduce expenditures would be to reduce
patronage. Indeed, he suspected that some appropriations
had been rapidly spent so as to avoid probable retrenchment.
One thing was certain, Bell averred: an efficient and far-
sighted Administration, desiring to face properly the conditions of the times, would never have permitted the expenditure of money for other than necessary objects.

Some congressmen who had voted for the deposit bill
were now apparently ready to sanction its repeal. Bell called
upon them to consider seriously whether they possessed the
right to rescind their action. Had not the states by their acceptance of the terms of the bill acquired certain rights to the
money involved? Having readjusted their fiscal affairs in expectation of receiving the fourth installment, the states would
have a just complaint should Congress abrogate the arrangement without even consulting them. Such a step, Bell
contended, would be a usurpation of power on the part
of Congress and a flagrant disregard of the rights of the
states.

To any and all who were serious in their demands for
retrenchment in Federal expenditures, Bell would say
"Now's the day, and now's the hour." The House must not
be deluded by those whose one great desire was the perpetuation of power. There was but one proper course open, Bell
concluded: the money supply must be shut off and the surplus
drained from the Treasury. Expenditures would then be
limited to bare necessities. Not until then would the Administration adhere to the republican principles it had so

long avowed.[18] Unable to block the proposal to postpone the payment of the fourth installment, Bell vainly attempted to have the House set October 1, 1840, as the date for payment.[19]

Anticipating an attempt to renew the charter of the United States Bank and in response to a number of memorials on that subject, Van Buren's friends on the House Ways and Means Committee, speaking through their chairman, C. C. Cambreleng, brought forward a resolution stating that the recharter of a national bank would be inexpedient. Wise proposed the addition of the words "at this time," and suggested a second resolution declaring that it would be expedient to re-establish a national bank if and when the people clearly manifested their desire for such an institution. Bell desired still another addition:

And that the adoption of the plan recommended by the President for the collection and disbursement of the public revenue through the agency of Sub-Treasuries, by means of which the public moneys would be under the unchecked control of officers holding their places at will of the Executive, and often his mere creatures and dependents, or the establishment of a bank, or any fiscal system in the nature of a bank, founded upon the credit and revenues of the Government, would be inconsistent with the spirit of a free constitution, and dangerous to the liberties of the country.[20]

While the House debated but took no action, Silas Wright of New York, in accordance with the wishes of Van Buren, had introduced a bill in the Senate to establish an independent treasury. Following a spirited discussion, highlighted by Calhoun's support and Clay's and Webster's opposition, the bill passed the Senate by a narrow margin. In the House the debate was brief; twenty-one conservative Democrats joined with the Whigs to send the bill to the table.[21] To repeat a Jackson term, the independent treasury had also been "Bellised."

[18] *Ibid.*, Appendix, 25–30.
[19] *Ibid.*, 25 Cong., 1 Sess., 90.   [20] *Ibid.*, 69–78.   [21] *Ibid.*, 100, 141.

The best that Van Buren's supporters could do was to secure the passage of a bill authorizing the issuance of $10,-000,000 of Treasury notes in denominations of not less than $50. Bell opposed this measure, also, characterizing it as a part of a scheme to destroy existing institutions, an initial step in the creation of a government bank.[22]

The special session adjourned on October 16. Seven weeks were to elapse before the opening of the regular session on December 4. Polk hurried home, hoping to assist in stemming the tide that was threatening to sweep his friend Grundy from the United States Senate. Grundy's aggressive support of Van Buren in the recent presidential contest made him a marked man in his home state; the victory of the White-Bell forces in the election of state legislators doomed him politically. Following the White victory in Tennessee, Grundy, conscious of his own predicament, adopted a temporizing attitude; yet he returned to the Senate and voted for the expunging resolution. The White supporters demanded that he be punished for his disloyalty to his colleague and subservience to the will of Jackson. The fact that Grundy's term would not expire until 1839 did not deter them; his successor must be elected in 1837.

If a senator should be chosen at that time, Grundy's friends feared that it would be Bell. Nevertheless, their hope was temporarily revived by a rumor of a breach between Bell and Foster. "All that I fear is that the breach will be healed," wrote a friend of Polk.[23] But the Democratic plan "to widen the breach if possible" fell short of its goal; Bell was not a candidate. Grundy's friends did not present his name to the legislature and Foster was elected over the Democratic candidate, William Carroll.[24]

The Democrats maintained that Bell, unable to dissuade Foster from being a candidate, was forced to postpone his

22 *Ibid.*, 23, 113–14, 120, 147.
23 Jonas E. Thomas to Polk, October 5, 1837, in Polk Papers.
24 Parks, *Felix Grundy,* 310–13.

own hopes. "We venture to express the opinion," hopefully announced John O. Bradford, the new editor of the *Union,* "that the election of Mr. Foster will be as gratting [*sic*] and mortifying to the feelings of Mr. Bell, as to any other man in the United States! Mr. Bell has found a successful competitor in a quarter where he least expected it. . . . We rejoice that he has been mistaken in his strength. The very man whose services he was commanding has blasted his prospects, and put his pretensions aside." The editor also ventured "to affirm, that if Mr. Foster's heart could be probed, he would pronounce Mr. Bell a cold, calculating, selfish, ambitious politician, regardless of friends or country, if he can but succeed." [25] At the same time, former President Jackson, basing his conclusions more on desire than information, pronounced Foster's election a "severe rebuke to Bell" and evidence of the legislature's loss of confidence in him.[26]

In spite of Democratic claims to the contrary, Bell was not interested in a senatorship at that time; he had unfinished work in the House. His immediate ambition was to wrest the speakership from James K. Polk. Instead of returning to Nashville at the close of the special session of Congress, he, in company with William J. Graves of Kentucky, set out on a tour of the commercial East. On the evening of November 10 the two were honor guests at a huge Whig celebration in Boston's Faneuil Hall. Following a complimentary introduction by Daniel Webster, Bell delivered an address, denouncing the Van Buren Administration in almost every sentence. The "profligate and unprincipled administration," he shouted, had already issued its decree, namely, "perish credit! perish commerce! down with the credit system!" As to the subtreasury proposal, no one could be deceived as to its paternity; it was the well-marked progeny of the patronage system, having as its object the aggrandizement of office-

---

[25] Nashville *Union,* October 28, 1837.
[26] Jackson to Blair, November 29, 1837, in Bassett (ed.), *Correspondence,* V, 520–21.

holders. Proceeding in "a fine strain of sarcasm," Bell next examined what he termed the inconsistencies in the monetary policy of the party in power. The verdict of the people was unmistakable, he concluded; the public was unwilling to entrust to officeholders the safekeeping of its money. In closing, Bell declared that although the distance between Massachusetts and Tennessee was great, the two were closely identified in their love for free government. Tennesseans were ready to unite with their New England brethren in resistance to the dangerous and absurd policies of the Democratic Administration.[27]

Following visits to Salem and Hartford, Webster, Graves, and Bell were in New York City by November 28, on which date Bell was honored with a dinner at the Astor House. The festival was "perhaps the most brilliant ever given in this city," declared the New York *American*.[28] Plates were ten dollars each, and "about 220, including the guests, sat down at half past seven o'clock and stayed all night!" [29] One newspaper reporter who tried to take notes on the revelry was ejected from the hall before he had consumed his ten-dollar dinner.[30] This convivial assemblage was interested in its own jollification, not in the edification of the outside world.

In response to a laudatory toast by Chairman Ogden Hoffman, Bell, exhibiting "great animation and ability," delivered an hour-and-a-half speech which brought forth thunderous applause.[31] A host of other speakers followed Bell and it was 2 A.M. before the "big gun," Daniel Webster, arose to make some "very brief" remarks, but when 4 A.M. arrived and "night was almost at odds with morning," he was still

[27] Boston *Atlas*, quoted in New York *Daily Express*, November 13, 1837; Boston *Daily Advertiser*, November 11, 1837. Quotations are from newspaper reporters.

[28] Quoted in *Niles' National Register*, LIII (1837), 210.

[29] Allan Nevins (ed.), *The Diary of Philip Hone, 1828–1851* (New York, 1927), I, 288. Hone was chairman of the committee on arrangements.

[30] *Ibid.*, 289–90.   [31] New York *Daily Express*, November 29, 1837.

speaking and no fewer than 150 persons had remained in their seats.[32]

The welcome accorded Bell in the stronghold of old Federalism was exciting news in Democratic circles. It frightened Polk's immediate friends, drove Jackson to still greater anger, and set the Administration press to howling louder than ever. The *Globe* announced that Bell had at last thrown off his mask and had journeyed to New England to offer up incense in praise of Federalist Daniel Webster.[33] Those Federalists who received Bell with open arms, exclaimed the Nashville *Union,* were the same men who had once thought it against moral and religious principles to celebrate their country's victories. And when Bell had assured them that Tennessee was identified with New England, those Federalists sent up a cheer, the like of which had not been heard in that section since the celebration of General Hull's defeat at Detroit.[34]

The news from the East stirred Jackson to more bitter letter writing. To his friends he poured forth his wrath against Bell for attending "aristocratic, federal, & shinplaster" meetings and making common cause with "Webster & the blue lights, abolitionists and vagrants." Nevertheless, he hoped that Bell's action might shock Tennesseans out of their delusion. Many who had conscientiously supported White would undoubtedly balk at the thought of being forced into the support of Clay or Webster. Even the Tennessee legislature, Jackson had heard, regretted its premature election of a United States senator. "Mark me—," he wrote Grundy, "Republican Tennessee will be herself again in less than two years." [35]

Before Jackson had finished his tirades against Bell's coa-

[32] Nevins (ed.), *Diary of Philip Hone,* I, 288–89.
[33] Washington *Globe,* November 20, 1837.
[34] Nashville *Union,* February 1, 1838.
[35] Jackson to Grundy, December 16, 1837, in *American Historical Magazine,* V (1900), 138; *id.* to James Buchanan, December 26, 1837, in Bassett (ed.), *Correspondence,* V, 522–23.

lescence with Federalists, Polk further stirred the Old
General by sending him some excerpts from Bell's speech in
the House during the extra session of Congress. Bell had
charged that Jackson's war on the United States Bank had
been prompted by his desire to establish another bank, based
upon government revenue and credit. Knowing Jackson's
sensitiveness on the subject of the Bank, Polk hoped to elicit
from him a vigorous denial of the charge and an even more
vigorous denunciation of Bell. Polk, like many other Democrats, still felt a need of support from the Hermitage. Jackson gave the desired response and authorized public use of
his letter. The views expressed in his veto of the Bank recharter bill, he said, were the same as those entertained at
the beginning of his Administration, and no one knew that
fact better than Bell. Therefore, the Congressman's false
statements could not be attributed to ignorance; they sprang
from a desire to satisfy "his morbid appetite for slander."
"All that I desire," announced the self-righteous Jackson, "is
truth and justice. This I do not expect from Mr. Bell." [36]

Meanwhile, other leading Tennessee Democrats were also
seeking to make political capital of Bell's alleged attempt to
marry their state to New England. At a meeting in Nashville,
resolutions were adopted declaring that "the gratulations of
fellowship and sympathy in a common cause recently exchanged between our representative, Mr. Bell, and the Hartford Convention Tories and Blue Light Federalists . . . are
not in unison with the feelings of the patriotic sons of Tennessee." Bell's recent actions, the resolution asserted, proved
what his speeches and votes in Congress had indicated: that
he had long been in sympathy with political groups whose
patriotism was open to question.[37] The author of these resolutions had undoubtedly been in communication with Old
Hickory.

There was some truth, however, in the Democratic rant-

[36] *Id.* to Polk, February 1, 1838, in Bassett (ed.), *Correspondence*, V, 533-35.
[37] Nashville *Republican Banner*, January 23, 1838.

ing about Bell's eastern tour. Now that he was a full-fledged Whig and still had his eye on the Speaker's chair, he went East to see and be seen. He did join hands with Whig leaders, some of whom had once been Federalists, and his speeches were intended as a manifesto of his complete break with the party in power. So great had been the decline of Jackson's political influence that the Nashville Congressman felt no special fear even in the General's home district.

The intense hostility between Bell and his Democratic protagonists permeated the next session of the House and rose to fever heat late in May, 1838. An Indian hostility bill was under discussion; and Bell proposed that, rather than driving the Indians off by military force, the President be authorized to spend $2,000,000 in persuading them to migrate. Hopkins L. Turney, a freshman Democratic representative from Winchester, Tennessee, apparently considering the discussion on an Indian bill an appropriate time to complete the scalping of Bell, launched a stinging attack upon the Nashville Congressman, whom he barely knew and with whom he never had had any dealings. Being familiar with Bell's recent speeches in New England, he began, it would "be criminal in me longer to remain silent." He had no objections to Bell's leaving the Democratic party, he said, but he most emphatically denounced him for accusing his former political friends of corruption and for attempting to undermine the existing government. There must be a reason for this alienation from his former friends. Could it be, Turney suggested, that an accommodation from the Bank had brought it about? Or was it an insatiable thirst for personal advancement that had induced him to welcome the embraces of his former political enemies? Only the record was needed, Turney said, to convict Bell of inconsistencies; accordingly, he spent the greater portion of two hours reading extracts from Bell's speeches.[38]

Flushed with anger at being thus attacked by one with whom he had had no previous difficulty, Bell replied in "gen-

[38] *Cong. Globe,* 25 Cong., 2 Sess., Appendix, 357-60.

tlemanly language, but in the tone which the most exasperated resentment assumes to express unmitigated contempt." [39]
Since Turney could not possibly have a "malignant feeling to
gratify," Bell began, it was evident that he had become "a
voluntary scavenger for other men's uses," a "fit and apt
conduit for the discharge . . . of hoarded and accumulated
malice and vindictiveness of others," "a tool of tools." Turney
interrupted, crying out, "It is false, the statement is false, and
my colleague knows it to be so." Swinging his arms in threatening gestures, he jumped from his seat as if to reach Bell
who was standing close by, only to meet a blow from Bell's
fist. Turney swung back as congressmen cried "Order!"
"Speaker!" "Sergeant-at-arms!" Speaker Polk rushed to the
Chair, turning out Benjamin Howard who had been presiding over the committee of the whole. Demands for apologies
were made from both sides of the House chamber, and both
Bell and Turney apologized, disclaiming "all intention of
disrespect to the House." [40]

Order having been restored, the committee of the whole
sat again, and Bell resumed his remarks. But John Quincy
Adams complained to his diary that the necessity of staying
within the rules of the House rendered the remainder of
Bell's discourse "stale and flat, like a pot of small beer after a
bumper of pure whisky." [41]

The principal source of the nation's ills, Bell charged, was
the fact that the people had elevated to the highest position
of trust persons who were destitute of skill, talents, and
patriotism. The President, through abuse of the appointive
power, had filled the prominent offices with incompetent and
untrustworthy partisans. The difficulties of the time were not
the result of faulty laws but faulty administration of them.
There was no wonder that the public interests had been
neglected for almost a decade; President Jackson had spent

[39] Adams (ed.), *Memoirs of John Quincy Adams,* X, 4.
[40] *Cong. Globe,* 25 Cong., 2 Sess., Appendix, 558; Adams (ed.), *Memoirs of
John Quincy Adams,* X, 4.
[41] Adams (ed.), *Memoirs of John Quincy Adams,* X, 5.

his time furnishing a prostituted press with vile propaganda under his own frank. The Indian war then raging in Florida was merely another example of official negligence and maladministration.[42]

Bell felt some humiliation over having resorted to fisticuffs in his clash with Turney, especially since he was so vigorously denounced in the Democratic press. He had been the object of a premeditated attack, he explained to an editor friend, and the Speaker made no effort to give him protection. Indeed, the House under the present Speaker was a scene of habitual disorder. He himself was an advocate of decorum, Bell said, and did not claim justification for his apparent breach of order, although many colleagues thought him justified; but few persons in his situation would have acted otherwise.[43]

Turney, on the other hand, gave no evidence of regret for any portion of his conduct. Though a political unknown, he had placed Speaker Polk under some obligation to him. Soon after arriving home, following the close of the session, he triumphantly reported to Polk that, from all he could learn, "my difficulty with Bell, has made me a captain in my district." [44]

Although desiring to hurry home following the close of the session of Congress, Bell took the time to return by way of East Tennessee. His Knoxville friends, having been notified in advance, arranged a public dinner in his honor; the supporters of White in the recent presidential campaign must be urged to persist in their opposition to Van Buren's Administration. In his after-dinner speech Bell assured his listeners that he could still have been Speaker of the House had he bowed to dictation and supported Van Buren. But he said that he preferred to be in the minority and have freedom of action than to be with the majority and forfeit that freedom.

[42] *Cong. Globe*, 25 Cong., 2 Sess., Appendix, 558–63.
[43] Bell to Editor, June 6, 1838, in Nashville *Republican Banner*, June 22, 1838.
[44] Hopkins L. Turney to Polk, July 30, 1838, in Polk Papers.

His views on the Bank, he explained, had not changed. Were he as mercenary as the friends of Jackson had charged, he certainly would never have turned to the Bank for assistance, for banks required that their loans be repaid with interest. It would have been far more promising to have turned to the Executive Department—"the notorious fountain of all corruption." There large salaries could be enjoyed without the thought of repayment or interest. There he could have bartered his support for favors far more lucrative than could be bestowed by any bank. Yet, regardless of whether he himself was pure or corrupt, no defects in his principles or character could restore an adequate currency, revive prostrate business, repair a violated Constitution, or end the corruption attendant upon the abuse of the patronage.

In the course of his remarks, Bell sounded the call to arms for the presidential election of 1840 at which time the Democrats were certain to make a great effort to regain Tennessee. Tennesseans must be alert, for *"the purchased and rewarded tools of power"* would attempt "to deliver over as penitents, the majority of the freemen of Tennessee, to be humbled, degraded and servile followers of him whom they have heretofore had spirit to oppose and set at defiance." [45]

Late in September Bell attended a big Whig rally at Murfreesboro where he began speaking immediately after lunch and continued until sunset.[46] He also made speeches at Pulaski, Brownsville, Bolivar, and Paris. Attempts were made by his friends to arrange for him to meet Polk at several political rallies throughout the state, but Polk was not interested.[47]

Back in Washington for the opening of the third session of the Twenty-fifth Congress on December 3, 1838, Bell intensified his attack upon the Van Buren Administration. On December 26 the House resolved itself into the committee of the whole for the purpose of considering the President's mes-

---

[45] Nashville *Republican Banner,* September 2, 1838.
[46] Laughlin to Polk, September 27, 1838, in Polk Papers.
[47] Memphis *Enquirer,* October 6, 13, November 3, 1838.

sage. Charles E. Haynes proposed a series of resolutions calling for a distribution of portions of the message among several committees. Bell offered no opposition to the resolutions, claiming a lack of preparation for a discussion, but for three hours he delighted the Whigs with a severe analysis of the President's message.[48]

Van Buren had stated that among the more prominent dangers which threatened the Republic was the anti-republican concentration of wealth. Bell replied that a far greater danger was the concentration of too much power in the hands of a few. He was no defender of any "selfish, exclusive, grasping, monopolizing, and anti-republican tendencies of mere wealth," but he wished to stress that these characteristics were much more descriptive of the concentration of political power. In the President's enumeration of the dangers which threatened the liberties of the people, why had he omitted the most deadly one of all—the "grasping and monopolizing tendency" of executive power? This attack upon so-called associated wealth and the President's attempt to pose as the friend of the common man were branded as cheap electioneering cant, beneath the dignity of the office of President.

Van Buren had congratulated the country on the extension of the suffrage and the consequent increase in mass participation in the affairs of the nation. In reply Bell charged that never before had the common people been so powerless. Instead of being the controlling element they were mere subjects who were expected to follow blindly the leadership of a mere handful of men—the leaders of the party in power. This deplorable condition was the result of skillful management and the sinister influence of an enlarged patronage. Instead of the people becoming more attached to their government, as the President had boasted, they were manifesting an increased distrust. Men of honesty and intelligence viewed the future with apprehension and fear.

[48] Adams (ed.), *Memoirs of John Quincy Adams*, X, 78.

The vicious patronage system, Bell charged, had already produced three Indian wars costing not less than $20,000,000. These wars were the result of "sheer neglect and culpable negligence of the Administration," notorious speculation in Indian lands, which would not have been permitted except for the inefficiency and dishonesty of public officials, and failure on the part of the executive to make judicious selections of Indian agents.

Van Buren had requested the creation of a congressional committee for the examination of the accounts of those officials entrusted with the handling of public money. Bell professed great astonishment at this request. Was the President so far departing from the policies of Jackson as to invite congressional assistance? Could this be a "new profession of faith" on the part of the Democratic party? No, there was no change of heart or policy, Bell explained. It was merely a plan to have congressmen serve "in the capacity of informers and catchpoles for the Executive," relieving him of the undesirable duty of scrutinizing the political and personal conduct of his favorites, yet taking from him none of his power of appointment and removal. If Congress wished to make use of investigating committees, Bell insisted that they be empowered to act without dependence upon presidential pleasure.

Van Buren had also renewed his request for the enactment of the subtreasury plan, but in doing so suggested that the plan would not necessarily preclude the use of any banks. Bell seized upon this explanation and branded it as a part of a scheme to subordinate all banks to executive will. Certainly the President would refuse to favor those banks which failed to do his bidding. This competition for executive favor would bring under control of the patronage system "the entire money-power of the country, public Treasury, banks, and all." Any person who refused to believe that the party in power would make the fullest use of this opportunity for intimidation, Bell explained, was ignorant of the dearth of principle which had characterized its policies and practices. On the subject of the spoils system, Bell never tired of talking. "It is the spoils principle—it is the principle of corruption itself which has been adopted by the party in power as the only effective party cement—it is the false, corrupt, and corrupting principle upon which the appointing power has been and continues to be exercised under the present scriptive dynasty—it is the practice of appointing desperate, worthless, and unprincipled men to office—men who, in general, possess no other merit than their partisan services and efficiency in elections. This, then, sir, is the great and fundamental evil." As for the defalcation in money on the part of dishonest officials, as bad as it might be, it was "but a fraction of the losses sustained by the People . . . by defalcations of a different kind—by defalcations in capacity, in requisite skill, and, above all in sound political principles, on the part of the Administration." [49]

In the only other speech of any length which Bell delivered during this short session he continued his attack upon the Administration. He seemed so obsessed with the alleged evils of Van Burenism as to be blinded to its good qualities. One suspects, however, that a major portion of this blindness was born of the necessity of concealing the lack of harmony and a constructive program on the part of the Whigs. Since the House had refused to make use of the power to impeach the President, even when there could be no question of his guilt, Bell said, that method of removal had just as well be deleted from the Constitution. Instead there ought to be substituted some method of compelling the President to give due regard to the sentiments of the people. Referring to the threat of war with Great Britain growing out of the Canadian revolution, and denouncing the actions of blundering officials, Bell cried out as if in anguish: "Must we continue patiently and quietly to behold the most important interests of the country

[49] Richardson (ed.), *Messages and Papers,* IV, 1700 ff.; *Cong. Globe,* 25 Cong., 3 Sess., Appendix, 359–66.

sacrificed—the whole power of the Government falling into contempt and disuse at the very moment when its controlling authority and influence are most required by the state of affairs?" Even Administration men, he said, admitted that in spite of the expenditure of millions of dollars the Canadian frontier was inadequately defended and the navy was in wretched condition.

Paradoxically, according to Bell's argument, the Union was threatened with dissolution as a result of the weakness of the central government, although the party in power possessed dictatorial powers. It was not more power that was needed, Bell asserted, but honesty, energy, and efficiency in the exercise of it. The whole situation, he thought, could be summed up in the statement that since the President had been elected by a combination of "political agitators and leaders . . . upon the principle of mutual favor, patronage, and support," he was honor- and interest-bound to reward them for their services. In the long run, it would be the people who would pay, by having their interests sacrificed upon the altar of political expediency. A few more years of such a policy and the American system of government would become so disreputable as to make its overthrow inevitable.[50]

As a minority leader Bell had demonstrated energy and tenacity. Ever ready to seize upon an Administration error or sign of weakness, he drove majority leader Cambreleng to anger and kept Speaker Polk in a state of uneasiness. Spurred on by assurance of support from his home district, he took particular delight in attacking the actions and impugning the motives of those who had contributed to the elevation of Van Buren. Contempt and scorn characterized Bell's utterances; partisanship charted his course. Through this period he added little to his statesmanship, but every one recognized his effectiveness as a leader of anti-Administration forces.

As the short session of the Twenty-fifth Congress drew to a

[50] *Cong. Globe*, 25 Cong., 3 Sess., Appendix, 366–69.

close, Polk prepared to relinquish both the Speakership and his seat in the House. He had already yielded to the solicitations of his Tennessee friends and agreed to become a candidate for governor. He alone, the Democrats assured him, could wrest from the Whigs the control of the government of his home state. Good party man that he was, Polk could not refuse to make the race, although he undoubtedly preferred the speakership to the governorship. Knowing his intentions, his enemies in the House prepared for a final humiliation. They would deny him the customary unanimous vote of thanks for his services. Seargent S. Prentiss of Mississippi assumed the lead, denounced Polk as the most partisan of Speakers, and demanded that the word "impartial" be stricken from the proposed resolution of thanks. Bell expressed the hope that there would be "no objections of a technical character" but joined Wise, Graves, Prentiss and fifty-three others including William B. Campbell and Christopher H. Williams of Tennessee, in voting against the resolution.[51] "The whole movement," declared the Washington *Globe,* "was prompted by the jealousy of Mr. Bell, and carried out by his Whig colleagues from Tennessee, and Messrs. S. S. Prentiss, Wise and Co." [52] Polk himself gave little evidence of concern and effectively turned the tide by ignoring the opposition and courteously thanking the majority for the "highest and most valued testimony I have received from this House."

During Bell's slashing attacks upon the Administration and all of its measures, the Democrats of his home state became even more determined to retire him to private life. Andrew Jackson, directing the activities of his plantation or relaxing in the comforts of his beloved Hermitage, had been constantly plagued by the thoughts of Bell's continued political success. Among the Old General's numerous enemies, the Nashville Congressman was perhaps the most detested and distrusted. Early in February, 1839, Jackson was in Nashville

[51] *Ibid.,* 25 Cong., 3 Sess., 251–52.   [52] Washington *Globe,* March 5, 1839.

"daily urging" his friends to exert pressure on former Governor William Carroll to announce for Bell's seat in the House. He dispatched his trusted nephew, Andrew J. Donelson, to call on Carroll and put an end to his "shuffling," but the former Governor could not be located. The Old General then became suspicious of Carroll's strange conduct. Had he speculated in lands while a commissioner, and was he afraid of being exposed by Bell?[53]

Polk too had been working on Carroll, and had been informed that unless his health greatly improved he would not be a candidate. Carroll suggested Burton as the one who could trouble Bell most, but at the same time, implied that the defeat of Bell by any candidate was very unlikely.[54]

Jackson was disgusted with Carroll. "*Shamefull* [*sic*] *tho true,*" he wrote Van Buren, it was doubtful whether Bell would have an opponent. There was still hope, however, that Burton would announce. Usually optimistic over the prospects of Bell's downfall but consistently a poor prophet, Jackson again predicted that Burton could easily defeat Bell.[55] Burton was hesitant. His political thirst had been satiated, he said, and his friends could not have made a more unpleasant requisition upon him. If he did decide to enter the service, he wished it understood that it would be "not as a volunteer but as a drafted militiaman who but rarely makes you know a good soldier." Where Bell was concerned, Burton observed, the people of Wilson County were covered by the "darkness of midnight," and he questioned any candidate's ability to dispel this shadow. However, Jackson, Polk, Donelson, and General Robert Armstrong continued to apply pressure and Burton finally yielded.[56]

[53] Jackson to Polk, February 11, 1839, in Bassett (ed.), *Correspondence,* VI, 4–5.

[54] Carroll to *id.,* February 8, 1839, in Polk Papers.

[55] Jackson to Van Buren, March 4, 1839, in Bassett (ed.), *Correspondence,* VI, 5–6.

[56] Robert M. Burton to Polk, March 24, April 4, 1839, in Polk Papers; Jackson to Van Buren, April 4, 1839, in Van Buren Papers; Jackson to Amos Kendall, April 19, 1839, in Bassett (ed.), *Correspondence,* VI, 9.

In preparation for an all-out effort to make "Old Democratic Tennessee . . . herself again," the Democrats imported a new editor for the Nashville *Union*. Owing to inconsistency and, at times, inefficiency in its editorial policy, this organ had not developed into the bulwark of Democracy which was intended by its sponsors. The new editor, Jeremiah George Harris of Massachusetts, recently editor of the *Bay State Democrat* and sometime editor of the New Bedford *Daily Gazette,* proved to be exactly what the Democrats ordered. For invective and vituperation he had no equal in the state, unless it was the East Tennessee editor, William G. ("Parson") Brownlow, whose best editorial work was still several years in the future. Harris took over the editorship of the *Union* on February 1, 1839, and immediately announced his intention to uproot "Federalism" in Tennessee. During the next three years the *Union* was never lacking in energy even if, like many other presses of both parties, it did play loosely with the truth.

Before mid-April, 1839, Tennessee politicians were in full action. Sensing the seriousness of the task which he had undertaken and realizing his lack of preparation, Burton urged Polk to furnish all kinds of speeches and documents bearing upon Bell's career. "I must have help," he pleaded. Polk would please supply direct references to Bell's vulnerable points, for all of his apostasies must be exposed.[57] With this material and a copy of Butler's *Life of Van Buren* in hand, Burton went forth to meet Bell on the stump in an active and animated campaign. All over Wilson County they sparred, with Bell centering his attack on Van Buren and Burton rapidly thumbing the pages of Butler in an effort to disprove Bell's accusations. A prominent Democrat, after listening to some of the speeches, notified Polk that "Mr. Burton needs more ammunition." [58]

A big political rally at Lebanon was planned for April 13.

---

[57] Burton to Polk, April 4, 1839, in Polk Papers.
[58] Isaac Golladay to *id.*, May 1, 1839, *ibid.*

Polk and Newton Cannon, candidates for governor, were to furnish the entertainment. Bell also made his appearance and mounted the platform as soon as the gubernatorial candidates had concluded their addresses. Beginning at 5:30 P.M. and attacking Polk "in his first sentence," he flayed the Democrats until dark, and then moved to the courthouse where he continued by candlelight. Burton was lost sight of except for his occasional stroll about the room in search of a drink of water. Polk, resenting Bell's constantly dogging his footsteps, wishfully confided to his wife that Burton had profited by Bell's course.[59]

From Wilson County, Bell and Burton moved to Davidson and continued their thorough canvass, discussing banks, currency, and the credit system. The campaign became so heated that Burton, professing to believe Bell was heavily armed, tried to borrow pistols, balls, and caps from Andrew J. Donelson.[60] During less exciting moments the candidates spent considerable time discussing the relative merits of Martin Van Buren and Henry Clay, for the Tennessee campaign was of more than local importance; it was a test of the strength of probable candidates in the next presidential campaign. " . . . as the [Tennessee] vote shall be in August next," Bell prophesied, "so will it be in 1840." Clay, realizing the importance of the Tennessee campaign, forwarded to Bell a summary of arguments to be used throughout the state, and Bell and his associates resolved to "carry the war into Africa." But the prosaic Cannon, no match for Polk in either ability or experience, fared badly in every joint discussion and eventually quit the stump entirely before the close of the campaign. Bell was thoroughly disgusted with the Governor whom he considered "too sluggish and selfsufficient" to be effective.[61] Yet, realizing that the defeat of Polk was his party's prime objective, Bell shouldered the major portion of the Whig

---

59 Polk to wife, April 14, 1839, *ibid.*
60 Burton to Donelson, May 5 [?], 1839, in Donelson Papers.
61 Bell to Henry Clay, May 21, 1839, in Henry Clay Papers (Division of Manuscripts, Library of Congress).

burden and brought all his power of oratory to play upon this "travelling missionary" of Van Burenism.

Dr. W. P. Sayle, apparently acting without Polk's consent, made preliminary arrangements for these two protagonists to meet at Lebanon on June 12. Polk was campaigning in the eastern section of the state when he learned that the plan had been made. He immediately rushed a letter to his wife at Columbia, enclosing a long list of journals, newspapers, and manuscripts which would be needed if he was to prostrate Bell. Polk's brother, William, must pack these materials in the sulky and meet him at Gainesborough.[62] Although Polk was willing, if not eager, the meeting was not held. Burton interposed an objection. If such a meeting must take place, he insisted that it be held at Nashville.[63] Burton had no desire to have his opponent return to Wilson.

Out at the Hermitage there was a constant stir during the summer of 1839 as delegations came and went. The Old Hero was quite active in his electioneering, especially among the older men who called to pay their respects. In spite of the feeble state of his health, he made his appearance at militia musters where he had not been seen in twenty years, and shook hands with old and young. Surely Tennessee would never humiliate this dying patriarch, whispered Democrats throughout the crowd, by contributing to the elevation of those who had sought to destroy him. Bell had no sympathy with such "pathetic rant," but he confided to Clay that should the Kentuckian carry Tennessee in 1840, the Old General would probably "burst a blood vessel & expire." [64]

Democratic ranting to the contrary, Bell's re-election was never seriously in doubt. Even Polk's friends conceded as much, although the scurrilous Harris, lashing the Whigs to fury, assured the readers of the *Union* that Burton had "literally dissected his opponent who has been schooled in the

[62] Polk to wife, May 28, 1839, in Polk Papers.

[63] *Id.* to *id.*, June 2, 1839, *ibid.*

[64] Bell to Clay, May 21, 1839, in Clay Papers.

sophistries of partizanship, and laid the diseased limbs of Modern Whigism bare to the bone." [65]

The election returns brought joy to Democratic circles; Polk was victor by a majority of three thousand, and both houses of the next legislature would be Democratic. Although the Whigs retained seven of the thirteen seats in Congress, Cave Johnson regained the seat he had lost in 1838, and Polk was succeeded by a stanch Democrat, Harvey M. Watterson. Vacationing with Grundy and Armstrong at Tyree Springs when the good news arrived, Jackson rushed his congratulations to Polk. Truly, "old Democratic Tennessee" was again in the Republican fold! Inspired by the joviality of the occasion, the Old General again felt like prophesying: "It will be at least a century before she [Tennessee] will permit herself to be again duped into her late false position by such jesuitical hypocrites and apostates as Bell White and Co." [66] Hastening to pass the good news to Van Buren, Jackson wrote with great satisfaction: "Judge White must resign, or he will feel the weight of instructions & a Senator elected over his head—the precedent set by our last Legislature will justify this procedure. My own opinion is, White will resign—Bell being disappointed in going into the Senate to fill White's vacancy, which was the price of his apostacy, if he is disappointed in getting into the Speaker's chair, will resign or *cut his throat* in despair & disappointment; and this catastrophy will end the existence of bluelight federalism in Tennessee." [67]

[65] Nashville *Union*, May 27, 1839.
[66] Jackson to Polk, August 13, 1839, in Bassett (ed.), *Correspondence*, VI, 18.
[67] *Id.* to Van Buren, August 12, 1839, in Van Buren Papers.

Chapter IX

BALLYHOO TRIUMPHANT

FOLLOWING the strenuous Tennessee campaign of 1839, Bell spent some time relaxing at his home in Nashville. He was physically exhausted and low in spirit. The Whigs in general had not measured up to his expectation. Either too confident of victory or naturally apathetic, the mass of the party had assumed little of the campaign burden. On August 10 he dispatched a letter to his friend William B. Campbell of Carthage, who had also been successful in retaining his seat in Congress, urging that the Campbell family pay the Bells a visit. There was need for conference among the Whig leaders, he explained, in order that each might "hear all that can be said" and that the group might decide what should or could be done. "If we cannot act in concert," he insisted, "it will be useless to act at all. I am *done done,* as a public man, unless we can have some better understanding with each other and all agree to give the *working men* more assistance. . . . A few of us have had to bear the brunt all the time and but few willing to do more than go out to a public meeting. . . . Let me know your griefs and consolations, what it was that hurt us most, where the weak points are etc." [1]

Not only Campbell but Christopher H. Williams of Lexington and Ebenezer J. Shields of Pulaski visited Bell, and extensive future plans were mapped. Within a month Whig rallies were in progress throughout the state. The big mid-state festival was held in Davidson County on October 25. Bell spoke for three hours on the opening day of the celebra-

[1] Bell to Campbell, August 10, 1839, in David Campbell Papers.

tion and concluded his remarks on the second. The greater portion of his speech was devoted to a review of Polk's "Address to the People of Tennessee" which had been issued at the beginning of the recent campaign. According to a friendly newspaper reporter, before Bell had "concluded this scathing review . . . what he left of that artfully concocted budget of gross and outrageous misrepresentations and false statements, we do not believe the most sycophantic follower of the Governor or The Party would take the gift of." [2]

Bell was invited to numerous rallies in other parts of the state. The eastern section he planned to visit on his way to Washington; West Tennessee he was unable to visit, but his letters of regret were designed to stir the Whigs to new endeavors. It was a deep humiliation, he wrote the Whigs of La Grange, to see "our hitherto proud and noble state *hitched* on the *tail* of power, and assurances given that hereafter she will be as *obedient* and *submissive* as *New Hampshire!*" Yet at worst, he believed, it was only a temporary humiliation made possible by overconfidence and apathy on the part of the Whigs. A state-wide diffusion of the flame of patriotism could effect a rescue from this disgraceful position. For the present, however, it must be admitted that executive power was absolute and patronage was rapidly becoming omnipotent.

During the past decade, Bell averred, national expenditures had doubled and the number of government officials and agents had increased by 50 per cent. Some of those officials had proved to be common thieves; others had held no scruples against interfering in elections in order to protect their jobs and salaries. Add to this combination the influence of a prostituted and pensioned press and the result was still only a partially complete picture of the corruption and inefficiency of the Van Buren Administration.[3]

While the Whigs attempted to stir up artificial enthusiasm the Democrats looked on with amusement and not too much

[2] Nashville *Republican Banner*, October 28, 1839.
[3] *Ibid.*, October 4, 1839.

concern; nothing new could be added to the attacks on the Van Buren Administration. Furthermore, the Democratic leaders in Tennessee knew that the new legislature would soon instruct Senators White and Foster to support those Van Buren measures which were known to be obnoxious to them. These gentlemen would probably resign, it was believed, rather than obey, and Grundy could then be restored to the senatorial seat from which he had been ousted by the Whig legislature in 1837.[4] White and Foster were instructed and both did resign rather than support the subtreasury bill.

Jackson was partially correct when he remarked that these Whig demonstrations were for effect outside of Tennessee. Bell still aspired to the speakership of the House, Jackson reasoned, and he could not expect enthusiastic general Whig support unless he demonstrated effective political leadership within his own state. Jackson hoped that every effort would be made to block Bell's elevation. If the Democrats could not elect their candidate, then they should unite on some Whig other than Bell.[5]

Bell did want the speakership and he had some reason to believe that, with Polk out of the way, he could secure a majority of the votes. He set out for Washington early in November. Before leaving Nashville he dropped a note to his friend Campbell, urging him to be present on the opening day of the session. One vote might turn the tide in a close election.[6] Traveling by coach rather than by boat, the Bell family made a leisurely tour through East Tennessee, where Bell spoke at no fewer than four towns. Continuing through Virginia in the same leisurely manner, his party did not arrive in Washington until late in November. His Democratic colleagues, already on the scene, steadily watched his every move from

[4] See Parks, *Felix Grundy*, 326 ff.

[5] Jackson to Blair, September 23, 1839, in Bassett (ed.), *Correspondence*, VI, 27–28; id. to Roger B. Taney, October 10, 1839, in *Maryland Historical Magazine*, IV (Baltimore, 1909), 308–10.

[6] Bell to Campbell, October 28, 1839, in David Campbell Papers.

the time he arrived in the city. Watterson reported that Bell "looks melancholy and like something hangs heavily upon his mind." It was rumored, he said, that the Whigs wished to drop Bell and run William C. Dawson of Georgia for Speaker. In case Bell should be dropped, some Democrats were urging that their party run Cave Johnson, since it was believed that he could get the votes of three Virginians—Robert M. T. Hunter, James Garland, and George W. Hopkins. This report of a disposition on the part of a few Whigs to set Bell aside was confirmed by Bell's friend William B. Campbell in a letter to David Campbell: "You know that Bell of Tenn. has been looked to by the whole Whig party throughout the union as the certain candidate for Speaker and the newspapers universally have spoke [n] the same language—but now a *few* . . . are making up an effort to lay him aside." This attempt, he thought, was producing much bad feeling. The Tennessee delegation did not propose to sit back and have their colleague "laid aside by the jealousy of a few." [7]

Democratic hope of victory over the divided Whigs was further strengthened as a result of the disputed election in New Jersey. Five Whigs, fortified with certificates of election signed by the governor, were opposed by a like number of Democrats who also claimed to be the legally elected representatives from that state. Owing to the unavoidable absence of a few Whig members from other states, certain Democratic leaders saw a possibility of a temporary majority for the party if the New Jersey Whigs were denied seats. Hugh A. Garland, clerk of the House, contributed to this plan by refusing to include the New Jersey Whigs in the roll call. This action threw the House into a great uproar. John Quincy Adams was eventually called to the Chair as temporary presiding officer. Wise moved that the New Jersey Whigs be seated; the Democrats demanded that the motion be tabled and that those

[7] Watterson to Polk, November 29, 1839, in Polk Papers; William B. Campbell to David Campbell, December 1, 1839, in David Campbell Papers.

whose seats were in dispute should have no vote. In spite of a favorable ruling from the Chair, the Whigs lost the battle.[8]

After a number of caucus sessions, the Whigs were still unable to agree on a candidate for Speaker. According to a Democratic account, Bell refused to be blurred off ; therefore, both he and Dawson were put forward by their friends.[9] The Democrats supported John W. Jones of Virginia. On the first ballot Jones received 113, Bell 102, and Dawson 11. The deadlock was finally broken on the eleventh ballot when enough Whigs shifted to Robert M. T. Hunter to give him a majority.[10]

John Catron, a close, if partial, observer, reported to Polk that the defeat had broken Bell. Upon learning that election was improbable, Catron said, Bell "behaved very badly, & gave great offense to many Whigs." [11] Bad behavior on Bell's part is both probable and understandable, but this Democratic version of his conduct is nowhere verified by a Whig source. In the absence of any statement from Bell, the only point which is certain is that he was angry. This wrath he immediately loosed on the Democrats. Speaking in opposition to a Democratic proposal to change the method of voting in the House from the ballot to viva voce, he charged that it was the purpose of the Administration to make every man walk the chalk. Indeed, public officeholding had already been reduced to the most degraded form of political subserviency. He would go still further and declare that no English monarch since the days of the Stuarts had more completely dominated his country than had the American Presidents during the past two administrations. Strong men who had the physical courage to face a cannon mouth had been seen to bow down rather than be denounced by the "party press." Such party despotism,

8 Aaron V. Brown to *id.*, December 7, 1839; Cave Johnson to *id.*, December 4, 7, 1839, *ibid.*

9 Johnson to *id.*, November 28, 1839; Watterson to *id.*, December 1, 1839, *ibid.*
10 Adams (ed.), *Memoirs of John Quincy Adams*, X, 163.
11 Catron to Polk, January 3, 1840, in Polk Papers.

Bell exclaimed, would ultimately make slaves even of strong men.[12]

Before the end of the session Bell again introduced his freedom of elections bill, but to no avail. It was lost by more than a two-to-one majority.[13]

On December 4, 1839, in the midst of the controversy over the speakership, which had made of the House a scene of "greatest disorder & confusion," the Whig national convention met at Harrisburg, Pennsylvania. Preconvention discussion had centered, for the most part, around the candidacy of Henry Clay, William Henry Harrison, and General Winfield Scott. Bell was definitely a Clay man. During the Tennessee state elections of 1839 he had sung the praises of the Kentuckian from many a stump. In the midst of the campaign he had written Clay that the main question before the people of Tennessee was "will they take Henry Clay to rule over them." [14] Bell's only concern in adopting this new course was the possible attitude of Hugh Lawson White, but White soon put him at ease.

One evening during the 1838–1839 session of Congress, Clay and Bell called on Henry A. Wise. They were seeking advice as to the best method of ascertaining White's plans for 1840. Both expressed great admiration for the Tennessee Senator but stated that, in their opinion, he had no chance to secure the Whig nomination. Wise advised an open and frank discussion, and Clay, particularly eager to secure White's support, persuaded Wise to talk with him. White was found to have no presidential aspirations. Even if there were a probability of his being nominated and elected, he had no desire to make the race. He would support Clay for the nomination, but owing to differences on national issues, he could not vote for him for President.[15]

Clay knew that his unconcealed position on national issues made him objectionable to certain factions of the party.

[12] *Cong. Globe,* 26 Cong., 1 Sess., Appendix, 187–89.   [13] *Ibid.,* 829.
[14] Bell to Clay, May 21, 1839, in Clay Papers.
[15] Wise, *Seven Decades of the Union,* 161–67.

Should the Whigs decide to evade these issues by announcing no platform, he would not be the most suitable candidate. As in the case of White, Clay's greatest interest in the election of 1840 was the defeat of Van Buren. Accordingly, he suggested to his friends in the Harrisburg convention that if they believed another could come nearer unifying the party, they should "discard all attachment or partiality for me." [16] Clay probably thought himself sincere in this message, but he undoubtedly considered himself best qualified to do the job. The convention gave Clay a plurality on the first ballot but finally nominated William Henry Harrison, an elderly man who had spent a half century in political and military life without establishing a claim to greatness in either. John Tyler, a state rights man, was named as vice-presidential candidate.

Clay was bitterly disappointed and, if Wise's account be accurate, behaved disgracefully.[17] Bell was also disappointed, but he left no record of his efforts in Clay's behalf or his own reaction to Harrison's nomination. After he had spent months in an attempt to convince the people of Tennessee that Clay was a man of superior qualities, the Kentuckian's own party had expressed a preference for one whose qualities were relatively unknown. An unfriendly observer thought Bell a badly broken man. "The truth is, he was a mere Clay man—and sunk with Mr. Clay on the occasion of the nomination, lower than his selfishness, & vindictiveness had previously sunk him." [18] This was wishful thinking, but two hard blows in succession likely left their mark on Bell.

Soon after the adjournment of the Harrisburg convention, the Whigs indicated the type of campaign they proposed to wage. In the absence of principles upon which there was common agreement, they decided it would be unwise to debate important national topics. The strongest points in favor of

[16] Stanwood, *History of the Presidency*, I, 193.
[17] Wise, *Seven Decades of the Union*, 172.
[18] Catron to Polk, January 3, 1840, in Polk Papers.

their candidate were his relatively unknown position on many public issues and his acceptable military record. This victor over the Indians at Tippecanoe Creek and the British in the battle of the Thames had long been an idol of hero worshippers. The Democrats had previously done well with just such a candidate in the person of Andrew Jackson. And to carry the analogy further, Harrison was also a true product of the West. Many remembered him for his fight in behalf of liberal land laws while a delegate from the old Northwest Territory. Much stress was placed on his simplicity, even though his Ohio home was elegant, if not palatial. He was presented as a man of the people asking for their support in regaining control of a government dominated by a party that had deserted republican principles. The Whig managers also reasoned correctly that what the average voter wanted was excitement rather than cold logic. In short, ballyhoo was to be substituted for sound thinking; songs and parades were to take the place of formal oratory.

As early as February, 1840, the Ohio Whigs set the pace for the demonstrations which were to follow. Adopting as their emblems the symbols of the true frontier—log cabins, raccoon skins, and hard cider—they made themselves hoarse singing the praises of "Tippecanoe and Tyler too." A still greater celebration was held in Baltimore on May 4. It was no coincidence that this was also the date for the assembling of the Democratic national convention in the same city.

Since there was no strong opposition to Van Buren's renomination, his endorsement by the convention was little more than a formality. There was considerable opposition to Vice-President Richard M. Johnson, however, and Polk's friends contributed a good part to it. Johnson, "a burly and slightly educated Kentucky Indian fighter," failing to receive an electoral majority in 1836, had been chosen by the Senate. Already hostile toward the Vice-President because he had failed to expose Bell in 1835–1836, the friends of the Tennessee Governor preferred to see the Kentuckian retired to private life, especially if the Governor himself could get the vice-presidential nomination. When these Polk supporters learned that he had no chance to win, they sponsored a successful movement to have the convention adjourn without making a nomination for vice president.

The Democratic attack on the Whig presidential candidate was formally launched by Felix Grundy in his "keynote" address before the Baltimore convention. Here was a candidate, he asserted, who feared to take a stand on public issues. Soon after the convention, Grundy boldly announced that an examination of Harrison's past record revealed membership in an abolitionist society and a willingness to spend public money in the interest of emancipation.[19]

The mention of friendship for abolitionists encouraged certain Tennessee Democrats in their determination to expose Bell's "true course" on that question. Their findings, a major portion of which were true, were published in a pamphlet entitled *A Looking Glass for the Federal Whig Leaders in Tennessee, or Facts for the People.* When the controversy over abolitionist petitions began in the House, it was revealed, Bell was either cautious or indifferent, usually refraining from voting. When, in 1836, William Jackson of Massachusetts presented a petition from his constituents, praying Congress to abolish slavery in the District of Columbia, his action precipitated a heated discussion on the right of petition. Proslavery extremists demanded that Congress refuse to receive such memorials since it possessed no constitutional power to carry out the request. Others, North and South, insisted that a refusal to receive would be a violation of the constitutional right of petition. Jackson's petition was received and tabled, and a few weeks later Henry L. Pinckney of South Carolina offered a series of resolutions, one of which was designed to establish a procedure for handling abolitionist requests. All petitions or memorials relating to slavery or its

19 *Niles' National Register*, LVIII (1840), 147–48; Nashville *Union*, July 16, 1840; Washington *Globe*, June 23, 1840.

abolition were to be tabled without being printed or referred
to a committee. This resolution, adopted by the House on
May 26, 1836, became known as the "gag resolution." Bell had
opposed suspension of the rules in order that the resolution
might be called up, and he refrained from voting on its
passage.

The gag resolution was renewed in January, 1837, but expired with the life of Congress on March 3; therefore, when
the new Congress convened in December, the controversy
was reopened. On December 20, William Slade of Vermont,
in presenting two memorials from his state, made himself so
obnoxious to the proslavery group that Speaker Polk ordered
him to his seat. The Southern congressmen hurried into caucus and decided to push through another resolution even
more stringent than the one that had expired. Bell later stated
that he objected to it "openly and strongly." He argued that
regardless of "whether the petitioners had strict right on their
side or not, sound policy dictated the reception and reference
of their petitions." The adoption of any other unusual course
would stimulate the abolitionist movement, furnish new cause
for agitation, and increase excitement rather than allay it.[20]

On the day following the caucus, when John M. Patton of
Virginia introduced the resolution agreed on, Bell alone of
the Tennessee delegation opposed a suspension of the rules;
he cast no vote on the passage of the proposal. As he later explained, in taking this action, he was conscious of a lack of
harmony with the opinion of his constituents; but believing
that their opinions had been formed without careful study, he
did not hesitate to trust "their better judgment, after they
should have more fully considered the subject." [21]

In 1838, Bell took a more decided stand and voted to table a
proposed gag resolution. Failing in this effort, he and Joseph
L. Williams of Tennessee voted against its passage. Again in
1840, Bell dared reaffirm his stand, causing Cave Johnson to

[20] Bell to George R. Gilmer, n.d., in Washington *National Intelligencer*,
August 8, 1840; Nashville *Republican Banner*, January 30, 1838; *Cong. Globe*,
33 Cong., 1 Sess., Appendix, 946; *Cong. Debates*, 24 Cong., 1 Sess., 4053-54.
[21] *Cong. Globe*, 33 Cong., 1 Sess., Appendix, 946.

remark that if this association with abolitionists did not ruin Bell politically "then I surrender my judgment." [22]

While Democrats were denouncing him as a friend of abolitionists, Bell was carefully considering what part he should take in the coming presidential campaign. He could not approve of the campaign of songs and parades planned by Whig leaders; such antics were foreign to his nature. Dignified even to the point of aloofness, he had no special talent for applying mass psychology. He never possessed the common touch. His preference was for the speaker's platform and he would have been pleased to meet the best the Democrats had to offer. But even he now realized that it would take more than well-polished speeches to oust the party in power. Voters must be reached and party tactics must be directed toward that end. Regardless of his lack of enthusiasm for the candidate and the program, Bell had no choice but to support them with a show of enthusiasm.

Before Congress adjourned on July 21, Bell was appointed a member of the congressional committee for the promotion of the election of the Whig candidates. It would take more than the efforts of those nine Whigs, sneered Andrew Jackson, to delude the people into believing Harrison "either a great general or civilian." [23] Detained on business, Bell remained in Washington until after July 30. Before leaving the city, he received a letter from East Tennessee friends urging that he meet Grundy on the stump at Jonesborough. Unable to reach Tennessee by the designated date, Bell suggested that Grundy be detained until he could arrive. In fact, he wished that both Polk and Grundy would arrange their schedules so as to make it possible for him to be present. This would be not only the republican way but also the best way "of eliciting the truth . . . and of preventing the intrusion of intemperate and violent passions in the canvass." [24]

Neither Grundy nor Polk arranged to meet Bell. Governor

[22] Jackson to Polk, May 24, 1840, in Polk Papers.
[23] *Id.* to Blair, May 24, 1840, in Bassett (ed.), *Correspondence*, VI, 61–62.
[24] Bell to Samuel Green *et al.*, July 24, 1840, in Jonesborough *Whig*, August 12, 1840.

Polk made only a few speeches during the presidential campaign, but even this limited action was sufficient to cause the Sevier County grand jury to denounce him as a nuisance.[25] The death of Hugh Lawson White on April 10 made it necessary for Bell to spend several weeks campaigning in East Tennessee. The mountain counties had long been a Democratic stronghold although there had been a recent deflection in favor of White. The friends of the late Senator must be rallied to the Whig cause.

As Bell approached the Tennessee border on his return trip from Washington, he was met at Leesburg by a large delegation which escorted him to Jonesborough where, according to "Parson" Brownlow, he delivered a speech which was "the spontaneous effort of a mind ample and inexhaustible in its resources." [26] For six weeks Bell fought to counteract the efforts of Alfred O. P. Nicholson and other prominent Democrats who had been sent into the eastern section to aid Andrew Johnson.[27] Lashing out at Bell for his interference in East Tennessee politics, one Democratic editor declared that his presence would make one thousand votes for Van Buren. "We thank the Federalists for bringing John Bell here. They will rue the day they did it." [28] Bell did not reach home until the first week in October.

During the summer Middle and West Tennessee had been aflame with Whig enthusiasm which had manifested itself in the form of most elaborate pageants. In the words of one Democratic observer, "The efforts of the Democratic orators and presses to advocate their principles was met and overwhelmed with log-cabin, hard cider, and coonskin displays by the organized and uniformed Straightouts, who made a perfect frolic of it." [29] In mid-June the steamer *Rio* arrived at the Nashville levee. On board was a Whig delegation from In-

[25] Phelan, *History of Tennessee*, 387.
[26] Jonesborough *Whig*, September 9, 1840.
[27] Orville Bradley *et al.* to Green and Thomas A. R. Nelson, August 23, 1840, in Thomas A. R. Nelson Papers (Lawson McGhee Library, Knoxville).
[28] Quoted in Nashville *Union*, September 14, 1840.
[29] Guild, *Old Times in Tennessee*, 159.

diana bringing compliments and presents from the Tippecanoe clubs in that state. Among the presents was a canoe in which was tied a live raccoon. On sight of this spectacle the crowd of assembled youngsters screamed with delight. Escorted by the Straight outs, resplendent in their "dark blue hunting shirts, trimmed with white coon-skin caps and copperas breeches," the raccoon was carried through the principal streets of the city and finally deposited atop a newly constructed log cabin on Market Street.[30] From far and near men came to view these emblems, so common to frontier life, yet so novel in a political campaign.

A few weeks later another steamboat from Louisville brought a many-colored ball "as big as a house," a gift from the Whigs of Muskingum County, Ohio. One Porter, a giant eight feet tall, was imported from Kentucky to "keep the ball rolling." Escorted by the uniformed Straight-outs, Porter rolled the ball up Broadway, turned to Capitol Hill by way of Senator Grundy's home, and thence to the public square. Even the Democrats admitted that the shouts from the accompanying throng "made the welkin ring." [31]

During the course of the campaign, Ephraim H. Foster was probably the most active of the Tennessee Whigs. Still smarting over his forced resignation from the Senate, he carried the story of Democratic corruption and inefficiency throughout Middle and West Tennessee. On August 17 he presided over the great Whig rally at Walnut Grove on the outskirts of Nashville. No fewer than eleven states sent delegations to this mammoth convention which was high-lighted by a speech by Henry Clay. The brilliance of the parade from uptown Nashville to the assembly ground was the subject of conversation for months, even years, to come.

Bell, campaigning in the eastern section, missed these jolli-

[30] *Ibid.*, 159–61. Guild recalled that the cabin had been constructed earlier in the day under the supervision of Bell and Dr. Boyd McNairy. He also stated that on this occasion Bell delivered a speech, addressing the raccoon as "his Majesty" and welcoming him to the state. Either this statement or the date is incorrect; Bell was in Washington in mid-June.

[31] Guild, *Old Times in Tennessee*, 161.

fications. His efforts, however, although not accompanied by so much ballyhoo, were well rewarded: East Tennessee gave to Harrison almost 60 per cent of its vote. Harrison carried the state by a majority of more than twelve thousand. Even Middle Tennessee, the Jackson-Polk-Grundy-Johnson stronghold, went for the Whig candidate by more than a thousand votes. The total vote of the state exceeded that in the recent governor's election by almost two thousand,[32] a rare occurrence in a presidential election and a testimony to the effectiveness of emotional appeal.

The victory of "Old Tip" over "Marty Van" electrified the Whigs throughout the Union. At last the reign of Andrew Jackson had been terminated. Truly a new day had dawned, a day that would bring to the Whigs not the inauguration of a definite national program but the fruits of public office which had so long been enjoyed by the Democrats. The perseverance of those Whig leaders who had been relentlessly pounding at the walls of the fort had indeed been rewarded.

To Bell the victory brought more than hope; it brought a vision. "Have we not acheived [sic] a glorious triumph? 10,000!!! What will Mr. Grundy say to this?" he asked an East Tennessee associate.[33] With skillful management, he believed Polk could be defeated for governor and he himself could be made Speaker of the House.[34] To defeat Polk, an effective man must be nominated; Cannon would not do. Such a victory would require the closest harmony among all Whigs. And party harmony, Bell reasoned, could be developed through the leadership of East Tennessee only. His plan, as explained in a letter to Thomas A. R. Nelson, was for that section to hold a convention and nominate a candidate for governor. The other sections, he believed, would then "acquiesce without a murmur, in their present fine temper." On the other hand, if left to make their own choice, Middle and

[32] Nashville *Republican Banner,* December 2, 1840.
[33] Bell to Nelson, November 9, 1840, in Nelson Papers.
[34] Adams (ed.), *Memoirs of John Quincy Adams,* X, 344.

West Tennessee Whigs would be badly divided. But who should be run? Bell declared that Foster was the man but doubted whether he would agree. He thought that he himself should not make the race.

It would be said that I had been called from Congress to beat Jimmy Polk. I cannot agree that our party has not in its ranks many men besides Foster and me either, who can do that Job for *Jimmy*—especially since the late result—10,000 majority. But *Jimmy* declares he will run the race out & we will have to beat him. I scarcely believe him, but we must be prepared to meet him. Who can do it among those who are willing to try? If the lot should fall on Middle Ten. the choice must be made out of one of three of our men, Caruthers, Jones, & Gentry. . . . Of the three who would accept the nomination, Caruthers possesses most ability & experience—Jones most vivacity, a better tact in pleasing the people on the stump, & a greater energy; while Gentry has most eloquence, keener invective and not less discretion than Caruthers.

Bell thought that since Gentry lived in the same county as Cannon, his nomination might draw off the Cannon support in case Cannon decided to run independently.[35]

Nelson, a resident of Jonesborough and probably the most capable among the East Tennessee Whigs, did not agree. He thought Bell himself should run against Polk. Bell protested, arguing that Foster could do a better job and could easily beat Polk. Besides, should he give up his seat in Congress and his chances to become Speaker, people would say that he was sacrificing possible promotion for the mere pleasure of destroying his old rival. Furthermore, Bell argued, the party should not insist that he forgo acceptance of the speakership or a cabinet position in order to become governor of Tennessee.[36]

There can be no doubt about Bell's desire for a cabinet post, even though, during the campaign, he had confided to Adams that to attain again the speakership "would be the summit of

[35] Bell to Nelson, November 8, 1840, in Nelson Papers.
[36] *Id.* to *id.*, December 21, 1840, *ibid.*

his ambition." [37] Writing from Washington, early in January, 1841, he unbosomed himself in a most revealing letter to his friend Robert P. Letcher of Kentucky:

I presume [John] White keeps you advised of all the *on dits* of the day here,—of the *under-current* plots and *counter-plots,* etc.,— so I shall say nothing of them. Of myself I will say, that I believe for the whole time since the opening of Congress the *rank* and *file* of our party here have been strongly in favor of my going into the cabinet. With not a few the feeling has been a positive one, not of mere acquiescence. Still, the great leaders evidently hang back.

Both Clay and Webster would be glad to have some more active or unscrupulous partisan (I know not which) than either of them think I could be made. Webster thinks I am, or will be, a decided partisan of Clay, and the latter thinks I would not go far enough, or be bold enough in his service. This is the gospel truth of the matter.

It is either so or General Harrison himself has objections, for I have learned that he, or his friends about him, have been long since well advised of the course of sentiment in regard to me. Yet the War Department is still held up for further development of public sentiment. I am growing pretty sick already of this thing of *office* in my own case, and the increasing tide of application[s] from new quarters that daily beats against my ears gives me spasms. In truth, I begin to fear that we are at last, or rather that our leading politicians in the several States are, chiefly swayed by the thirst for power and plunder. . . . God help us all and keep us, I pray.[38]

By the time Harrison arrived in Washington on February 9, party leaders had about selected his cabinet for him. Clay had declined to become Secretary of State, preferring to remain in the Senate, and Webster had been designated for that position. It appears that Webster, upon the request of Harrison, then took the lead in selecting persons for the other posts. According to Wise, the method used in forming the Cabinet was shocking.[39] In spite of Bell's misgivings, he was eventually

[37] Adams (ed.), *Memoirs of John Quincy Adams,* X, 344.
[38] Bell to Robert P. Letcher, January 13, 1841, in Mrs. Chapman Coleman, *The Life of John J. Crittenden* (Philadelphia, 1871), I, 136–37.
[39] Wise, *Seven Decades of the Union,* 180. For Webster's influence in the

selected as Secretary of War, probably due to the work of Webster.[40] Since Bell's eastern tour in 1837, the two had been close political, if not personal, friends. Certainly both Clay and Webster recognized the service performed by Bell in delivering Jackson's Tennessee into the ranks of the Whigs. There is no reason to believe that Clay did not favor Bell's elevation; but Harrison, fearing a possible Clay attempt to dominate the Administration, kept the Kentuckian at arm's length.[41]

The offensive and defensive groups had exchanged positions. Those Whigs who had so vigorously denounced the Democratic practice of appointing congressmen to office were now open to their own criticism; four of the six new cabinet members were members of the Twenty-sixth Congress. Hordes of other Whigs "rushed pell-mell to Washington, every man with a raccoon's tail in his hat," according to Wise, "and tugged at the string of the latch out at the White House door, as if sure enough it was a log cabin." [42] "In confidence," wrote one Whig editor who had attended the inauguration of Harrison, "I tell you that the rush of the Whigs for office, is beyond any thing you could have immagined [sic]—even disgraceful." [43] He believed that the new Administration would make a "clean sweep" of officeholders.

The Old Hero at the Hermitage chuckled over the news of Bell's appointment. This incident was all that was needed, he reasoned, to open the eyes of the people. No longer could they fail to see that Bell's apostasy and his denunciation and slander

selection of the cabinet, see Harrison to Webster, December 1, 1840; Webster to Harrison, December 11, 1840; Harrison to Webster, December 27, 1840, in *Writings and Speeches of Daniel Webster* (Boston, 1903), XVIII, 90–97.

40 Other cabinet appointments were Francis Granger of New York, Postmaster General; John J. Crittenden of Kentucky, Attorney General; Thomas Ewing of Ohio, Secretary of the Treasury; George Badger of North Carolina, Secretary of the Navy.

41 Among other persons who recommended Bell for a cabinet post was Zachary Taylor. Taylor to Ethan Allen Hitchcock, May 19, 1841, in Zachary Taylor Papers (Division of Manuscripts, Library of Congress).

42 Wise, *Seven Decades of the Union*, 179.

43 William G. Brownlow to Nelson, March 8, 1841, in Nelson Papers.

of Democratic officeholders were merely the efforts of a hypocrite to secure an office for himself.[44] Too long had John Bell been "wilfully, wickedly and knowingly" circulating falsehoods and breathing partisan slander. Had the office of Secretary of War been tendered this apostate when he was recommended by Judge White, Jackson asserted, Bell would never have allied himself with "blue light Federalists." Would people who professed moral and Christian principles continue to express confidence in such an office seeker?[45] The Old General thought not; so while the Whigs were celebrating the inauguration of the new President, he was penning a few words of consolation to the retiring Chief Magistrate. Within two years, Jackson assured Van Buren, Bell would be abandoned by those whom he had deluded and "your merits will be proclaimed by all the honest and moral portion of our Country."[46]

Bell entered upon the duties of his new office with characteristic enthusiasm and industry. He had a job to do and wished nothing more than an opportunity to work. During the coming weeks his old friends seldom saw him. Some were offended by his aloofness and apparent selfishness.[47] He was not enthusiastic enough about handing out jobs, and was secluding himself from office seekers. Characteristically, Bell failed to realize that to have loyal friends one must be a friend at all times and not just when convenient. He immediately dismissed two clerks in the War Department, not in order to replace them with Whigs, but because he considered them surplus.[48] A thorough study of the spoils system had not impressed upon him the fact that victorious Whigs, like victorious Democrats, would demand the fruits of their victory. In short, Bell was not a good politician. With a mind

[44] Jackson to Van Buren, March 4, 1841, in Bassett (ed.), *Correspondence*, VI, 92.
[45] *Id.* to Polk, March 20, 1841, *ibid.*, 95–96.
[46] *Id.* to Van Buren, March 4, 1841, *ibid.*, 92.
[47] Arthur Campbell to David Campbell, March 22, 1841, in David Campbell Papers.
[48] Brownlow to Nelson, March 8, 1841, in Nelson Papers.

"essentially analytical and logical," he could sketch broad
over-all plans, but he was never the equal of Polk in attending to the minute details necessary for the realization of those
plans. Probably most important of all, he was lacking in that
attribute known as human sympathy.

The rays of the midnight light in the War Office soon became a familiar sight to Washington residents; Bell was preparing a report to the President. But on April 4 all work in
executive offices came to a sudden halt; the President was
dead. Despite his heralded physical vigor, Harrison had contracted pneumonia on March 24 and proved deficient in re-
serve strength. The cabinet hurriedly dispatched messengers
to Williamsburg to summon Vice-President Tyler. For the
first time in American history the Vice-President was to complete the unexpired term of a deceased President.

The new President requested Harrison's entire cabinet
to remain in office. And Bell, for one, although he knew that
Tyler was at heart a Democrat, was not displeased with the
prospects for a harmonious Administration. He thought
Tyler appeared quite happy and "not at all displeased with
his fortune." The President seemed conciliatory and would
probably steer clear of extremes. In fact, Bell thought everything was "quite as fine as could be expected." [49]

Further evidence of his confidence is found in his interest
in the Tennessee elections of 1841. Before becoming ill Harrison had issued a call for a special session of Congress to
convene on May 31. Since the terms of Tennessee's congressmen had expired on March 4 and the regular election was
not scheduled until late in the summer, it was necessary, if
the state was to be represented, to call a special election. All
Whigs must rally to the support of the Administration, Bell
wrote his friend Nelson. Under no circumstance should two
Whigs be candidates for the same office and the members of
the party must put forth their best efforts to make Tennessee a moral force in both houses of Congress. Only with the

[49] Bell to Letcher, May 2, 1841, in Crittenden Papers.

finest co-operation within the party, Bell concluded, could the Administration "give practical effect to those great principles for which we have been so long contending." [50] The spring election of Tennessee congressmen resulted in the selection of eight Whigs and five Democrats. Bell's district remained loyal to the Whigs, electing Robert L. Caruthers of Lebanon.

Before Congress convened on May 31, Henry Clay, having advised Harrison to call such a session and, eager to direct its course, had prepared a legislative program. As leader of the nationalists, the largest group within the Whig party, the Kentuckian intended that he himself, not the state rights Tyler, should lead the party. Although Harrison had declared his intention to serve a single term only, the new President had not committed himself. If Clay's presidential aspirations were to be realized in 1844, then he must keep Tyler in check.

Clay's legislative program was embodied in a group of resolutions presented to the Senate on June 7. The Subtreasury Act was to be repealed, a national bank chartered, the tariff increased, and the profit from the sale of public land distributed among the several states. Since this program had not been presented during the recent campaign, Clay's personal friends were the only ones in any way obligated to support it. Tyler, in his message to Congress, pronounced the Subtreasury system unsatisfactory; but he also made it clear that in case Congress saw fit to adopt a substitute plan, care must be taken not to violate the Constitution by infringing upon the rights of the states.[51] Within a week the first of Clay's objectives had been attained: Congress, with the President's approval, had repealed the Subtreasury Act.

Then came the test of strength. On June 12, Thomas Ewing, Secretary of the Treasury, in response to a request from the Senate and with the endorsement of Tyler, pre-

[50] Id. to Nelson, April 24, 1841, in Nelson Papers.
[51] Richardson (ed.), Messages and Papers, IV, 1893 ff.

sented a plan for the establishment of a national bank. A central bank was to be located in the District of Columbia, but no branch bank might be established within any state without that state's consent. This was not Clay's idea of a national bank; he saw no need for consulting the states. Unable to secure the omission of this restriction on branch banks, however, he accepted a midway proposal apparently suggested by John Minor Botts of Virginia. In case a state legislature, during its first session following the passage of this bill, should fail specifically to deny permission to establish a branch of the bank, permission would then be considered as granted. Thus amended, the bill passed the Senate on July 28 and was rushed through the House by August 6.[52]

When the bill reached the President he called his cabinet members into conference and an extensive discussion followed. According to Webster, the cabinet was unanimous in recommending that the bill be signed.[53] If this statement be correct, the President was already out of harmony with his constitutional advisers. Although he kept the bill nine days before sending in his veto, his mind had been made up by the time he received the bill. On the morning of August 16, the day the veto was sent to the Senate, Ewing called upon the President and found him putting the finishing touches on his message. Bell soon joined them, and the bank bill became the topic of discussion. Bell remarked that he expected the veto to "create a great sensation in Congress" but not so great as it would have a few days earlier. He hoped that the Whig members of Congress would receive the news calmly, especially since the veto did not destroy all hope of creating a bank of some form. Tyler replied that he had delayed the delivery of his message to allow time for congressmen to quiet themselves. He had already indicated to Congress the type of bank he would approve, and if the Whig

[52] *Cong. Globe,* 27 Cong., 1 Sess., 260, 303.
[53] See Webster's "Memoranda respecting the Bank Bills & the Vetoes," in Daniel Webster Papers, IV (Division of Manuscripts, Library of Congress).

majority wished it, such a bank could be created in three days.[54]

Tyler's veto of the bill was no surprise to Congress; neither was Clay's inability to pass the bill over his veto. The Whigs, however, were greatly stirred, some going so far as openly to denounce the President as a traitor to the party. Yet despite their raving, most Whigs were conscious of the necessity of an attempt to repair the breach within the party. A caucus was convened and John Sergeant of the House and John M. Berrien of the Senate were delegated to confer with the President and then to frame a bill that would be acceptable to him. Conferences with Tyler were held on August 17 and 18. He refused to suggest a definite plan and pointed to his first message as a sufficient guide for Congress. Tyler also conferred with his cabinet on the eighteenth. According to Webster and Ewing, he expressed his approval of a "Bank of issue, deposit, and exchange, without power of discounting promissory notes. And for such a Bank he did not intimate that he requested the assent of the States." Furthermore, Tyler requested Webster and Ewing to convey indirectly these views to congressional leaders. Accordingly, they conferred with Sergeant and Berrien.[55] On August 20, Sergeant introduced in the House a bill to create a Fiscal Corporation. It passed the House on August 23 and the Senate on September 3.[56] Clay gave the bill mild support but Tyler's friends in both houses, having been notified of his disapproval, fought to prevent its passage. Whether Tyler had been misunderstood by his cabinet or had changed his mind is still a question; however, according to statements by Webster and Henry A. Wise, the President used them as intermediaries in conveying his disapproval to several Whig congressmen. Tyler himself later stated that no fewer than fifty

[54] "The Diary of Thomas Ewing, August and September, 1841," in *American Historical Review* (New York, 1895–), XVIII (1912), 99. Quotations are Ewing's words.
[55] *Ibid.*, 100–103; Webster's "Memoranda."
[56] *Cong. Globe*, 27 Cong., 1 Sess., 370–72, 423.

congressmen were fully aware of his objections. He did not believe that there was a single Whig member of Congress who was unaware of the certainty of a veto. Even Ewing admitted that on the day following the introduction of the bill, while he, Bell, and Tyler were at the Arsenal inspecting "some experiments with improved rockets," the President intimated that he would veto the measure.[57]

With the introduction of the Fiscal Corporation bill other government business had come to pretty much of a standstill. Everyone sensed that a crisis was at hand. Clay was undoubtedly determined to force Tyler either to conform to the nationalist program or forfeit his standing within the party. Tyler was equally as determined to remain loyal to his state rights views, regardless of the consequence. Ewing confided to his diary that "Mr. Clay was evidently hurrying matters to a catastrophe; intending to . . . force him [Tyler] to approve or Veto—in the latter event compel the Cabinet to resign." [58] Other Clay friends within the cabinet likewise knew that they must soon choose between the two antagonists. Cabinet meetings were characterized by a feeling of a lack of frankness and confidence between the President and his advisers and even among the advisers themselves. Somebody had been divulging cabinet secrets, for Clay had stated in the Senate that the cabinet was unanimous in advising Tyler to approve the bank bill. Some of Bell's enemies circulated a rumor that he was the one who was keeping Clay informed, but they submitted no proof.[59] The tenseness of the situation, however, was somewhat relieved by an enjoyable party at Bell's Washington home on the evening of September 2. The President was among the guests.[60]

Tyler kept the Fiscal Corporation bill for six days before

[57] *Niles' National Register*, LXI (1841), 54–55; Lyon G. Tyler, *The Letters and Times of the Tylers* (Richmond, 1884–96), II, 88, 98–102; "Diary of Thomas Ewing," *loc. cit.*, 107; Webster's "Memoranda."

[58] "Diary of Thomas Ewing," *loc. cit.*, 105–106.

[59] Cave Johnson to Polk, July 17, 1841, in Polk Papers.

[60] "Diary of Thomas Ewing," *loc. cit.*, 107.

sending his veto message to the House. In the meantime, Clay continued to exert indirect pressure upon his friends in the cabinet; they must prepare to resign en masse in case of another veto. Bell and Ewing had already been conferring with each other as to their future course. To resign, they concluded, would be to prove "false counsellor to the President —near his person—admitted to his secret councils, and at the same time conniving with and abetting his most bitter adversary." On the other hand, to remain would draw from their political associates a charge of having abandoned principles for the "love of office." And probably most important of all, in the words of Ewing: "We would be made the constant object of attack by the papers on both sides in politics, and probably be at last compelled to resign or be displaced, with injured characters, and minds soured and discontented." [61] Bell confided that he would not consider a veto of the Fiscal Corporation alone sufficient cause for him to resign. However, in case Tyler should veto the land bill also, the President's betrayal of the party would be clearly in evidence and the entire cabinet should resign. In any event, Bell, aware of Clay's political ambition, declared that he would take no part in any immediate movement to nominate Clay for the presidency.[62]

The land bill to which reference was made was also a part of Clay's program. For a decade he had been advocating distribution of the proceeds from the sale of public lands. Such a division of money among the states would probably reduce the Treasury surplus to a point where an increase in tariff rates would be necessary. Furthermore, placing Federal funds in state hands would defeat Jacksonian prohibition on local internal improvements at Federal expense by enabling the states to develop the projects. Since the Deposit Act of 1836 had been limited to the existing surplus only, the adoption of a permanent plan was desired. The new bill, provid-

61 *Ibid.*, 105–106. Ewing stated that Bell concurred in this opinion.
62 *Ibid.*, 106.

ing for the distribution of the expected surplus, was passed only after it was agreed that the tariff should not be increased above the 20 per cent maximum set by the compromise of 1833.[63] Bell, cognizant of Tennessee's interest in internal improvements and personally interested in land speculation in other states, had changed his mind since the day of Jackson's veto of the Maysville Road Bill. But he had consistently approved of distribution.

Tyler signed the land bill and on September 9 informed the House of his veto of the Fiscal Corporation bill. In the evening of that same day, the cabinet, with the exception of Granger, assembled for dinner at the home of Badger. Webster, upon finding that Clay was among the guests, did not remain long. During the evening Crittenden, Badger, Ewing, and Bell decided to resign their cabinet posts. It was later alleged that Clay spent the evening entertaining the Badger family and therefore took no part in the conference of cabinet members.[64] Even if absent in body he was certainly present in spirit. How else could his appearance at the Badger home on that particular evening be explained?

On September 11 all members of the cabinet, except Webster, sent in their resignations. Two days later Congress adjourned, and on the same day the Clay Whigs, meeting in public caucus, repudiated Tyler and publicly announced that he was no longer one of them.[65] Ewing's letter of resignation, a copy of which was released for publication, was a lengthy defense of the part he had taken in the bank struggle. It was not the veto that caused his resignation, he said, but the President's "personal indignity" toward him. At the request of Ewing, Bell confirmed this revelation of cabinet secrets, and in a letter to the *National Intelligencer*, he stated

[63] Benjamin H. Hibbard, *A History of the Public Land Policies* (New York, 1924), 184–87.
[64] George R. Poage, *Henry Clay and the Whig Party* (Chapel Hill, 1936), 100–101.
[65] *Niles' National Register*, LXI (1841), 35–36; George T. Curtis, *Life of Daniel Webster* (New York, 1870), II, 207–209.

that his own resignation was the result of "pre-existing causes." [66] In a private letter to Ewing, written after more than a month's reflection, Bell declared Tyler both "knave & fool." "We did what we could not help doing, & save our own self respect. If we had been better *politicians* & worse *men* we might have been still in public life." [67]

Webster published over his signature a statement that he saw no adequate reason for a disruption of the cabinet, and then wrote for the *Madisonian,* the Tyler organ, an unsigned article entitled "The Ex-Members' Publications Abbreviated." [68]

We should more readily incline to suppose there might be some reason for the retirement of the four members of the late Cabinet, if they could agree on such reasons among themselves. But, unhappily, they entirely differ, each has a ground of his own, & no sooner does one come forth to show his cause than another follows with a different showing.

Mr. Ewing, who leads off, rejects the Veto, as ground of resignation, & goes out on 'personal indignity.'—

Mr. Crittenden follows, & having no complaint to make of personal indignity, he goes out on the Veto—

Then comes Mr. Badger, who does not go out, on the Bank question, but because the case is one of 'a measure, embraced, & then repudiated—efforts promoted, & then disowned—services rendered, and then treated with scorn and neglect'—

That is to say, Mr. Badger resigned because the President trifled with his cabinet.

But now hear Mr. Bell—

'Nor was it because the President thought proper to trifle with or mislead his Cabinet, as there is but too much reason to believe he intended to do, in the affair of the late Fiscal Bank that I resigned my place.—

[66] *Niles' National Register,* LXI (1841), 33–34, 53–54; Washington *National Intelligencer,* September 22, 1841.

[67] Bell to Thomas Ewing, October 23, 1841, in Thomas Ewing Papers (Division of Manuscripts, Library of Congress).

[68] The manuscript of this article is among the Daniel Webster Papers and was published in Claude H. Van Tyne (ed.), *Letters of Daniel Webster* (New York, 1902), 238.

There were other & pre-existing causes, for such a course, &c.'
What these 'other & pre-existing causes' are or were, Mr. Bell
does not inform us. In regard to these, the world is yet to be enlightened.[69]

Clay was delighted with the mass resignation of the cabinet.
"What wonderful but mortifying & humiliating disclosures
are made of the President by Ewing, Bell & Badger," he wrote
John M. Berrien. And a few months later, again referring to
Tyler, he further commented: "We could get along with a
man who was only fool or knave, or mad; but the extraordinary occurrence of all three of those qualities combined
in one person is intolerable." [70]

Regardless of any public statement to the contrary, it was
with reluctance that Bell resigned his cabinet post; he liked
his job.[71] On May 31 he had submitted to the President a
report making some general recommendations in the interest
of public defense and internal improvements.[72] The "dictate
of patriotism," he informed the President, demanded that
due provision be made against the infliction of a national insult through the possible seizure of "even one of our strongholds by a powerful enemy." Owing to recent improvements
in the application of steam power to ocean navigation and
the increase in the "destructiveness of shells," our system of
defense, although still under construction, had become out-
moded. It could not be doubted, he explained, "that the
cause of humanity will be promoted in proportion as the existing systems and means of defensive warfare are perfected
by new improvements." Only through such improvements
could the weaker nations of the earth enjoy their "forms of
society and government" and could wars be rendered less

[69] Washington *Madisonian*, September 25, 1841; Daniel Webster Papers.

[70] Clay to John M. Berrien, October 7, 1841, July 21, 1842, in *Georgia Historical Quarterly*, XXIX (Savannah, 1945), 25–27.

[71] Bell had hoped to use a portion of his salary to pay some pressing debts.
Bell to Letcher, January 28, February 9, 1841, in Crittenden Papers.

[72] Nashville *Whig*, June 25, 1841; Nashville *Union*, June 21, 1841; Washington *National Intelligencer*, June 8, 1841.

frequent. Accordingly, he requested an appropriation of $12,186,547 to be used in the rapid completion and armament of defense projects then under construction, even though they would be defective "as a perfect system of national defence."

Since taking over the War Office, Bell explained, he had used all available funds on the improvement of the fortifications on the Atlantic coast. This he deemed wise in view of the "unsettled and threatening aspect of our foreign relations." [73] He was pleased to report that, with the co-operation of New York, the defenses on Staten Island had been placed in good repair.

In the interest of both efficiency and economy, Bell had suspended the civilian superintendents of the national armories. Officers of the Ordnance Department had been placed in charge. Civilian superintendents, Bell explained, had demonstrated a lack of "proper qualifications." "Some degree of science, as well as a practical knowledge in the construction and use of arms" he considered "indispensable requisites" of an efficient superintendent. Another objection to the use of civilians, he asserted, was the "defective and inadequate control" which the War Department was able to exercise over them. He desired to see the armories "separated, as far as possible, from all connexion with the party politics of the day."

The $30,000 appropriated by the last Congress for the purpose of repairing the Potomac Bridge had not been spent. The expenditure of such a small sum on so huge a project would be a waste of money. Congress should appropriate such additional funds as were necessary for "repairs on a safe and durable plan." Bell expressed considerable interest in the expenditure of the $75,000 recently provided for the removal of obstructions from the Red River. Much good was expected from this worth-while undertaking. A competent officer had been placed in charge of the work, but had not yet reported on his progress. Bell's interest in the improvement

[73] Reference was to the controversy with Great Britain growing out of the McLeod case and the Maine boundary dispute.

of Red River antedated his appointment to the War Office. In 1840 he and his brother James had begun the purchase of extensive tracts of fertile but wild lands in Caddo Parish, Louisiana, near Shreveport.[74] This speculation was begun with the expectation that the state and Federal governments would co-operate in removing the obstacles to commerce on the Red River. Since financial embarrassment was one reason for Bell's eagerness for a cabinet post, one suspects that he was not averse to using his position in the furtherance of his own private welfare. It is significant that the Red River project was the only one for which Bell expressed great enthusiasm.

As for Indian affairs, Bell had nothing definite to report. Alleged misuse of Indian funds was under investigation. A later report might be expected. No further report was issued by Bell, but later, during the bank crisis, he presented to the cabinet a rather extensive plan for future defensive fortifications. Tyler and his cabinet, however, were too much absorbed with other matters of more immediate importance.[75]

The Whig press made frequent mention of the business-like atmosphere which surrounded the War Office. The Democrats, on the other hand, were not impressed, except by the cold formality within the "princely quarters" of Bell the "unapproachable." Indeed, declared an unfriendly Tennessean, the Secretary of War was "enjoying all the honors and luxuries of a little monarch. . . . If you call to see him, you are met by a white servant—you must give your name, and if his majesty is in the humor, you are ushered into his sanctum sanctorum, where he is sitting on his throne, or in

[74] Caddo Parish, Louisiana, Conveyance Records, Book A, 264.

[75] "Diary of Thomas Ewing," *loc. cit.*, 105. It was Bell who recommended Winfield Scott for promotion to the position of Major General of the Army following the death of General Alexander Macomb in June, 1841. Scott to Bell, June 27, 1841; Bell to President John Tyler, June 29, 1841, in Charles Winslow Elliott, *Winfield Scott: The Soldier and the Man* (New York, 1937), 399–400. Scott later confidentially stated that, with a "little more experience," Bell would have done well as Secretary of War. See memorandum by Scott, dated July 16, 1850, in Millard Fillmore Papers (Buffalo Historical Society).

his soft cushioned rocking chair, or his splendid sofa, and he receives you with all the grandeur of an eastern monarch. If he happens not to be in the humor his white servant notifies you that his master does not see company." [76] It must have required a wonderful imagination to see a resemblance between the quarters of a cabinet member and those of an oriental monarch.

Bell stated a fact when he said that he did not resign his post in Tyler's cabinet because of the veto. He approved a bank in principle, but there is no evidence that he had any clearly developed ideas on the subject. It is quite probable that he agreed with Tyler in the President's preference for a bank which had no power to deal in local discounts. That was certainly the view of many of his friends. Yeatman, Woods and Company, in which the Bells were interested, desired no additional competition in local banking circles. It was rumored that the late Thomas Yeatman always kept a spy in the United States Bank. Furthermore, no Whig in Tennessee, not even Bell in the Nashville district where businessmen had been much concerned over the derangement of the currency, had dared make a bank the principal plank in his platform.

As for the pre-existing causes of which Bell spoke, they were mere subterfuge to conceal the real reason for his resignation. His failure to identify these causes, even when challenged in the press, is proof that they did not exist. The truth was, Bell yielded to the personal and political pressure exerted by Henry Clay. As recorded by Ewing shortly before the resignations, Clay sometimes "exacted great sacrifices of his friends and was willing to sacrifice nothing to them." [77] Ewing also correctly observed that Bell was not so strong in his support of Clay as was generally supposed. He was none too eager to sacrifice so much for the ambitions of the Kentuckian.[78] On the other hand, family ties, a long period of

[76] Nashville *Union*, July 19, 1841.
[77] "Diary of Thomas Ewing," *loc. cit.*, 110.   [78] *Ibid.*

personal and political friendship, and regard for the future played their part. Mrs. Bell was said to have remarked that in case the bank should be vetoed her husband must resign.[79] Moreover, Bell, during recent campaigns in Tennessee, had spent his time denouncing the Democrats and singing the praises of the great Kentuckian. Could he now nullify his own words by repudiating Clay's leadership and remaining loyal to a President whose only hope for the future lay in reunion with the Democrats? Certainly, without the support of the Clay group, no Whig could be elected to succeed Tyler. Thus the Secretary of War, inwardly denouncing both Tyler and Clay for their unwillingness to compromise, reluctantly returned to private life and to the practice of law, a profession for which he no longer had a great amount of enthusiasm.[80]

On his way home via Wheeling and the Ohio River, Bell wrote Ewing:

I had an awful time in selling off & sending off my large home full of furniture. Catch me in such a fix again, who can! I will never be the slave of one man again—nor have my interests as well as my feelings so exclusively dependent upon any upstart tyrants [sic] will. But thank God, I am now free,—& I mean to keep so. I begin to feel my new liberty. I feel tolerably free from party shackles also I can tell you—not that I think of turning against the whigs—but I do think of telling them shift for yourselves so far as I am concerned. . . . I have made nearly half my own state my eternal and implacable enemies & many elsewhere—& all for what? To be the victim of self-willed & selfish leaders. I will none of it more.[81]

[79] Cave Johnson to Polk, August 15, 1841, in Polk Papers.
[80] Years later Henry A. Wise recalled that Bell "was opposed to the retirement, and desired that the subject of the bank might be postponed, on condition that in the meantime no hostile movement should be made on the Cabinet; and Mr. Crittenden himself supposed to be most under the influence of Clay, playfully inquired whether he might not in honor remain until the stock of wine he had laid in was consumed; but Mr. Clay was inexorable." Wise, Seven Decades of the Union, 191.
[81] Bell to Ewing, October 26, 1841, in Ewing Papers.

Chapter X

IN THE "BOSOM OF PRIVATE LIFE"

TENNESSEE had but one senator at Washington during the called session of the Twenty-seventh Congress. The term of Alexander Anderson, who was serving out the unexpired term of the late Hugh Lawson White, came to an end on March 4, 1841; and Governor Polk, fearing a charge of extravagance, refused to call the legislature into special session for the purpose of filling the vacancy.

Already the simplicity-minded Whigs, continuing their tactics of 1840, had nominated James C. Jones as Polk's opponent. "Lean Jimmy" Jones, tall and stringy, weighing only 125 pounds, was a master of mimicry, swagger, and general tomfoolery. At times, however, he showed evidence of considerable ability. Polk himself had used sarcasm and mimicry with some success against the slow-witted and ponderous Cannon in 1839. But campaigning against Jones was truly a new experience for the Governor; his sallies backfired and his wit proved stale. Even his friends soon realized that the dignity of the parliamentarian was too apparent through his thin veneer of showmanship. Goaded, misrepresented, and belittled by Jones, Polk became disgusted, angry, and self-conscious. Truly an able debater was being heckled almost to the point of despair. On one occasion, after Polk had completed a very serious speech, Jones arose, pulled a raccoon skin from his pocket, and began stroking the fur. With one eye on Polk and the other on the audience, he queried: "Did you ever see such fine fur?" [1]

[1] Guild, *Old Times in Tennessee,* 159.

One who heard many of his campaign speeches later re-marked of Jones: "He got down in the very life and hearts of people. It was the seasoning and the dressing of the food that he served, together with the delightful service of it, and not the dainty and superior quality of the material, that gave to it its flavor and its piquancy." [2] Polk fought back with sarcasm and ridicule, but with little effect. It was only during the more serious discussions that he showed definite superiority. But judging from the returns of the August election, there must have been few serious discussions; the vote attested the preference for entertainment over dignified de-bate. Polk was defeated; the Whigs won control of the lower house of the legislature; and in the senate the Democratic majority was reduced to one. [3]

When the new legislature convened early in October, 1841, it took its politics very seriously. Two United States senators were to be selected. In addition to the seat vacated by Ander-son, the one held by Alfred O. P. Nicholson, a Polk-appointed successor to the late Felix Grundy, automatically became vacant with the meeting of the legislature. In the past, sena-tors had been selected by the two houses meeting in joint ses-sion. A continuation of this practice would have resulted in the selection of two Whigs. The Democrats of the Senate sud-denly decided that proper procedure required the two houses to act separately, and by a vote of 13 to 12, they declined to go into joint session with the Whig-controlled house.

During the pre-election discussions, the Whigs, demand-ing both seats as a part of the reward for victory, were pretty well agreed on Ephraim H. Foster and Spencer Jarnigan. The Democrats, on the other hand, hoping that their persistence might lead to a compromise and the selection of one from their own ranks, favored Nicholson, Hopkins L. Turney, or Polk. In view of the latter's defeat in the recent race for

[2] Oliver P. Temple, *Notable Men of Tennessee from 1833 to 1875* (New York, 1912), 252.

[3] Eugene I. McCormac, *James K. Polk: A Political Biography* (Berkeley, 1922), 180–88.

governor, many of his friends, unwilling to see him retire to private life, demanded that he be sent to the Senate. As for Polk himself, he undoubtedly wished to be senator, but the possibilities of his being elected were so slim as to cause him to hesitate to take the chance; another defeat might ruin his political future. Accordingly, he remained at Columbia, declining to go to Nashville and work in his own behalf.[4] Still, in spite of Polk's apparent inactivity, there was a fear among some Whigs that his friends would apply sufficient pressure to elect him. John England, a Whig representative from White, had already stated his willingness to support Polk, and it was believed that Craven Sherrill of Bledsoe would sell his vote to Polk's friends for a thousand dollars.[5]

By the time the legislature convened, Bell had resigned from Tyler's cabinet, and many of his friends were demanding that he be sent to the Senate. As in the case of Polk, Bell probably desired a senatorship and felt that he should be rewarded for his recent sacrifice. At the same time, he did not expect to be chosen, and he knew that an attempt to upset Whig plans might result in an irreparable breach within the party and ruin his future prospects. He, therefore, remained in Washington until late in October and made no effort to enter actively into the senatorial contest. Before leaving Washington he confided to Thomas Ewing that he had become "perfectly cool" over the recent happenings in the capital. "We are doomed I take it, for a long time at least, to private relations. I hope you do not regret it—I do not. . . . I go home to attend to my own until such time as I shall see that I can operate to some effect for the good of our cause. Then will I make the usual sacrifice—not until then. I have spent one small fortune—& when there is propriety [?] in it will spend another." [6]

[4] See Powell Moore, "James K. Polk and the 'Immortal Thirteen,'" in East Tennessee Historical Society's *Publications* (Knoxville, 1929–   ), No. 11 (1939), 20–33.
[5] C. W. Nelson to Thomas A. R. Nelson, October 6, 1841, in Nelson Papers.
[6] Bell to Ewing, October 23, 1841, in Ewing Papers.

Meanwhile, the legislature remained in deadlock; the "immortal thirteen" refused to budge. A Democratic proposal to elect Thomas Brown, Whig, and Turney, Democrat, met with little favorable response. The Whig press of Nashville continued to clamor for Foster, for it was he who had been driven from the Senate by Democratic instructions. Bell's arrival in Nashville on November 19 further complicated matters. A shift of considerable Whig support to him made the Democrats even more adamant than ever. Of all the Whigs, Foster and Bell were the most despised and feared; under no condition would the Democrats agree to elect them.

Even prior to Bell's return to Tennessee, prominent Whig newspapers outside of Nashville had become sponsors of his candidacy. In many cases, his name was linked with that of Foster, and his own merits were particularly stressed. East and West Tennessee editors proclaimed their willingness to forgo sectional claims to a senatorship if such was necessary to the election of Bell. "I go for John Bell against any man in the state," announced the fiery "Parson" Brownlow, "[and] . . . he shall have my humble support, as long as I conduct a paper, or as long as he signs his name, John Bell *of Tennessee.*" [7]

All the while, the Whig press of Nashville ignored Bell, scarcely noticing his return to the city. In securing for Allen A. Hall an appointment as chargé d'affaires to Venezuela Bell had deprived himself of his strongest press support in Nashville. Both the *Whig* and the *Republican Banner* had become strong supporters of Foster and their editors feared Bell's appearance on the scene might prove a barrier to Foster's return to the Senate. If only one Whig senator could be elected, Foster must be the one. Goaded by the Democrats and ignored by a formerly favorable press, Bell's embarrassment became so great that self-defense demanded a public statement. The occasion for such a statement was furnished

[7] Jonesborough *Whig,* October 20, 1841; Memphis *Enquirer,* quoted in *ibid.;* Lebanon *Chronicle,* quoted in *ibid.;* Knoxville *Post,* October 6, 1841.

when a few Nashville friends offered him a public dinner. Bell declined the dinner. Friends and neighbors who freely exchanged their views during the course of everyday life, he said, had no need for such formal affairs. "Without pretending indifference to the honors and distinction of public station," he explained, "I can truly say that I return to the bosom of private life without regret—not disqualified, I trust, either for its pursuits or its pleasures by habit contracted in public employment."

As for the senatorships, he insisted that the Whigs should elect those two gentlemen upon whom they had previously agreed. He wished for them "increase of days and honors so long as they shall continue faithful champions of Whig principles and policy." Although conscious that his acquiescence in this decision would probably terminate his political career, he expressed a desire to contribute something toward the moderation of the "rage of disappointed expectants." Many prominent Whigs had assured him, he said, that his exclusion from a senatorial seat, to which many thought him entitled, was not intended as either a censure or an expression of distrust. Since the general public had not been apprised of this fact, he thought justice demanded that it be made known.[8]

A week later a dinner invitation from Lebanon gave Bell another opportunity to speak out. He was again in private life, he wrote, because he had sacrificed the "distinction and emoluments of office" rather than become a "passive instrument of personal designs and projects." In making this decision he felt positive that Whigs of his district would appreciate the motives which prompted his action.[9]

The Whig press of Nashville continued its silence, entirely ignoring Bell's Nashville letter. After the lapse of more than a month his reply to the Lebanon committee was finally printed, without comment, in the *Republican Banner*. The

8 Bell to S. V. D. Stout *et al.*, November 22, 1841, in Knoxville *Post*, December 1, 1841, and in *Niles' National Register*, LXI (1841), 231.
9 *Id.* to Jordan Stokes *et al.*, November 29, 1841, in Nashville *Republican Banner*, December 31, 1841.

Democrats were amused and hopeful. The Old Hero at the Hermitage felt some satisfaction. This was deserved compensation for Bell's service as a "Clay spy upon Mr. Tyler." [10] "Parson" Brownlow was resentful of the treatment Bell was receiving. Since when did Nashville Whigs become so interested in East and West Tennessee, inquired the "Parson," that they hesitated to support Bell for fear of doing an injustice to other sections of the state? He wished to announce that East and West Tennessee knew their own minds and desired to reward John Bell for his efficiency and loyalty.[11] Foster and Jarnigan were eminent, exclaimed the Trenton *Journal,* but Bell was pre-eminent. He was the "originator and the sustainer, aye, the main prop of the Whig party in Tennessee." [12]

Furthermore, Brownlow insisted, all other cabinet members forced from office by that "contemptible fool" Tyler were already being adequately cared for by their political friends. And in Bell's case, the only noticeable opposition came from a Nashville clique which, by threat of the loss of state printing, had won over the press of that city. This was certainly base ingratitude on the part of the *Republican Banner,* charged Brownlow, since that "blessed print" had been "fed and clothed from the pocket of John Bell." Not so many months earlier, it was he who had spent three thousand dollars of his own money to save that paper from bankruptcy.[13]

While Whigs quarreled among themselves, the Democrats rejoiced over the apparent destruction of Foster and over Bell's inability to unite his party. Polk and his friends were particularly pleased with the break between the two Whig leaders. "Thank God and the immortal thirteen," exclaimed J. George Harris, "Ephraim's fiddle is broke." But he cautioned the Democrats to beware of Bell. "The tricks, the in-

[10] Jackson to Lewis, November 18, 1841, in Ford Collection (New York Public Library).
[11] Jonesborough *Whig,* December 29, 1841.
[12] Quoted in *ibid.,* December 22, 1841.
[13] Jonesborough *Whig,* December 29, 1841.

trigues, the appliances, and the serpentine winding" being resorted to by Bell were "numberless and astonishing." Harris feared the effects upon some Democrats and predicted an early proposal of some form of bargain.[14] Another Democratic leader feared that the "immortal thirteen" were playing into Bell's hands; in their attempt to destroy Foster they were making the election of Bell probable.[15] A similar belief was expressed by Polk's brother who was in Nashville collecting information. He suspected that a number of Democrats, in their desire to destroy Foster, were disposed to take up Bell.[16]

Other Democrats expressed an almost opposite view. Turney felt certain that Bell could not get more than a dozen Whig and five Democratic votes. Thus if there was to be any compromising, it must be on either Foster or Brown. James Walker, Polk's brother-in-law, was just as convinced that the Democrats would not take up Bell under any condition. They had no intention of "rewarding apostasy, and whitewashing the traitor who had caused all the trouble in Tennessee politics." It would be better to have no senator at all than to elect Bell.[17]

The Bell proposal, which the Democrats had prophesied, was brought forward early in January, 1842. William Ledbetter, speaking in behalf of the Rutherford and Wilson delegations, offered to support any Democrat for one of the Senate seats if the Democrats would support Bell for the other.[18] Nothing came of the proposal; Polk, the guiding hand in Democratic affairs, refused to have any part in the elevation of Bell. The legislature adjourned without electing, and for the next two years Tennessee had no representation in the United States Senate. The Old Gentleman at the Hermitage found cause to rejoice. "Bell and Foster may now be

14 Harris to Polk, December 13, 15, 1841, in Polk Papers.
15 Catron to Mrs. James K. Polk, n.d., in *ibid.* This letter is bound under January 7, 1840, but probably should be 1842.
16 William Polk to Polk, December 15, 1841, *ibid.*
17 Turney to *id.,* December 26, 1841; Walker to *id.,* January 13, 1842, *ibid.*
18 Laughlin to *id.,* January 10, 1842; J. P. Hardwicke to *id.,* January 9, 1842, *ibid.*

said to be in dry dock," he exclaimed, "examined and condemned as unfit for repairs." Again he pronounced the last words over deceased Whiggery in Tennessee.[19] The Whigs of Memphis met in caucus and adopted a resolution requesting Senators Henry Clay of Kentucky and William C. Preston of South Carolina to look after Tennessee's interests in the Senate.[20]

In addition to blocking the election of senators the "immortal thirteen" rejected Governor Jones's nominations to the board of directors of the Bank of Tennessee. Then when the Whigs charged corruption and demanded an investigation of the institution, the same "thirteen" also blocked this proposal. This was certainly bad politics for one as shrewd as James K. Polk, especially in view of the fact that he planned to run again for governor in 1843. This series of political blunders on the part of the Democrats gave Governor Jones sufficient grounds for a bold denunciation of those who nullified his constructive efforts. A Democratic attempt to divert public attention from state to national issues was only partially successful; the deadlock between governor and legislature was closer to the average voter than the deadlock between President and Congress. In the election which followed, Polk was defeated for a second time and the Whigs also won control of both houses of the legislature.

The new legislature convened on October 2, 1843. A group of Bell's friends addressed a letter to him requesting permission to use his name as a candidate for the Senate. Bell replied that he considered the Whigs of East Tennessee entitled to one of the seats; therefore, it would be necessary for either him or Foster to decline the proposed honor. Since Foster had previously been driven from the Senate, Bell was quite willing that the Whigs should honor Foster with re-election. He wished, therefore, "to relieve the Whigs of the legislature, so far as I am concerned, of all embarrassment

[19] Jackson to Blair, May 23, 1842, in Bassett (ed.), *Correspondence,* VI, 152–53.
[20] Washington *National Intelligencer,* February 13, 1842.

in settling the claims, either personal or sectional, to the vacant stations." [21] Bell having voluntarily eliminated himself, the Whigs then chose Foster and Jarnigan to be United States senators.

In declining the probability of an election to the Senate, Bell stated that he needed additional time to rescue his private business from the disorder which had resulted from a long period of neglect. He also conceded the superior claims of Foster and some candidate from the eastern section. These reasons must have been unsatisfactory to Bell's friends unless they knew more than was published. To decline a senatorship was to decline the highest office in the gift of the people of Tennessee. He certainly could not have been playing for higher stakes. Furthermore, the reputed wealth of his wife could scarcely have become so diminished as to necessitate his retirement from public life. A more satisfactory explanation comes from an intimation that even some of his friends did not favor his selection. "Bell has not achieved the advantage over Foster which we apprehended," wrote Meredith P. Gentry to William B. Campbell, "but on the contrary . . . was compelled to concede the superior claims of Foster. . . . So you will perceive that our 'cock did not walk' to the extent that we feared." [22] Undoubtedly these two prominent Whigs were displeased with Bell's retirement from the cabinet.

Bell was apprised of this attitude. He then withdrew his name rather than wreck the party by widening the breach between himself and Foster or by alienating Whig supporters in East Tennessee. It seems quite probable that he was sincere when he remarked that this meant the end of his public career.

Already, on January 10, 1843, Bell had published an announcement that he and F. Gorin, late of Kentucky, had formed a partnership for the practice of law in Davidson and

---

[21] *Niles' National Register*, LXV (1843), 137–38; Jonesborough *Whig*, October 16, 1843.

[22] Gentry to Campbell, October 17, 1843, in David Campbell Papers.

adjoining counties. Offices had been established in the new Campbell Building on Cherry Street.[23] Having temporarily abandoned politics, he turned his full attention to the practice of his profession and the management of his iron and coal business. Unfriendly persons, however, soon started a rumor that he was none too successful at either and would re-enter politics with the hope of securing either a foreign mission or a seat in the Senate. From the same source there also came a report that Bell had lost heavily from speculation in coal.[24] Beginning in 1842, he had acquired extensive coal lands lying on Tradewater River in Crittenden County, Kentucky. The records of this business venture are too meager to verify or disprove this story of heavy loss from speculation.

The nomination of Henry Clay and James K. Polk as candidates for the presidency in 1844 dispelled any notions Bell may have had of permanent retirement from politics. Any lack of enthusiasm for Clay was more than offset by Bell's inveterate hate for Polk. Four months before the parties made their nominations, the Tennessee Whigs had designated Bell as a candidate for elector-at-large.[25] The Democratic press immediately reopened its heaviest fire on him. How could the former Secretary of War explain his charge of corrupt bargain made against Clay during the campaign of 1827? The mystery of the White campaign of 1836 had at last been brought into clear view, announced the Nashville *Union*. White was not privy to that attempt to destroy the Jackson party; it had all been the work of Clay and Bell. The former wished to remove the venerable Jackson from his path to the presidency; the latter, having been elected Speaker by the opposition, felt the necessity of eliminating Polk, the trusted lieutenant of the Old General. Both Clay and Bell were willing to make use of White's popularity in order to achieve their objectives.

23 Nashville *Whig*, January 10, 1843.
24 Balch to Van Buren, March 4, 1844, in Van Buren Papers.
25 *Niles' National Register*, LXV (1844), 343.

Therefore, Polk's recent nomination could be nothing short of wormwood and gall to his arch rival.[26]

Would Bell please explain his association in Congress with John Quincy Adams and William Slade, New England abolitionists, inquired the same press. It was rumored that Bell had been writing letters to Vermont urging the election of Slade as governor.[27] Bell ignored the charge!

Every conscientious Whig in Tennessee was active during the campaign. This was truly the most severe test to which they had ever been subjected. Having twice defeated Polk in his race for governor, the Whigs could conceive of nothing more humiliating or destructive to their morale than for Tennessee to contribute to his elevation to the presidency. Bell deserted his law practice and spent the major portion of five months in active canvass. His magnanimous gesture in withdrawing from the Senate race in favor of an East Tennessean greatly increased his popularity in that section. Neither had the friends of the late Hugh Lawson White forgotten Bell's loyalty to their leader even in the face of Jackson's threats. Consequently, Bell did much of his campaigning in the mountain counties, the bailiwick of Andrew Johnson who had recently come into prominence as a member of the "immortal thirteen." Assisting Johnson in that area was Hopkins L. Turney, long a Clay-Bell antagonist and at that time a Democratic candidate for elector-at-large.

"This is a grand rally, and all creation are invited to attend it," cried Brownlow in announcing a three-day Whig celebration at Greeneville. "We are authorized to say, that there will be meat and bread, and 'chicken fixin' in abundance for strangers, and every whig house in town will be open for their accommodation. On the second day, a barbecue will come off, worth seeing, and certainly worth eating. Come Whigs of Carter, Johnson, Sullivan, old Washington, Hawkins, and 'all the region round about,' prepare your tent

26 Nashville *Union and American*, June 1, 27, September 4, 1844.
27 *Ibid.*, September 13, 1844.

clothes, wagons, bacon hams, and travelling utensils, and go to Greeneville." John Bell would be there ready to hold forth against any and all "locofocos." [28]

Later in the campaign, Brownlow again burst forth with enthusiasm. He had just returned from Elizabethton where Bell and Turney had entertained the people. As Bell approached the town he had been met by hundreds of horsemen and pedestrians with music and flying banners. The parade had continued through the town to an orchard beyond, where the speaker's platform had been erected. There Bell delivered a speech which, according to Brownlow, "for eloquence, point, efficiency, and animation," had "never been equaled in that gallant country." He denounced Tyler's treaty for the annexation of Texas; advocated a high tariff as a means for raising revenue and for protecting labor and industry; and went on record as favorable to the establishment of a bank, the distribution of the proceeds from the sale of public lands, and internal improvements at Federal expense. Thus he endorsed the Clay program in its entirety. This was apparently the first time he had openly advocated a protective tariff, but the growth of protectionist sentiment in the Nashville area and his own connection with the iron industry made the change understandable.

When Turney accused his opponent of being mortified at the nomination of Polk, Bell replied, in the language of Brownlow, that on the contrary, he was highly pleased; for "after a [Democratic] nomination had been given to a third or fourth rate man, who had never originated any measure or policy, and who had no other merit than that of having been a sort of toady, or button-hole, coat tail man, hanging on to Gen. Jackson, there was now a chance for any of us!" [29]

The Turney-Bell joint speaking arrangements were discontinued in Middle Tennessee. Turney charged Bell with arranging the Whig program so as to preclude Democratic

[28] Quoted in *Niles' National Register*, LXVI (1844), 34.
[29] Jonesborough *Whig*, August 7, 1844.

participation. Bell denied responsibility for the selection of dates and places, but practically admitted that the Democrats had been shut out. He was ready, he declared, to meet Turney or any other Democratic speaker but not under the conditions which had prevailed at certain meetings in East Tennessee where Democratic leaders, fearing the convincing power of Whig orators, had urged their followers to boycott the meetings. Bell wished to speak to Democrats as well as Whigs. In no other place where such a course was pursued, would he allow Turney or any other Democrat any time on the program. In adopting such a policy, he insisted that he did not mean to insinuate Democratic inferiority; he suspected Democratic fear of the superiority of Whig principles and policies.[30]

Never had Bell fought harder; never had his personal feelings been more involved in a political struggle. His was no labor of love for Clay but rather a labor of hate for Polk. "His [Bell's] bosom is hotter than the centre of Aetna when it is pouring forth its burning lava," Alfred Balch reported to Polk. Yet in spite of this Whig heat, Balch predicted that the Democrats would carry Tennessee by a "majority which will astonish our adversaries." "It seems to me," he concluded, "that a victory in Ten. will kill John Bell outright and downright." [31]

The election returns proved Balch a poor prophet. Polk lost his home state by the narrow margin of 113 votes,[32] although he was elected to the presidency. Disappointed by national defeat but unperturbed by Democratic shouting, the Tennessee Whig electors made ready to carry out their constitutional duty. Assembling at Bell's home on Broad Street, they entered four open carriages, and accompanied by fifty other carriages, a band, two uniformed companies, and numerous other pedestrians, they proceeded up to and around the Square and thence to the State House. Bell was

[30] Quoted in *ibid.*, October 9, 1844.
[31] Balch to Polk, September 19, 1844, in Polk Papers.
[32] Stanwood, *History of the Presidency*, I, 223.

made chairman of the group and each elector solemnly cast his votes for Clay and Frelinghuysen. That night a Whig jollification was staged in uptown Nashville, and on the following evening Mrs. Foster complimented the electors with a "splendid supper." The ceremonies came to an end on the next evening when the electors and other prominent Whigs enjoyed a "magnificent entertainment" at the home of the Bells.[33]

For the next three years Bell took little part in politics, devoting his time to his family, the practice of law, and the management of his iron and coal business. In addition to his interest in the Cumberland Iron Works in Stewart County, he continued to expand his activities in Kentucky.[34] He was also interested in railroad construction, especially in the proposal to link Tennessee with the east coast. In 1845 he, Jones, and Foster were among the delegates to the southern railroad convention which met in Memphis. Late in the same year the Tennessee legislature incorporated the Nashville and Chattanooga Railroad Company, and Bell was made a member of a board of commissioners to receive subscriptions for shares, arrange for a survey of the route, and investigate the probable cost of construction.[35]

Little is known of the home life of John and Jane Bell. The fact that she accompanied him to Washington and was active in social affairs there indicates that she was more forceful and influential than the first Mrs. Bell. The Bells were a religious family, although it was late in life before Bell himself became affiliated with the First Presbyterian Church of Nashville. Nevertheless, the strict moral code by which Bell was always governed was a result of his Presbyterian background.

According to family stories, Bell was kind and considerate as a husband, father, and master. The only concrete evidence, however, of his paternal interest and solicitude is a single let-

33 Nelson to Brownlow, n.d., quoted in Jonesborough *Whig,* December 18, 1844.
34 For list of purchases see Polk-Yeatman Papers under date of May 8, 1856.
35 Hamer, *Tennessee,* I, 422, 429-30.

ter to his stepson Henry C. Yeatman. Shortly after Bell's marriage to Mrs. Yeatman he was made legal guardian of her minor children. In 1849, Henry wished to leave college and accompany his older brother Thomas on a trip to Europe. Bell wrote him a fatherly letter strongly advising against such a course. To enjoy to the fullest the cultural advantages which old-world travel had to offer, Bell insisted, Henry must be well grounded in "the elements of many branches of science" and must have acquired other accomplishments expected of a traveler of his means. His deficiency in these requisites would produce a lack of confidence and boldness which frequently caused one to avoid more genteel companions and "seek the society of inferior men—of the idle—& not improbably the wild and dissolute." Furthermore, if Henry left college before preparing himself for a profession, how did he intend to spend the future? "To be merely a gentleman of leisure & pleasure is disgraceful." Besides, did he think that the fortune inherited from his father would be sufficient without being properly invested and managed? Should he trust his money to the management of others, middle age would find him a poor man. Rather than see Henry go to Europe merely to satisfy curiosity and to seek pleasure, Bell preferred that he join the rush to California. In the West there would at least be opportunity for developing one's natural faculties, character, and constitution. But the best course of all would be to remain in college. Change his course of study and even his college if he wished, but continue his mental and cultural development.[36]

Bell was not active in the state campaign of 1845 when Aaron V. Brown defeated Foster for the governorship and the Democrats also won a slight majority in each house of the legislature. His name was put before the legislature, however, when that body took up the selection of a successor to Foster whose senatorial term had expired. The Democratic caucus agreed upon Alfred O. P. Nicholson, a

[36] Bell to Henry Yeatman, May 31, 1849, in Polk-Yeatman Papers.

BEAR SPRING FURNACE, CUMBERLAND IRON WORKS

close friend of President Polk, but there was some dissension within the ranks and a few Democrats refused to be bound by the caucus. For four days the balloting continued with three Democrats—Nicholson, Turney, and William C. Dunlap—and Bell receiving support. There was no chance of electing Bell and the forty-seven Whigs eventually joined with six Democrats and elected Turney. Nicholson received the votes of forty-five Democrats and one Whig. In view of the close friendship between Nicholson and Polk, this was an indirect blow at the President.[37]

Shortly after the close of the senatorial contest Congressman Joseph H. Peyton of Sumner County died. Under the recent rearrangement of congressional districts, that county had been added to the Nashville district. A group of Whigs from Smith County (also a part of the new district) nominated Bell to fill the Peyton vacancy, and the Nashville press opened his campaign. Although Bell was away on a business trip to the east, the Nashville *Whig* claimed to have assurance that he would become a candidate. On the strength of this statement, Washington Barrow, a newly announced candidate, offered to withdraw his candidacy and stated that his opponent Edwin H. Ewing was ready to do likewise.[38] But when Bell returned to Nashville on December 6 he found Barrow and Ewing engaged in a heated contest. In alarm, he rushed a letter to William B. Campbell of Carthage. The Whig candidates were endangering the safety of the district, he insisted. His own return to Congress at that time, even if elected, he explained, "would be next to absolute ruin to my private affairs." Besides, it was too late to get the word around. Therefore, the safe thing to do was to put full strength behind Ewing.[39] Bell then announced through the *Whig* that he did not wish to return to Congress, and urged the support of Ewing.[40]

37 Hamer, *Tennessee*, I, 312; Tennessee *House Journal*, 1845, pp. 79 96.
38 Nashville *Whig*, November 27, 1845.
39 Bell to Campbell, December 8, 1845, in David Campbell Papers.
40 Nashville *Whig*, December 9, 1845.

Chapter XI

"STRANGLE THIS HYDRA"

ON March 26, 1847, the Tennessee Whigs assembled in convention to name a candidate for governor. Directly following this revival of Whig enthusiasm the *Republican Banner* proposed Bell as a candidate for the state house of representatives. This announcement was correctly considered a forewarning of the former Secretary of War's decision to emerge from retirement. No active campaign was necessary; those who had sent him to Congress for seven consecutive terms supported his candidacy for the legislature.

Many East Tennesseans expressed pleasure over Bell's election. He was more than just a resident of Nashville, commented the Knoxville *Tribune,* he was "John Bell of Tennessee." Such a man, the editor thought, could be depended upon to help his fellow citizens in their fight for such legislation as would tend to bring them progress and prosperity.[1] It must have been Bell's past record as an advocate of internal improvements that so endeared him to East Tennessee at this time. Many West Tennesseans, on the other hand, did not share this enthusiasm. The Memphis *Daily Appeal* charged that Bell's election was a part of a plan to plunge the state further into debt through a decision of the legislature to invest money in "the utopian scheme of constructing the Nashville and Chattanooga Rail Road." Such a scheme would greatly benefit Nashville property holders provided they could "gull the people of Tennessee into a debt to construct

[1] Quoted in Jonesborough *Whig,* May 5, 1847.

it." Already, the major portion of the state debt, the editor insisted, was for improvements around Nashville.[2]

Owing to a serious illness in his family, Bell was absent when the legislature convened on October 4, 1847. Nevertheless, the Whig caucus unanimously requested him to accept a nomination for the speakership of the house. Since the Whigs were in a majority, acceptance of such a nomination would have been tantamount to election. Bell declined the honor, however, with the explanation that he preferred to be "tongue-loose" upon the floor.[3] He was active during the early days of the session, but he was ever mindful of the important political service to be performed by that body—the selection of a United States senator.

Senator Spencer Jarnigan had irritated many of his fellow Whigs in Tennessee by his vote in favor of the Walker tariff of 1846 [4] and was apparently scheduled for retirement to private life. Almost a month before the legislature convened, Brownlow, editor of the Jonesborough *Whig,* announced his support of Bell as a successor to Jarnigan. Tennessee had never fittingly honored this great son, explained Brownlow; therefore, East Tennessee was willing to relinquish its claim on the senatorship in favor of "John Bell of Tennessee." [5] Two weeks later the "Parson" reported that on a tour of five eastern counties he had found the Whigs "to a man" for Bell. All favored the "great Internal Improvement man," "the *founder* of their party in the State." [6] Brownlow himself advocated Bell's selection because of his great talents, his prominence throughout the nation, and his unrewarded service to the party.[7]

It is doubtful whether Brownlow correctly represented the

[2] Memphis *Daily Appeal,* September 23, 1847. A movement was on foot to have the legislature vote to assume a deficit of $500,000 in the construction cost of this railroad.

[3] Memphis *Daily Eagle,* October 8, 1847.

[4] For a good description of Jarnigan's action, see Daniel Webster to Fletcher Webster, July 29, 1846, in Van Tyne (ed.), *Letters of Daniel Webster,* 337–39.

[5] Jonesborough *Whig,* September 8, 1847.

[6] *Ibid.,* September 22, 1847.   [7] *Ibid.,* October 13, 1847.

opinion of a majority of the East Tennessee Whigs. There was no great hostility to Bell in that section, but many Whigs urged that the senatorship should go to an easterner. A failure to agree on a single candidate, however, resulted in the nomination of several East Tennessee Whigs.

In the western section of the state there had been an even earlier boom for Bell. In December, 1846, the editor of the Memphis *Daily Eagle* had announced to his readers: "There are now in the U.S. Senate three of Gen. Harrison's cabinet —Webster, Crittenden, Badger. A *fourth* of them *should* be there—we mean John Bell." [8] Again, as in the case of Brownlow, it is doubtful whether the editor represented the wishes of a majority of the Whigs of his region; sectional pride demanded that a Western man be sent to the Senate. There was also a similar pride in Middle Tennessee where sentiment was divided among Bell, Foster, and Gustavus A. Henry. Yet even if the mid-state Whigs united on one candidate, his selection was impossible without assistance from one of the other sections.

On October 28 the two houses of the legislature assembled in joint session for the purpose of selecting a senator. Robertson Topp of the western section led on the first ballot and was closely followed by John Netherland and William B. Reese of the eastern division. The mid-state Whigs were not yet ready to show their hands; therefore, they widely scattered their votes and Bell received only seven. Five ballots were taken during the day, and when the legislature adjourned, the vote stood: Topp 19, Netherland 16, Reese 15, and Bell 3. [9]

For several weeks the deadlock remained unbroken. On the twenty-first ballot the name of Christopher H. Williams, another West Tennessean, was presented, and he received 34 votes. Bell had now fallen to one. The deadlock continued, and Williams' name was withdrawn following the twenty-

8 Memphis *Daily Eagle,* December 10, 1846.
9 Tennessee *Senate Journal,* 1847, pp. 140–46.

third ballot. There was then a rush to Bell, carrying his total
up to 25 on the twenty-fourth ballot, while Netherland stood
at 26 and Topp fell to 4. The struggle appeared to have resolved itself into a race between Bell and Netherland; but on
the twenty-ninth ballot, Netherland's support shifted to James
A. Whitesides, another East Tennessean, and by the thirty-
second, Whitesides had a total of 34 votes. On the following
ballot most of Whitesides' votes shifted to Reese, carrying his
total to 25, while Bell, who had once gone as high as 30, had
now also fallen to 25.

During this shifting and maneuvering, according to Brownlow, the several candidates had been on the scene "with collars
open, sleeves rolled up, and wine and liquor, in abundance,
inviting supporters from all ranks in politics, and bowing,
scraping, and smiling to every man they met—even to Locofocos." [10] Although not an avowed candidate, former Governor
James C. Jones of Memphis made his appearance in Nashville
and remained several days. Some of Bell's friends reported
that Jones was spending his time advising against the selection
of a Middle Tennessee man; and Bell suspected that the
former Governor himself had some hope that his own name
might be used to break the deadlock. Bell remarked privately
that Jones "should have been either with his sick family or
soliciting subscriptions for the railroad for which he is to be so
richly paid." [11] Foster was also on the scene. He had little
chance of being chosen, but he quietly worked against the
selection of Bell. Henry too was present but took no part in
the maneuvering; however, Bell suspected him of a secret
desire to see an East or West Tennessee man chosen so that
"Middle Tenn. including himself might have a chance . . .
4 years hence." [12]

In the meantime, the public had begun to complain about
the waste of time and money. The Franklin *Weekly Review*

[10] Jonesborough *Whig*, December 1, 1847.
[11] Bell to William B. Campbell, December 23, 1847, in David Campbell
Papers. Jones had been appointed financial agent for the Nashville and Chattanooga Railroad.   [12] *Ibid.*

suggested that the way to put an end to this troublesome and expensive sectional quarrel was to elect John Bell, a man who had "a character as broad as the whole State, who would faithfully represent it in all its parts." [13] From East Tennessee, Brownlow, through the columns of his *Whig*, continued his vigorous support of Bell. And from the western section, the editor of the Memphis *Weekly American Eagle*, who had joined the movement for a West Tennessee man, announced that he had been overwhelmed with demands that he change his views and advocate the selection of Bell. The editor felt positive that four fifths of the people in Middle and West Tennessee now favored the election of Bell.[14]

The sectional legislators were reluctant to give up the struggle. In vain did West Tennessee again present the name of Williams; his vote never exceeded 36. Balloting continued through the day on November 22, and as the lamps were lighted in the capitol, legislators refused to support a motion to adjourn. Spectators, sensing a determination on the part of the legislators to terminate the contest, postponed their supper and remained on watch. On the forty-eighth ballot Bell received 51 votes and was declared elected.[15] The arguments and promises used by Bell in securing the election are not recorded. Neither do we know what position he took on national issues. The Nashville *Union* later claimed that he promised to support the Mexican War, but this same press failed to mention such a promise during the campaign. Since Bell was elected by a Whig legislature it is not likely that a statement on war policy was required.

"As is often the case in less important matters," commented the Democratic Nashville *Union*, "Middle Tennessee, by prudence and caution, secured the prize, when the other sections had wasted their strength in quarreling for it." [16] Bell privately expressed the opinion that, considering the opposi-

[13] Quoted in Jonesborough *Whig*, November 17, 1847.
[14] Memphis *Weekly American Eagle*, October 27, 1847.
[15] Tennessee *Senate Journal*, 1847, p. 291; *House Journal*, 1847, p. 449; Memphis *Daily Eagle*, November 27, 1847.
[16] Nashville *Union*, November 24, 1847.

tion encountered, his selection was "the most singular result in the history of elections." [17] Far in the eastern section of the state, Brownlow received the election news with delight. He exclaimed that Tennessee had chosen a man "of commanding appearance the soul of chivalry—bold, brave, and dignified —affable in his manners—and of great energy and perseverance." He suspected that President James K. Polk would not be pleased with this selection.[18] Not all East Tennessee Whigs joined Brownlow in his enthusiasm; many were unable immediately to forget their disappointment. A small public meeting at Knoxville adopted resolutions disapproving of the selection made by the legislature. The Knoxville press admitted Bell's merits, but continued to insist that an Eastern man should have been chosen.[19] Even in Middle Tennessee there was some dissatisfaction among the Whigs. On the day following the election, Boyd McNairy wrote to John J. Crittenden: "John Bell is elected our Senator, beware of him. . . . Never was a man elected under such circumstances. . . . He has broken down the Whig party in Tennessee—Old Jackson told the truth about him, *for Self* he would do any thing. . . . I repeat watch *John Bell* by day & by night, if the Lady will let you do it by night." [20] Unfortunately, McNairy failed to give details on the way in which Bell had broken down his party.

Although the Democrats applauded the dissension within the ranks of the opposition, they generally agreed that the foremost Whig had been chosen. If Democrats must battle Whigs, announced the Columbia *Beacon,* "we had rather combat with the Eagle than bandy blows with the pigmy sparrow." [21] A veteran Tennessee Democrat then residing in Washington observed that "the *Folks* hereabouts of the Whig

[17] Bell to William B. Campbell, December 23, 1847, in David Campbell Papers.

[18] Jonesborough *Whig,* December 1, 1847.

[19] *Politician and Weekly Nashville Whig,* December 3, 10, 1847; John F. Henry to Whigs of East Tennessee, in Nashville *Whig,* January 6, 1848.

[20] McNairy to Crittenden, November 23, 1847, in Crittenden Papers.

[21] Columbia *Beacon,* quoted in *Politician and Weekly Nashville Whig,* December 3, 1847

family were for Foster but the upper crust prefer Bell." It was his own opinion that Bell had "native and acquired talent & dignity of character beyond them all." [22]

The news of Bell's election elicited favorable comments from the Whig leaders throughout the nation. "As a man, he is true and able; as a Whig, he is faithful and fearless," declared the New York *Tribune*. "The Whigs of the nation will hail this event with joy," prophesied the Cincinnati *Chronicle*. The Baltimore *Patriot* likewise thought the election of Bell would produce much rejoicing within the Whig camp. [23]

A serious illness detained Bell at his home for several days following his election to the Senate. He was unable to appear in person before the legislature and thank the members for the honor bestowed upon him. He recovered sufficiently, however, to take his seat in the Senate on December 13. Even before Bell's arrival in Washington there was some hope within Administration circles that he might be inclined to support the President's policies. At least it was thought advisable to be courteous to him. Daniel Graham, a close friend of Polk, expressed the hope that the intense partisanship which had characterized Bell's earlier congressional career had softened with the passing of years. Graham advised Thomas Ritchie, editor of the Washington *Union,* "to forbear any rasping or irritating remarks personally or politically toward Mr. Bell, & let him be judged by the fruits which he may bear in the future." [24] Such an attitude on the part of leading Democrats was evidence that Bell had not yet committed himself.

At the time Bell took his seat in the Senate, President Polk was nearing the close of his third year in office. The United States was in the midst of the war with Mexico. Following the annexation of Texas during the closing days of the Tyler Administration, war became inevitable when the United

[22] Daniel Graham to Nicholson, December 3, 1847, in Alfred O. P. Nicholson Papers (New York Historical Society).
[23] Quoted in *Politician and Weekly Nashville Whig,* December 3, 1847.
[24] Graham to Nicholson, December 3, 1847, in Nicholson Papers.

States insisted upon the Rio Grande River as the boundary between Texas and Mexico. Antislavery men in general had opposed annexation and were joined by a considerable number of proslavery Whigs who, instead of being expansionists, feared the national disturbance which was certain to accompany further acquisition of territory. Although the Whig generals, Winfield Scott and Zachary Taylor, won brilliant victories, the Mexican government refused to make peace on the terms offered. Whig congressmen, continuing their opposition to the whole Mexican affair, were reluctant to vote the men and money necessary to a more vigorous prosecution of the war.

Bell opposed offensive war against Mexico. Producer of coal and iron, friend of business and financial interests, speculator in undeveloped lands, and advocate of railroads and other internal improvements, he dreaded the effects of needless controversy. Though the owner of a large number of slaves, which he worked in his mines and rolling mill, he could see no essential connection between the perpetuation of slavery and the acquisition of territory in which slavery could never be profitable. What support the Administration could expect from the new Senator was a matter for speculation. He and Polk had not been on speaking terms since the controversy over the speakership in 1834.

On December 27, 1847, Daniel Saffrons of Gallatin, Tennessee, called at the White House. He had come, he said, in the hope of arranging a renewal of social intercourse between the President and the newly elected Senator from Tennessee. Saffrons explained that he had talked with Bell and had found him willing to support the Administration policies relative to the war and the tariff. He had suggested that Bell should call on Polk at an early date, and should the Senator decide to do so, he hoped the President would extend an invitation to dinner, at which both Whigs and Democrats would be guests. According to Polk's account, he gave assurance of a courteous and kind reception in case Bell did him the honor of calling.

He wished Saffrons to understand that, although he and Bell had long been bitter political antagonists in their home state, he harbored no ill feeling toward the Senator, and was willing to forget unpleasant memories.[25] With this assurance, Saffrons departed.

Two days later he was again at the White House. He had conferred with Bell again and had been reassured of the Senator's intention to support the Administration's war and tariff policies. In fact, Saffrons was confident that Bell would vote for any amount of money and any number of men that the President thought necessary to victory in Mexico. The President again stated his willingness to meet the Senator halfway. After Saffrons had departed, Polk confided to his diary a suspicion that both of Saffrons' visits had been made at the instance of Bell.[26]

Saffrons reported to Bell immediately after the conference at the White House. By that time Bell had either changed his mind or he had been misrepresented by Saffrons. At any rate, the Senator became uneasy from fear that Saffrons had pledged him to go all out in support of the Administration. Bell then hastened to call on Hopkins L. Turney, the Democratic Senator from Tennessee, and to request that he go to Polk and correct any wrong impressions for which Saffrons might have been responsible. Turney went to the White House that evening and reassured Polk of Bell's desire for better relations; but he also told the President that Bell wished it clearly understood that he intended to act with the Whig party.[27]

On the morning of January 4, 1848, Bell made a personal appearance at the President's mansion. According to Polk's account of the visit, the Senator, though apparently embarrassed at first, was soon put at ease by the manner of the President. Polk assured Bell that he was willing to forget the past and ready to renew the friendly relations of earlier years. Bell

25 Milo M. Quaife (ed.), *The Diary of James K. Polk During His Presidency, 1845 to 1849* (Chicago, 1910), III, 258–60.
26 *Ibid.*, 264.   27 *Ibid.*, 264–65.

expressed the same desire and stressed the fact that after the two should retire from public life they would live as neighbors in Nashville; [28] he preferred their neighborly relations to be pleasant. The two then engaged in a half-hour discussion of topics of general interest. As Bell was preparing to take his leave, Polk suggested that Mrs. Polk would be pleased to see Mrs. Bell. Bell's reply to this suggestion gave the President the impression that Mrs. Bell was a bit reluctant but would call at an early date. Polk recorded in his diary: "I suppose the difficulty [with Mrs. Bell] consisted in the pride which ladies sometimes feel, which makes them reluctant to yield to each other, and the fact that the established etiquette of the Presidential office required the first call from Mrs. Bell." [29] The supposition was correct; Mrs. Bell was a very proud lady. The visit was probably never made.

These conferences had taken place after President Polk's third annual message had been presented to Congress on December 7, 1847. The greater portion of the message was devoted to the Administration's Mexican policy. Following a brief survey of the progress of the United States armies, Polk reaffirmed his desire for an honorable peace at the earliest possible date. Such a desire, he explained, had prompted him to send a peace commissioner to accompany General Scott's army in its invasion of Mexico. Polk stated that he considered territorial indemnity the only type of indemnity that could be exacted from Mexico, for that country's inability to make payments in money was well-known. Since the territory demanded was more extensive than might reasonably be required as indemnity, Polk said that he was willing to offer "such additional pecuniary consideration as was deemed reasonable." In view of the fact that Mexico had refused to make peace on reasonable terms, the President urged that "we

[28] Polk had recently purchased the old home of the late Senator Felix Grundy, located on the site of the present Polk Apartments at the corner of Seventh Avenue and Union Street. Bell lived only a few blocks away on Broad Street.

[29] Quaife (ed.), *Diary of James K. Polk*, III, 284–85.

should press forward our military operations and levy such military contributions on the enemy as may, as far as practicable, defray the future expenses of the war." And "taking the full measure of indemnity into our hands," the United States should enforce such terms of peace as honor might demand.[30]

In support of the President's desire for a complete victory over Mexico, Lewis Cass, from the Senate Committee on Military Affairs, presented a bill providing for the raising of additional troops.[31] On February 2, 1848, Bell began a two-day speech in opposition to this bill. The people in his home state, he explained, had strongly supported the war in spite of the questionable motives back of its origin; however, since the public had read the President's recent message, there had been some change in opinion. Bell said that he would not take the time to inquire into the President's responsibility for the war or whether or not it could have been avoided, although he thought "it might and should." He had no sympathy for Mexico and was not inclined to hold that nation blameless, but he could understand how Mexico might feel that the annexation of Texas "was not a very neighborly act on our part." Regardless of Mexican guilt, however, the punishment had been sufficient. We as conquerors should make no demands the compliance with which would prove "dishonorable or ruinous to Mexico."

In Bell's opinion, the evils which would result from a further prosecution of the war would prove greater than could ever be compensated by territorial acquisition. Among those people who shared this opinion, he asserted, could be found citizens from all sections of the Union, some of whom had "given freely of their blood and treasure." "I verily believe," Bell exclaimed, "that two-thirds of the people of this country are in heart opposed to the policy of this war, . . . and but for the tyranny of party, the force of party obligation, and the power of Executive influence, could they be allowed

30 Richardson (ed.), *Messages and Papers*, VI, 2382 ff.
31 *Cong. Globe,* 30 Cong., 1 Sess., 63.

to speak—satiated with the glory already acquired, the honor of the country already amply vindicated—they would strangle this hydra to-day." In the interest of harmony and the welfare of the Union, these people were appealing to the President to sacrifice national and personal glory. If their appeal should be denied, Bell warned that there would surely come a day of reckoning for those who were responsible for the needless shedding of blood.

If the Administration really desired peace on the basis of the cession of New Mexico and California, inquired Bell, then why not order the American armies to fall back to the borders of those provinces? Such a withdrawal would greatly reduce both bloodshed and expenditures. Casting his eyes in the direction of Senator Henry S. Foote of Mississippi, a Polk supporter, Bell inquired whether other territory was desired. Foote replied that he would be satisfied with New Mexico and California, but that he doubted whether the existing Mexican government could assure respect for a treaty made on that basis. Then what assurance would be demanded, asked Bell, looking in the direction of Lewis Cass, chairman of the military affairs committee. Cass was not inclined to reply until he knew where Bell was leading. A few moments later he did interrupt to say that "security for the future" was the only assurance demanded. Bell then stated that he supposed the President intended to continue the war until a government capable of guaranteeing security should make its appearance.[32]

Before the Senate adjourned for the day, Cass explained that in his opinion future security required that the United States should take Mexican territory as far as the Sierra Madre. That range with its few passes would furnish the necessary natural barrier. Since Mexico had rejected the American peace terms, Cass could see no alternative but "to push our operations . . . till an honorable peace is obtained."[33]

On the following day Bell again took up the fight. If Ameri-

[32] *Ibid.,* Appendix, 189–92.   [33] *Ibid.,* 194.

can troops were to occupy Mexican territory until a suitable government was organized in that country, he prophesied that thousands of "youthful, ardent, and enterprising" Americans would rush into the occupied areas for the purpose of becoming proprietors of farms, mines, and industries. Once a number of those citizens were established on Mexican soil, the troops could not be removed, leaving them without protection. Thus necessity would compel the United States to hold permanent sovereignty over all occupied territory. Bell asserted that permanent occupation would be the closing act of the drama and the consummation of the President's policy as expressed in his message.

In case the Administration's policy should be successful and the United States should acquire Mexico, Bell wished to know what would be done with it. Would it be divided into states? If so, he thought that would mean the addition of at least twenty new states in which republican government must be guaranteed among millions of Indians and half-breeds. As many as eighty representatives and forty senators would be added to Congress. Then, becoming sarcastic, Bell congratulated the Senate upon the prospect of the addition of representatives of mixed races. He felt certain that the "novelty of their complexion" would give "new interest and attraction."

Bell prophesied that Europe would look on "in quiet complacency" while the United States, by extravagant conquest, placed a permanent drain on its own resources and weakened itself as a military power. The policy of the United States toward the Spanish Americans, Bell averred, seemed to be to protect them against all other powers, while at the same time reserving the privilege "to despoil them at discretion." "You will have no partners in the work of territorial spoliation; you claim a monopoly of the spoil and plunder of America."

Bell explained that he realized that anyone who spoke of controlling the spoils system would be branded as belonging to a bygone period, yet he could not refrain from making some observations relative to the effects on the patronage which would result from the conquest of Mexico. There would be the appointment of governors, judges, and many minor officials. "John Bull need not swell himself out, and vaunt himself so lustily any longer. We, too, shall have our Indies; our subject millions; our rich provincial governments; our large standing army." We, too, would witness "generals returning from distant provinces laden with wealth and honors, making their triumphant progress through the country, and suing for the consulship." What a spectacle would be witnessed on levee occasions at the imperial palace, the White House; "what a glitter of epaulets; what a clatter of dangling swords, what a waving and doffing of red and white plumes!" And what a scene when the new governors should assemble at the palace "to kiss hands" before leaving for their assignments!

Bell also expressed fear of the effects of conquest upon the American system of government. He explained that already the competition for the presidency was so great that every election threatened to destroy our system. What would be the condition when the President of a far-flung empire should command an army of fifty thousand soldiers plus innumerable civil officials? We might continue to be republican in name, but Bell wished to warn that the title of republic "long survived the crushed liberties of the people of Rome."

"Sir, if any should now desire to know my poor opinion upon the proper mode of terminating this war, I say to them, make the best treaty with any existing Government you can. If you must have the territories of New Mexico and California, get a cession of them; if you cannot do that, come back to the Rio Grande—to the boundary you claim title to, and thus save your honor.

"My advice is, Stop the War! Flee the country as you would a city doomed to destruction by fire from Heaven!" [34]

No doubt the war party, both inside and outside of Congress, felt the sting of Bell's thrusts. The Administration press was quick to denounce him as a deserter from a cause which

[34] *Ibid.*, 197–99.

he had promised to support. Bell "has played the demagogue after the tallest model," announced the Nashville *Union*. It was charged that, during his campaign for election to the Senate, he had promised to support the war and had condemned Clay's Lexington manifesto. It was further claimed that, soon after arriving in Washington, Bell had assured the President of his support. One editor, however, expressed a belief that he had the proper explanation for Bell's shift. When the Senator was making such promises he was looking to General Zachary Taylor as the Whig candidate for the presidency in 1848 and knew that the General would favor extensive territorial indemnity; but when Bell arrived in Washington and found Clay the most likely candidate, he soon deserted both Taylor and indemnity and placed himself upon the Clay platform.[35] This was almost the reverse of the truth.

On the other side, Thomas Corwin, commenting on the second portion of Bell's speech, declared that his "exordium and preliminaries were perfectly Delphic." [36] And several Whig editors expressed great satisfaction over what they termed Administration contortions. One reporter pronounced Bell's speech "a glorious harangue." Another thought it transcended anything he had heard upon the war. "He has *wilted* the laurels of all who have preceded him," declared a third. One correspondent gave a careful description of Bell's manner as well as his speech: "The cast of Mr. Bell's mind is eminently philosophic and statesman like—his views are necessarily broad, bold and comprehensive, and he announces them with a purity of language and style that would do credit to a state paper. Courtesy, and parliamentary dignity, mark every action and word—add to this fluency of diction, animation, a well modulated voice, singular powers of combination and method, and you have an imperfect idea of the elements

[35] Nashville *Union*, February 12, 23, 29, March 3, 1848; Memphis *Daily Appeal*, March 9, 1848.

[36] Thomas Corwin to James A. Pearce, February 4, 1848, in *Maryland Historical Magazine*, XVIII (1923), 342.

that make up one who is enrolled in the honored calendar of American statesmen." [37]

It so happened that on February 2, the day Bell began his two-day denunciation of the Administration's war policy, the Mexican government signed the treaty at Guadalupe Hidalgo, ceding New Mexico and California to the United States. When the treaty came before the Senate for ratification Bell voted in the affirmative. He later explained that he did so "under a solemn feeling of responsibility and conviction that if the war went on, we would be compelled to take all Mexico and incorporate it into this confederacy." Such a step would be ruinous, he said, and "Mexico would be the grave of our liberties." He pronounced the acquisition of New Mexico and California a curse, and prophesied that the Wilmot Proviso would be applied. Thus, in supporting the treaty, he contended that he voted for the lesser of two evils. He preferred annexing New Mexico and California to continuing the war and eventually annexing all of Mexico.[38]

The famous Wilmot Proviso had injected the question of slavery extension into the discussion of territorial adjustment several months before the signing of the treaty with Mexico, and though it was never accepted by the Senate, it remained as a threat to the proslavery cause. The actual acquisition of New Mexico and California increased the intensity of the slavery struggle. President Polk was an expansionist, but he gave no evidence of a special desire to see slavery extended into the newly acquired territory.[39] He was soon convinced that the pro- and antislavery extremists would never be able to agree on the question of slavery in the territories of New Mexico and California. He did not believe there would ever be any extensive importation of slaves into those territories, yet his proslavery sympathies caused him to doubt the advis-

[37] Nashville *Republican Banner*, February 16, 1848, quoting New York *Journal of Commerce*, New York *Mirror*, and Philadelphia *Daily News*; Philadelphia *North American and United States Gazette*, February 5, 1848.
[38] Statement in Nashville *Republican Banner*, September 29, 1848.
[39] McCormac, *James K. Polk*, 616 ff.

ability of congressional restriction on slavery south of 36 degrees, 30 minutes. Such an attempt to restrict, he feared would endanger the Union.[40] He stated definitely that he would accept either an extension of the Missouri Compromise line or a proposition to allow the people of the territories to decide the question for themselves.[41]

As weeks passed and Congress still took no action relative to governments for the territories, Polk became anxious lest the rapidly increasing population of California should cause that region to take matters into its own hands to the extent of setting up an independent government. He was beginning to suspect that the friends of President-elect Zachary Taylor would welcome such action since it would relieve the General of embarrassment over the Wilmot Proviso.[42] It must have been by this line of reasoning that Polk reached the decision to recommend the admission of California as a state. Accordingly, he persuaded Stephen A. Douglas to sponsor a bill admitting California and providing a territorial government for New Mexico. Douglas sought to have his bill sent to the Committee on Territories, of which he was chairman, but Andrew P. Butler of South Carolina objected and the bill went to the Judiciary Committee. This committee made an adverse report and presented a majority resolution calling for the creation of territorial governments for New Mexico and California.[43]

It was late in January, 1849, when the California bill was brought before the Senate. Slightly more than a month remained in the session. The opposition sought to delay action by urging that the remainder of the session be spent in the passage of the civil and diplomatic appropriation bill. But a group of proslavery men and their "doughface" friends refused to be sidetracked. When the appropriation bill was called up in the Senate committee of the whole on February

40 Richardson (ed.), *Messages and Papers,* VI, 2458.
41 *Ibid.,* 2491–92.
42 Quaife (ed.), *Diary of James K. Polk,* IV, 231–33.
43 *Cong. Globe,* 30 Cong., 2 Sess., 190–92.

22, Isaac P. Walker of Wisconsin proposed a rider which called for the application of the Constitution and all applicable United States laws to the territories of New Mexico and California.[44] This action would have given to the territories the benefits of law and order and yet evaded the question of slavery.

For once in recent years, John Bell at least partially agreed with James K. Polk. Bell wished to see California admitted to the Union, but showed no interest in the President's plan for a territorial government for New Mexico. The California case was urgent; New Mexico could wait. Accordingly, Bell moved to alter Walter's amendment so as to provide for the admission of California as a state. Butler protested that the proposal was out of order but the Chair sustained Bell. John P. Hale of New Hampshire then appealed to the Senate to override the decision of the Chair. Butler, not wishing to see the controversy carried further, sought to withdraw his question of order, but John M. Berrien of Georgia declared such a withdrawal to be out of order. John C. Calhoun denounced Bell's proposal as incongruous with the original proposition. "I appeal to the Senate," he shouted, "that if there ever was a case of incongruity, this is one." "I call the Senator to order," cried Bell, who explained that it was not the question of incongruity but the appeal from the decision of the Chair which was before the Senate. But the question of incongruity was somewhere laid down in Jefferson's *Manual,* insisted Calhoun. Bell retorted that he knew the rules and demanded that his proposition be disposed of by a vote of the Senate.[45] This verbal battle so confused Samuel S. Phelps of Vermont that he confessed he did not "understand the question before the Senate." [46]

Bell offered to withdraw his amendment if the Senate would assure him that the California bill would be taken up as soon as the general appropriation bill was passed. Such assurance not being received, he explained that his amendment was

44 *Ibid.,* 561.   45 *Ibid.,* 561–62.   46 *Ibid.,* 562.

offered in order that he might have an opportunity to speak.[47] He then launched an attack upon the recent report made by the Judiciary Committee. The report had stated that Congress possessed no power to create a state, such an act being left to the people of the territory from which the state was to be carved. Bell took the opposite view, contending that Congress alone could create a state. In support of its position, the committee had pointed out that it had been the custom in all cases where states were carved from territory ceded by other states or by foreign countries to require a period of territorial government before admission as states. This Bell denied. He pointed to the case of Kentucky which, he maintained, was ceded to the Federal government by Virginia and admitted as a state without having gone through a territorial stage. If this could be done in the case of Kentucky, then why not in the case of California which was certainly more urgent. In view of the rapid increase in population in California, Bell prophesied that, should the government fail to provide some kind of restraint within the next eighteen months, the territory would be "overrun with hordes of reckless adventurers, rendering it almost a moral impossibility that a constitution could be formed and maintained." [48]

Berrien denounced Bell's argument as "suicidal." Were senators and the American people as a whole willing to share their birthright with the people such as those described by the Senator from Tennessee? Certainly such people must be restrained, but why could it not be done by a territorial government rather than by admitting them into the Union? The Judiciary Committee was right. Such people should be kept "in a state of pupilage until they shall be better qualified to enjoy the privileges of American citizens and to become members of this Union." Furthermore, Berrien insisted, Congress could not make those people into a state even if it chose to do so. The Constitution conferred upon Congress the power to admit states but no power to create any. The framers inten-

47 *Ibid.*, 565–66.   48 *Ibid.*, Appendix, 253–54.

tionally omitted such a grant, he believed, in obedience to "the principles of popular sovereignty . . . which required that those who are to constitute the State are alone competent to organize it." [49]

Bell's amendment was defeated 99 to 4, Augustus C. Dodge of Iowa, Solomon W. Downs of Louisiana, and Douglas of Illinois voting with Bell in the affirmative. Walker's amendment was accepted by the committee of the whole, but was later stricken from the bill. Thus the Thirtieth Congress and the Polk Administration came to an end, leaving New Mexico and California without organized governments. The Memphis *Eagle* probably expressed the dominant sentiment in the South when it remarked: "We regret sincerely that no government was provided for so important a territory [California] but our regret is modified by the satisfaction we feel in remembering that the opportunity to fasten an insult upon the South was not ungenerously seized upon." [50]

In the meantime, the Whigs had elected Zachary Taylor President. Bell was among the original Taylor men in Tennessee. He realized that, even though many Whigs had opposed the war with Mexico, there was no reason why his party should not capitalize on the popularity of one of the successful Whig generals. As early as May 8, 1847, he publicly announced his hearty support of Taylor for President.[51] Clay's friends in Tennessee became alarmed. Boyd McNairy notified John J. Crittenden that Bell was against their friend Clay. Bell's manipulations in his recent fight for a seat in the Senate, plus his support of Taylor, McNairy contended, had greatly weakened the Whig party in Tennessee.[52] There were some, at least among the Democrats, who suspected that in spite of Bell's public statement in favor of Taylor, his personal predilections were for Scott. Daniel Graham, who had known Bell since boyhood, prophesied that before Bell joined in any political battle over the presidency he would "examine the outworks with the

[49] *Ibid.*   [50] Memphis *Daily Eagle,* March 12, 1849.
[51] *Ibid.,* May 20, 1847.
[52] McNairy to Crittenden, November 23, 1847, in Crittenden Papers.

eye of an Engineer." Graham had observed that "since the days of Vauxhall . . . [Bell] has no palate nor brain for *'running his head against a bomb proof battery.'* " [53]

McNairy and Graham were correct in their belief that Bell would not support Clay. Soon after taking his seat in the Senate, Bell wrote William B. Campbell that he had found Clay's political strength to be even weaker than was expected. The practical politicians within the Whig party were more interested in availability than "personal performance." Clay had considerable strength among the Quakers and other anti-war groups but they were in a minority. From what Bell could learn, Northern Whig leaders preferred General Scott; however, General Taylor was the greater favorite in the South and with the masses in the North.[54]

Four months later Bell again reported his impressions. He thought Clay was "prepared to cut loose from the South and rely upon the free states to elect him." He believed that Taylor was the South's only hope. Even if Taylor were elected, Bell feared the General would be "the last of the Mohicans." Yet there was hope that Taylor might "by his justice, moderation and firmness stay the tide of fanaticism at the North." Most of the "Clay storm" in the North, Bell insisted, was for the purpose of destroying Taylor rather than electing Clay. Other leaders in the Clay movement had wished only to compliment the aged Whig leader, expecting that he would accept the glory but retire in favor of Taylor. Indeed, this expectation had been encouraged by Clay. Bell knew the fanatics of the North were all opposed to the General, but he believed that even though the politicians preferred a Northern man many of them would not hesitate to support Taylor. He had found

[53] Graham to Nicholson, December 3, 1847, in Nicholson Papers. There was some talk of a Scott-Bell ticket. "If I had the power to make a ticket today," wrote Congressman Washington Hunt of New York to Thurlow Weed, "I should say Scott for Prest. and John Bell for V.P. That would give us Tennessee— He would give us more strength than any man except Crittenden, and it is more important to fortify in Tennessee than in Ky." Hunt to Weed, May 19, 1848, in Thurlow Weed Papers (University of Rochester).

[54] Bell to Campbell, December 23, 1847, in David Campbell Papers.

only three members of Congress who thought Clay would have a chance of being elected should he get the Whig nomination.[55]

After the lapse of another month Bell was still hopeful of Taylor's nomination but had lost all hope of Northern support. The "North are now bent on having a Northern man," he informed Campbell. He believed Northern Whigs would accept Clay, however, since they considered him a Northern man on the question of slavery. But even they knew Clay could not be elected. There were some indications that the Northern Whigs might take up John J. Crittenden who they considered held Clay's views on the question of slavery. But Bell doubted whether Crittenden would attempt "to trip up the heels of old Zach." In his opinion Crittenden would make "the most negative sort of a Whig President." [56] There was also a personal side to Bell's opposition to Clay and Crittenden. He confided to Campbell that if either of the two should be made President the Foster-Jones clique would be their chosen friends in Tennessee. Still, Bell insisted that his real opposition was based on the fact that he would prefer "a Northern man with Southern feelings to a Southern man with Northern feelings." Crittenden's actions during the past year had convinced Bell that the Kentuckian was "playing this game." As to the Democratic nomination, he still suspected that Polk had hopes. The President's statement to the contrary was pronounced as "all fudge." [57]

When Taylor was nominated by the Whigs and the Democratic nomination went to Lewis Cass, Bell was enthusiastic in his support of Taylor. In an address before a political gathering at Murfreesboro, he praised the General as one who always acted for the welfare of his country, and who, despite

---

[55] *Id.* to *id.*, April 13, 1848, *ibid.*

[56] *Id.* to *id.*, May 23, 1848, *ibid.* Bell either was strangely unaware of Crittenden's activities in behalf of Taylor or chose to ignore them. See William O. Lynch, "Zachary Taylor as President," In *Journal of Southern History* (Baton Rouge, 1935–), IV (1938), 279–94.

[57] Bell to Campbell, May 23, 1848, in David Campbell Papers.

his lack of political experience, possessed the endowments requisite for the "highest civil office in a period of peril." Bell did not "regard the sink or swim with one man [Clay] principle an article of Whig faith. We were not bound to adhere to one man through life, although we might be to one woman!" He did not wish to detract from the merits of Clay, but he felt that many men were fixed in their hostility toward the Kentuckian. General Taylor was a man in whose support "the honest and patriotic of all parties could unite." [58]

Bell's enthusiastic support of Taylor for the nomination and during the campaign which followed elicited much comment. His critics charged that he was angling for a cabinet post. Bell made an effort to check this rumor with a definite statement that he preferred his seat in the Senate to any cabinet position.[59] Following Taylor's election, however, Bell's friends revived the subject and strongly advocated his appointment. "Parson" Brownlow took the lead. "For moderation, calculation, foresight, firmness, energy and great caution," he declared, Bell had no superior. There was no man to whom Taylor was quite so much indebted as to Bell for his efforts at the Philadelphia convention and in the campaign in Tennessee.[60] At least one East Tennessean wanted Bell appointed to a cabinet post in order to create a senatorial vacancy which might be filled by a man from that section. He also felt confident that, as a cabinet member, Bell would not neglect East Tennessee, especially in view of the fact that numerous indignation meetings had been held in that section following the Senator's election.[61] It was also rumored that Bell would probably be the next minister to Great Britain.[62] There is no evidence that Bell desired either a cabinet or

[58] Quotations are from summary of Bell's speech as reported in the Nashville *Republican Banner*, September 29, 1848.

[59] Bell to Campbell, April 13, 1848, in David Campbell Papers.

[60] Jonesborough *Whig*, November 29, 1848. At the Philadelphia convention the Tennessee delegation was unanimous in its support of Taylor.

[61] Landon C. Hoss to Nelson, December 1, 1848, in Nelson Papers.

[62] New York *Herald*, quoted in Memphis *Daily Eagle*, April 19, 1849.

foreign post, but undoubtedly he did expect to wield considerable influence in Administration circles.

William B. Campbell, Tennessee's Whig hero of the Mexican War, prophesied that Taylor would rely heavily upon
Bell and Congressman Meredith P. Gentry, but that their
Whig enemy, former Governor James C. Jones, would be
completely overlooked.[63] Some Tennessee Whigs, however,
were not pleased with the prospects of a President under Bell's
influence. Boyd McNairy, a friend of Jones, wrote Crittenden
that he "did not admire such leaders as John Bell and A. A.
Hall—the former, a cold-blooded heartless man—the latter, a
drunken Gad-fly." McNairy claimed that if Jackson had given
Bell an appointment he would have remained a Democrat.[64]

With the election of Taylor, the Whigs again returned to
power after years of absence from the government payroll.
Brownlow journeyed to Washington for the inauguration,
and, incidentally, to view the patronage possibilities for his
friends in East Tennessee. He was delighted to learn of the
esteem in which his friend Bell was held in Washington circles.
From what the "Parson" could learn, Bell ranked "no. 1 in
the Senate." He reported that some of the ultra proslavery
men had made an effort to prejudice the President-elect
against the leader of the Tennessee Whigs, but they had failed
utterly. Instead, no sooner had the General taken up quarters
in the city than he sent for Bell to advise with him.[65] Two
weeks after the inauguration Brownlow was even more impressed. "Bell is regarded as the right arm of the administration in the Senate," he wrote Thomas A. R. Nelson, "and
evidently has great influence with the President and his cabinet." [66] Apparently many others shared Brownlow's opinion,
for long before the inauguration Bell had been overwhelmed

[63] Campbell to David Campbell, May 14, 1849, in David Campbell Papers.
[64] McNairy to Crittenden, December 12, 1848, in Crittenden Papers. Allen A.
Hall, a Nashville editor, had been a supporter of Bell since 1827. He was also
one of the original Taylor men in Tennessee.
[65] Brownlow to Nelson, March 2, 1849, in Nelson Papers.
[66] Id. to id., March 19, 1849, ibid.

by office seekers from many states. Bell did not welcome these requests for the use of his influence. To him dispensing the patronage was an unpleasant task. Even his close friends, who felt that they had a just claim on his services, often complained of his apparent lack of interest in their elevation to lucrative positions.

In his inaugural address, Taylor referred to the appointing power as imposing upon the President "delicate and onerous duties." And he promised that as far as was possible to secure adequate information, he would "make honesty, capacity, and fidelity indispensable prerequisites to the bestowal of office, and the absence of either of these qualities shall be deemed sufficient cause for removal." [67] Taylor was not a politician and apparently did not realize the extent to which the spoils system had become established. Those Whigs who had worked for his election were expecting reward for themselves and their friends, and probably no one was more seriously concerned than Bell. Since the Administration of Andrew Jackson, Tennessee had been accustomed to most favored consideration when appointments were being made. Now that the Whig party had come to power, many Tennessee Whigs demanded a wholesale dismissal of Democrats and a continuation of most favored consideration in matters of appointments. Bell knew that his state no longer had reason to expect special consideration, and he feared the political results. Should Tennessee's quota of officeholders be substantially reduced, he feared that the Whigs might suffer in popularity. He confided to friends that he expected removals to be made but only for interference in elections, incompetency, or lack of fidelity. [68]

Bell was much concerned over the dispensing of patronage in East Tennessee. That section had given him little support in his recent election; in fact, his only prominent newspaper support had come from Brownlow's Jonesborough *Whig*.

[67] Richardson (ed.), *Messages and Papers*, VI, 2544.
[68] Bell to William B. Campbell, April 14, 1849, in David Campbell Papers.

Consequently, Bell realized the advisability of increasing his popularity in the eastern section, especially in the Knoxville area. While attending Taylor's inauguration, Brownlow expressed a desire to move his *Whig* from Jonesborough to Knoxville. Bell and Congressman Meredith P. Gentry encouraged the move, agreeing to endorse Brownlow's note covering the cost of two new presses. Brownlow later stated that he had intended paying for the presses out of the money received for doing government printing. He also claimed that Gentry and Bell promised to secure for him that portion of the printing which should be allotted to East Tennessee.[69]

If Bell made such a promise, further reflection caused him to change his mind. He needed support from more than just the *Whig;* therefore, he arranged for a division of the printing contracts among the *Whig,* the Knoxville *Register* and the Knoxville *Tribune.* Brownlow was awarded the printing of mail contracts, but in a spirit of protest, he refused to accept the printing offered him, and opened up a newspaper attack upon Bell and the Taylor Administration.[70] More than a thousand dollars' worth of printing had been given to the *Register,* Brownlow asserted, "with a view to *buy up its support for those Tennessee Whigs, whose election to Congress, and to the United States Senate it has heretofore opposed.*" His *Whig* was the "People's paper," he declared, and he pledged himself to use its columns "to expose the frauds, villainies, and corruptions of both Whigs and Democrats, no matter who [*sic*] we give offense to, or who [*sic*] we may injure." [71] It is evident that Brownlow's earlier enthusiasm for the Taylor Administration had greatly subsided.

In the meantime, a storm had broken in the United States Senate. On December 24, 1849, James W. Bradbury, a Democrat from Maine, introduced a resolution requesting the President to submit to the Senate copies of all charges which

[69] Brownlow to Nelson, May 30, 1851, in Nelson Papers.
[70] Bell to *id.,* January 28, 1850, *ibid.*
[71] *Brownlow's Knoxville Whig,* February 2, 1850.

had been preferred against civil officials who had later been dismissed. The President was also asked to furnish information concerning the number of hearings granted to accused officials and the total number of removals which had been made in each department.[72] Speaking in defense of his resolution, Bradbury explained that it was his purpose to seek information rather than opinion. He charged that President Taylor had not remained true to his promise "to act independently of party"; however, he thought that the great number of removals had been less a result of Taylor's insincerity than of charges preferred against officeholders by Whigs who hoped to get jobs. If that was true, the Senate needed such information before confirming new appointments. He considered it the duty of the Senate to advise with the President on such matters, and, to him, "advise" meant more than mere confirmation of presidential nominations. In order to exercise judgment, the Senate must have before it the facts; therefore, the Senate had a right to request the President to furnish such information as might be in his possession.

Bradbury further charged that Taylor had removed more officeholders in one month than Andrew Jackson had in a year. He said that he could think of only one old officeholder still on the job in the state of Maine. Those who had been dismissed were men of high character and efficiency, and it was his purpose to find out why such men had been removed.[73] In retirement at Clarksville, Tennessee, former Postmaster General Cave Johnson was making a similar complaint. The new Postmaster General, he charged, had already made more removals in Tennessee in three months than he did in four years.[74]

Daniel Webster commented that he considered the President's power over officeholders to be "one of the existing evils of the time, and one which endangers the harmonious action

[72] *Cong. Globe,* 31 Cong., 1 Sess., 74–75.
[73] *Ibid.,* Appendix, 47–52.
[74] Johnson to Buchanan, June 17, 1849, in James Buchanan Papers (Historical Society of Pennsylvania).

of the Government''; however, since all Administrations had resorted to removals, he considered the spoils system to be an established practice. The power of removal was definitely among the powers of the President and could be exercised by him even in complete disregard of the wishes of the Senate.[75]

Bell came to Taylor's defense, but gave no figures on the number of removals. He thought there could be no fair comparison of the removals made by Jackson and Taylor; Jackson had found all offices filled with men of his own party, while Taylor had found but few Whigs in office. Bell denied that Taylor had made wholesale removals because of difference of opinion. The principal cause for removal, he asserted, had been interference in elections. Bell conceded the right of officeholders to vote as they pleased, ''but active participation —intermeddling in election; taking part at public meetings, making party speeches, and drumming up votes at the polls'' was denounced as ''inconsistent with the regular, faithful and satisfactory discharge of official duties.'' No Democratic officeholder need worry, Bell advised, as long as he was faithful and skillful in the performance of duty and did not meddle in politics. He contended, however, that from the Whig viewpoint, it was unfair for the Democrats who had monopolized the offices during the Democratic Administration to continue their monopoly during a Whig Administration, while Whigs were to receive appointments only when cause could be shown for removing Democrats. Should the Democrats continue their policy of considering public office as a part of the fruits of victory, Bell feared that the Whigs would be forced to do likewise in spite of their opposition to such a practice. Rather than to see such a condition prevail, he preferred to see Congress regulate by law this dangerous power of removal. Either that power must be regulated by Congress or it would soon regulate Congress.[76] Bell's proposal had the mark of sincerity. Whether he believed congressional regulation would result in more efficiency in the public service is not clear, but there is

---

[75] Cong. Globe, 31 Cong., 1 Sess., 1125–26.   [76] Ibid., Appendix, 500–504.

238 JOHN BELL OF TENNESSEE

no doubt about his eagerness to lessen the pressure of office seekers.

The Bradbury resolution failed, but the question of removals was again before the Senate in May, 1850. A bill to establish a Board of Accounts had been reported, and it was specified in the bill that the members of the board should serve a term of twelve years, subject to removal by the President. James Whitcomb of Indiana attacked this provision on the ground that a long term would not remove the members from executive pressure unless the power of removal should be denied to the President. Robert M. T. Hunter of Virginia interrupted to explain that the reporting committee had considered senatorial approval as a requirement for removal, but had abandoned the idea because of conflicting constitutional views on the removal power of the President. Hunter further explained that it was hoped that the specification of a long term would impress upon the executive the congressional desire for an independent board, and that it would cause the President to be cautious in his removals.[77]

Henry S. Foote, a Democrat from Mississippi, facetiously remarked that he was opposed to any attempt to limit the removal power of the President since he expected the Democrats to return to power following the election of 1852. Stephen A. Douglas wished to deny to the President the power to remove the officials in question.[78] Bell returned to his former argument, insisting that if the purity of American institutions was to be safeguarded, the Senate should not delay further a definite stand on the subject of the President's removal power. He explained that he had always considered as erroneous the earlier congressional decisions that the President's power of removal could not be limited. He now wished to see Congress reverse itself, he said, and was ready to deny to the President the power to remove the board members in question. "I should consider it as one of the signs of real progress," he added, "if we could come to this decision . . . that

[77] *Ibid.*, 31 Cong., 1 Sess., 931.   [78] *Ibid.*, 934.

both Houses of Congress have power over appointments and
removals, and to say to the President . . . 'You shall not remove persons from office except with the assent of the
Senate.' " In making such a statement, Bell was not expressing
a lack of confidence in President Taylor, for he added: "I do
not believe that a more honest man lives than the present
incumbent of our presidential chair. Nevertheless, I would
control him in the exercise of this power, and not only him,
but all his successors." [79]

While the Senate debated the President's power of removal,
the fiery Brownlow intensified his attack upon the Taylor
Administration. In publishing Bell's speech in defense of the
Administration, Brownlow explained that he did so as courtesy to the Senator and his constituents rather than as a defense
of Taylor and his "fence-riding" cabinet. He further suggested that, after the close of the session, Bell should return
home by way of East Tennessee that he might mingle with the
Whigs of that section and "hear them curse and denounce
this Administration." [80]

[79] Ibid., 935.   [80] Brownlow's Knoxville Whig, June 8, 1850.

Chapter XII

THE SPIRIT OF COMPROMISE

A NEWCOMER to Washington circles sat in the Senate gallery on the opening day of the Thirty-first Congress, December 3, 1849. Later he described the famous figures he saw below. "On the right of the main aisle were to be seen the massive head and deep-set eyes of Webster, the tall and commanding figure of Clay, the dark but genial face of Corwin, the white head of 'Honest John Davis,' the calm and cautious visage of John Bell, the scholarly looking head of Berrien, the tall forms of Mangum and Dayton, and the merry smile of John P. Hale; on the left, the portly form of General Cass, the towering bulk of General Houston, . . . the classic head and genial face of Colonel Benton, the long, grey locks and sharp attenuated features of Calhoun, the erect, slender figure of Jefferson Davis, the swarthy, foreign-looking face of Pierre Soulé, the energetic, black-clothed 'Little Giant' Douglas, the dark, curling locks of Hunter, and the silver-haired familiar face of Daniel S. Dickinson." [1] These were to be prominent participants in the Senate battle over the Compromise of 1850; and in the development of the spirit of compromise the work of John Bell of Tennessee as a leader of the moderate or middle-of-the-road Southerners on the question of slavery in the territories was to play an important part.

Since President Taylor was a Louisiana slaveholder and the

[1] Frederick W. Seward, *Reminiscences of a War-Time Statesman and Diplomat, 1830–1915* (New York, 1916), 70. Seward had just come to Washington to serve as secretary to his father, William H. Seward, a newly elected senator from New York.

father of the first wife of Jefferson Davis, his proslavery background and his silence on the important national issues gave hope to the ultra proslavery men that he might espouse their cause. The moderates hoped that his reputation for "justice, moderation and firmness," might incline him to check the extremists of both the North and the South. This was Bell's impression when, a few weeks after the inauguration, he confided to his friend Campbell: "I believe Gen. Taylor is entirely sound on every point." [2]

Taylor's only annual message to Congress was presented early in December, 1849. He informed Congress that the people of the California territory, being "impelled by the necessities of their political condition," had formed a constitution and would soon ask for admission into the Union as a state. There was reason to believe that the people of New Mexico would soon do likewise. These people were establishing republican forms of government founded upon such principles as seemed to them "most likely to effect their safety and happiness." By extending to them this privilege, "all causes of uneasiness may be avoided and confidence and kind feeling preserved." In the interest of harmony and tranquillity "we should abstain from the introduction of those exciting topics of a sectional character which have hitherto produced painful apprehension in the public mind." [3]

The President was not interested in the creation of any territorial governments. Immediate admission of California and New Mexico as states would eliminate all need for a Wilmot Proviso or an extension of the Missouri Compromise line. Although he wished to see the people of these territories found their new state governments upon such principles as would "most likely effect their safety and happiness," he had no desire to see the principle of popular sovereignty applied to them while they remained in a territorial stage. His message offered no encouragement to those proslavery men who hoped

2 Bell to Campbell, April 13, 1848, April 14, 1849, in David Campbell Papers.
3 Richardson (ed.), *Messages and Papers,* VI, 2556–57.

to use the admission of California as a means toward the securing of slavery in New Mexico.

On January 23, 1850, the President sent to the Senate a supplementary message explaining and defending his action in sending a representative to California and New Mexico to encourage the residents to hasten the formation of state constitutions. In taking this step he "was actuated principally by an earnest desire to afford to the wisdom and patriotism of Congress the opportunity of avoiding occasions of bitter and angry dissension among the people of the United States." He was convinced that the admission of these territories as states would "remove all occasion for the unnecessary agitation of the public mind." [4]

Taylor's failure to take cognizance of the numerous other issues which clouded the political skies indicated that he did not fully grasp the complexity of the problems which faced the new Whig Administration. In addition to the question of slavery in the territories, the boundary between Texas and New Mexico was in dispute. Abolitionists were demanding that slavery be abolished in the District of Columbia. The proslavery South was demanding that its property in slaves be better protected by a more adequate fugitive slave law.[5]

But the venerable Whig leader, Henry Clay, though broken in health, was very much alive to the dangers which threatened not only the new Administration but the Union itself. The coolness which characterized the relations between Taylor and Clay denied to the inexperienced President the counsel of the veteran statesman, but it in no way affected Clay's love for the Union. He believed it his duty to make every possible effort to bring opposing factions together in a plan which would relieve the tension and save the Union from destruction.

Having conferred with Daniel Webster and received encouragement from him,[6] Clay resolved to try a compromise

---

[4] *Ibid.*, VI, 2565–66.   [5] *Cong. Globe,* 31 Cong., 1 Sess., 91, 119, 165–71.
[6] Curtis, *Life of Daniel Webster,* II, 397.

plan. On January 29, 1850, he introduced in the Senate a
series of resolutions providing for the admission of California
as a free state; creation of a territorial government for the remainder of the territory acquired from Mexico, without restriction as to slavery, settlement of the Texas–New Mexico
boundary dispute by ceding a considerable portion of the territory to New Mexico and compensating Texas for the relinquishment of its claims; abolition of the slave trade but not
of slavery in the District of Columbia; passage of a more adequate fugitive slave law; and noninterference by Congress
with the slave trade between the states.[7]

On February 5, Clay spoke in support of his resolutions.
In great earnestness he appealed to men both North and
South to compromise their differences in the interest of the
preservation of the Union. Why insist upon a Wilmot Proviso when slavery would never exist in these territories anyway? In view of all the benefits enjoyed by the South in the
case of Florida, Louisiana, and Texas, why should proslavery
men threaten extreme measures at the prospect of the first
reverse? He begged extremists, both North and South, to pause
before their actions led to "certain and irretrievable destruction."[8]

Clay's compromise proposals pleased very few, North or
South. Most Northern senators insisted on restricting slavery
in the territories. The more extreme among them also objected to the passage of a more vigorous fugitive slave law, and
demanded that slavery, not just the slave trade, be abolished
in the District of Columbia. The majority of the Southern
senators realized that California would inevitably become a
free state, but they objected to the method used in framing
its proposed free-state constitution. Some would agree to
the admission of California under this constitution, but all
demanded that there should be no restrictions on slavery in
the territories of New Mexico and Utah. Furthermore, when
those territories should present themselves for statehood,

---

[7] *Cong. Globe*, 31 Cong., 1 Sess., 244–47.   [8] *Ibid.*, Appendix, 115–27.

they must be admitted either with or without slavery according to the desire of the inhabitants.[9]

The success of Clay's compromise plan depended largely
upon the attitude of the Administration. The coolness between the President and the Senator from Kentucky did not
help the situation. Had Clay's proposals been made by some
person in a position similar to that occupied by Bell, the
chance of winning Administration support would have been
improved. Bell's known conservatism on the question of the
extension of slavery and his friendly relations with Taylor
gave him a position of some importance. During the first
month of the debate, he was busily engaged in compiling the
opinions of "at least a dozen honorable Senators" who like
himself disapproved of parts of Clay's plan and had no particular desire to follow his leadership. This group, later characterized by Bell as "partial friends," believed that a plan offered by a man in Bell's position would aid the "prospect of a
satisfactory adjustment." [10]

Bell placed his compilation of opinions before the Senate
on February 28 in the form of a set of proposals. By way of introduction, he expressed the belief that no proposition offered by a Southern man would have any "particular weight
or influence" in adjusting this controversy. Such a proposition must come from the North, the section which possessed
the power to settle these questions. Nevertheless, he wished
to present a plan of compromise.

The resolution by which Texas was made a state in the
Union, Bell explained, had provided that, with the consent
of that state, as many as four states might be carved from her
territory. Those new states which should be carved from the
territory south of 36 degrees, 30 minutes were to be admitted
either with or without slavery according to the wishes of the
inhabitants. Therefore, he proposed that as soon as the legis-

---

[9] Alexander H. Stephens, *A Constitutional View of the Late War Between the States* (Philadelphia, 1870), II, 200–201.
[10] *Cong. Globe,* 31 Cong., 1 Sess., Appendix, 1089.

lature of Texas should give its consent, the western boundary
of that state should be set at the Trinity River. All territory
claimed by Texas which lay West of the Trinity and south of
34 degrees should be admitted into the Union as a separate
state either with or without slavery as the inhabitants preferred. It was rumored that should such a proposed state apply for admission, the North would disregard the provisions
of the Texas resolution. "It is for the purpose of meeting and
quieting this apprehension of the South, and for the soothing
effect which the admission of such a state into the Union now
would have, that I have thought proper to propose it."

It had long been the practice to balance the admission of a
free state with the admission of a slave state. Of course this
practice could not be continued indefinitely, but Bell reasoned that it might be used at least once more by carving a
new state from Texas to balance the admission of California
as a free state. He envisioned the carving of at least ten new
free states from the territories within the next decade, but he
was unable to see the equivalent in slave states. He therefore
insisted that his proposal be accepted "in conformity with
ancient practice, which must soon be abandoned." There was
no assurance that the Texas representatives in Congress
would support the plan or that the legislature of that state
would give its consent; but, even though such consent might
be refused, "here is a peace offering" which would bear witness to Northern desire for justice. The responsibility for
failure would rest upon the shoulders of Texas and the
South.

Bell further suggested that when that portion of the proposed new state which lay west of the Colorado River should
have a population equal to the number required for a representative in Congress, it should be cut off and admitted as a
state either with or without slavery. It would certainly be a
slave state but that fact should not unduly alarm Northern
senators since when this state should be admitted it would
be the "last of its race." As long as the Union should last

there could never be another slave state. Local hostility would prevent any further division of Texas.

Texas should also be requested to cede to the United States its claim to all territory north of 34 degrees and west of the Colorado. For this cession Texas would receive a stipulated sum of money to be applied on its debts. The cost to the United States, Bell thought, would be a minor matter if such a cession could be the means of helping to preserve the Union. Should Texas agree to cede this territory, it was to be joined with New Mexico and the whole to be given a territorial government without restrictions on slavery. This territory was destined to be free; therefore, restrictions on slavery would be "both objectionable and unnecessary." "While the present organization of material creation stands, African slavery can never find a foothold in New Mexico." All labor demands there would be met by Indians and immigrant whites. "Why then, upon the vague fear in the minds of gentlemen that some contingency—the bare conjecture of an accident now inconceivable to the imagination—should the fate of the Union, or its continued harmony, be jeoparded by insisting upon a slavery restriction clause?" Even if the Missouri Compromise line should be extended it would be a "barren victory." The principle would be preserved, but there would be no territory to which to apply it. "I regard the establishment of the Missouri Compromise line as a thing of no value —a working of benefit of no kind."

Bell thought that a suitable government without restrictions on slavery should be provided for the remainder of the territory lying between California and New Mexico. California he would admit as a free state under its proposed constitution, but henceforth no territory should be permitted to frame a constitution "without the consent and authority of Congress." [11]

---

[11] *Ibid.*, 31 Cong., 1 Sess., 336–39. For a map showing the proposed division of Texas into states, see William C. Binkley, *The Expansionist Movement in Texas, 1836–1850* (Berkeley, 1925), 208.

Bell purposely omitted from his resolutions any proposals relative to fugitive slaves and slavery in the District of Columbia. He expressed his confidence that when the California and New Mexico controversies should be settled, other differences could be easily adjusted. It was his wish that his resolutions be referred to the Committee on Territories, of which Douglas was chairman. But Henry S. Foote of Mississippi proposed that they be sent to a special committee of thirteen which should carry on an investigation with a view to presenting a plan for the "adjustment of all pending questions growing out of the institution of slavery." Thus there was precipitated a running debate which continued until April 19 before the proposed committee was finally selected.

There was difference of opinion as to what prompted the introduction of this second plan for settlement. Bell explained that he made no claim to authorship of his resolutions. He would not claim that even a single proposition was "entirely original." Most, if not all, of these proposals had "passed through the minds of at least a dozen honorable Senators." [12] By some persons the plan was considered a result of consultation among Southerners who preferred an extension of the Missouri Compromise line, but realized they could not get it.[13] If a new free state was to be forced upon them they hoped to offset it by the immediate admission of a slave state also. Others saw in Bell's plan the substance of a "modified form of the executive policy." [14] This belief was strengthened by the fact that the chief organ of the Administration, the Washington *Republic,* gave its enthusiastic support to the Bell proposals.[15]

For more than six weeks the best talent in the Senate debated every phase of the slavery controversy. Calhoun, on the threshold of the grave, left his bed in order to oppose com-

12 *Cong. Globe,* 31 Cong., 1 Sess., 436.

13 Washington Correspondent of the Charleston *Courier,* quoted in *Republican Banner and Nashville Whig,* March 12, 1850.

14 Stephens, *Constitutional View,* II, 205.

15 Washington *Republic,* March 1–14, 1850.

promise. He sat with grim determination while his last defense of the South was read to the Senate by James M. Mason. Claiming that the balance which had once existed between the sections had been upset by legislation unfavorable to the South, he asserted that if the equilibrium should be further disturbed by the admission of California as a free state, the South could no longer hope for justice within the Union.[16]

Webster gave his support to compromise. He believed that the Wilmot Proviso was unnecessary and could serve no purpose other than to humiliate the South. The activities of the abolitionists had been productive of no good, he said, but to the South he gave warning that peaceable withdrawal from the Union was impossible.[17] He had listened with interest to the arguments by Bell, and he was forced to admit the binding character of the Texas resolution. "I know no way, I candidly confess, in which this Government, acting in good faith . . . can relieve itself from that stipulation and pledge." [18] This confession on the part of Webster gave increased hope to the less radical Southerners. "We have a tolerable prospect for a proper settlement of the slavery question," wrote Robert Toombs. "I should think it a strong prospect if it were not that the Calhoun wing of the South seem to desire no settlement and may perhaps go against any adjustment which would likely pass. The settlement will probably be in the main on the basis of Bell's proposition as backed by Webster." [19] The Northern press opened an attack upon Webster for his apparent support of Bell's proposal for the division of Texas, but the Washington *Republic* hastened to his defense. "The most perverse ingenuity cannot alter, mystify, or change the interest or signification of the words employed" in the resolution under which Texas was an-

16 *Cong. Globe,* 31 Cong., 1 Sess., 451 ff.
17 *Ibid.,* 476 ff.   18 *Ibid.,* 479.
19 Robert Toombs to Linton Stephens, March 22, 1850, in Ulrich B. Phillips (ed.), *The Correspondence of Robert Toombs, Alexander H. Stephens, and Howell Cobb,* American Historical Association, *Annual Report,* 1911, II (Washington, 1913), 188.

nexed. Webster and Bell were correct. "The people [of Texas] MAY form States—Congress SHALL admit them, on the condition and guarantees prescribed." [20]

Douglas gave his support to a part of Clay's compromise proposals, but William H. Seward and Salmon P. Chase vigorously denounced the institution of slavery, those who advocated its extension, and the compromise proposals in general.

The chief opposition to the creation of the proposed committee of thirteen came from those senators who wished to consider the California question separately. Roger S. Baldwin of Connecticut protested against connecting California with other controversies, and argued that since the President had asked that California be admitted immediately, his request should be considered. "I am opposed to this mixing of subjects which have no affinities," declared Thomas Hart Benton, "and am in favor of giving the application of California . . . a separate consideration, and an independent decision, upon its own merits." [21]

Douglas pointed out that there were bills pending before the Senate touching all of the topics included in both the Clay and the Bell resolutions, and remarked that he could see no good reason to have a committee report others of the same nature. He wished to see the resolutions tabled and the bill to admit California considered.[22] A few days later Benton also attempted to have Foote's proposal set aside and the California bill called up, but failed by four votes. The clash between Benton and Foote became so heated as to cause both momentarily to lose control of themselves. Benton's threatening movements in the direction of Foote caused the latter to draw his pistol. No shots were fired, Henry Dodge of Wisconsin restraining Benton, Dickinson taking the gun from Foote, and Butler persuading him to take his seat.[23] Amid

20 Washington *Republic,* March 14, 1850.
21 *Cong. Globe,* 31 Cong., 1 Sess., 656.
22 *Ibid.,* 662.   23 *Ibid.,* 762.

scenes such as this, the Senate voted to send both the Clay and the Bell resolutions to a select committee of thirteen.[24]

While the Senate had been debating, preparations were being made for a Southern convention to meet at Nashville to chart the proper course for the South.[25] The Whig press in Tennessee at first gave lukewarm support to the convention idea, but later denounced it as a disunionist movement sponsored by Democrats. Bell's Nashville organ, the *Republican Banner and Nashville Whig,* was especially vigorous in its denunciations. The Democratic press attributed the *Republican Banner's* "miraculous summerset" to the influence of the "potential voice" of Bell. It suspected Bell of being the author of the Tennessee opposition to the convention.[26] So far as was indicated by his press, Bell took no part in the plans for the convention. Instead, he expressed "liberal confidence" in the North's desire to settle great national questions "upon an equitable and liberal basis." He hoped that some good might come out of the convention, but he insisted that his opinion had no influence in determining the outcome.[27]

The convention met on June 3, 1850, but proved to be less radical than its original sponsors probably had intended. The growing interest in compromise had cut heavily into the ranks of those who had once leaned toward a more sectional mode of settlement. The most radical recommendation adopted by the convention was one for the extension of the

[24] The committee consisted of Clay, Daniel S. Dickinson of New York, Samuel S. Phelps of Vermont, Lewis Cass of Michigan, Daniel Webster of Massachusetts, Bell of Tennessee, Berrien of Georgia, Willie P. Mangum of North Carolina, Solomon W. Downs of Louisiana, James M. Mason of Virginia, William R. King of Alabama, James Cooper of Pennsylvania, and Jesse D. Bright of Indiana.

[25] See Dallas T. Herndon, "The Nashville Convention of 1850," in Alabama Historical Society, *Transactions* (Montgomery, 1897–1904), V (1904), 203–37.

[26] *Republican Banner and Nashville Whig,* January 28, 1850; Nashville *Union,* March 13, 1850. For a discussion of Tennessee's part in the convention, see St. George L. Sioussat, "Tennessee, the Compromise of 1850, and the Nashville Convention," in *Mississippi Valley Historical Review* (Cedar Rapids, 1914–), II (1915), 313–47.

[27] *Cong. Globe,* 31 Cong., 1 Sess., 438.

Missouri Compromise line, a proposal which no longer had a chance to pass Congress.

In the meantime, the committee of thirteen made its report on May 8. In substance its recommendations and the accompanying bills were the same as Clay's resolutions. The first three resolutions were incorporated in one bill; the next two in separate bills.[28] A death blow was dealt the heart of Bell's proposals when it was recommended that the question of carving new states from Texas should be postponed until the people and legislature of Texas requested it. There was little hope that Texas would ever voluntarily make such a request. The acceptance of this recommendation destroyed the last chance for the admission of another slave state.

Even before the committee made its report, Taylor had decided against the Clay compromise. The General had come under the influence of William H. Seward of New York. Seward favored the Wilmot Proviso, but being unable to bring Taylor around to this view, he joined with him in a "plan of non-action." [29] When the *Republic,* the Administration's Washington organ, came out in favor of compromise and attempted to show that the committee's proposals differed from the President's plan in detail only, Taylor became so angry as to demand either a change in editors or the establishment of a new organ. Editors Alexander C. Bullitt and John N. Sargent were induced to resign, and Allen A. Hall, Assistant Secretary of the Treasury and former Nashville editor, took over the editorial chair.[30] Hall was a close friend of John Bell and had been his stanch supporter in the long Bell-Polk controversy. Early in the Taylor Administration Bell had been partly responsible for the appointment of Hall to the position in the Treasury Department, an act which

28 For the committee report, see *Senate Reports,* 31 Cong., 1 Sess., No. 123.

29 Salmon P. Chase to Charles Sumner, April 13, 1850, in Edward G. Bourne (ed.), *Diary and Correspondence of Salmon P. Chase,* American Historical Association, *Annual Report,* 1902, II (Washington, 1903), 208.

30 Washington *Republic,* March 14, 1850; Poage, *Henry Clay and the Whig Party,* 229-31.

made the Tennessee editor the "happiest man" Bell had ever seen.[31] Many who did not know the facts believed Hall's recent promotion to have been due to Bell's influence. The truth was that Bell had no knowledge of the matter until Hall informed him of the offer and requested his advice as to whether to accept. When Taylor's cabinet quarreled with the editors of the *Republic* and decided to make a change, Hall was available and had attracted favorable attention as a result of some articles he had written on the Nicaraguan question.[32] Although generally recognized as a man of some ability, his intense partisanship and intemperate habits had caused him to be detested by the Democrats and disliked by many Whigs. Dr. Boyd McNairy denounced him as a "drunken Gad-fly," and Cave Johnson described him as a "drunken vagabond tho. a smart fellow," wholly unfit for responsible office.[33]

Before the resignation of the editors, Clay, believing that the attitude of the *Republic* probably indicated a change on the part of the President, opened the debate with a conciliatory speech. But when the President unmasked himself the Kentucky Senator did likewise. On May 21 he opened up a severe attack upon Taylor for his opposition to the compromise and his policy toward New Mexico. The nation had five bleeding wounds, he explained. The President's plan to admit California would heal one only, leaving the "other four to bleed more profusely than ever." The President would do nothing for the territories or to settle the other controversies. Meanwhile, New Mexico was being governed by an army officer. "Stand up, Whig who can—stand up Democrat who can," cried Clay, "and defend the establishment of a military government in this free and glorious Republic, in time of profound peace!" And the President pro-

---

[31] Bell to William B. Campbell, April 14, 1848, in David Campbell Papers.
[32] *Id.* to Nelson, May 4, 1851, in Nelson Papers; "Americus" to Brownlow, May 20, 1851, in *Brownlow's Knoxville Whig*, July 19, 1851.
[33] McNairy to Crittenden, December 12, 1848, in Crittenden Papers; Johnson to Buchanan, June 17, 1849, in Buchanan Papers.

posed to continue this type of government until New Mexico was admitted as a state.[34]

Debate on the committee's recommendations and the accompanying bills continued for almost five months. Every senator who felt a desire to speak was given an opportunity. On July 3 Bell began a three-day argument, in which he explained that from the day he learned that the Polk Administration would demand further acquisition of territory from Mexico, he had had a "pretty clear perception of the dissension likely to grow out of it." He stated that as soon as the treaty was signed he began advocating a speedy settlement of a nature which would make it "final and irrevocable, leaving no open questions to irritate and fester in the public mind." This conviction had prompted him to oppose the Clayton compromise proposals in 1848,[35] which could have had no other result than a postponement of a decision on a question which would become more and more aggravated each day. For this reason, he said, he had advocated during the last Congress that these territories be admitted as states, leaving the question of slavery to be settled by the inhabitants. Had his course been adopted, the territories would now be enjoying the protection of organized government and much of the dissension between North and South would have been repressed. He had been severely assailed for his efforts in behalf of such a settlement, but he still insisted that the plan violated "no principle of the Constitution and no well-settled sentiment of right or justice."

As to the bills then before the Senate, Bell asserted that he had not committed himself. Before he could give his complete approval these bills must be reshaped. In their present form, he feared they would not produce the harmony prom-

[34] *Cong. Globe,* 31 Cong., 1 Sess., Appendix, 615.

[35] The Clayton compromise proposal provided for the creation of territorial governments for California and New Mexico, and forbade the territorial legislatures to pass laws relative to slavery. Disputes over slavery were to be tried in the territorial courts with the right of appeal to the United States Supreme Court. This proposal was adopted by the Senate, but was tabled in the House. *Cong. Globe,* 30 Cong., 1 Sess., 1002–1005.

ised by their sponsors. They still contained "elements of continued agitation and discord." The whole plan proposed by the committee was lacking in comprehensiveness. When giants like Clay, Webster, Cass, and Foote put their heads to a task the public had a right to expect something better than it got. The plan they presented was nothing more than a "piece of political joinery." He predicted that unless a more comprehensive and permanent plan should be adopted, a "controversy would arise in the South which would shake the fabric of this Union" to its very foundation.

Bell expressed regret at having presented his plan of compromise. It did not correctly present his views, he said, but he was still convinced that the proposal to divide Texas was sound. Although some members of the committee had denounced it as "impolitic and injurious," he still insisted that such a division would discharge an obligation and defeat an evil by anticipating it. This was an adjustment which must be made within the next few years, so why attempt to settle other questions and leave Texas to disturb the harmony?

Bell came to the defense of President Taylor's action relative to California. The President by encouraging California to request admission to the Union had violated no law, nor had he been guilty of usurpation. The Chief Executive had merely recommended the formation of a state constitution. Congress alone could give vitality to this document. Surely the President's action had placed no restrictions on the action of Congress. Bell regretted to see members under the leadership of Clay make the antagonism of the two plans appear as an issue between Congress and the President.[36]

Clay, shaking his head in protest, exclaimed that he would have been glad to see the President adopt either one of two courses—keep silent or support a plan of compromise. But instead "war, open war, undisguised war, was made by the administration and its partisans against the plan of the committee." If he understood the President's action correctly,

[36] *Ibid.*, 31 Cong., 1 Sess., Appendix, 1091.

Taylor refused to support any plan other than his own. But Clay served notice that he would defend the plan of the committee "against a thousand Presidents, be they whom they may." In that case, Bell replied, the whole matter resolved itself into the question of "whether Mahomet will go to the mountain, or the mountain shall come to Mahomet." Which was the mountain and which was Mahomet he would not undertake to determine. "I beg pardon," retorted Clay, "but I only wanted the mountain to let me alone." [37]

Clay averred that the plan presented by the committee would have passed both houses without serious difficulty had the President supported it or even kept silent. This Clay believed to be the opinion in the mouth of "every member of Congress." Jefferson Davis protested. Nothing like that had ever been in his mouth. He wanted his constituents to understand clearly that he was not under executive influence. In fact he knew of no executive influence. "I do," exclaimed Foote, who went on to say if Bell wished to make an issue of it, he would prove that the cabinet had threatened members with the loss of their seats if they dared oppose the President. "I dare him [Bell] to make that issue," he screamed.[38]

But Bell was cautious. Not wishing any proof from Foote, he sought to dismiss the subject with a statement that he had no knowledge of any effort to influence. Foote countered by asking about the dismissal of Bullitt and Sargent, editors of the *Republic.* Had they not been dismissed for expressing sentiments favorable to the committee's plan? Was not that sufficient evidence of influence? [39] Bell had retreated into a corner and must fight his way out. The editors of the *Republic,* he explained, were generally considered to be in close touch with the President. Since opinions expressed by them were interpreted as having come from the President, they should have correctly ascertained his views before expressing theirs. Instead, they had published misleading sentiments, causing the public to believe that President Taylor ap-

37 *Ibid.,* 1091–92.   38 *Ibid.,* 1093.   39 *Ibid.*

proved of the plan presented by the committee. For this violation of trust they should have been retired from the press.

Bell insisted that the President's determination to stand by his own plan did not constitute an attack upon the committee's plan. Clay's attitude toward Taylor had forced the latter either to stand firm in his own views or to surrender and "cease to be the President of the United States." [40] While Bell was making this vigorous defense of the President, it is unlikely that he was ignorant of the fact that Taylor was planning a cabinet shakeup, and was reported to be seriously considering a man from Kentucky or Tennessee as the successor to Attorney General Reverdy Johnson.[41]

Returning to a consideration of the compromise proposal, Bell argued that the organization of a territorial government for New Mexico was no substantial concession to the South. If he could have his way he would adopt "the spirit of the Missouri Compromise," setting aside a definite part of the territories to which a slaveholder might go with safety. If slavery should become established in the territory of New Mexico, was there any guarantee that Congress would ever admit that territory as a slave state? The chance that slavery would ever become established there was very slender, but it was enough to cause continued agitation in both the North and the South. On the other hand, if Congress would immediately admit New Mexico as a state "one of the bleeding wounds of the country" would be healed. The President had proposed such an admission without congressional interference on the question of slavery. The President's plan would close the controversy, but the committee's plan would merely prolong it. His only interest in the matter, Bell insisted, was to restore "mutual trust and confidence" between the sections. He thought the committee's plan would not accomplish this result.[42]

[40] *Ibid.*, 1094.
[41] Harriet A. Weed (ed.), *Autobiography of Thurlow Weed* (Boston, 1883), 590–91.
[42] *Cong. Globe*, 31 Cong., 1 Sess., Appendix, 1095–98.

It is clear that Bell's interest in the committee's compromise proposals centered around the one concerning New Mexico. He had but little to say about the others. The only point of his own plan of compromise which he wished to preserve was the division of Texas.[43] When this was rejected he lost interest in the Texas–New Mexico boundary dispute. As a slaveholder Bell felt compelled to defend the institution against the attacks by abolitionists. In spite of the preachings of "fanatic priests, or more learned and rational divines," he still preferred to interpret the law of God by the revelations of the history of mankind. History did not reveal a parallel to the growth and development of the African Negro under the supervision of his white master. Regardless of what greatness the future might hold for the Negro race, these people were not yet "prepared for any great change in their condition." It was but "an arrogant and presumptuous arraignment of the ways of Providence . . . for feeble man to declare, that that which has been permitted to exist and prosper from the beginning, among men and nations, is contrary to its will." [44]

It seems clear, also, that Bell was uncertain as to the course he should follow. He repudiated the plan he had offered because it did not correctly present his views. Once he had been willing to compromise his opinions in the interest of settlement. But the committee rejected the heart of his plan. Now he questioned the desirability of making any settlement which would be only temporary. While speaking in favor of his plan, he had denounced the proposal to extend the Missouri Compromise line as being of no benefit to either side. That was when he had had plans for carving two new slave states from Texas and leaving only that portion of New Mexico in which slavery would not likely exist. Now he suggested that should New Mexico not be admitted as a state the Missouri Compromise line should be extended so that the slaveholder might have a place where he could go with safety. But he was certain of one thing: he wished to see both California and New Mexico immediately admitted. In his opinion this action would bring to an end one important cause of agitation. This desire to prevent further agitation resulted from a conservatism which had been increasingly evident in Bell's public life since 1832. The accumulation of property in various forms was having its effect.

The position which Bell occupied, "apart from the acknowledged sagacity of his character and the comprehensiveness of his views," was sufficient to ensure large audiences both on the floor of the Senate and in the gallery.[45] His audience shared his uncertainty. Frederick Seward observed: "John Bell's speech was able and scholarly, and intended to be impartial, but seemed not even to satisfy himself. On the first day of its delivery, people in the galleries said, 'Bell is for it.' On the second day they said, 'Bell will vote against it.' On the third that he 'cannot make up his mind.' " [46] General Winfield Scott observed that Bell had "lost ground with northern whigs, by speaking a little on both sides of the Compromise bill." [47] All observers must have realized, however, that the compromise was receiving some hard blows from an Administration man. After listening to the first three hours of Bell's speech, the Washington correspondent of the Charleston *Courier* reported that the prospects for compromise grew worse and worse.[48]

The friends of the Administration were highly pleased with Bell's defense of the President's plan, even though many did not approve of the suggested extension of the Missouri Compromise line. Men like Bell were "perceptibly decreasing in the public councils," declared a correspondent of the Philadelphia *North American*. He was the leader among "a

[45] Philadelphia *North American and United States Gazette,* July 8, 1850.

[46] Seward, *Reminiscences,* 80.

[47] Memorandum by General Scott dated July 16, 1850, in Millard Fillmore Papers.

[48] Charleston *Courier,* July 4, 1850, quoted in Knoxville *Register,* July 20, 1850.

few who examine great measures, not for their momentary effect, but for their future influence upon the country." Among our public men, there were none who enjoyed "a higher reputation for integrity of purpose; for zeal in the cause which he espouses, for fidelity to his friends; for disinterestedness; for sound national opinion and for devoted patriotism." This speech by Bell "increased his already well-established reputation"; the courage and dignity which characterized his manner, even when he was opposed by a "combination of talents," ensured him the "respect of all parties, and the gratitude and confidence of the Whigs of the whole Union." [49] The editors should have said the Administration Whigs.

A group of Bell's associates insisted that he present a substitute for the compromise proposed by the committee. If such a substitute provided for the extension of the Missouri Compromise line and the South could be lined up in its support, there would be some hope of success. Might not Bell's loyalty to the Administration and his hostility toward Clay be sufficient to win Taylor's approval? [50] Those who reasoned thus must not have known of the extent to which William H. Seward was influencing President Taylor. There is no proof that Bell seriously considered offering such a substitute proposal; but if he did, he abandoned the plan upon the death of the President on July 9.

The death of President Taylor removed the greatest barrier in the way of compromise. Millard Fillmore, the new President, was a political enemy of Seward and opposed most of the things for which he stood. This fact alone was probably sufficient to bring about an abandonment of the position taken by Taylor. There was increasing evidence, however, that the "omnibus" character of the bill which had been designed to carry the principal part of the committee's plan into effect

[49] Philadelphia *North American and United States Gazette,* July 8, 1850.
[50] Charleston *Courier,* July 7, 1850, quoted in Knoxville *Register,* July 20, 1850.

would result in its defeat in the Senate. The combined strength of those groups which opposed the bill for different reasons was too much for the best efforts of Henry Clay. On July 31 the provisions were stricken from the bill one by one. Clay, broken in strength and spirits, departed for Newport to recuperate, and Douglas assumed the leadership.[51] Commenting on the senatorial reaction to the defeat of the omnibus bill, the Washington correspondent of the New York *Express* thought Bell to be "half-sorry, but two-thirds glad." But "there sat Old Hal [Clay], as melancholy as Caius Marius over the ruins of Carthage." [52]

The provisions of the omnibus bill were reintroduced as separate bills and passed. Bell voted in favor of the admission of California and for the proposed settlement of the Texas-New Mexico boundary dispute. He cast no vote at all on the bill establishing a territorial government for New Mexico. No division was recorded on the passage of the fugitive slave bill, but Bell voted in favor of passing it to a third reading.[53] A feeling of helplessness and the fact that the Whigs of his home state were holding numerous mass meetings in favor of the compromise assisted Bell in making up his mind to vote for these bills.[54]

The last of the compromise bills to be acted upon was the proposal to abolish the slave trade within the District of Columbia. Bell did not agree with the "many distinguished and eminent" men who insisted that Congress did not possess the power to regulate slavery within the District. According to his interpretation of the Constitution, Congress had the same power over the subject within the District that the states had within their borders, but when he considered the probable effect upon the adjoining slave states, he had grave doubts as to the advisability of the exercise of this power. A power

51 George Fort Milton, *The Eve of Conflict: Stephen A. Douglas and the Needless War* (Boston, 1934), 72.
52 New York *Express*, August 2, 1850.
53 *Cong. Globe*, 31 Cong., 1 Sess., 1555, 1573, 1588, 1660.
54 Nashville *Daily Gazette*, June 2, 1850.

might be ever so clear and "yet the exercise of it very unjust and oppressive, and very mischievous too."

If it would put an end to abolitionist agitation Bell would favor abolishing slavery within the District. He could see little prospect of this, however, since Senator Chase had already served notice that there was more to be expected on the slavery question. What was the limit to which the North intended to go? Could the South "ever expect repose from these agitations?" Had it not been for "ill-judged agitation" and the "officious intervention of northern fanatics" the more offensive features of the institution would long ago have been ameliorated. Attacks by abolitionists had made new restraints upon slaves imperative.

The only way to end the agitation once and for all, Bell concluded, was to abolish slavery within the District and remove from it all people of color. If slaves should be freed and allowed to remain within the District it "would soon come to pass that Congress itself would not find it convenient, if safe even, to sit here beset and surrounded by an overgrown population of colored inhabitants—degraded in caste, and for the most part idle, vicious, and mischievous—desperate paupers, sustained by the sympathy of one section and exasperated by the opposition of the other." [55]

At one time during his remarks Bell stated that in "deference to the sensibilities of our northern friends" he would vote for the bill. But before the vote was taken he had changed his mind. When the bill was called up for final reading on September 16, Bell joined with eighteen other Southern senators in voting in the negative.[56]

Many Tennessee Whigs had not appreciated the position taken by their Senator on the question of the compromise. As the session of Congress drew to a close and Bell prepared to meet the opposition at home, he felt the need of an explanation of his conduct. Half in defense of his actions and half

[55] *Cong. Globe*, 31 Cong., 1 Sess., Appendix, 1668–69.
[56] *Ibid.*, 31 Cong., 1 Sess., 1830.

as a warning of dangers to come, he addressed an open letter to the citizens of Tennessee: "The crisis is not past; nor can perfect harmony be restored to the country until the North shall cease to vex the South upon the subject of slavery; and that can never be, while the animating principle of party organization and cohesion continues without change or modification." The country is ever in danger when excess party spirit and ambition bring about a loss of dignity and "degenerate into factions." This "danger becomes imminent and extreme when sectional interests—sectional jealousies, inflamed by a diversity of social relations—become elements of political strife. . . . I am no ultraist, and favor no extreme measures. A spirit of conciliation and forbearance is demanded by patriotism and the exigencies of the times, as well on the part of the South, as on that of the North; but there is a difference between a policy dictated by a spirit of forbearance, and *quietism,* which may seem to approve, and would, inevitably, invite aggression." [57]

[57] Memphis *Daily Eagle,* September 27, 1850.

Chapter *XIII*

"BRAKEMAN UPON THE WHIRLING TRAIN"

ALTHOUGH not as close to the new Chief Executive as he had been to Taylor, Bell found no serious fault with the new Administration. "As for yourself," he wrote to President Fillmore, "since your accession to power & the avowal of the principles and policy of your admn. I have never, for a moment, wavered or faltered in the sentiment that it was my duty to give you a cordial & earnest support. In the conversations I have had with you, I have been perfectly candid, and I have seen no cause to change my mind or feelings." In patronage matters he found both the President and the cabinet generally co-operative. At times, however, he became a bit irked at his inability to see Fillmore when he wished; the President was either in conference with his cabinet or out of his office. And on one occasion, when the Postmaster General persisted in reading a newspaper during an interview, Bell picked up his hat and walked out.[1]

Regardless of the opposition resulting from his stand on the compromise, Bell's greatest worry was the patronage. Tennessee Whigs, already differing on the compromise, became even more divided in the scramble for office. The chief dispenser of the patronage became the principal target; distinct Bell and anti-Bell groups soon made their appearance. A few uncertain but hopeful office seekers, desiring to keep a foot in each camp, solicited Bell's assistance and at the same time requested that their letters be destroyed lest the correspondence later come to public view and embarrass

[1] Bell to Fillmore, April 29, 1851, in Fillmore Papers.

them in their home section.[2] Many who failed to secure jobs joined the anti-Bell forces. Bell privately complained that apparently all applicants believed that he possessed the power to place them in lucrative positions if he so desired.[3] Even William B. Campbell, who had probably been Bell's closest political friend in his home state, privately remarked that the Whigs then in control of Tennessee politics were an unprincipled clique. "There does not live a more cold hearted, selfish and artful scoundrel than John Bell. I think well of Mr. Fillmore & his cabinet, but they ought not to be ruled by John Bell in Tennessee matters." [4] Evidently Campbell himself had suffered a disappointment, for, two years earlier, he had stated that Bell and Gentry, both *"peculiar* friends of the President," were men of "high talents." [5]

From Mississippi, Texas, Arkansas, and California numerous former Tennesseans wrote Bell, insisting that he was the only senator who could aid them in securing appointments.[6] The Democrats also added their bit to Bell's discomfort. The new chief justice of Minnesota Territory, Cave Johnson complained, had been an iron molder at Bell's ironworks. Deserting the heat of the foundry for Blackstone, he had entered the Tennessee legislature and contributed toward Bell's election to the Senate. Another incompetent rewarded by the Whig Senator! [7] And in two unpleasant conferences, Congressman Andrew Johnson, adopting what he himself characterized as the tactics of a bully, warned Bell that East Tennessee would hold him strictly accountable for dismissals as well as for appointments in that section.[8] Overwhelmed with complaints, appeals, and threats, Bell, in an attitude bordering

[2] *Id.* to Nelson, December 17, 1850, in Nelson Papers.
[3] *Id.* to *id.*, November 6, 1850, *ibid.; id.* to William B. Campbell, January 25, 1851, in David Campbell Papers.
[4] William B. Campbell to David Campbell, February 9, 1851, *ibid.*
[5] *Id.* to *id.*, May 14, 1849, *ibid.*
[6] Bell to William B. Campbell, January 25, 1851, *ibid.*
[7] Cave Johnson to Buchanan, August 13, 1849, in Buchanan Papers.
[8] Andrew Johnson to D. T. Patterson, May 30, 1850, in Andrew Johnson Papers (Division of Manuscripts, Library of Congress).

on despair, exclaimed, "God help me under such circumstances." [9]

Brownlow continued his press attack upon Bell even though the latter had been compelled to pay the note which he had endorsed when new presses were purchased for Brownlow's *Knoxville Whig*. Each announcement of the appointment of one of the "Parson's" enemies was the occasion for another tirade and if it was another promotion for Allen A. Hall the editor's fury was unbounded. In private correspondence, Brownlow complained of being mistreated by the Whig leaders, and he swore to "pay them back." "My greatest concern now is to get out of the grasp of Bell and Gentry," he wrote Thomas A. R. Nelson, "and this I will do if it costs me my office." He would surely pay what he owed them by the following winter.[10] Brownlow's wrath did not begin to subside until reliable persons assured him that Bell had not been responsible for the elevation of Hall.

While showing great concern over the attitude of the *Knoxville Whig*, Bell was also conscious of the precarious condition in which the national Whig party had been placed. Further local division would only hasten the party's demise. During and immediately following the struggle over the Compromise of 1850, Whigs of the South were embarrassed by the antislavery sentiments of their political brethren in the North. It was difficult for proslavery Whigs to explain away the antislavery utterances of such a political associate as William H. Seward. It had become apparent that unless an end could be made to the slavery controversy, Whigs from the North and the South could not long continue to function as one party.

Bell had prophesied that the Compromise of 1850 would not heal the nation's wounds. By the early part of 1851 he was contemplating the formation of a conservative Union party to which could be attracted the moderates of both

9 Bell to Nelson, November 6, 1850, in Nelson Papers.
10 Brownlow to *id.*, May 30, 1851, *ibid.*; Bell to *id.*, May 4, 1851, *ibid.*

parties, North and South. His idea found little support even within his own state. Charles Ready, a prominent Whig of Murfreesboro, advised Bell that such a plan was "impracticable and inadmissible, if it were practicable." Conservative Whigs and Democrats would no more mix than "oil and water." [11] Thomas A. R. Nelson, a Whig leader in East Tennessee, was quite willing to see the Whig party become the "chosen Champion of the Union," but he was opposed to changing the name. The old party must continue to stand firm in the "sturdiest hostility to the annexation of Texas and the Mexican War and the train of evils which has followed." He explained that all Whigs who had distinguished themselves in the late war could be praised, while all blame for the war and the threat of disunion was placed upon the shoulders of those "nullifiers" who had sought to use the annexation of Texas as a means of building up Southern strength against the North. [12]

Receiving little encouragement, Bell temporarily abandoned his new party idea and plunged into the state campaign of 1851. He urged the popular William B. Campbell, who was a hero of the Mexican War, to desert the bench of the circuit court and become the Whig candidate for governor. When Campbell finally agreed, Bell became an adviser on campaign strategy. Owing to serious illness in his home plus a fear that his personal appearance as a campaigner might arouse "a spirit of jealousy in some other leading Whigs," he made no active canvass; but he urged Campbell to give full publicity to his "opinion on the subject of internal improvements and especially in relation to the projected railroads in East Ten." [13] Bell was also much interested in the election of members of the state legislature. The term of the Democratic Senator, Hopkins L. Turney, would expire in 1851, and the

[11] Charles Ready to Bell, January 3, 1851, in John Bell Papers (Division of Manuscripts, Library of Congress).

[12] Nelson to *id.*, January 10, 1851, *ibid.*

[13] Bell to Campbell, January 25, March 20, July 5, 1851, in David Campbell Papers.

new legislature would select his successor. A Democratic legislature would mean the continuation of a Democrat in the Senate. Furthermore, that same Democratic legislature might even choose Bell's successor in 1851 even though his term would not expire until 1853. That is what Bell's Whig friends had done to Senator Felix Grundy in 1837.[14]

The Whigs won control of both the executive and legislative branches of the state government, but their victory did not repair the breaks within their ranks; they immediately began a squabble over who should succeed Turney in the Senate. All efforts to make a caucus nomination failed, and the names of no fewer than six members of the party were presented to the legislature. Bell took no public stand in favor of any candidate, although there is evidence that he favored Thomas A. R. Nelson.[15] Undoubtedly Bell's lack of activity was prompted by a fear that those who had opposed his stand on the Compromise of 1850 might try to force his retirement from the Senate.[16] Certainly he did not approve of the selection of James C. Jones of Memphis, which eventually came as a result of what Brownlow termed "unholy and unnatural combinations."

When Bell returned to Washington late in the fall of 1851, the national outlook did not appear too dark. There was some friction over the enforcement of the fugitive slave law in certain Northern states; however, there was reason to believe that the general acceptance of the Compromise of 1850 might prevail. In January, 1851, thirty-four Southern senators and congressmen, representing both parties, had joined with ten from the free states in signing a pledge not to support for office any man who did not accept the finality of the compromise or did not oppose all forms of "agitation upon the subject of slavery." Bell stated that he favored such an idea, but hesitated to sign because he "thought the movement not

14 Parks, *Felix Grundy*, 309-13.
15 R. H. McEwen to Nelson, September 13, 1851, in Nelson Papers.
16 Andrew Ewing to Donelson, October 12, 1851, in Donelson Papers.

quite such in point of support as to make it effective." He suspected that it was a part of a plan to nominate Clay for the presidency.[17]

Owing to the temporary lull in the territorial controversy from 1850–1854, Congress was able to devote more of its time to the question of internal improvements. Most sections of the Union had long been conscious of the need for overland and water routes to markets, and many of the states had spent heavily on the construction of roads, canals, and railroads. Neither had the Federal government ignored these needs. In spite of constitutional scruples against spending Federal money on improvements of a local nature, millions had been spent on projects which had been classed as having national importance. This fact caused many petitioners for Federal aid to insist that their projects were of national significance. And of those who were bothered by constitutional scruples, some made a distinction between Federal grants of money and grants of public lands. The Constitution might limit the power of Congress to spend public money, they insisted, but there was no limitation on the power to dispose of public lands.

The states of the Mississippi Valley, except Kentucky and Tennessee, still contained millions of acres of Federal lands. Representatives from those states had long advocated the cession of all public lands to the states in which they lay. When Congress failed to sanction this plan, the sponsors of internal improvements in those states urged Federal grants of land as subsidies of their projects, especially railroads. The first of such grants came in 1850 when Stephen A. Douglas sponsored a bill to subsidize a proposed Illinois Central Railroad, which would eventually connect Lake Michigan with the Gulf at Mobile.[18] Each land state through which it ran was to receive Federal grants of land, in alternate sections, six miles deep on each side of the line. The participating

[17] Bell to William B. Campbell, January 25, 1851, in David Campbell Papers.
[18] A similar bill had passed the Senate in 1848 but had failed in the House.

states—Illinois, Mississippi, and Alabama—were to sell these lands and apply the proceeds to the cost of construction. As was calculated by Douglas, the inclusion of Mississippi and Alabama brought support from many who had long been advocating a Mobile and Ohio line.[19]

Bell could see no constitutional objections to granting Federal lands for such a purpose, and he declared that this particular project gave evidence of "great public utility." Lands should never lie idle, he said, when they could be put to public use; and by public, he meant a great portion of the nation. Such a railroad would "contribute imperceptibly to swell the tide of general prosperity." Still, the Senator from Illinois, he argued, ought not to propose to limit the land grants to three states when the line must pass across five. What about Kentucky and Tennessee? Certainly the proposed railroad would be of greatest value only when the entire line was completed. It was true that no Federal lands were located in Tennessee and Kentucky, but why could they not be given lands lying in other states? After all, the public domain was the property of all the states, not just those in which the lands happen to lie; therefore, he proposed that Tennessee and Kentucky receive grants similar in amount to those to be made to the other three states.

William R. King of Alabama objected and accused Bell of an attempt to defeat the bill. Tennessee, he said, had already greatly profited by the government extinction of Indian titles in that state. This remark brought protests from both Bell and Turney. Bell insisted that Tennessee's income from the Indian lands had not been enough to defray the cost of litigations over titles. And Turney added that the lands actually received by the state were not equal in value to the sections given to other states for school purposes. King then shifted to another point. To grant lands to states in which they did not lie, he asserted, would raise an embarrassing question relative

19 Roy M. Robbins, *Our Landed Heritage: The Public Domain, 1776–1936* (Princeton, 1942), 160–63.

to the powers of Congress, resulting in a division among the members and in the defeat of the bill. He appealed to Bell "as a friend of the work" to withdraw his amendment.

James Shields of Illinois joined King. He requested, "as a special favor," that Bell withdraw the proposal and allow the bill to pass. If this were done, Shields would support a bill to give Tennessee and Kentucky enough Illinois land to build their portion of the railroad. But to deny to Tennessee and Kentucky assistance equal to that given the other three states, exclaimed Jacob W. Miller of New Jersey, would be a "partial administration of the public property." Jefferson Davis of Mississippi, however, thought the two propositions quite different. To grant to Tennessee and Kentucky lands lying in other states would be the same as appropriating money from the Treasury, an action which he could not support.[20] Before the debate closed, several other senators had had their brief say; and in the end, the bill passed, but Kentucky and Tennessee got no lands.

The success of the Illinois Central bill brought forth numerous similar proposals. In 1852, Iowa asked for a million and a half acres for railroad construction; Missouri asked for almost two million; and Michigan sought an appropriation of $400,000 to build a canal around St. Mary's Falls. On all such bills, Bell's position remained the same: he favored grants of land to both land and landless states, but he opposed appropriations of money. While speaking on the Iowa bill he was a bit severe in his denunciation of those who opposed grants to landless states. If, as was being argued, railroads greatly increased land values within the regions through which they were constructed, then why should landless states be deprived of participation in this prosperity. There was "no logic, no reason, no justice in this limitation," he exclaimed. It was "simply a policy founded upon a cool, clear, and selfish calculation of local interest." Public lands were the property of all the states, he continued; therefore, the lands in Illinois were

[20] *Cong. Globe,* 31 Cong., 1 Sess., 867–70.

just "as much the property of Tennessee and Kentucky as Illinois." If those lands were appropriated, it must be for the mutual benefit of all states.[21]

Bell opposed the Michigan canal bill because it called for an appropriation from the public treasury. He could see how such a canal would be desirable, yet he could not believe it essential to national defense. Many other important canal bills had already been defeated by Congress. The same treatment had also been given the bills asking for appropriations to clear obstructions from the Ohio and Tennessee rivers. He said that he could not support an appropriation for a St. Mary's Falls canal as long as a million and a half dollars was being lost annually because of obstructions in the Ohio River. Furthermore, regardless of whether Congress did or did not possess the power to make appropriations for roads and canals, he opposed such a practice on the ground that it would lead to profligacy and dissatisfaction. Federal funds could never be properly distributed by such a method.[22]

While Congress debated internal improvement bills, the nation was preparing for another presidential election. As early as March, 1851, Bell was engaged in extensive correspondence with prominent Tennessee Whigs, especially editors, urging them to give a "cordial support" to the present Administration and pointing out that, owing to "the uncertain chances of listing Mr. Webster or Mr. Clay, however deserving they may be," the Whigs should center their efforts on Fillmore for 1852. Bell was careful, however, not to assail or proscribe General Winfield Scott or any other prominent Whig, "except only such as manifest a determination to favor or continue the slave agitation." [23] Two months earlier, Bell had confided to William B. Campbell his predictions and preferences for 1852. He predicted that General Winfield Scott and John J. Crittenden would be the ticket, although he preferred Fillmore if there was a chance to elect him. He consid-

21 *Ibid.*, 32 Cong., 1 Sess., Appendix, 197–98.   22 *Ibid.*, 947.
23 Bell to Fillmore, April 29, 1851, in Fillmore Papers.

ered the nomination of Clay or Webster to be "out of the question." However, owing to Webster's "well-timed modification of his views on the subject of the Wilmot Proviso," Bell declared that he deserved "the lasting gratitude of the South, and the presidency itself, if sufficient strength could be rallied to elect him." [24]

In spite of their disunity, the approach of the election of 1852 made it necessary that the Tennessee Whigs attempt to clarify their position on national issues, especially on the question of slavery. In February, 1852, the Whig-controlled legislature adopted resolutions condemning the activities of the abolitionists, expressing deep devotion to the Union, and pronouncing the Compromise of 1850 the final word on the slavery controversy.[25] Bell assured Fillmore that on the question of slavery the Tennessee Whigs were "undivided & sound," but it would be very difficult to persuade them to support any favorite of the free-soil Whigs, "especially of N.Y. and Mass^{tts}." [26]

The Whigs, seeking to make the fullest use of their surviving hero of the Mexican War, nominated Scott for the presidency. There was some talk of Bell for vice-president. In presenting such a suggestion to the public, the New York *Courier and Enquirer* pronounced a flattering eulogy on the Tennessee Senator:

John Bell is one of the soundest Whigs and the most conservative statesman [*sic*] of the day; and when Mr. Clay shall be no more, and Mr. Webster . . . shall have passed . . . John Bell, if spared . . . , will be their most prominent representative in the Councils of the Nation, and will worthily uphold the great conservative principles which Webster and Clay have so ably maintained. . . . Already does he occupy in the Senate, the conservative ground which so emphatically belonged to Webster and Clay; and although he does not possess the brilliant intellect of either of

[24] *Id.* to Campbell, January 25, 1851, in David Campbell Papers; copy of *id.* to J. H. McMahan, ?, 1851, *ibid.*
[25] *Acts of Tennessee,* 1851–1852, pp. 719–21.
[26] Bell to Fillmore, April 29, 1851, in Fillmore Papers.

these great statesmen, yet his conservatism, his devotion to the constitution, his firmness, and statesman-like qualities, give him an influence in the Senate . . . which at this moment appertains to no other Senator. Unmoved by personal ambition, he is the very man of all others who is most likely to have thrust upon him the Whig nomination for the Vice Presidency.[27]

When Scott failed to declare his unconditional support of the compromise, the Tennessee Whigs became badly confused. Congressman Meredith P. Gentry and Christopher H. Williams, who had worked to prevent the nomination of Scott,[28] and the eccentric "Parson" Brownlow openly repudiated the candidate. Bell begged Gentry and Williams not to break with the party, but to no avail.[29] Bell himself, professing disapproval of some tactics used in securing the nomination for Scott, confided to William B. Campbell that he had "no heart in the business." A continued illness made it impossible for the Senator to be active in the campaign, even if he had so desired. During the past year he had been so ill that he had at times been "privately resolved to resign." [30] His friendship for Fillmore brought him an offer of the office of Secretary of the Navy in July, 1852. The offer was declined, however, with the explanation that "during the brief period which must, in any event, terminate my public service," he believed it inadvisable to change positions.[31]

Congress did not adjourn until August 31, and Bell remained in Washington several weeks after the close of the session, recuperating from the strain of his activities and building up strength for the trip home. He arrived in Nashville on October 18. Prior to his arrival the streets had been decorated with flaming banners announcing that John Bell was "coming to town." At the city limits he was met by a huge crowd of "most respectable" citizens, who formed an escort-

[27] Quoted in Memphis *Daily Eagle and Enquirer*, May 30, 1852.
[28] *Cong. Globe*, 32 Cong., 1 Sess., Appendix, 871-73, 708-12.
[29] Bell to William B. Campbell, September 3, and ?, 1852, in David Campbell Papers.   [30] *Id.* to *id.*, ?, 1852, *ibid.*
[31] Bell to Fillmore, July 8, 1852, in Fillmore Papers.

ing procession consisting of thirty military, twenty-six foot-
men, eighteen buggies, and one barouche.[32] A friendly editor
commented that Bell's escort was probably not as large as
the one which had previously met Senator Jones, but was
much more respectable. He was glad to see that so many people still possessed enough discrimination to "judge between
the true talents of Bell, and the froth of Jones." [33]

The trip home must not have greatly aggravated Bell's illness, for he made a political speech at the Nashville courthouse on the evening of his arrival. By way of introduction,
he expressed serious concern over his failing health and his
inability to be active in the campaign. He was pleased to
learn, however, that "able expounders of the principles of
Whig faith" were already active throughout the state. His support of Scott, he explained, dated back to the early part of
1851; however, he never ceased to look with favor upon Daniel Webster, that senator who, on March 7, 1850, "announced
his support of the Compromise measure—bared himself to
the attacks of the opposition, and defied its assaults where it
was fiercest, in his own State, and proclaimed to the world
that he would, on such a question, know no North, no South,
no East, no West, but stand by the Constitution and the
Union." By that stand Daniel Webster had placed all Southern Whigs under obligation to him.

Bell said he knew that some of his political friends were
opposed to co-operating with antislavery Whigs. Some, so he
was informed, even preferred to support Franklin Pierce, the
Democratic candidate, rather than to encourage the antislavery group by voting for Scott. They argued that the correct procedure was to put an end to all co-operation with free-
soil men, regardless of party. But knowing that the Democrats
were also infected with free-soilism, Bell declared that he
preferred to stand by one whom he believed to be "sound
upon the mischievous sectional issue." [34] Such moderation on

[32] Nashville *American,* October 19, 1852.   [33] *Ibid.,* October 20, 1852.
[34] Summary of speech in *Republican Banner and Nashville Whig,* October
25, 1852.

the part of the leader of the Tennessee Whigs might have been due to his illness; still, one gets the impression that he was more concerned about the condition of his party in Tennessee than over the election of Scott. Bell always considered his participation in the organization of the Whig party "the proudest circumstance" of his career.[35]

James C. Jones, the other Tennessee senator, actively supported the party's nominee, a fact which did not stimulate Bell's enthusiasm for the cause. Bell considered Jones a "stump stereotyped speaker," without depth or substance.[36]

In spite of the division among the Whigs, Scott carried the state by almost two thousand votes, but his overwhelming defeat in the nation as a whole deprived his local supporters of cause of rejoicing. The campaign increased the confusion and distrust among Tennessee Whigs; and this was especially serious in view of the fact that 1853 was the year for state elections. Gentry suspected that Jones and Bell were conspiring to destroy him politically because of his opposition to Scott. His suspicion of Bell was unfounded; still both Gentry and Williams, sensing political isolation, decided not to become candidates for re-election to Congress.[37] During the winter of 1852–1853 it was general talk throughout the state that the Whig party was dead. Even Bell admitted privately in February: "I think I see signs of a more decisive breaking up of our party in Tenn. in the next election than I have seen at any time heretofore." [38]

Late in 1852 Bell made a business trip to New Orleans. While in the city he was invited to attend a public dinner to be given in his honor. He declined the dinner, but took advantage of the opportunity to address a note of encouragement to the Louisiana Whigs. He appealed to all to remain loyal to the original principles of their party and to demonstrate to the nation that the Whig organization had not

35 Ibid.
36 Bell to William B. Campbell, September 3, 1852, in David Campbell Papers.
37 Id. to id., January 6, 12, February 5, 1853, ibid.
38 Id. to id., February 5, 1853, ibid.

ceased to be effective. When referring to principles, Bell explained, he did not mean "the establishment of a United States Bank, or the prosecution of a system of Internal Improvements." Such things as these were not principles; they were "only the modes or forms of effecting great objects." "Principles lie deeper, and embrace multitudes of modes and forms." Bell admitted that the political outlook was not bright; still he insisted that the Whigs, working from their subordinate position, could serve as a "brakeman upon the whirling train." Regardless of what the future held for the Whigs, he hoped they would never "wage a factious opposition, or fail to do full justice and yield a cordial support to those measures of the incoming administration which may appear to be dictated by wise and patriotic views." [39]

When the Tennessee Whigs assembled for their state convention late in April, 1853, to nominate candidates for state offices, their political outlook was gloomy. During the past two years they had enjoyed control of both the legislative and executive branches of the state government; but Governor Campbell had declined to make the race for re-election. In an effort to revive party enthusiasm, Bell hurried home from Washington to attend the convention. Declaring that "there must and will be two parties in every free country," he assured the delegates that there were principles and policies "closely identified with the permanent success of republican institutions, which will survive every defeat which, like the Phoenix, will continue to rise again, however crushing and exterminating their overthrow may sometimes appear." The name of the party might be changed, he said, but the fundamental principles of the Whigs could never be destroyed.[40] Bell's opponents reminded the public that the Senator's efforts to convince the people that there was still a Whig party were due primarily to the fact that his own re-

[39] Quoted in *Brownlow's Knoxville Whig*, January 1, 1853.
[40] Summary of Bell's speech as reported in *Republican Banner and Nashville Whig*, May 3, 1853.

election to the Senate would be determined by the next legis-lature.[41]

The Democratic press gleefully announced the demise of "whiggery" in Tennessee, and the results of the state election came near to verifying the claim. Great was the humiliation of the Whigs and the exultation of the Democrats when it was announced that the "Eagle Orator," Gustavus A. Henry, had been defeated by Andrew Johnson, "the plebeian," in the race for governor. In the Tennessee legislature the Whig majority was reduced to thirteen in the lower house, and the Democrats obtained a majority of one in the senate.[42] "The masses have done the work," exclaimed an excited Demo-crat. The day laborer and the mechanic had delivered a fatal blow to Whig power.[43] The only consolation left the Whigs was in the fact that when the two houses should meet in joint session the Whigs would be in the majority. If they worked in harmony, they could continue to control both seats in the United States Senate. But the Democrats, knowing the seri-ousness of the divisions among the Whigs, expected to pos-sess the balance of power, and prophesied some "fun and devilment" in the coming session of the legislature.[44]

The fact that the two senators were from the middle and western sections of the state produced a feeling in the east-ern section that the time had come for one of its sons to be honored. When Bell's term expired in 1853, harmony might have been restored if he had agreed to step aside in favor of a man from East Tennessee. The condition of his health would have given ample excuse for his wishing to retire, had he wanted one. The most popular East Tennessee Whig was Thomas A. R. Nelson of Jonesborough who had been de-feated for the Senate in 1851. Long a close friend of Bell, Nel-son hesitated to oppose him, but contributed his part to the confusion by allowing his name to be put before the legisla-

[41] Nashville *American*, May 4, 1853.   [42] Hamer, *Tennessee*, II, 492.
[43] S. R. Anderson to Nicholson, August 16, 1853, in Nicholson Papers.
[44] *Ibid.*

ture.[45] The situation was further clouded when Gustavus A. Henry assumed the attitude that his fellow Whigs should make him senator in compensation for the humiliation he had suffered from his defeat in the race for governor.[46] Henry's home was at Clarksville in the middle section of the state; therefore, he would not be acceptable to those who demanded a senator from the East. Working through Felix K. Zollicoffer, Bell attempted to persuade Henry not to enter the race. On the other hand, Henry's friends insisted that Bell should not seek re-election. Bell replied that even if he did withdraw, the Democrats would support Nelson or Gentry in order further to humiliate Henry.[47]

Long before time for the election, Bell abandoned any idea that he may have had of retiring. A few weeks' vacationing at Montvale Springs, Blount County, East Tennessee, improved both his health and his political ambition. As Gentry remarked, "Old veteran politicians cling to political existence with a tenacity like that of the drowning man who catches at a straw." [48] In the face of opposition within his own party in the eastern and middle sections of the state, Bell realized that his hope of re-election lay with the legislators from West Tennessee, many of whom were Democrats. Since Senator Jones was from Memphis, the western section of the state would not likely have a candidate in the coming election.

Taking advantage of the fact that the Southern and Western Commercial Convention was scheduled to meet in Memphis early in June, 1853, Bell deserted his mountain retreat and hastened to Memphis, where he "just dropped in to visit and listen to the convention—not speak." As was to be expected, however, Whigs and Democrats alike demanded a word from him before the convention adjourned. In responding to this demand he stated that he considered the conven-

[45] A. Nelson to Thomas A. R. Nelson, September 1, 1853, in Nelson Papers.
[46] Henry to id., August 29, 1853, ibid.
[47] Bell to William B. Campbell, August 14, 19, 1853, in David Campbell Papers.
[48] Meredith P. Gentry to Nelson, March 20, 1852, in Nelson Papers.

tion a great gathering of delegates from the southern geographical division of the Union, but that it should in no sense be looked upon as "contemplating offence to other sections." All sections, he said, should be interested in projects for the development of communications. He attributed the wealth of the North to its geographical position and its commercial navy, and pointed out that the surplus derived from these advantages had been invested in "improvements of the useful branches of science." He suggested that the hope of the South was the adoption of the spirit of enterprise found in the North, and expressed the opinion that nothing was quite so important in the development of Southern resources as the construction of a railroad connecting the Mississippi valley with the Pacific. The vastness of such a project made it national in character and importance, he explained; therefore, government and individual enterprise should be united in the accomplishment of so great an undertaking.[49] This railroad speech removed all possibility of doubt about Bell's support in West Tennessee. The people of that section earnestly hoped that when such a railroad should be built Memphis would be the eastern terminus.

Outside of Tennessee the party press showed concern over the possibility that Bell might be retired to private life. The New York *Courier and Enquirer* expressed the hope that the Whigs would not deprive the Senate of "one of its most valuable and honored members." The editor had no interest in local jealousies, he said, but he knew that there was no man in public life who was "less of a demagogue; none, in habits of mind, of feeling, of language and of action, more of a statesman," than John Bell.[50] The Philadelphia *Inquirer* insisted that the Whigs keep their best men in office. Bell should be re-elected because he was "highly intellectual," "a far-seeing statesman," and "an eloquent speaker." [51]

[49] Summary of Bell's remarks as reported in Memphis *Daily Appeal*, June 10, 1853, and in *Republican Banner and Nashville Whig*, June 20, 1853.
[50] Quoted in *Republican Banner and Nashville Whig*, September 15, 1853.
[51] Quoted in *ibid.*

When the two houses of the legislature convened in joint session in October, 1853, for the purpose of electing a senator, the Whigs were still badly divided. An attempt to reach a caucus decision on a senatorial nomination failed,[52] and the names of Nelson, Henry, and Bell were placed before the assembly. In order to avoid the appearance of complete defeat, the Democrats proposed Cave Johnson of Clarksville, a former congressman and Postmaster General in Polk's cabinet. There was no hope of electing Johnson, yet the division among the Whigs gave to the Democrats the balance of power. They used this power with considerable pleasure as the contest continued for many ballots, casting a few votes for one Whig and then another, but being careful not to give any candidate enough to elect.

The three Whig candidates were on the scene and soliciting votes. "Parson" Brownlow's correspondent observed Bell "moving gracefully, but constantly through the crowd of members and citizens."[53] Nelson's friends claimed that the Democrats promised him their support when the proper time should arrive,[54] but the time apparently never came. Some Democrats had expected Nelson's backers to concede defeat and shift their influence to Henry.[55] There was also some expectation in Democratic circles that neither of the three candidates would be elected and that it would be necessary to bring in a fourth man, probably John Marshall of Franklin.[56] Gentry, by a previous announcement that he would not be adverse to accepting a senatorship from the hands of the Democrats, had ruined his chances to get Whig votes.[57]

[52] Foster was supporting Henry, but was reputed to have threatened to withdraw his support if Henry agreed to a caucus. John K. Howard to Nicholson, September 21, 1853, Nicholson Papers.

[53] *Brownlow's Knoxville Whig*, October 8, 1853.

[54] Brownlow to Oliver P. Temple, October 26, 1853, in Oliver P. Temple Papers (University of Tennessee Library).

[55] Howard to Nicholson, September 21, 1853, in Nicholson Papers.

[56] *Ibid.* Marshall was a first cousin of Bell.

[57] S. R. Anderson to A. O. P. Nicholson, August 16, 1853; John K. Howard to *id.*, September 21, 1853, in Nicholson Papers.

When the Democratic legislators had toyed with the Whigs as long as they desired, the westerners led enough votes into the Bell ranks to re-elect him. From "first to last, the Western District Democrats have been for Bell," complained Brownlow who was still a bit irritated over the patronage controversy. "They have but *one idea* and that is the Pacific Railroad, and its terminus at Memphis—and Bell is their man for the scheme." [58] Cave Johnson attributed Bell's reelection to activities of the A. O. P. Nicholson faction of the Democratic party. A serious rift had developed between Nicholson and former Governor Aaron V. Brown.[59] There was some truth to the charge of Nicholson's friendship for Bell. Since 1847 the two had been friendly and had corresponded occasionally.[60] It is certain that the election contributed nothing toward a restoration of harmony within the ranks of the Tennessee Whigs. Henry went home "mortified, disappointed, and mad at the whole world." [61]

While the legislature was wrangling over the election of a senator, the other members of the Tennessee congressional delegation were preparing to take their seats in the Thirty-third Congress. With the re-election of Bell the Whigs still held both seats in the Senate; but the House delegation was composed of five Democrats and five Whigs.[62] Four of the five Whigs were from the middle division of the state, and the fifth was from West Tennessee.

Soon after his arrival in Washington, Bell sensed the fact that President Franklin Pierce did not command the undivided support of the Democratic leaders, and he hoped to

[58] Brownlow to Oliver P. Temple, October 26, 1853, in Temple Papers.
[59] Johnson to Buchanan, November 20, 1853, in Buchanan Papers.
[60] Bell to Nicholson, December 30, 1847, in Nicholson Papers.
[61] Brownlow to Temple, October 26, 1853, in Temple Papers.
[62] Whigs: William Cullom of Smith County, Robert Bugg of Giles, Felix Zollicoffer of Davidson, Charles Ready of Rutherford, and Emerson Etheridge of Weakley. Democrats: Brookins Campbell of Washington, William Churchwell of Knox, Samuel Smith of Bradley, George W. Jones of Lincoln, and Frederick P. Stanton of Shelby. Campbell died before qualifying and was succeeded by Nathaniel Taylor, a Whig, thus increasing the Whig total to six.

see the Whig party profit from the dissension which had developed. "The Whigs who are prudent will take no active part against the adminn. for the present," he advised, "but let the elements of distraction accumulate before they make a combined attack." [63] But before the Whigs could prepare for a combined attack upon the enemy, Stephen A. Douglas brought forward the Kansas-Nebraska Bill, which upset the sectional truce and doomed the Whig party as a national organization.

[63] Bell to William B. Campbell, December 16, 1853, in David Campbell Papers.

Chapter XIV

IN INTEREST OF SECTIONAL HARMONY

A BILL to organize a Nebraska territory had been introduced by Douglas during the second session of the Thirty-second Congress, but it had been neither fully debated nor brought to a vote. As explained by its author, the purpose of the bill was to make possible the establishment of a line of settlements from the Mississippi to the Pacific and to furnish adequate protection to "emigrants, travelers, and traders." This was not the whole story, however, for Douglas was under considerable pressure from the advocates of a transcontinental railroad, especially those who desired to see Chicago become the eastern terminus of such a line. The existence of settlements along the proposed route would make construction more feasible, less difficult, and more profitable. Bell was among those who had registered opposition to the territorial proposal, basing his objection on the contention that it violated the government's legal obligations to the Indians who had been given perpetual possession of that area. The question of slavery was not a part of the original bill or the discussion thereon.[1]

The new bill as originally introduced by Senator Augustus C. Dodge of Iowa, December 14, 1853, also provided for the establishment of a territorial government for Nebraska; but as it came from the Committee on Territories, of which Douglas was chairman, it specified that the question of slavery should be settled by the inhabitants when ready for statehood. Thus the committee had incorporated in the bill the

[1] *Cong. Globe,* 32 Cong., 2 Sess., 1115-16.

territorial principle set forth in the Compromise of 1850.
Since Nebraska lay north of the line 36 degrees, 30 minutes,
the provisions of this bill ignored the Missouri Compromise
of 1820. The passage of such a bill was dependent upon
Southern support, and it was with the hope of securing such
assistance that Douglas agreed to the application of "squatter sovereignty." Southern expansionists and advocates of a
southern Pacific railroad must be compensated for their support. But even "squatter sovereignty" was not enough to
please the Southern ultras; they would support nothing less
than an outright repeal of the restriction on slavery north of
36 degrees, 30 minutes. Such a repeal amendment was prepared by Archibald Dixon, a Kentucky Whig and the successor to Henry Clay.[2] In order to secure Southern support,
Douglas was forced to accept Dixon's proposal and return the
bill to the Committee on Territories for its approval.

Except for Dixon's insistence on the incorporation of the
repeal provision, the Whigs had little part in the shaping of
the Kansas-Nebraska Bill, and it soon became apparent that
they were far from united in their attitude toward it. The
Northern Whigs were unanimous and consistent in their opposition, while a majority of the Southern wing of the party
seemed favorably disposed, and eventually voted for its adoption. Nowhere was the lack of Southern unanimity more
strikingly demonstrated, however, than in the case of the
Tennessee Whigs in both houses of Congress.

Bell was a member of the Senate Committee on Territories,[3] but he was visiting his mines in Kentucky at the time
the committee began its deliberations on the original bill.
He returned to Washington in time to make a hurried examination of the new proposal, and immediately questioned
the advisability of disturbing the Missouri Compromise. He
finally agreed to the incorporation of the Dixon amendment,

[2] Mrs. Archibald Dixon, *The True History of the Missouri Compromise and
Its Repeal* (Cincinnati, 1899), 430 ff.

[3] The other members were Sam Houston of Texas, Robert W. Johnson of
Arkansas, George W. Jones of Iowa, and Edward Everett of Massachusetts.

but he did so, he later said, "with the express reservation of the privilege of opposing the passage of the bill," should he, upon a more careful examination of its contents, consider it his duty to do so.[4] Having made this reservation he then proceeded to maintain a studied silence until the closing hours of the Senate debate on the bill.

The amended bill, as reported by the Committee on Territories, provided for the division of Nebraska into two territories—Kansas and Nebraska. All decisions relative to slavery were to be made by the inhabitants of those territories, the Missouri Compromise being declared "inoperative."[5] The antislavery forces immediately sprang to arms in defense of the compromise. Salmon P. Chase and Charles Sumner requested Douglas to delay action on the bill for a few days in order that they might have time to study it. Douglas agreed. Nevertheless, on that same day there appeared in the press "The Appeal of the Independent Democrats," a document apparently written by the abolitionist Joshua Giddings and revised by Chase.[6] Designed to stir antislavery sentiment in the free states, this "Appeal" denounced the bill as "a gross violation of a sacred pledge; as a criminal betrayal of precious rights," and pictured Douglas as a schemer against liberty.[7]

After a delay of a week, Douglas opened the debate on January 30, 1854, with a defense of the bill and a severe denunciation of the signers of the "Appeal." Chase replied on February 3, calling upon the Senate to "Maintain Plighted Faith," arguing that the Compromise of 1820 constituted a compact between slave states and free states.[8] Chase was fol-

[4] *Cong. Globe,* 33 Cong., 1 Sess., Appendix, 408. According to Everett, Houston was also absent when the committee was considering the original bill. Paul R. Frothingham, *Edward Everett, Orator and Statesman* (Boston, 1925), 353.
[5] *Cong. Globe,* 33 Cong., 1 Sess., 222.
[6] J. W. Schuckers, *Life and Public Services of Salmon Portland Chase* (New York, 1874), 141.
[7] *Cong. Globe,* 33 Cong., 1 Sess., 281–82.
[8] *Ibid.,* Appendix, 133 ff.

lowed by Sumner and Benjamin F. Wade. Wade asserted that the Missouri Compromise had attained "a character not much less important or sacred than that of the Constitution itself," and predicted that nothing short of dire calamity would follow the destruction of that sacred agreement.[9]

Bell's colleague, James C. Jones, immediately became involved in the discussion. He was among those who had been consulted by Dixon before the repeal amendment was submitted;[10] consequently, when such antislavery champions as Chase, Sumner, and Wade launched a vitriolic attack upon the proponents of repeal, he reacted with a spirit akin to that of an author. Wade's speech was denounced as a "tirade of abuse," and Jones declared that although in the past he had worked side by side with the Senator from Ohio in an effort to uphold Whig principles, that co-operation ended when Wade began an attack upon the rights of the people. It had never been a principle of the Whig party, Jones contended, "to inveigh against the institutions," inherited from the fathers of the country; and he added, "I utterly repudiate and scorn . . . I spit upon and despise any such doctrine as that, when applied to the Whig party." Although he respected those great men whose names were connected with the passage of the Compromise of 1820, he believed that the question of repeal must be decided by the living. As a senator, therefore, he intended to represent his constituents correctly, and to do this, he said, "I must vote for myself, and not for the dead."[11]

This indication of a clash between Northern and Southern Whigs was a source of much pleasure for the Democratic press. The Nashville *Union and American* had predicted that as soon as some question involving the finality of the Compromise of 1850 should arise in Congress, Whig unity would no longer exist. Although it deprecated the revival of the

[9] *Ibid.*, 33 Cong., 1 Sess., 337 ff.
[10] Dixon, *True History of the Missouri Compromise*, 443.
[11] *Cong. Globe*, 33 Cong., 1 Sess., 340–43.

slavery controversy, it was pleased to see "a touchstone applied to whiggery." The editor further predicted that support of the Kansas-Nebraska Bill by Southern Whigs would put an end to their alliance with free-soil Whigs and destroy the party. He added that any person who aspired to the presi dency would do well to watch his steps with regard to this bill, and that Senator Bell would therefore be on his guard.[12]

Jones's friends in the Tennessee legislature quickly rallied to his support. On February 27, H. R. Lucas presented a resolution to the lower house, expressing approval of the course pursued by Jones in his support of the Kansas-Nebraska Bill. E. James Lamb, a Democrat, immediately offered a substitute approving the bill and declaring the "principle contained in said bill in regard to the question of slavery to be just, equitable, and in conformity to the federal constitution, to the treaty by which said territory was acquired, and to the compromise of 1850." Lamb further proposed that Tennessee's senators be instructed and the congressmen requested to give the bill "their zealous support." [13]

While these resolutions lay on the table, the press took up the discussion. The *Union and American,* a Democratic paper, not wishing to give any endorsement to a Whig senator, denounced the Lucas resolution as "entirely personal and invidious," and expressed its approval of the substitute offered by Lamb.[14] The Nashville *True Whig* came out in support of the Kansas-Nebraska Bill. But the *Republican Banner and Nashville Whig,* a supporter of Bell, was not yet ready to endorse the position taken by Jones or to give its unqualified approval of the bill before the Senate.[15] Bell had not yet committed himself, and until he did, this paper considered the bill in too much of a state of immaturity to justify the instructing of senators. This position was denounced by

12 Nashville *Union and American,* February 9, 1854.
13 Tennessee *House Journal,* 1853–54, pp. 979, 1094–95.
14 Nashville *Union and American,* February 28, 1854.
15 *Republican Banner and Nashville Whig,* March 4, 1854.

Lucas, who declared the editor of the *Republican Banner* to
be only "a fossil remain of whiggery." [16]

On March 4 the resolutions were called up and tabled.
Meanwhile, Joel J. Jones, a Democrat, had introduced in
the state senate a set of resolutions similar to those offered by
Lamb in the house, and these were quickly passed by a vote
of 20 to 1.[17] When they were taken up in the house, only
forty-seven members were present and voting. These voted
approximately three to one in favor of the resolutions. But
the presence of fifty members was required for a quorum; so
the Speaker ruled that since no quorum was present the
resolutions were defeated and the proceedings void, and the
clerk was instructed not to record them in the journal.[18] It is
evident that Bell's friends, not wishing to embarrass him with
instructions or endorsements, were responsible for the defeat
of these resolutions.

Meanwhile, in Washington, Bell maintained his silence.
By the latter part of February the debate in the Senate had
become warm. Douglas, pushing the bill with all of his power,
had met with strong opposition from Chase and Sumner. The
National Intelligencer, which was considered by many to be
the mouthpiece of the Whigs, came out in opposition to the
bill. Southern Whig leaders became worried, and apparently
under the leadership of Robert Toombs they were called into
caucus. Two things must be done: pressure must be put on
the *Intelligencer* to change its attitude, and those Southern
Whigs who had not committed themselves must be lined up in
support of the bill.

Both Jones and Bell attended the meeting, but Bell suspected a trap to force him to commit himself and left without
taking a seat. The caucus adopted a resolution authorizing
Senator George Badger of North Carolina to state on the
floor of the Senate that the Southern Whigs were united in

[16] Nashville *Union and American,* March 5, 1854.
[17] Tennessee *Senate Journal,* 1853–54, p. 713.
[18] Nashville *Union and American,* March 9, 1854.

support of the principal features of the Kansas-Nebraska Bill.
The caucus also appointed Bell as one of a committee of three
to confer with the editors of the *Intelligencer*. Bell later
stated that he never served on any such committee, and that
he had not authorized Badger to commit him in favor of the
bill.[19]

Bell did not break his silence until March 3. In an extended
speech on that date, he explained to the Senate that he was
not convinced of a need to create any new territorial governments. In the vast territory which it was proposed to organize,
there was "no white population to demand the protection and
security of a territorial government." According to his information, as late as the past October there had been only three
white persons in the territory, exclusive of officials, soldiers,
missionaries, and traders. Neither was he convinced that the
deficiency in good land in the border states was so great as to
produce "a necessity for this measure arising from the pressure of population." To the sponsors of this grand scheme he
wished to say: "Wait a season; be not so impatient to build
up a great northwestern empire. In due time all your great
plans of development will be accomplished, without any great
sacrifices of any kind, and without conflicting with any other
great public interests. . . . In a very few years the advancing
lines of settlement on both sides of the Rocky Mountains, but
moving in adverse directions, will meet, overtake, and destroy both the buffalo and the Indians in their last retreats."

Bell insisted that the government should not take a step
that would violate the agreements entered into with the Indian tribes which had moved to western lands. Although the
proposed territorial organization excluded those regions held
by the Indians, the two races would again be brought close
together. Experience had proved that, under such conditions,
the Indians "were sure to contract all the vices, without
adopting any of the virtues of civilized communities." For

[19] See remarks by Toombs and Bell in *Cong. Globe,* 33 Cong., 1 Sess., Appendix, 755–58, 939 ff.

twenty years the territory west of Arkansas and Missouri had been designated as a place of permanent residence for those Indians who agreed to migrate to it. He pointed out that the line 36 degrees, 30 minutes, divided this Indian country into two almost equal parts, although very few Indians had migrated north of that line. The proposed bill would organize the northern part and leave the southern portion to the Indians. This would deny to the South all hope of creating another slave state. He insisted that justice would require the North to compensate the South for the loss by voluntarily conceding the creation of a slave state north of 36 degrees, 30 minutes, should slavery be adapted to that region.

Bell further contended that the Federal government had promised to observe "faithfully and rigidly" all engagements entered into with the Indian tribes in this territory. One of these engagements was that "those tribes should never be exposed to the evils of a white population around them, and that no *Territorial or State* government should ever be organized or established including their lands within its boundaries." He maintained that every tribe which had migrated west of the Mississippi after 1830, had done so under this guarantee, yet the Kansas-Nebraska Bill proposed to include these tribes within the territories and to open up to white settlers all of the lands not allotted to or occupied by the Indians. The "whole scope and object" of the bill, Bell averred, was undoubtedly in "direct and open violation of those engagements."

Following this digression on the Indian problem, Bell returned to the main theme of his speech by revealing to the Senate that a number of his Southern friends had stated in "private and friendly conversation" with him that any man from the South who failed to support the Kansas-Nebraska Bill would be a traitor to the interests of his section. They had told him that regardless of scruples, he must offer no objection to the passage of the bill; but he was not willing to go that far until the question had been given a fair consideration. He would agree with the advocates of the bill that its passage would be in keeping with the principle of congressional noninterference which had been established in 1850; that the restrictions set up in the Missouri Compromise were in violation of the cession treaty with France; and that the compromise was unjust to the South. Likewise he was compelled to agree that Congress did not possess the power to establish the restrictions incorporated in that compromise. At the same time, he must admit that the compromise had been accepted by the South. On the other hand, it had never been acquiesced in by the abolitionists and the "more mischievous type of anti-slavery agitators." Such men as Chase and Sumner, he charged, had already exhibited in the Senate that they repudiated all compromises and would never cease their agitation until slavery should be abolished in all of the territories. They professed no war on the Constitution, he said, but they would not hesitate to destroy it if such was necessary in order to destroy slavery. In view of these facts, he questioned "the expediency of disturbing the Missouri Compromise under existing circumstances." He could see no "practical advantage or benefit to the country, generally, or the South in particular."

On the other hand, Bell continued, he saw possibilities of even greater danger to the interests of the South if the bill should be passed. Suppose, he suggested, that one of the territories created by the bill should immediately pass a law establishing slavery. Would the North quietly acquiesce, or would the passage of such a law sound the "tocsin for a general rally of all the worst elements of the Abolition faction . . . stimulated and supported by numbers of northern citizens who have heretofore given no countenance to their excesses?" Even if no such law should be passed, would not the mere repeal of the Missouri Compromise cause a "deep-rooted hostility to slavery and the whole South?" He said that he was not especially concerned over the group to which Chase and Sumner belonged, because, regardless of what happened, they would continue their agitation. Indeed, nothing would disappoint them quite so much as the defeat of the Kansas-Nebraska Bill. The group about which he was concerned was composed of the "sober-minded and reflecting" people of the North who, although opposed to slavery, had taken no part in the ravings of the abolitionists. Those people had no desire to violate engagements or to withdraw constitutional protection from slaveholders within the states, but they were decidedly hostile toward the extension of slavery into territory which heretofore had been designated as free, and he feared the consequence if they should be stirred to action.

Granting that the Missouri Compromise had been unjust to the South, Bell pointed out that the extent of that injustice was the prohibition of slavery north of the compromise line, a region to which slavery was not adapted. It was his prediction that slavery would never be established in Kansas, and that even Missouri would "eventually give up her slaves to Texas and other regions where the soil is better adapted." Of what value to the South, therefore, he asked in conclusion, would be the establishment of the principle of nonintervention when there were no other territories to which to apply it.[20]

In Tennessee, the *Republican Banner and Nashville Whig,* which had been advising caution until the bill could be analyzed thoroughly, took its cue from Bell and joined the opposition. Southerners had a right to take their slaves into any territory, it declared, and neither Congress nor a territorial legislature could constitutionally prevent it. The doctrine that a territorial legislature could prohibit slavery was denounced as indefensible in both principle and practice. The "squatter sovereignty" principle in the bill was no concession to the South, it said, but was "a mockery and a humbug, and not worth the South's acceptance." Slaveholders could not win in a race with nonslaveholders for the possession of Kansas. Before slaveholders "could get up in the morning, eat

[20] *Cong. Globe,* 33 Cong., 1 Sess., Appendix, 408–15.

our breakfast, yoke the oxen, and get off the 'darkies', the Yankees with the assistance of the squatters, would possess the land and have their quarantines established." Taking up Bell's concluding suggestion, the editor stated that if the principle of squatter sovereignty should be accepted by the South, "it requires no great sagacity to perceive that there will never be another slave State formed out of any territory we now possess or which we may hereafter acquire." [21]

In the meantime, the Senate, after adopting an amendment by John M. Clayton of Delaware, limiting suffrage in the proposed territories to citizens of the United States,[22] had passed the bill on March 3 by a vote of 37 to 14. Jones obeyed the decision of the caucus and voted with the majority. Bell persisted in his opposition and was the only Southern Whig to vote in the negative.[23]

In the House of Representatives, William A. Richardson of Illinois, a Douglas lieutenant, assumed sponsorship of the bill. Over his protest, it was referred to the committee of the whole instead of the Committee on Territories. There it remained until May 8. This delay allowed ample time for the "Appeal" to take full effect in the free states, as well as to give President Pierce time to apply party pressure to the wavering Democrats. It also gave time for congressmen to convince the people back home or be convinced by them.

The Democratic press in Tennessee, apparently unanimous in support of the bill, labored to convince the people that the bill under consideration did not provide for squatter sovereignty during the territorial stage. This resulted in a spirited controversy between the Nashville *Union and American* and the *Republican Banner and Nashville Whig*. The latter, ably supported by the Shelbyville *Expositor,* stood by Bell in opposition to the bill. "Who wants the Missouri compromise repealed?" inquired the *Republican Banner.*

[21] *Republican Banner and Nashville Whig,* March 7, 8, 9, 13, 1854.

[22] The original bill proposed to extend the suffrage to all residents of the territory who had declared their intentions to become citizens.

[23] *Cong. Globe,* 33 Cong., 1 Sess., 532.

The editor asserted that such a thing had not been thought of by the people of the South, and since it had been proposed they had shown not the "slightest excitement in relation to the matter." To the people the thunder being manufactured in Washington was as artificial as that produced in the theater. "President-making and party supremacy are the considerations which lie at the bottom of this most mischievous, unnecessary and uncalled for measure." [24]

The Nashville *True Whig* and the Columbia *Intelligencer* joined with Jones in support of the bill. The *Intelligencer* explained that it did not believe Jones to be Bell's superior in statesmanship, but in the case of the Kansas-Nebraska Bill, Jones's course had been more "manly and nearer the true Southern tone." [25] What position many of the other Whig papers took is not known; [26] the Democratic press, as late as May 21, 1854, pronounced them either "absent" or "not voting." The *Union and American* predicted, however, that when those papers did take a stand most of them would undoubtedly follow John Bell to the wrong side. [27]

During the weeks covered by the debate in the House, Senator Bell had time to reflect upon the course which he had pursued. His position was fully explained in letters to political friends. He said that when the Whigs of the South were rushing "headlong" to join in the support of the bill, he was "really desirous of not breaking the ranks"; however, when he learned that three Whig members of the Tennessee delegation in the House were also opposed to the bill, he "resolved to obey the dictates of [*his*] own judgment" and join them in their opposition. From the beginning, he explained, he had considered the repeal proposal "most foolish and mischievous," and he now confided that he suspected Jones's support as being purely a political move. Jones probably had

[24] *Republican Banner and Nashville Whig*, March 29, April 7, 1854.
[25] Quoted in Nashville *Union and American*, May 21, 1854.
[26] Extant files of other Tennessee newspapers are incomplete for the year 1854.
[27] Nashville *Union and American*, May 21, 1854.

not believed that Douglas would ever take up Dixon's proposal, and when it was accepted, he felt that he could not then change his position. Bell also expressed to his friends a belief that the original plan was got up for the purpose of "counter excitement" in order to get public attention off the fact that the Administration had appointed "so many free-soilers and abolitionists to office." Although not especially interested in what happened to Pierce, Douglas could not afford to let the party be ruined. As for the Southern support of the bill, Bell thought it came as a result of a feeling of pride in Southern principles; yet he suspected that a few supporters were looking for an issue on which the Union could be dissolved. He also suggested that one of the designs of the bill "was probably to put an extinguisher upon the Whig party—and as many of the Whigs of the South took the bait, it may have that effect." [28] It apparently never occurred to him that railroad interests might have had some part in the origin of the Nebraska bill.

The supporters of the bill in the House finally succeeded in terminating debate on the evening of May 22, and it was quickly passed by a vote of 113 to 100. The Whig members of the Tennessee delegation were divided in their attitude. William Cullom, Emerson Etheridge, Nathaniel Taylor, and Robert M. Bugg voted in the negative. Charles Ready and Felix Zollicoffer joined the four Tennessee Democrats in support of the bill.[29]

Since the House had stricken out the Clayton amendment restricting the suffrage to citizens, the bill went back to the Senate for concurrence. Here Bell immediately opened another long denunciation. He charged that the type of non-interference provided for in the bill was not the same as that established in 1850. The principle of 1850 forbade the ter-

[28] Bell to R. T. Saunders, April 21, 1854, in *Olympian Magazine*, I (1903), 351; *id.* to James McCollum, May 9, 1854, in Miscellaneous Papers, Tennessee Historical Society Collection.

[29] *Cong. Globe*, 33 Cong., 1 Sess., 1254. Only three other Southern Whigs —one from Louisiana and two from North Carolina—voted against the bill.

ritorial legislature to legislate on slavery, leaving it to the people to settle the question at the time of admission into the Union. The Kansas-Nebraska Bill proposed to repeal all restrictions on slavery, and at the same time it specified that the inhabitants, through their representatives, should decide the question of slavery. With this system, Bell held, the first legislature could abolish slavery and the second re-establish it, thus keeping up a "perpetual struggle." Yet sponsors of the bill declared it to be a "measure of peace!"

Toombs interrupted, charging that Bell was allied with Northern agitators in an effort to perpetuate *"this prohibition on his own section,* although high-minded, noble, generous, and patriotic men of the North feel and see its injustice, and labor for its overthrow." He further charged that, at the beginning, Bell had co-operated with friends of the bill, but later made an about-face and called into question the motives of those with whom he had co-operated.[30] Bell admitted attending two meetings called by friends of the Nebraska bill. Those meetings, he explained, had been held immediately following speeches by Sumner and Chase, which expressed sentiments "repugnant and offensive to southern Senators." He denied having taken any part in those meetings; and again he insisted that he was not present when he was designated as a member of the committee to wait upon the editors of the *Intelligencer* or when Badger was instructed to commit the Southern Whigs in favor of the bill. Bell further asserted that no senator had mentioned any resolution to him or inquired about the success of the committee; neither had Badger consulted him before making the statement about Whig unity. Badger interrupted to explain that he had not thought it necessary to consult the senator since the vote of the Whig caucus had been unanimous. Clayton tried to patch up the difference between Bell and Badger, but gave up when Bell challenged his statement that all Whig senators had agreed that the Missouri Compromise should be

[30] *Ibid.,* Appendix, 939 ff.

repealed.[31] By the time the Senate adjourned for the day, Bell had worked himself up to a high point of excitement. He apparently believed that the Whig supporters of the bill, failing in their effort to bind him, were determined to ruin him.

On the following day Bell renewed the fight. Toombs's accusation of an alliance with abolitionists was denounced as "worthy only of the shallowest and lowest demagogue." Struggling as if to convince himself as well as others, Bell insisted that by opposing the bill he was not "misrepresenting the sentiments" of his constituents. They had long ago "disavowed and repudiated" the doctrine of squatter sovereignty; and prior to the introduction of the Kansas-Nebraska Bill, not one Whig or Democratic organ in Tennessee had ever "uttered a syllable of complaint against the Missouri restriction act, or even suggested the idea that it was proper or desirable to repeal it." Regardless of what their "first impressions or impulses may have been," Bell said that he had no fear of his constituents once they were made to understand the question. And true to the practice of politicians, he professed great confidence in the "good sense of patriotism" of the people. It was upon their "noble traits of character," he explained, that he and his colleagues in the House had relied to sustain them in their opposition to the bill. He warned that his constituents were watching not only the North but also certain suspicious persons in neighboring Southern states. Tennesseans would always stand by the South in resistance to all forms of oppression or infringement; yet they would "never countenance any movement on the part of their southern brethren, which they apprehend will lead to a separation of the Union." [32]

No one present could have had any doubts about the object of Bell's closing remarks. Toombs had both irritated and frightened him, and Bell was countering with a veiled accusation that Toombs was plotting to destroy the Union. Toombs then thought it necessary that he give his version of the Whig

---

[31] *Ibid.*, 33 Cong., 1 Sess., 1311.   [32] *Ibid.*, Appendix, 938 ff.

caucus. He told the Senate that the meeting was "public and patriotic" and had no "personal and private object." He said that he had presided over the meeting and had been responsible for the resolution instructing Badger. He felt positive that Bell was present and "did not utter publicly one word in opposition." Bell interrupted to declare that any statement that such instructions were given in his presence was an "infamous falsehood." John B. Weller, the presiding officer, called for "order! order!" Bell repeated his charge and added, "I cannot sit quietly and allow any man to profess to treat me with contempt." Cries for "order" came from senators all over the chamber. But "there is a boundary to proceedings here," exclaimed Bell. "Will Senators permit the rules to be violated this way?" inquired the presiding officer. Bell broke forth again: "I pronounce the statement to be an infamous falsehood." "The Sergeant-at-Arms must preserve order!" instructed the presiding officer. "The Senator ought to be required to take his seat," yelled Lewis Cass. Bell took his seat, grumbling, "I cannot bear everything."

Toombs continued his explanation. He pronounced as "mere fancy" Bell's professed belief in a conspiracy to trap him. No one had stated definitely that the Senator from Tennessee was present when Badger was instructed; therefore, Bell was denouncing points which had not been made. "If so, I take them back," Bell replied. He admitted that he was "more sensitive than was necessary," and was willing to "take it all back." [33]

Throughout the debate Bell had exercised more energy than was his custom. He surprised both friends and opponents. That he was a man of ability had long been generally conceded; however, his associates also recognized in him a "certain modesty of temperament" and indecisiveness in movement. His indecision was in evidence during the early days of the debate, but later he threw off all restraint and battled aggressively. As a Democratic senator later remarked, he

[33] *Ibid.*, 755-58.

"fearlessly and vigorously essayed to throttle the monster of sectionalism on the floor of the Senate, ere yet, like Eolus, he should succeed in unchaining all the winds of heaven once more, which had been now for nearly four years quietly sleeping in their caves." [34]

A correspondent of a prominent New York newspaper who had carefully observed the members of Congress during the recent debate made particular mention of Bell, William Cullom, and Emerson Etheridge. These Tennesseans, he announced, were among the "noblest specimens of a genuine manhood." "Their indignant denunciations and their lofty bearing would, if any thing could, shame every Northern doughface out of Washington. Governor Jones will stand almost alone in Tennessee. He was the first silly pigeon to fly under the net." [35]

Several weeks after the passage of the Kansas-Nebraska Bill, Bell gave a detailed explanation of the position which he had taken in the whole controversy. He said that although he was aware of a great risk of losing support in Tennessee and throughout the South, his only regret was that he had not attacked the bill at the beginning. [36] He confessed that timidity and a reluctance to separate from other Southern Whigs had been the cause of his earlier indecision; and he now believed that there had been an "ingeniously arranged plan" among some of the Southern Whigs to force him to support the bill or to destroy him. In fact, he added, he even suspected Toombs and a few other zealous supporters of the bill of a desire to destroy the Whig party and to form a new one. Although he was not convinced that the party had received

[34] Henry S. Foote, *War of the Rebellion; or Scylla and Charybdis* (New York, 1866), 193–94.

[35] James S. Pike, *First Blows of the Civil War* (New York, 1879), 221. This report to the New York *Tribune* was dated March 20, 1854.

[36] On March 4 Edward Everett recorded the observation that "Houston of Texas and Bell of Tennessee, members of the Committee on Territories, both voted against the bill. Had they done so in committee, it would not have passed, but Bell took care to be absent at his mines, and Houston (so Douglas told me) neglected to attend." Frothingham, *Edward Everett*, 353.

its death blow, he thought that the course pursued by the Whigs of the Northern states would be the determining factor. He had confidence in the Whigs of Massachusetts, Pennsylvania, and Ohio, but he doubted those of New York. "If these great States do not play the fool," he reasoned, "the lesser ones will be brought into moderate counsels." Probably the worst the Whigs had to fear, he concluded, was "that the next House of Reps will have a larger addition of abolitionists and may bring mischief upon us" by attempting to rescind the repeal of the Missouri Compromise.[37] In Tennessee the press was still arguing the merits and demerits of the Kansas-Nebraska Bill. The Memphis *Enquirer* praised John Bell for his "manly opposition," and prophesied that his popularity would be greatly increased.[38] On the other hand, the Murfreesboro *News* denounced him as a "dough face" who had let his aspiration for the presidency overcome his loyalty to his section.[39] The Shelbyville *Expositor* appealed to Whigs to cease their denunciation of the Kansas-Nebraska Bill, lest those Whigs who had supported it should feel compelled to "defend themselves from the imputation of being duped and cheated, or of having wilfully and knowingly contributed their influence to the success of a measure injurious to their section of the Union." [40] Probably the most prophetic observation came from the pen of Bell's friend, the editor of the *Republican Banner and Nashville Whig:* "The vote *in Congress* on the Nebraska bill will be the great weapon which will be used by our Democratic opponents, from this time forward . . . to cripple and destroy the Whig party in this State. . . . It will be used to defeat the re-election, as well of those Southern Whig Representatives who voted *for* the bill, as those who voted against it!" [41]

Actually, however, it is not possible to determine just what

37 Bell to William B. Campbell, August 10, 1854, in David Campbell Papers.
38 Quoted in *Republican Banner and Nashville Whig,* August 2, 1854.
39 Quoted in Nashville *Union and American,* June 16, 1854.
40 Quoted in *ibid.,* June 9, 1854.
41 *Republican Banner and Nashville Whig,* June 2, 1854.

direct effect the Kansas-Nebraska struggle had upon the political careers of those Tennessee Whigs who had participated in it. Ready and Zollicoffer, who had voted for it, were re-elected to the next two Congresses and then retired. Of the four who voted against it in the House, Etheridge was re-elected to the Thirty-fourth Congress and defeated for re-election to the Thirty-fifth; Cullom and Taylor were defeated in the election of 1854; and Bugg was not a candidate for re-election. These facts would seem to indicate punishment of opponents of the bill; but the additional fact that all six of these men were succeeded by Democrats suggests that it was the disappearance of the Whig party as a factor in Tennessee politics rather than individual positions on the bill that caused their retirement. This explanation would seem to be further supported by the fact that while Bell's opposition to the bill was to be used as an excuse for defeating him when he came up for re-election to the Senate in 1859, Jones, who had supported the bill, was retired at the expiration of his term in 1857. They, too, were succeeded by Democrats. Thus, even though the division of the Tennessee Whigs on the issues involved in the Kansas-Nebraska question may not have been the actual cause of the death of the party within the state, it was at least a warning sign that the end was near. And in that respect it stands out as a striking illustration within a single state of the condition of the party itself in the nation as a whole.

Chapter XV

WITH "PAINFUL SOLICITUDE"

BELL was sick in body and spirit when he returned to Nashville early in the fall of 1854. Long speeches, the excitement of personal controversy, and political uncertainty had drawn heavily upon his strength. Still he must have expected a speedy recovery, for he accepted an invitation to deliver the principal address at a dedication ceremony at the University of Nashville on October 4. That struggling institution, the successor to Cumberland College, had seen many lean years since the day of Bell's graduation. In 1850 an epidemic of cholera and the resignation of President Philip Lindsley had resulted in a temporary suspension of operation. By 1854, however, an effort was being made to revive and expand the activities of the University. Among other improvements, a department of law was to be organized.[1] Bell, probably the most distinguished living alumnus of the University, was a logical choice for speaker on such a celebrated occasion. Although it was doubtful whether the state of his health would permit his participation, he remained hopeful until the morning of the ceremonies. At the last moment, he yielded to the advice of his physician to avoid unnecessary mental or physical exercise, sent his regrets, and remained in bed.[2]

The days of Bell's confinement must have been spent in meditation upon his political future. He knew that the passage of the Kansas-Nebraska Bill had destroyed the Whig party as a national organization. Always lacking in unity and

[1] Alfred L. Crabb, *The Genealogy of George Peabody College for Teachers* (Nashville, 1935), 24–26.
[2] *Brownlow's Knoxville Whig,* October 14, 1854.

long in the process of disintegration, it could not stand the strain of the slavery controversy. The demise of their party and the rise of the Republicans left the conservative Whigs of the South in a dilemma. For Southern slaveholders to go over to the sectional Republican party was unthinkable. To many it was equally out of the question to join the Democrats, since the Southern wing of that party was also tainted with sectionalism. Some felt that the only choice remaining was an alliance with the "Know-Nothings."

The Order of the Star Spangled Banner, a secret organization commonly referred to as the "Americans" or "Know-Nothings," was organized late in the 1840's. Its program of intolerance of aliens and Catholics proved very popular in some sections. Although there were few aliens or Catholics in Tennessee, by 1855 most of the prominent Whigs of the state had joined the order; but Bell moved with caution. Meredith P. Gentry, backed by the Know-Nothings, announced as an opponent of Andrew Johnson for the governorship. Bell took no active part in the campaign, although it is reasonable to suppose that he preferred Gentry. The heated campaign between Johnson and Gentry marked the zenith of Know-Nothingism in Tennessee, even though Johnson proved to be the winner.

In September, 1855, Bell addressed a Know-Nothing mass meeting at Knoxville. Never before in thirty years of public life, he told his audience, had he "been so fearfully impressed by the dangers which impended over the country as at the present time." A crisis was at hand and our frame of government was facing a severe test. Passions in all sections were distempered and explosive. He could see no safety for liberty, rights, or property except "in the stern and successful maintenance of the constitution and the Union." Should these be destroyed, he warned, chaos and anarchy would reign until a Caesar or a Napoleon should establish a despotism.

There could never be "peaceful or bloodless" division of the Union, Bell asserted. Let no one be duped by dreamers and visionaries who argued that states could "enjoy their separate liberties and independence, in peace and security." Although those who openly advocated immediate disunion were few in number, there were others who were madly pursuing schemes which could have no other consequence. A few agitators, he insisted, could cause more trouble than could be put down by the greatest of statesmen. There was still hope, however, that the patriotism of the masses might prove equal to the occasion when it was realized that the Union was "likely to fall victim to the schemes of political gamesters."

Since Bell was speaking to a Know-Nothing audience, he apparently felt compelled to refer to the principles upon which that organization had been formed. Although not a member of the party, he explained, he endorsed its "great and leading principles." Accordingly, he launched an attack upon the practice of allowing aliens to vote in American elections; yet he did not openly advocate exclusion of naturalized foreigners and Catholics from the privilege of voting and holding office. Indeed, he was careful to evade a discussion of the anti-Catholic portion of the Know-Nothing program. Neither was there anything in his speech nor past record which could be considered as a sanction of the policy of secrecy.

It is evident that Bell felt himself cramped by the narrowness of the party's principles, but at the same time he envisioned its development into a truly national conservative organization. He expressed the hope that "when sufficient time and reflection shall have been allowed, the creed of the American party will reflect faithfully every truly American principle and sentiment." The Whig party was dead, he explained, and since the new Republican party was organized on a single principle, it could not endure unless the Union should be divided. Therefore, he hoped to see the American party take a position opposite the Democrats as a great national organization. For the sake of the Union, he insisted that the new party exhibit a spirit of tolerance on the question of slavery. An attitude of defiance would be unwise and "wholly

useless." There was little hope for harmony within the ranks
of the Democrats since that party included a "hot headed class
which is distinguished by the fierceness of their opposition to
the north." On the other hand, within the ranks of the American party were to be found "the truest friends of the Union
and such as have maintained a resolute opposition to all dis-
organizing doctrines of nullification and secession—all the
more temperate and considerate portion of the southern
people, who have cultivated a fraternal feeling between the
two sections of the Union." [3]

Bell was feeling his way. He hoped that the Americans
might prove to be the truly conservative party which he had
advocated as early as 1851. Yet he recoiled at proscription and
secrecy. While awaiting further developments, he would venture a semblance of support yet stop short of membership.

The Americans were definitely playing for Bell's active
participation. All other prominent Tennessee Whigs except
James C. Jones had already lined up. Brownlow had not only
become an enthusiastic American; he had placed "John Bell
for President" at the head of the editorial column of his *Whig*.
The New Orleans *Delta* also joined in the movement in favor
of the only statesman "who combines an intimate acquaint-
ance with our political administration . . . with a sufficiency
of intellectual and physical vigor," while the St. Louis *Intelligencer* declared him the unquestionable "head of the American Senate, in all that illustrates and adorns that body." [4]

What interest Bell took in the possibility of a nomination
is not known; there is no reason to believe that he expected
it. Although his position on the Kansas question might bring
him some Northern support, he knew that his enemies were
numerous, even among the Tennessee Whigs.[5] Brownlow
confided to him that, while he believed either Bell or Millard

[3] *Ibid.*, November 3, 1855; *Republican Banner and Nashville Whig,* October
21, 1855.
[4] *Republican Banner and Nashville Whig,* June 10, 1855; *Brownlow's Knoxville Whig,* March 24, 1855.
[5] John M. Lea to Bell, December 19, 1855, in Polk-Yeatman Papers.

Fillmore could carry Tennessee in the coming presidential election, he must frankly admit that the leaders of both the old Whigs and the Americans preferred Fillmore. This, he thought, could be explained by the fact that several Tennesseans aspired to the vice-presidency and that they knew Bell's nomination would blast their hopes. Andrew Jackson Donelson and Thomas A. R. Nelson, Brownlow added, had been selected as Tennessee delegates-at-large to the American national convention. He thought Nelson probably would not go; still, if he did, he would likely be against Bell for President. Of course Brownlow would go to the convention and do all he could. The only consolation the editor could offer his friend, however, was that Bell was more popular with the masses of the people than he was with party leaders.[6] But from faraway San Francisco, Balie Peyton sent more encouraging news. Bell's nomination would be "eminently popular" with the American party in California.[7]

The national convention of the American party met in Philadelphia on February 22, 1856, and nominated Millard Fillmore and Andrew J. Donelson. It does not appear that Bell was seriously considered. The party platform declared that "Americans must rule America," and advocated exclusion from public office of all who recognized allegiance or obedience to a foreign prince or potentate or who refused to recognize their state and Federal constitution "as paramount to all other laws of political action." No definite commitment was made on the slavery question, although the Administration was denounced for its territorial policy.[8]

There was nothing in this platform to which Bell could seriously object; neither was there anything to elicit an outburst of enthusiasm. He remained reluctant, and his reluctance was strengthened by the general outlook which he described as "gloomy and threatening in the highest degree." While

6 Brownlow to *id.*, January 15, 1856, in Bell Papers.
7 Peyton to *id.*, February 3, 1856, *ibid.*
8 Stanwood, *History of the Presidency*, I, 261–63.

seated at his desk in the Senate chamber and listening to the display of sectional animus, he wrote: "We can calculate upon nothing with any confidence, which may bring back peace and harmony to the country." There was little hope for the Fillmore-Donelson ticket. He feared that the trouble in Kansas had greatly strengthened the Republican cause. If the Republicans should prove to be "patriotic and wise enough to nominate John McLean," he felt sure that they could carry every Northern state. Yet should they take up John C. Frémont, they would do no more than defeat the Americans and elect a Democrat.[9]

When the Tennessee Americans asked Bell to represent them at a convention to be held in New York early in June, 1856, he declined, explaining that his presence could serve no "useful or valuable purpose." Even though he planned to make a trip to New York anyway, he did not wish to have his first appearance in a "convention of the order" mean nothing more than having his name "enrolled as a delegate." [10] The cautious Senator was still in doubt.

The trouble in Kansas, to which Bell alluded, had indeed reached an alarming state. No sooner had the Kansas-Nebraska Bill become a law than the struggle for Kansas had begun. Proslavery men from Missouri and the South vied with antislavery men from the North and East. With the aid of armed voters from Missouri, the proslavery group gained control of the territorial legislature, in March, 1855, and proceeded to adopt drastic measures in defense of slavery. The free-soilers backed by substantial Eastern support refused to recognize the authority of the legislature, called a convention at Topeka, and drew up an antislavery constitution for a proposed state of Kansas. On January 24, 1856, President Pierce sent to Congress a special message, reviewing the situation in Kansas and denouncing the emigrant-aid companies of the East for their interference in the affairs of the territory. Re-

9 Bell to William B. Campbell, May 29, 1856, in David Campbell Papers.
10 *Ibid.*

gardless of the alleged "irregularities" in the election of the legislature, he said, it was too late to question its legality; therefore, he considered "the legislative body thus constituted and elected" as the "legitimate assembly of the Territory." The action of the Topeka convention was declared revolutionary in character, motive, and aim; and, the President continued, should it "reach the length of organized resistance by force," it must be considered as "treasonable insurrection." With the hope of putting an end to "internal agitation and external interference" in Kansas, Pierce recommended the passage of an act enabling the inhabitants of the territory, as soon as their number should justify, to convene a duly elected convention for the purpose of framing a constitution, preparatory to admission into the Union as a state.[11]

On March 12, Douglas, from the Committee on Territories, made a report on the situation in Kansas, and five days later presented a bill prepared by his committee. The bill provided that whenever the census, taken by the authority of the legislature and under the supervision of the governor, should show that the population of Kansas had reached 93,420, there might be assembled a convention, the delegates to which were to be chosen by white males above twenty-one years of age and of three months residence in the territory.[12] A long debate followed, and the Republican senators made the most of the opportunity to increase their strength through the exposure of the "crimes" of Kansas. The most celebrated speech was that delivered by Charles Sumner, which resulted in a severe caning at the hands of Preston S. Brooks.

Bell did not speak until July 2, even though he had been watching the "progress of the disorders in Kansas with the most painful solicitude." As had become his custom, he wanted to settle the question immediately and permanently. He said that he objected to the proposed population requirement for statehood on the ground that such a total could not

[11] Richardson (ed.), *Messages and Papers*, VII, 2885 ff.
[12] *Cong. Globe*, 24 Cong., 1 Sess., 693.

be reached in a shorter time than four years. Some sources of trouble might be removed by halfway measures, he admitted, but "dissension and discord will still continue, not only in Kansas, but throughout the country, until Kansas shall become a state." He was fearful of the consequence should this agitation and excitement be extended into still another presidential campaign. In fairness to all concerned, he insisted that all "unconstitutional and tyrannical" laws be repealed; that a new constitutional convention be assembled; and that Kansas be admitted as a state, "without reference to the amount of population." Bell agreed with Senator Henry S. Geyer, who said that the threatening aspect of the slavery controversy was a result of party struggle for power. He respected those who had moral and religious sentiments on the question of slavery, but he most emphatically rejected Senator Seward's statement that abolitionism was " 'the result of the irrepressible uprising of the spirit of freedom' "; he denied that the North had "a monopoly on the spirit of freedom." Slavery might be a blemish. Still, it was a part of the social and economic structure; and he had nothing in common with those who would raze the structure in order to eliminate an imperfection.

Bell was not disposed to argue the merits or demerits of the activities of either faction in the Kansas struggle, inclining to accuse both of indiscretions, but he placed the responsibility upon the shoulders of a blundering Congress. Coming to the heart of the controversy, he concluded: "On the question whether Kansas shall be a free or a slave State, as a representative of southern interests, my preference, of course, is for a slave State. But, sir, if in a fair competition it must be so, let it be a free State; let it be retroceded to the Indians, the aboriginal occupants of the soil; let it become another Dead sea, rather than continue the pestilent source of mortal disease to our system." [13]

Congress debated until August 18, 1856, and then ad-

[13] *Ibid.,* Appendix, 781–88.

journed, making it possible for members to return home and participate in the political campaign, and leaving Kansas to "bleed." In the meantime, the Republicans had nominated John C. Frémont for the presidency, and the Democrats had named James Buchanan as their candidate. Bell remained in Washington for about a month after the close of the session, sounding out public opinion and catching up with his correspondence. He had received an invitation to return to Knoxville and address another mass meeting. Duties at Washington during the closing days of the session prevented his acceptance, but in reply, he sent a letter setting forth his fears for the safety of the Union. He could see no assurance against the outbreak of civil war unless all true patriots rallied to the support of the Union rather than to party. The Union was definitely in danger, he insisted, and its dissolution would be the greatest calamity which could befall either the South or the North. He had "no faith in the political metaphysics of those, who seek to establish a peaceful mode of breaking up the Union, by deducing from the Constitution a right of secession." Such a doctrine he denounced "as equally unsound, delusive and mischievous. Delusive, because it can have no efficacy in preventing civil war; and mischievous, because it tends to mislead, and seduce the people of a State into a revolutionary measure, for insufficient cause, under the false idea of immunity from the ordinary hazard of a revolt against an established Government." The only way the American Union could be dissolved was by revolution!

Bell told his Knoxville friends he understood that some Southern Whigs were advocating support of Buchanan in order to defeat the Republican ticket. Such a movement, he thought, would brand Buchanan as the choice of the slaveholders and thus line up a solid North in favor of Frémont; therefore, his advice was "to stand fast by Fillmore and Donelson, and to spare no effort, to secure their election." [14]

[14] Bell to Rolfe S. Saunders *et al.*, August 26, 1856, in *Brownlow's Knoxville Whig*, September 13, 1856.

Although Bell's letter was political in its nature and was intended for publication, its contents were consistent with the opinions privately stated by its author. Writing to William B. Campbell, Bell expressed the opinion that Fillmore was gaining strength; still, he could see nothing more favorable than a defeat of Frémont and an election by the House of Representatives. In case the Democrats should win, Bell doubted Buchanan's ability to prevent the "ultraism of the leading spirits of his party" from plunging the country into war; a Frémont victory would "bring on a fearful crisis." Bell had "no thought that Fremont's *election* by *itself* ought to draw off the South." The wise course would be to wait and see what the Republicans proposed to do.[15]

Bell returned to Nashville on September 26 and was received with a gratifying ovation. Across the streets had been suspended huge banners bearing the inscriptions "Welcome to the great Bell of Tennessee" and "Honor to John Bell, Fillmore, Donelson and the Union." A huge crowd met him at the railway station, and he rewarded the group with a three-hour speech, repeating much that he had said in recent letters and addresses and urging an all-out effort to elect Fillmore and Donelson.[16] Throughout the campaign, Bell was in demand as an adviser and participant at Fillmore barbecues and mass meetings in several states,[17] but the records do not reveal that he was excessively active.

Many Tennessee Whigs abhorred the intolerance expressed in the Know-Nothing principles, and hesitated to support this new party merely for the pleasure of defeating the Democrats.[18] Some of this number, under the leadership of James C. Jones, who continued to style himself "an old fashioned, old school, Henry Clay, Heaven-descended and consecrated

15 *Id.* to William B. Campbell, September 10, 1856, in David Campbell Papers.

16 *Republican Banner and Nashville Whig*, September 27, 28, 1856.

17 Henry Branch *et al.* to Bell, March 20, 1856; L. P. Sanderson to *id.*, June 26, 1856; Bing Fiond[?] *et al.* to *id.*, September 16, 1856, in Polk-Yeatman Papers.

18 James M. Calhoun to *id.*, July 17, 1856, *ibid.*

Whig," [19] went over to the Democrats and helped to give that party's electoral ticket its first victory in Tennessee since 1832. The American party carried only one state, and thus was eliminated from serious competition as a national party. Buchanan had won, but the heavy vote cast for Frémont gave warning that the Democrats had better act with wisdom.

Bell had scarcely returned to Washington again to do battle for a fair deal on the Kansas question when a slave insurrection panic swept the area in which his Tennessee iron mines and works were located. A large number of his slaves were alleged to have been connected with the conspiracy. Fearing the spread of the panic, the principal newspapers of the region made no mention of the affair until pressed by out-of-state editors. The Nashville *Union and American* then reluctantly admitted that there had been plans for an insurrection, but that the conspirators had been apprehended and turned over to the authorities for punishment.[20] However, the Baltimore *Sun,* citing an unnamed Tennessee newspaper as its authority, stated that five of Bell's slaves had been killed by a mob and that the courts had ordered four others to be hanged. The Senator's loss was estimated at $10,000.[21] Bell's reaction to this unfortunate affair is not recorded, but his friend Balie Peyton, writing from San Francisco, probably expressed Bell's sentiments as well as his own: "I am sorry to see that you have lost some of your negroes in Tennessee. I am opposed to lynching negroes, because if guilty there is no difficulty in their legal punishment." [22] A contemporary, writing some twenty years later, gave a vivid picture of both the hysteria which seized the whites and its gruesome results:

> In 1856 a plot was discovered among the slaves of Stewart County for a general uprising of the race and the striking of a blow for freedom. A feeling of unrest and apprehension prevailed among

[19] Hamer, *Tennessee,* I, 507.
[20] Nashville *Union and American,* December 20, 1856.
[21] Baltimore *Sun,* December 24, 1856.
[22] Peyton to Bell, February 4, 1857, in Bell Papers.

the white people throughout 1854 and 1855, it being evident to a careful observer that mischief was brewing among the blacks. They would hold meetings on Sundays and of nights in secret places, and were instigated by several white men who claimed to be preachers. The plot was disclosed to the white citizens in December, 1856, and a vigilance committee was at once organized at Dover. Slaves from all parts of the county were arrested and carried before the committee, and under pain of severe punishment or death were made to confess. The object was that on a given day slaves would arise, overpower their masters, arm themselves, and push across the country to Hopkinsville, Ky., and then march into Ohio, where they supposed they would be free. Six of the ringleaders were captured and hung by the vigilants at Dover a few days before Christmas, in 1856, and a large number were severely whipped. To make the execution of the negroes impressive a citizen of Dover cut off the heads of the dead slaves, and hoisting them on poles paraded the streets, during the day of the hanging, displaying the ghastly, gory objects to the terrified negro population.[23]

As was common in such cases of "conspiracy," the whites had discovered the "plot" before the day of slaughter arrived! Bell was now more convinced than ever that an immediate and just settlement of the slavery issue was essential to a preservation of both property and the Union.

With this impression fresh in mind, he turned again to the discussion on "bleeding" Kansas. What would the new Administration do about Kansas and the slavery question in general? Bell prophesied that the Southern "fire eaters" would probably meet the Northern Democrats on some "half way course" in order to hold the party together and in power. He suspected that most of the Southern ultras would hesitate to make a firm stand on *"extreme ground,"* fearing that such a course might strengthen their opponents in the North. When Bell spoke of ultras, he did not mean to include the most extreme element in the South; that group, he contended, would stop at nothing short of disunion. As to the Republicans, Bell thought they would adopt a waiting policy until the Demo-

[23] Goodspeed, *History of Tennessee* (with sketch of Stewart County), 900.

crats had charted their course. If that course should be one "favorable to peace and harmony," then the moderate Republicans would modify their course and seek a "union with the Americans and old Whigs of the South." This was wishful thinking on the part of Bell, yet he was not carried away by his thoughts; for he added that should Buchanan adopt a course similar to that followed by Pierce, the Republicans would "adhere to their present organization" and hope for a victory in 1860.[24]

James Buchanan took office on March 4, 1857, and two days later Chief Justice Roger B. Taney delivered the majority opinion in the famous Dred Scott case. The Court denied Scott his freedom; and going further into the general question of slavery, declared that since slaves were property and since persons could not be deprived of property without "due process of law," Congress could not prohibit slavery in a territory; therefore, the Missouri Compromise had been unconstitutional during its entire life. Regardless of the intention of the justices or the correctness of their reasoning, the Dred Scott decision did nothing to allay the strife in Kansas.

Buchanan sent Robert J. Walker of Mississippi to the Kansas Territory to assume the governorship. Walker arrived in Kansas on May 26, 1857, and found preparations underway for the election of delegates to a constitutional convention. The election was held on June 15, but the free-soilers, in spite of the Governor's insistence, refused to participate. The convention, meeting at Lecompton, drew up a proslavery constitution; however, instead of submitting the entire document to the people for ratification, the convention voted to refer only the section which would have permitted future importation of slaves. Under this plan, regardless of the action of the voters, property in slaves already in Kansas would be protected. Governor Walker vigorously protested against such proslavery tactics, and not receiving the proper backing from Buchanan, resigned in disgust.

[24] Bell to William B. Campbell, January 19, 1857, in David Campbell Papers.

In the meantime, Tennessee was going through one of its most bitterly contested state elections. Robert Hatton, Whig and American, was opposing Isham G. Harris, Democrat, for the governorship. Governor Andrew Johnson was not a candidate for re-election; his eyes were on the United States Senate. But he could reach this goal only if the Democrats controlled the Tennessee legislature. Bell, although not a candidate for any office at that time, became the principal object of Democratic attack as the leader of the old Whigs. To further discredit him would contribute to Whig-American defeat. Johnson boldly denounced all Northern Know-Nothings as abolitionists, and implied that no friend of the South could co-operate with them. The Nashville *Union and American,* a Democratic organ, insisted that every effort ought to be made to elect a Democratic legislature and thus prevent John Bell from going back to the Senate to join hands with the "Black Republicans." He was accused of abandoning his former position on the subject of distribution, of favoring the extension of the suffrage to aliens, of desiring to be a dictator within his own party, and of being an abolitionist.[25]

Bell fought back, denying that he had abandoned distribution, and asserting that unless there was a great change in the condition of the Treasury, plans for distribution would be continuously advocated in Congress and before the people. Much of the Mexican War debt had been paid and government expense had been reduced, he explained, yet revenue from customs and the sale of public lands continued to flood the Treasury. He opposed a great surplus in the Treasury because it tempted Congress to approve of "extravagant and wasteful expenditures." One way to reduce the surplus, he pointed out, was to reduce the tariff, and some reductions had already been made. It is significant that Bell stopped short at this point, not wishing to recommend a drastic reduction. Conditions were just right for distribution, he continued, just as they had been when "Henry Clay and the Whig party never

[25] *Republican Banner and Nashville Whig,* May 17, 26, June 4, 7, 1857.

failed to press it." Beginning in 1850, Congress had made some heavy grants of land to the newer states to encourage the building of railroads. Some of those grants, Bell explained, were so large that the income from the railroads would possibly give to the fortunate states perpetual relief from the necessity of taxing their citizens; consequently, the older states, which had not shared in this bounty, had a just claim on the surplus in the Treasury. Until that inequality should be remedied, Bell said that he favored reserving $5,000,000 in the Treasury and distributing the remainder. Such a distribution, he calculated, would, in the future, give to each state about $400,000 annually for each millon of population.[26]

As to granting the suffrage to aliens, Bell vigorously denied that he had ever favored it. It was the Democrats, he averred, who were guilty. Had not the original Kansas-Nebraska Bill been a Democratic measure and had it not proposed that suffrage be extended to all who had signified their intention to become citizens? Yes, he had voted against the bill which included the Clayton amendment; however, it was the House, not the Senate, that killed the amendment. Nevertheless, he said he was not seriously concerned whether or not aliens were permitted in the territories; but he did consider as "monstrous" the doctrine that states possessed the "constitutional power" to confer the suffrage upon aliens. Such action, he maintained, tended to nullify the importance of the residence requirement for citizenship, and did not respect the power of Congress to pass uniform laws of naturalization.[27]

Harris defeated Hatton by more than eleven thousand votes, and the Democrats also placed a substantial majority in both houses of the state legislature. These Democratic representatives were not long in getting down to work. The senatorial term of James C. Jones had expired. Andrew Johnson was selected to succeed him; Jones failed to receive even

[26] See Bell's Nashville speech delivered on July 18, 1857, and published in *Republican Banner and Nashville Whig*, August 1, 1857.
[27] *Ibid.*

one vote.[28] John Bell was next on the list. Although his term did not expire until 1859, his bitterest opponents demanded that his successor be selected in 1857. The *Republican Banner* vigorously charged that such a choice would be unconstitutional since the Constitution provided for the selection of senators every six years.[29] The Knoxville *Register* was not certain that such an election was literally unconstitutional, but it was "at variance with the *spirit* of the constitution and with the true theory of our representative government." [30] The majority of the legislators, however, were in no frame of mind for delay. There was a precedent for their proposed action, and it had been established by the Whigs themselves.

In mid-October a questionnaire was sent to each prospective candidate for the senate, and on October 29 the two houses convened in joint session for the purpose of making a selection. Dr. J. W. Richardson of Rutherford County begged for a postponement until November 3 in order to give the candidates ample time to answer their questionnaires. He said that he felt certain Senator Bell would give a full and satisfactory reply, and that in such a critical period, he thought Tennessee ought to be made "a wall of fire" between Southern ultras and Northern fanatics. He was joined by W. L. McConnico of Rutherford and Williamson, who declared the proposed election to be unnecessary and inexpedient. But the best Bell's friends could do was secure an adjournment for lunch. In the afternoon W. C. Whitthorne of Maury read Alfred O. P. Nicholson's reply to the questionnaire and placed his name in nomination. Apparently no reply was received from Bell; Dr. Richardson nominated him anyway.[31] R. C. Saunders of Smith brought laughter to the house and at the same time expressed the feelings of Bell's friends when he said: "We on this side of the House, were called upon the other day to dance to the tune of a vacancy occasioned by the

---

[28] Tennessee *House Journal*, 1857–1858, p. 36.
[29] *Republican Banner and Nashville Whig*, September 19, 1857.
[30] Knoxville *Register*, October 29, 1857.
[31] *Republican Banner and Nashville Whig*, October 28, 29, 1857.

expiration of a term of office. The tune, though no favorite of ours, owing to the circumstances was one which necessity required, one which the Constitution sanctioned, and to it we gave the best we had on hand. But we are called upon now, sir, to dance—no; but to shuffle to a tune of an entirely different nature, and I for one most frankly confess I can't take the step." [32] Then declaring the whole procedure unconstitutional Saunders took his hat and walked out.[33] The voting was completed in short order; Nicholson receiving 58 and Bell 35.[34]

[32] *Ibid.,* October 29, 1857.
[33] Tennessee *House Journal,* 1857–1858, p. 92.
[34] Tennessee *Senate Journal,* 1857–1858, p. 81.

Chapter XVI

A FAIR DEAL FOR KANSAS

THE Thirty-fifth Congress was scheduled to open its first session on December 7, 1857. Bell left Nashville about the middle of November; he had much business to attend to. In addition to his irritation over the action of the legislature, things were not going well at his mines, and during the late campaign in Georgia Senator Toombs had given him some hard blows. Bell could do nothing about the action taken by the legislature, but he could give his attention to the other two matters. He wrote his friend Campbell that he intended to spend about two weeks at the mines and arrive in Washington around December 1. He wished Campbell to meet him there and serve as his second, for he felt bound to call Toombs "to account" and thought that the Georgian could not "get out of a fight." Campbell was the only one to whom Bell thought he could turn; Southern senators and congressmen would hesitate to take part in an affair against one of the "strong men on the slavery question"; and it would not do to use a Northern man, even if he could find "one of pluck." [1] Campbell's reply has not been preserved. According to Brownlow, Bell dispatched a note to Toombs, inquiring whether he had made the statements recorded in the Atlanta *Intelligencer*. Toombs made a verbal reply through Alexander H. Stephens, but Bell refused to accept it. Toombs then sent a note denying that he had made any such statement and informing Bell that he had instructed the editor to correct the mistake.[2] This apparently ended the controversy.

[1] Bell to Campbell, November 13, 1857, in David Campbell Papers.
[2] *Brownlow's Knoxville Whig*, October 20, 1860.

In his first annual message to Congress on December 8, 1857, President Buchanan made it clear that he intended to support the action of the Lecompton convention in Kansas. "A large portion of the citizens of Kansas did not think it proper to register their names and to vote at the election for delegates," he informed Congress, "but an opportunity to do this having been fairly afforded, their refusal to avail themselves of their right could in no manner affect the legality of the convention." As to the proposed method of ratification, he pointed out that the Kansas-Nebraska Act provided that the portion of the constitution relating to slavery, not the constitution as a whole, should be submitted to the people for ratification; therefore, the method adopted by the convention was in accordance with the law. The provision safeguarding the rights of property in slaves already in Kansas was declared to be "just and reasonable." [3]

The ratification election was held in Kansas on December 21, and the proslavery constituton was approved by an overwhelming majority, the free-soilers again not voting. On February 2, 1858, Buchanan sent to Congress a special message, transmitting a copy of the Lecompton constitution, and recommending that Congress dissipate the "ominous clouds which now appear to be impending over the Union" by admitting Kansas as a state "during the present session." [4]

One week after the delivery of the President's special message, the Tennessee legislature, still hot on Bell's trail, adopted a set of resolutions instructing the state's senators and requesting its members of the House to vote for admission of Kansas under the Lecompton constitution. These resolutions, which in their original form had requested Bell's resignation,[5] also included a long preamble condemning the Senator's conduct since 1854. The Missouri Compromise was denounced as a "palpable wrong" against the slaveholders,

3 Richardson (ed.), *Messages and Papers*, VII, 2980–85.
4 *Ibid.*, 3002–3012.
5 Tennessee *Senate Journal*, 1857–58, p. 151.

and the Kansas-Nebraska Act was accepted with "unqualified approbation." Bell was denounced for his failure to resign after having stated on the floor of the Senate that, should the time ever come when his views and course were out of harmony with and unacceptable to his constituents, he would consider his resignation as imperative. Certainly that time had arrived. Was not the result of the late election in Tennessee sufficient proof of public disapproval of his course? [6]

The resolutions precipitated a lively debate in the legislature. As a result of his public course and his failure to resign, Bell had "lost every spark of *personal* as well as *political* honor," exclaimed state Senator W. C. Whitthorne; and if Bell had been living at the time of Christ, "Judas Iscariot would have lost his thirty pieces of silver." From the other side, A. F. Goff of Davidson wanted to know what this nondescript, mongrel resolution was supposed to do. Was it to instruct, request, or concur? He believed in the legislature's power to instruct, he explained, but not to issue "ex post facto instruction." He denied that Tennessee had ever signified unqualified approval of the Kansas-Nebraska Act. Bell had proved a good prophet, he thought, for all of the unhappy results predicted by the Senator had come true. [7]

Other able defenders of Bell's public career were W. L. McConnico of Rutherford and Williamson, Dr. J. W. Richardson of Rutherford, S. S. Stanton of Jackson, and R. C. Saunders of Smith. The last became eloquent and eulogistic. Likening Bell's opponents to Brutus and Cassius, he cried: "Aye, they professed to love him, but forced by the same high sense of duty to their country they slew him." "You have no love for John Bell," he yelled to the Democratic side of the chamber. "Your professions are hollow hearted and empty, and while you pretend to be actuated by patriotism, you are really prompted by jealousy—green-eyed jealousy." And continuing his Shakespearean parallelism, he remarked:

[6] Quoted in *Cong. Globe*, 35 Cong., 1 Sess., 804.
[7] *Republican Banner and Nashville Whig*, January 16, 17, 1858.

So, you, when you enter the Senate Chamber . . . there [you will] find John Bell, the noblest Tennessean of them all, bending in deep meditation upon some great measure, involving the dearest interest of his country, or scanning with an eye which amounts almost to prophesy [*sic*], the result of the passage or defeat of some great measure which strikes perhaps at the foundation of the government. Or perhaps you will find him on his feet, with his eyes fixed upon the eagle, which stands with wings half-poised, ready to take its flight from a dismembered Union, calling with overpowering eloquence upon his compeers, to rally to the rescue, and keep together that beautiful sisterhood of stars which have glittered in one group for three quarters of a century. While the noble Senator is pleading for the Union and the Senate is sitting spell bound by his eloquence, plunge the steel to his heart, to that heart, whose palpitations have ever beat in unison with the interest of his country. And when the noble Senator falls, he will like Caesar cry *et tu Brute,* or rather, Is it a Tennessean? Is it a Tennessean?

This great man, like the great Caesar, also has a will, concluded Saunders; he would leave to his country the benefits of "his services in its councils for forty years, and a fame as unperishable as its own everlasting hills." [8] Votes, not oratory, were to decide the issue; the resolutions were adopted 52 to 27.[9]

On February 23, Bell, in a manner more like a Roman gladiator than a fallen Caesar, exhibited to the Senate what he described as a set of resolutions instructing him how he should have acted with regard to a bill which had become a law four years earlier. These resolutions also informed him that his position with regard to the Kansas-Nebraska Bill had been repudiated by the people of Tennessee. Bell told the Senate he denied that either of the three elections since 1854 had been considered as a referendum on the Kansas-Nebraska Act. In 1855, he contended, Americanism was the "staple of the discussion"; in 1856 there was some discussion of the bill, but other issues superseded it in importance when the Demo-

8 *Ibid.*, March 20, 21, 1858.
9 Tennessee *Senate Journal,* 1857–58, p. 520; *House Journal,* 1857–58, p. 55.

crats began to plead for Whigs and Americans "to waive all party prejudices" and help them defeat Frémont and disunion. In spite of the resulting defection of some Whigs and Americans, Bell explained, Fillmore received about 66,000 votes, only about 7,000 fewer than Buchanan; and this, too, after Fillmore had stated that had he been in Congress in 1854, he would have voted against the Kansas-Nebraska Bill. It was true that the Democrats had been victorious in the state election of 1857, but Bell attributed their victory to the "discouraged and depressed" condition of the opposition. In neither of those elections, he asserted, had the Kansas-Nebraska Act been the main issue; and he still believed that, in the absence of party influence, the freely expressed opinion of a majority of the Southern people would be that "the repeal of the Missouri compromise [was] the most unfortunate measure ever sanctioned by Congress."

Bell insisted that the quotation from his speech of 1854 had been garbled and that the resolutions had no other purpose than to discredit him. "But, sir, I thank God," he added in an air of self-righteousness, "that neither my character nor my honor is in the keeping of such men. I regard the preamble and the first two resolutions as a gratuitous insult . . . entirely characteristic of those who plotted it."

The doctrine of the right of instruction, Bell argued, had lost most of its strength; it was not supported by the Constitution; it had long ago been abandoned by the Whigs; and the Democrats had sometimes obeyed and sometimes disobeyed. He looked upon legislatures as "political juntas" dominated by party interests, and he could see no more reason for holding senators responsible to legislatures than for holding the President responsible to the electoral college. A legislature had a right to express its views; beyond that, it had no power in national matters.[10]

Andrew Johnson came to the defense of his Democratic friends in Tennessee. He expressed regret at not having "been

10 *Cong. Globe,* 35 Cong., 1 Sess., 804–806.

spared the performance of this painful duty" of replying to his colleague. During the course of the debate on the Kansas-Nebraska Bill, he explained, the Tennessee senate had passed a resolution approving of the principle of squatter sovereignty; and, in the house, a resolution endorsing the Dixon amendment had received the vote of every Whig present. Was that not sufficient reflection of public opinion? In the election of 1855, Johnson said he canvassed the state from "Johnson County to the Chickasaw Bluffs," and everywhere he went, he found the leading issue to be the Kansas-Nebraska Act. The same was true in 1856, and in 1857 the opponents of the act were overwhelmed.

The trouble with Senator Bell, Johnson averred, was that he was constantly "looking North." No one living in the South had ever gone quite so far North; no Southern man had made such a strong bid for Northern support. In fact his colleague's public career reminded him of a little verse:

> He wires in and wires out,
>   Leaving the people all in doubt
> Whether the snake that made the track,
>   Is going North or coming back.

All the while, Bell's anger continued to rise. He was exasperated at being classed as a traitor to the South; he was furious at being referred to as a snake; and all this from one upon whose plebeian background the aristocracy never ceased to look askance. When Johnson continued to refer to him as his competitor, Bell lost control of himself and yelled out that he was not the Senator's competitor in any respect. The Senate broke forth in laughter. Johnson flushed with anger; he took this remark as a slur, which is the way it was probably intended. He had had many competitors, he retorted, who, in ability, were not inferior "even to the honorable Senator's own conception of himself." "A gentleman and well-bred man will respect me, and others I will make do it: 'Upon what meat doth this our Caesar feed, that he is grown so great?' "

Johnson was thoroughly aroused. "If you have never been my competitor," he shouted at Bell, "your equals have"; and, in a manner reflecting both wrath and egotism, he added, "and in the conclusion of their contest they adjusted their robes and prepared themselves for their fate." And then, as one fighting to overcome an inferiority complex, he yelled to the whole Senate: "I stand here, in a senatorial sense, the compeer of any Senator."

Bell was on his feet again. Johnson's remarks were denounced as the bitterest, most insulting, and most personal "that malice, premeditated malice, and determination could invent." At that point several senators broke in with demands for adjournment. Bell agreed, being assured of the floor on the following day.[11]

The next day Bell thanked the Senate for its vote to adjourn before he had, in a moment of excitement, demeaned himself in a regrettable manner. Johnson then explained that it was not his intention to attack Bell's "personal integrity or his private character"; he merely wished to deal with him as a political representative. In that case, retorted Bell, the Senator was either ignorant of his own language or of what constituted an attack upon one's private character. Was it not personal to accuse one of a lack of principle, of being a political aspirant, and of trying to hold to the South with one hand and to the North with the other? Referring to Johnson's threat to make all men respect him, Bell declared that after the Senator's "speech of yesterday, I cannot respect him until he gives proper explanation of it; and now, or at any time, let him attempt to make me respect him." The Chair, Asa Biggs presiding, interrupted to state that Johnson's remarks had not been "strictly in order" and neither were Bell's since they were "calculated to excite personal feelings." Nevertheless, Johnson might reply if he would stay in order.

Johnson spoke at some length, covering familiar ground, and concluding with stinging braggadocio:

11 *Ibid.*, 806–13.

I feel now that I have pursued my colleague almost too far; for, from the contortions and restlessness manifested by him, I am not mistaken by the results. I know . . . when I have issues that will hold. . . . I look, politically speaking, on my honorable colleague as now being down. He is now out of power, and he that is down can fall no lower. I am a humane man. I look upon him in his prostrate condition with all the tender sympathies of humanity . . . I will not mutilate the dead, nor add one additional pang to the tortures of the already—condemned.

"I had rather be myself dead than that man living," screamed Bell. "I may be dead, politically speaking; but that is the position of honor when times turn up such members of the Senate as he is." [12]

Bell was certainly down, but the old Whig press made it clear that he could not be counted as out. That Andrew Johnson was acting "true to his low, groveling instincts," exclaimed the Lynchburg *Virginian,* was evidenced by the fact that not even senatorial courtesy could restrain his "vulgarian character." The Memphis *Eagle and Enquirer* denounced him as "an ill-bred, vulgar blackguard" and "an unprincipled political scoundrel." The affair between the two Tennessee senators, the editor insisted, brought out the difference between great statesmen and "groveling demagogues." The Cincinnati *Gazette* thought Bell made it perfectly clear that Johnson was a scoundrel and was sadly lacking in veracity.[13]

As has been indicated, the controversy between Johnson and Bell grew out of the instructions in favor of the admission of Kansas under the Lecompton constitution. Bell made it quite clear that he had no intention of obeying; and when the Kansas proposal was brought up, he launched a long and dry, but very methodical, discussion of the whole Kansas question. He pointed to the irregularities which had been resorted to by both factions, and suggested that Buchanan's sanction of this most recent fraud was a result of "positive and imperious

12 *Ibid.,* 830–38.
13 Quoted in *Republican Banner and Nashville Whig,* March 17, 1858.

requisition" on the part of men like Toombs. He could join those men, he said, in defense of every Southern right, not wishing to see the Southern states "truckle or surrender" or "yield one jot or tittle of their rights." What he could not do was support a measure which would create strife and yet be of no practical value, even if adopted. Both the North and the South should concern themselves only with whether or not the Kansas constitution had been "fairly formed." If it had, then neither the presence nor the absence of a slavery clause should have any bearing on its acceptance. He could not accept the Lecompton constitution since it did not have the approval of the people of Kansas. In fact, he did not consider that the people of that territory had made application for admission into the Union.

The surest way to block the progress of slavery agitation and reduce the strength of the Republican party, Bell asserted, would be to reject the proposed admission of Kansas under the Lecompton constitution. All who were interested in putting an end to agitation should support a proposal to send this constitution back to Kansas for popular ratification or rejection. As things now stood, he concluded, "Two adverse yet concurrent and mighty forces are driving the vessel of State toward the rocks upon which she must split, unless she receives timely aid—a paradox, yet expressive of a momentous and perhaps a fatal truth." [14]

Bell took a calm and sober view of the Dred Scott decision. In a speech delivered in Nashville a few months after the announcement of the decision, he had praised the Supreme Court as "the true bulwark of the constitution and of our system of Government." [15] During the course of his speech on the Lecompton constitution, he refused to go into a discussion of the principles set forth by the Court. He merely stated that if these principles were sound, they would stand; if not, they would "yield to further and closer investigation." If

[14] *Cong. Globe*, 35 Cong., 1 Sess., Appendix, 131–40.
[15] *Republican Banner and Nashville Whig*, August 1, 1857.

there had been an obiter dictum, no harm had been done, for the same questions would arise again and require a readjudication. As to the power of Congress to legislate on the question of slavery in the territories, he did not regard the matter as permanently settled. Congress, being a political body, would continue to legislate as the majority saw fit. Therefore, if the decision had inflicted no injury on either the North or South, he queried, "why should it be made a pretext for continuing this dangerous slavery agitation?" [16]

When the Lecompton bill came up in Congress, Bell lined up with Douglas, who had vigorously denounced Buchanan's Kansas policy and as a result had been driven from Administration circles, and with John J. Crittenden of Kentucky, upon whom the mantle of Henry Clay had fallen. They, in turn, were joined by three Democrats from the middle and far west and by the entire Republican delegation. Nevertheless, the friends of the Lecompton bill, under the leadership of Toombs, Jefferson Davis *et al.,* and with Administration backing, passed the measure on March 23, by a vote of 33 to 25. Crittenden and Bell were the only Southern Whigs to vote in the negative.

In the House the bill was amended, making the acceptance of the Lecompton constitution contingent upon its prior ratification by the people of Kansas. Should the people approve the constitution, the President was given authority to admit Kansas by proclamation. If they rejected it, they might form another constitution. The Senate refused to concur in the amendment and called for a conference committee. Out of this committee came the so-called English bill. Along with the Lecompton constitution, the people of Kansas were to be offered a substantial grant of public lands, but the two must be accepted together. Failure to ratify the constitution would block the admission of Kansas until its population should reach the total required for a representative in the House.

Bell opposed this bill also. He contended that because of

16 *Cong. Globe,* 35 Cong., 1 Sess., Appendix, 140.

"defective execution of the law" the Lecompton convention was irregular; therefore, its work was invalid and the alleged ratification was fraudulent. Why had not the territorial archives been opened and full information presented to the Senate? He insisted that there was before the Senate no constitution which had been presented by the people of Kansas. On the contrary, they had expressly "repudiated and rejected" the one now under consideration.[17]

Bell placed no stress, however, on the charge of bribery which some anti-Lecompton men were hurling at the proposed land grant. In fact, he suggested that the grant was no greater than the one made to Minnesota. He would applaud the framers of this bill, he said, if he thought that they had been actuated by a sincere desire to end the controversy; but, in his opinion, the bill would do nothing more than prolong the controversy into another presidential election, and increase antislavery sentiment.[18] He was not far wrong. The English bill passed; Kansas rejected the proposal by more than nine thousand majority; and the problem remained unsolved.

A sincere regard for justice, a real fear for the safety of the Union, and a belief that property in slaves was being endangered by continued agitation had prompted the conservative Bell to take this stand on the Kansas question. He believed in slavery, but only for those who wished to own slaves; he could see neither justice nor wisdom in an effort to force the institution upon unwilling settlers. In his opinion Southern ultras were as aggressive and as dangerous as Northern abolitionists. Perhaps in no other debate during his public career did he appear to a better advantage. One who observed and listened to the Kansas debate from the Senate gallery later remarked: "In his personal appearance in the Senate, Mr. Bell is noticeable. Though his hair is grey, the fire of his eye is undimmed,

---

17 The free-soil legislature had submitted the Lecompton constitution to popular vote on January 4, 1858, and it had been rejected by more than 10,000 majority.

18 *Cong. Globe,* 35 Cong., 1 Sess., 1877–80.

and the freshness of his countenance is youthful. Few men in the Senate speak so vigorously as he. His voice is sonorous and loud, and the energy of his tone, his style, and his gesticulation remind one of an orator of thirty." [19]

None but a "bigoted and prejudiced partisan" could question their "superior statesmanship and patriotism," exclaimed the Knoxville *Register*, upon receipt of copies of the Lecompton speeches of Crittenden and Bell. "We are not given to man-worship, nor have we sworn allegiance of opinion to any man, for we regard no man as infallible. But we have ever regarded John Bell as a 'safe counselor in the affairs of the nation.' . . . Truckling demagogues and soulless politicians have usurped the seats of honor and power, while the good and the great of the nation are almost universally in retirement. Let us, therefore, esteem the more highly the noble few that remain. . . . Hear him [Bell], for his cause. Judge him, and judge him impartially, that you may do him justice." [20]

The Memphis *Weekly Appeal* struck a different note. John Bell stood abandoned and alone, the editor triumphantly remarked, having been deserted by the last man of the Tennessee delegation at Washington. All had learned that to follow him meant political death, and they had no desire to fall with him. Bell himself, the editor concluded, was about the only remaining monument of his own apostasy.[21]

According to a Chinese proverb, responded the Memphis *Eagle and Enquirer*, "mountains are measured by their shadows, and great men by their slanderers." If that be true, the editor commented, then Bell was the greatest man since Clay and Webster; for the Democrats held for him a greater hatred than "the most abject, ignorant and servile minion of Popish idolatry ever entertained toward good ole Martin Luther."

[19] David W. Bartlett, *Presidential Candidates: Containing Sketches, Biographical, Personal and Political, of Prominent Candidates for the Presidency in 1860* (New York, 1859), 151.
[20] Knoxville *Register*, March 25, April 22, 1858.
[21] Memphis *Weekly Appeal*, April 3, 1858.

Indeed, the "Locos" were afraid of John Bell and had been ever since, as a young man, he defied the "Lion of the Hermitage" and succeeded in winning a glorious victory.[22]

As was to be expected, the Nashville *Union and American*, the leading Democratic organ in Middle Tennessee, sarcastically denounced Bell for his professed patriotism and his great desire to save the people from self-destruction. And when the news arrived that Bell had also voted against an Administration bill to repeal fishing bounties, the editor remarked that the opposition was made up of all the "Black Republicans, and Bell, Crittenden, and Houston—a triumvirate of traitors." [23]

Congress adjourned on June 14, 1858, leaving the members free to become active participants or interested observers in the state campaigns of the summer and fall. Of special importance was the campaign in Illinois, during which Lincoln and Douglas engaged in their celebrated debate; in Pennsylvania, where the anti-Administration coalition won an overwhelming victory; and in New York, where Seward delivered his "irrepressible conflict" speech, a stinging denunciation of the Democratic party and its defense of slavery. No important state elections were held in Tennessee; nevertheless, there was no evidence of a political holiday. Early in the summer Crittenden and Bell were invited to New York to partake of a public dinner to be given in their honor. The rumor spread, especially within Democratic circles, that a new political party was in the process of formation. "The times are certainly most sadly out of joint," remarked the Memphis *Appeal,* "when statesmen of the South can command the admiration, approving smiles and good dinners of such men as *Horace Greeley, Truman Smith* and *Erastus Brooks.*" [24] The dinner was not held, neither of the honorees

---

[22] Quoted in *Republican Banner and Nashville Whig,* September 25, 1858.
[23] Nashville *Union and American,* June 1, 18, 1858.
[24] Memphis *Weekly Appeal,* June 29, 1858.

being able to attend, but Bell, in sending his regrets, appealed for an abandonment of sectionalism.[25]

On December 6, 1858, the Thirty-fifth Congress convened for its second session, the last in which Bell was to participate. The President's annual message was read on the same day. Buchanan expressed no regrets over the course which he had pursued relative to Kansas. In fact, he said, he had "never performed any official act which in the retrospect has afforded me more heartfelt satisfaction." Had Kansas been admitted as a slave state and had a majority of the voters of the new state been dissatisfied, they could have easily amended their constitution, abolishing slavery. Kansas would then have been a free state; as it was, she was only a free territory.

United States relations with Spain in respect to Cuban affairs, the President told Congress, remained unsatisfactory. The Spanish system of government made it difficult to secure redress of grievances growing out of intercourse between the United States and the island. "The truth is," he explained, "that Cuba, in its existing colonial condition, is a constant source of injury and annoyance to the American people." He called attention to his predecessors' unsuccessful attempts to acquire Cuba by negotiation and stressed the benefits which would accompany United States' possession of the island. Before negotiations were reopened, however, he suggested that Congress make available a sum of money to be used as an advance payment, pending the Senate's ratification of a treaty of acquisition.[26]

In accordance with the President's wishes, a Cuba bill was introduced by Senator John Slidell of Louisiana, on January 10, 1859; and two weeks later, the bill, with minor changes, was reported from the Committee on Foreign Relations. Thirty million dollars was to be placed at the disposal of the President for use as an advance payment in the purchase of

25 Bell to L. Bradish *et al.*, June 17, 1858, in *Republican Banner and Nashville Whig*, June 27, 1858.
26 Richardson (ed.), *Messages and Papers*, VII, 3039-3042.

the island. No figure was set as the maximum amount to be paid for Cuba; however, the committee report suggested that the island might cost as much as $125,000,000.[27] Seward, although a member of the committee, made an immediate attack on the bill and the report, and called attention to the hostility which had already been generated in Spain as a result of the President's suggestion. Seward had visions of Buchanan's offering to pay $250,000,000 or more for Cuba.[28]

In general the division on the Cuba bill was much the same as on other recent measures involving the slavery question. The Republicans were bitterly opposed; the rabid proslavery group, desiring additional slave territory to offset the loss of Kansas, strongly advocated it; and the more conservative men were divided. Douglas supported the bill; Crittenden opposed it on financial grounds; and Bell opposed it for many reasons. In the first place, Bell said that $30,000,000 was too much money to be placed at the disposal of a President. That amount was sufficient to support the army and navy for two years, and that was all any despot or traitor could ask. Although the present executive might be trusted, he felt no assurance that his successors could be.

This plan to acquire Cuba, Bell asserted, was just another step in the course of that "reckless and aggressive group" which had demanded 54 degrees, 40 minutes in the Oregon country and had become disgusted at being forced to accept 49 degrees, the same that had pounced on Mexico and announced that expansion was the mission of the Republic, a destiny which could not be avoided. This was the same spirit, he exclaimed, which had led to the announcement that should Spain fail to yield to negotiations relative to Cuba, "the object of self-preservation, on the part of the United States, would force us to wrest it by violence from her control."[29]

Bell referred to the committee report as a "skillfully-drawn

[27] *Cong. Globe*, 35 Cong., 2 Sess., 538.   [28] *Ibid.*, 539.
[29] Referring to the Ostend Manifesto of 1854.

paper," appealing to "what is supposed to be the pre-
dominant and characteristic trait of our population—cupid-
ity, or the lust for gain." The report held that the acquisition of Cuba would be of great benefit to all sections of the
Union. There would be trade and commerce for the North
and East, markets for the products of the Northwest, and a
more extensive and profitable use of Southern slave labor.
Indeed, Bell said that he could find but one weak point—no
provision was made for the iron interests of Pennsylvania.
He thought, however, that this deficiency might be "compensated by the promise of cheap sugar." Assuming a more serious manner, he explained that what the country needed was
not more territory but relief from sectional strife, allowing
the people fullest enjoyment of what they already had.

Bell maintained that it was to the advantage of the United
States for Spain to retain possession of Cuba as long as her
policy was not injurious to the South. He was conscious of the
strategic location of the island and of its commercial advantages; at the same time he was also conscious of the difficulty which would be encountered in defending the island in
time of war. In his opinion, it would be unwise to accept
Cuba even as a gift unless we were sure of a friendly attitude
on the part of Great Britain and France. Should the United
States be forced to defend even its present coast against Great
Britain alone, he estimated that it would necessitate a fleet
of no fewer than two hundred "war-steamers—those terrible
engines of destruction." Why further complicate the problem
of defense by annexing territories beyond the needs of the
American people?

Past experience, Bell asserted, had proved that the problems of government multiplied in about the same proportion to expansion, for the greater the distance, the greater the
problems of administration, both civil and military. He had
heard it said in the Senate that the United States might some
day make extensive annexation in the tropics; against this
he wished to warn that the tropics "are to us forbidden fruit,

and the primeval curse announced as the penalty of disobedience will surely fall upon us as a free people, if we are guilty of this great transgression. The day that we pluck that fruit we die." [30]

The Cuba bill was never brought to a vote and was eventually withdrawn by Slidell. It had become hopelessly tied up with a homestead bill which had already passed the House. Each apparently destroyed the other's chances of passage. Republican leaders sought to have the Cuba bill set aside so that the homestead bill might be taken up. Toombs protested the sidetracking of an important question of foreign policy in order to take up "land for the landless." To this Benjamin Wade replied that the question was whether there should be "land to the landless" or "niggers to the niggerless." [31] The line was clearly drawn: if Southern expansionists could not have Cuba, then their opponents should not have the advantages that might come from free lands. Both the Cuba and the homestead bills were doomed.

Bell was not opposed to the principle of granting lands to the landless, yet he had no hope that those for whom the relief was intended would be able to take advantage of the government's generosity. On a previous occasion he had argued that the penniless would not possess the means even to reach the land, to say nothing of acquiring the tools necessary for cultivation. He suggested, therefore, that a certificate for a quarter section of land be granted to each family which was unable to acquire the means for removal and that such certificates be made transferable.[32] No such provision having been incorporated, Bell consistently opposed the homestead proposal.

Although Bell had opposed most of the expansionists' schemes, he was eager to develop means for adequate defense of all annexed territories. He advocated the construction of

[30] *Cong. Globe*, 35 Cong., 2 Sess., 1340-45.
[31] *Ibid.*, 1353-54.
[32] *Ibid.*, 33 Cong., 1 Sess., Appendix, 1105.

a Pacific railroad because he believed it essential to the defense of the west coast. And owing to the gigantic nature of such a project and to the fact that a broad strip of unproductive country must be traversed, he thought the undertaking too great for private enterprise. He estimated that it would be "a measure of economy" if the government should invest as much as $150,000,000 in such a railroad. Under the existing inadequate system, he explained, it was costing no less than $12,200,000 annually to transport the mails to and from the west coast and to send supplies to the Indian frontiers. What would be the cost of transporting military supplies should a strong maritime power attack California or Oregon? Indeed, such a task could not be accomplished; the United States would be defeated in that area.[33]

Bell did not want the government to do the actual construction of the proposed railroad. He preferred the granting of government subsidy to private corporations. He thought that would eliminate the twin dangers of patronage and extravagance. Probably the clearest understanding of Bell's ideas on the railroad question can be found in a substitute bill which he presented in the Senate. He suggested that Congress ask for bids on three lines—northern, middle, and southern—connecting the Mississippi valley with the west coast, each bidder specifying the termini of his proposed line and the general route to be followed. Each bidder would also state the "amount, or extent and description of the aid, facilities, and privileges which will be expected or required of the Government, whether consisting of lands or money, or both." Other information was to be supplied: the proposed rates for hauling the mail and military and naval personnel and supplies, and the date at which the bidder would be willing to surrender the line to the government if such a surrender should be desired.[34]

Such bids, if submitted at all, Bell explained, would give the advocates of each of the three routes an equal opportunity

33 Ibid., 35 Cong., 2 Sess., 107–108.   34 Ibid., 422.

to have their case presented to the public; and "Congress will have the very best test as to what are the cheapest and most eligible and practicable routes." [35]

In Bell's remarks on the railroad question he was careful not to take a sectional stand. This was in keeping with the advice of friends who had resolved to secure for him a presidential nomination in 1860. Duff Green wrote Bell that, while he himself was "deeply interested" in the southern route, he did not wish to see Bell advocate a sectional measure in the Senate. "You are now as I believe the only southern man who can if nominated get the vote of Pennsylvania." A sectional speech, however, would "dwarf" Bell to a sectional man and destroy his chances.[36] Regardless of the need for a bill similar to the one offered by Bell, the sectional rift in Congress rendered the passage of any transcontinental railroad bill improbable.

The second session of the Thirty-fifth Congress came to an end on March 3, 1859, and so did the senatorial career of John Bell. He was almost sixty-three years of age, not in robust health, yet by no means ready to die, either physically or politically. Many, in bidding him good-by, either in person or through the press, predicted his early return to Washington in an important capacity. The *New Hampshire Cabinet* and the Concord *Statesman* both proposed him for the presidency in 1860, and the Nashville *Union and American* immediately denounced those papers as "Black Republican." [37] "True to the Democratic policy of viewing everybody and everything through the glasses of niggerism," responded the Memphis *Bulletin*, the *Union and American* construed "every northern compliment to Mr. Bell's worth as nothing but so much additional evidence of his unsoundness on the said everlasting slavery question." The editor thought Bell "too great a patriot for democratic toleration." [38]

35 *Ibid.*   36 Green to Bell, January 15, 1859, in Bell Papers.
37 Nashville *Union and American*, December 14, 1858.
38 Quoted in *Republican Banner and Nashville Whig*, December 22, 1858.

The Democrats, especially in the Nashville district, were afraid of Bell. Ever since the day he defeated Grundy he had commanded a respectable following in his home section. He had led Middle Tennessee into the Whig ranks, and not even the halo about the public career of Old Hickory could dim the light of the man who had successfully defied him even in the Hermitage district. Only a certain amount of frigidity and austerity [39] in Bell prevented him from being a great leader of men.

Fearing that, upon retirement from the Senate, Bell might announce his candidacy for a seat in the House, the Democratic press kept its guns trained on the Senator. The public was continually reminded of his alleged treason to the South and his failure to recognize that he was the servant of the people. "The People! I am the People, says Bell, the——Tennessean!" exclaimed the *Union and American*.[40] Why all of this froth? inquired the *Republican Banner*. It was a result of the fact that "John Bell dared to stand up in the face of a frenzied sectionalism and tell the South the *truth*." [41] If the Senator thought he had been treated with undue harshness, replied the Democratic press, then let him run for governor instead of for Congress. "*His* issue is with the people of the entire State, and not of a Congressional district." [42] There is no evidence that Bell aspired to be either a congressman or a governor.

[39] Lewis L. Poats to Nelson, August 24, 1853, in Nelson Papers.
[40] Nashville *Union and American,* June 18, 1858.
[41] *Republican Banner and Nashville Whig,* September 5, 1858.
[42] Nashville *Union and American,* September 16, 1858.

Chapter XVII

THE CONSTITUTION AND THE UNION

FOLLOWING the crushing defeat of the Know-Nothings in 1856, those Tennessee Whigs who still refused to join the Democrats referred to themselves as the Opposition. On February 12, 1859, a large Opposition meeting at the Nashville courthouse adopted resolutions denouncing the ruinous policies of the Buchanan Administration, expressing regret at Bell's retirement from the Senate, and nominating the former Senator as a suitable candidate for the presidency.[1] When Bell arrived in Nashville these friends greeted him with a reception which partisans claimed exceeded anything witnessed in Tennessee since the campaign of 1840.[2]

In the spring of 1859, Bell made a combined political and business trip to points east. On April 27 he spoke at a reception given in honor of Henry C. Carey at La Pierre House in Philadelphia. From there he journeyed to New York, where he addressed a gathering of old Whigs. Conservatives, he declared, regardless of whether they were called Whigs, Americans, or by some other name, had the same great object—the preservation of American institutions and the Union. He would not say that the people were incapable of governing themselves, but he warned his hearers that unless a popular will to preserve the Union was reflected in politics the Union could not endure.[3]

His eastern trip was probably more of a private than a public nature. Things were still not going well at his Ken-

---

[1] *Republican Banner and Nashville Whig*, February 13, 15, 1859.
[2] *Ibid.*, April 3, 1859. [3] *Ibid.*, May 8, 1859.

tucky mines. He had recently incorporated his holdings there but was still the owner of almost all of the stock. According to his own figures, he had put more than $100,000 in cash in these mines and improvements. During the 1850's he had continued to acquire additional tracts of land and now possessed 1,000 acres of fine coal lands.[4] Yet in spite of this huge investment, production of coal did not exceed 150 tons daily. Facilities were available for handling double that amount. Consequently, Bell was in search of a manager who could substantially increase production and relieve him of all worry. Appeals were made to business and political friends in Philadelphia and New York to assist in securing such a person.[5] What success he had is not recorded, but Bell's income from these mines was not greatly increased.

Bell's land speculation in Louisiana had also brought him little profit and much worry. Improvements on Red River had not been adequate and the proposed railroad had not been constructed through that section. With the death of James Bell in 1841, the burden had been shifted to John. From the beginning of their purchases there the Bells had encountered great confusion. At one time John Bell found himself paying taxes on another's land; again, another man's land was advertised for sale to pay Bell's taxes. Litigations over titles were continuous, and whatever profits Bell might have made were consumed by court costs and attorney fees. At the time of his death in 1869, he still owned a tract of this Louisiana land, at least a part of which was sold for taxes in 1882.[6]

Reports from Stewart County, Tennessee, were more favorable. The ironworks there had been greatly expanded

[4] See indentures in Polk-Yeatman Papers.
[5] Bell to Coryell, May 28, 1859, in Collection of the Historical Society of Pennsylvania.
[6] R. C. Downes to Bell, January 10, May 10, 1852; M. R. Douglas to id., February 26, 1852; Sheriff M. Watson to id., February 11, 1855; R. G. Harper to id., November 5, 1855, May 14, 1857; G. A. Martin to id., May 18, 1857, in Polk-Yeatman Papers; Caddo Parish Conveyance Records, Book A, 264, 266; Book C, 657, 735; Book G, 274; Book M, 95, 736; Vol. I, 156, 499.

since Bell had become part owner. In 1847 the Woods brothers and the Bells had purchased the Stacker interests. An inventory made by James Woods and reported to Bell in 1852 showed that the company, now known as the Cumberland Iron Works, owned more than 51,000 acres of land, a rolling mill, four furnaces—Dover, Bear Spring, Randolph, and Bellwood—365 slaves, and a huge amount of iron in various forms. The total value of all property of every kind was estimated at $504,875.36. In 1852 Henry C. Yeatman, Bell's stepson, purchased a one-sixteenth share in the company for $80,000.[7] Judging from the great expansion of the Cumberland Iron Works, the concern must have been efficiently managed. The Woods brothers should be given the major portion of the credit for this success.

Regardless of the urgency of private business, neither Bell's friends nor his enemies would permit him to retire from politics; neither is there evidence that he wished permanent retirement. His Northern tour gave additional ammunition to his Southern enemies. "H. G. Robertson, the sapheaded editor of the Greeneville *Democrat,*" complained "Parson" Brownlow, told all over East Tennessee that Bell had confided to a General Brazelton that he expected to get the Republican nomination in 1860. Brownlow pronounced Robertson's statement an *"infinite infernal lie,"* and set out to find Brazelton. No such statement had been made, Brazelton assured the "Parson." Bell had merely expressed a belief that Northern conservatives would co-operate with conservatives from the South, and had admitted that his name had been proposed as a possible conservative candidate.[8]

Meanwhile, Horace Greeley, editor of the New York *Tribune,* was toying with the idea of a possible union of the Republicans with other political groups. He thought that there might be co-operation among those who had opposed the Kansas-Nebraska Bill and the Lecompton and English bills

<hr/>

[7] James Woods to Bell, September 4, 1852, in Polk-Yeatman Papers.
[8] *Brownlow's Knoxville Whig,* July 5, 1859.

and those who had objected to further acquisition of foreign territory for the purpose of increasing the amount of slave territory. In listing the names of those who fell within this group and who would be acceptable to the Republicans, Greeley mentioned both Bell and Emerson Etheridge of Tennessee. He then inquired whether Seward, Chase, and Bell had not occupied the same position on the above questions.[9]

Greeley's sincerity in mentioning Bell as an acceptable candidate is questionable; six months later he was definitely opposed to the Tennessean. "Before you say much more about John Bell," he wrote his veteran reporter, James S. Pike, "will you just take down the volumes of the *Congressional Globe* for 1853–4. . . . I venture to say that Bell's record is the most tangled and embarrassing to the party which shall run him for President of any man's in America. And as to his wife owning the slaves—bosh! We know Bell *has* owned slaves—how did he get rid of them? That's an interesting question. We know how to answer respecting Bates." [10] Six days earlier Greeley had publicly announced that Edward Bates of Missouri was "the man for the hour." [11]

In the congressional election in Tennessee in 1859, Bell's name was almost as prominent as if he had been a candidate; the former Senator's prospects for 1860 must be ruined. His alleged leaning toward the "Black Republicans" was thoroughly publicized by the Democrats. To this charge Thomas A. R. Nelson replied that "if Mr. Bell is thus nominated by a Convention of Black Republicans, and the Opposition of the South, and the Black Republicans will drop their abolition tendencies, I will support him." [12] In Middle Tennessee especially Bell's opponents tried desperately to destroy his influence, but the old Whig districts stood firm; and throughout the state the Opposition party won six out of the ten

[9] New York *Tribune*, July 25, 1859.
[10] Horace Greeley to James S. Pike, February 26, 1860, in Pike, *First Blows of the Civil War*, 499–500.
[11] New York *Tribune*, February 20, 1860.
[12] Quoted in Hamer, *Tennessee*, I, 515.

congressional seats. Bell was jubilant; he felt that he had been vindicated. The power of the Democracy had been broken, he declared to a gathering of "the boys" at the City Hotel in Nashville.[13]

On August 19, Bell participated in a torchlight celebration at Knoxville. Nelson presented him as the "Nestor of the Whig party," and Horace Maynard referred to him as the man whom the Democrats had slandered from the beginning to the end of the recent campaign. Bell made a short speech stressing the differences between the parties and declaring that the only binding tie among the Democrats was the "cohesive power of plunder." To those who had denounced him for friendship with Republicans he announced that he was willing to co-operate with anyone, even the "profligate leaders of Democracy in Tennessee," for the sake of the Union.[14]

Following the Knoxville meeting Bell hurried across the state to address a gathering at Memphis. At the conclusion of his speech he was presented with a bouquet, and in the course of the presentation remarks, the name of the late Andrew Jackson was mentioned. This gave Bell an opportunity to pronounce a eulogy on the Old Hero. According to an enthusiast, his remarks "thrilled through the audience like the strains of sweet music through the dreams of a sleeping girl. With uplifted hands he prayed that the Hero of the Hermitage might come forth from his grave in the hour of the Union's peril. The effect was electrical. Tears were freely shed. . . ."[15]

Among moderates outside of Tennessee there was great interest in Bell's fight for political existence. His conservatism on the slavery question had won for him a number of admirers in the North. In August, 1859, he received a communication from Senator James R. Doolittle of Wisconsin relative to the possible acquisition of a piece of territory in

[13] *Republican Banner and Nashville Whig*, August 9, 1859.
[14] *Brownlow's Knoxville Whig*, August 20, 1859.
[15] Memphis *Bulletin*, quoted in *Republican Banner and Nashville Whig*, August 30, 1859.

the western hemisphere to be used in colonizing free Negroes. Doolittle was a former Democrat who had left his party
as a result of the repeal of the Missouri Compromise and had
been sent to the Senate by the moderate Republicans in 1857.
The establishment of such an asylum for free Negroes, Doolittle apparently believed, would eliminate the South's principle objection to voluntary emancipation. He wished to know
whether Southern conservatives would approve of such a
plan. Bell thought they would, since, in his opinion, the
South would receive greater benefits from it than would the
North. However, he was not convinced that Doolittle could
secure the support of his Northern friends, "flushed as they
are with the hope of victory." At any event, Bell replied, if
he and Doolittle "were duly empowered upon this subject"
he believed they "could adjust all the grounds of difference
& discord between the *conservative* opposition North & South,
in twenty four hours."[16]

In many sections of the North the name of the conservative
Tennessean was being used in connection with the approaching presidential election. By November, 1859, the Philadelphia *North American* had announced in favor of Bell for
President. His close friends in Tennessee began to ponder
the advisability of opening a campaign in the key state of
Pennsylvania. The brilliant and courageous Balie Peyton,
recently returned to Gallatin after a six-year residence in
California, took the lead. For almost thirty years this "noble
chevalier of the olden times" had done yeoman service for
the Whig cause. Ever an ardent admirer of Bell, he had been
indefatigable in his support of the political aspirations of
the leader of the Tennessee Whigs. Henry A. Wise, one of
Peyton's close associates, once remarked that if Balie had ever
"read any thing" he would have been one of the great men
of his time.[17] Peyton, like Bell, had viewed with great concern

[16] Bell to James R. Doolittle, October 18, 1859, in *American Historical Magazine*, IX (1904), 275–76.

[17] Robert Hatton to wife, April 24, 1860, in James Vaulx Drake, *Life of
General Robert Hatton* (Nashville, 1867), 274.

the growth of sectionalism and the apparent disintegration of the old parties. In view of the existing conditions, he decided that he and Bell should "go to *Philadelphia* & throw all our weight & strength, fearlessly & boldly, into the breach, with a view to the formation of a conservative, national, union, opposition party." Philadelphia was unquestionably the place "to set the ball in motion," he reasoned, for many residents of that city were known to be favorably inclined toward Bell; all that was needed was a few demonstrations and some stirring speeches. And the resourceful Peyton had a plan for providing these needs. Jesse Peyton, a Philadelphia relative, had suggested that Balie himself be honored with a public dinner in Philadelphia and that Bell, Edward Everett, William C. Rives, and other conservatives, including the Opposition members of Tennessee's congressional delegation, be invited as guests. Balie Peyton was eager to carry out the plan and insisted that Bell accompany him to Philadelphia both as a companion and an adviser. Without Bell's counsel, Peyton feared that he might *"play hell,"* for he planned to "take most decided ground against all mere sectional parties North & South." [18]

Apparently Peyton had already arranged for the dinner before writing to Bell, for on the following day, a Philadelphia committee, headed by Henry C. Carey, sent Peyton an invitation to a public dinner to be given in his honor on January 14. His Northern friends wished an opportunity to congratulate him upon his return from the Far West, the invitation announced, and to convey through him "assurance of the cordial good will and fraternal feeling they entertain for their countrymen generally who reside in that section of the Union to which you belong." Peyton replied that he would be "but too happy to supply the occasion for such assurance, of the sincerity of which I entertain no doubt." [19]

[18] Peyton to Bell, December 17, 1859, in Bell Papers.
[19] Henry C. Carey *et al.* to Peyton, December 18, 1859; Peyton to Carey *et al.*, December 28, 1859, in *Republican Banner and Nashville Whig*, January 20, 1860.

Whether Bell went to Philadelphia as Peyton's adviser is not known; he did not attend the dinner. Instead, he sent a letter in which he expressed great confidence in the people of Pennsylvania. Although the "threats of disunion continually resounded on the one side, [and were] responded to by defiance on the other," he looked with hope and confidence "to the great and powerful commonwealth of Pennsylvania, to her well known loyalty and devotion to the Constitution and the Union—a loyalty and devotion, I trust and believe as immovable as her own mountains—to avert a fatal issue." [20]

The dinner was held in the Philadelphia Academy of Music. Although a downpour of cold rain made the day the most "forbidding and comfortless" in many years, several hundred enthusiasts splashed through the mud to the Girard House to serenade the most distinguished visitor, the venerable John J. Crittenden; and at four o'clock in the afternoon, 378 guests sat down to dinner in the banner-draped hall of the Academy. On the wall was displayed Nagle's full-length portrait of Henry Clay, underneath which was inscribed:

A union of hearts
And a union of hands
And the flag of our Union forever.[21]

There was some speaking and much handshaking, but no new party was organized.

Catching a bit of the enthusiasm generated at Nashville and Philadelphia, Brownlow and his associates held a Union mass meeting at Knoxville on January 19, and adopted resolutions declaring that they knew "no North, no South, no East, no West, but one common country, whose integrity the Constitution alone secures, and whose varying interests the Union harmonizes and protects." [22]

[20] Bell to Carey et al., January 3, 1860, in Chattanooga Gazette, January 28, 1860.
[21] Philadelphia North American and United States Gazette, January 16, 1860.
[22] Republican Banner and Nashville Whig, January 21, 1860.

On January 6, 1860, the *Republican Banner and Nashville Whig* raised the Bell standard and was quickly joined by no fewer than a dozen other presses in the larger towns of the state. Outside of Tennessee a number of conservative newspapers representing many sections also announced their support of Bell. "There is nothing of the demagogue about him," declared the New Orleans *Bulletin.* "He rises above sectionalism and the tricks of the demagogue," announced the Boston *Courier.* "No public man of our time exhibits a more unspotted political career," asserted the New Orleans *Bee.* Similar statements came from the editors of the Philadelphia *Enquirer,* the Baltimore *Patriot,* and the Cincinnati *Gazette.*[23] And on January 23 the Baltimore *American* published a long article in the interest of Bell.

On January 11 the Opposition members of the Tennessee legislature held a caucus in the senate chamber and adopted resolutions calling a state convention for February 22, advocating the holding of a national convention, and proposing Bell for the presidency.[24] Andrew Jackson Donelson, a nephew of Rachel Jackson and onetime secretary to Old Hickory, made a public appeal for support of his fellow Tennessean. Should Bell be elected to the presidency, Donelson had no fear for the Union cause, for he knew him to be *"one of the ablest and purest patriots that the country has produced."* It was true that Bell's support of Hugh Lawson White instead of Martin Van Buren had alienated him from General Jackson. "But he [Bell] never failed to manifest sentiments of respect and gratitude for Gen. Jackson, and he has often expressed his regret that the hero was not now with us, still guarding the country from the perils brought upon it by modern Democracy." [25] A clever bid for the support of the older members of the Democratic party! Apparently the persons concerned had conveniently forgotten Donelson's earlier

[23] Quoted in *Brownlow's Knoxville Whig,* February 11, 1860.
[24] *Republican Banner and Nashville Whig,* January 12, 1860.
[25] Donelson to Jere Clemens, February 16, 1860, in *Brownlow's Knoxville Whig,* March 31, 1860.

reference to Bell as one "damned with treachery and intrigue." [26]

The Tennessee convention assembled on February 22. Most of the counties were represented, the mid-state counties sending especially large delegations. The assembly was called to order by W. L. Martin of Wilson, and Jere Clemens of Shelby was made chairman. Resolutions were adopted asserting that " the true test of devotion to the Union is the practice of ready obedience to the requirements of the Constitution," denouncing slavery agitation as being "fraught with infinite mischiefs" without promise of profit to any section, and advocating a tariff sufficient to give adequate protection to American labor. John Bell, the convention announced, because of his "superior qualifications" and experience, his "broad and expansive patriotism," and "his unswerving devotion to the Union and the Constitution," was the man best suited for the presidency of the United States. The convention also went on record in favor of a national convention, selected delegates to the proposed convention, and instructed them to support Bell.[27] The Tennessee nominee was not present when nominated, but had remained in easy reach. He was immediately notified, and delivered a short address of appreciation before the convention at its evening session.[28]

On the same day that the Tennessee convention held its session, John J. Crittenden, William C. Rives, Francis Granger, William A. Graham, Washington Hunt, Henry Fuller, John P. Kennedy, William G. Brownlow, Jere Clemens, and twenty-one other prominent leaders from among the old Whigs and Americans issued an appeal "To the People of the United States." Bell's signature was not among the thirty and there is no evidence that he had any part in the plan, although he undoubtedly knew what was being planned. Neither the Democrats nor the Republicans could be "safely

26 *Id.* to Polk, September 24, 1835, in Polk Papers.
27 *Republican Banner and Nashville Whig*, February 23, 1860.
28 *Ibid.*

entrusted with the management of public affairs," announced the appeal; therefore, a new party must be organized. Such a party should have as its cardinal principles the removal of the slavery question from party politics, development of national resources, maintenance of honorable peace with all nations, strict enforcement of the laws and the powers of the Constitution, and respect for state rights and reverence for the Union. The conservative elements in all the states were urged to select delegates to a national convention which was to be held in Baltimore.[29]

If such a party was to be organized on the basis of these principles, its logical leader was the venerable Crittenden, the acknowledged successor of Henry Clay. And had he desired to become the party's presidential candidate, he could easily have had the nomination. But neither he nor his family wished it. In midsummer, 1859, his daughter urged him not even to consider making a race. To her he replied that she had never given him "*wiser* or nobler advice." [30] Early in 1860, however, considerable pressure was brought upon him to accept a nomination. "You are the candidate of the National Americans here," wrote a Massachusetts admirer, "and they will not look elsewhere until you direct them to do so." [31] But Crittenden remained firm even under the pressure of his friends, advising them repeatedly that he would not accept a nomination. He was tired of public life, and disgusted "with the low party politics of the day, and the miserable scramble for place and plunder." He was looking forward to the close of his senatorial term and his return to the repose of a private citizen. His only wish with regard to the new party, he said, was that it "act wisely and prudently." He did not much care who was nominated, he remarked, "so that I can escape and get off smoothly." [32]

29 Washington *National Intelligencer*, February 23, 1860.
30 Crittenden to Mrs. Ann Mary Coleman, July 2, 1859, in Coleman, *Crittenden*, II, 178.
31 Amos Lawrence to Crittenden, January 6, 1860, *ibid.*, 183.
32 Crittenden to ? Hunton, April 15, 1860, *ibid.*, 192-93.

Secretly, General Winfield Scott was hoping for another chance at the presidency. He neither expected nor desired anything at the hands of the existing parties, he confided to Crittenden, but in case he should be brought forward (presumably by a new party), he would make his stand on the Constitution and on the "known antecedents of my public life." [33] Crittenden may have mentioned Scott to some of his friends, for Amos A. Lawrence remarked that Massachusetts Americans were not interested in the nomination of Scott unless Crittenden chose to recommend him.[34]

The friends of the picturesque Sam Houston were insisting that he was the most "available" of all possible candidates. The exciting career of this warrior-statesman was well known to all, and in Washington he had almost become an institution unto himself. In his adopted state of Texas, an enthusiastic group of admirers, while celebrating the anniversary of the battle of San Jacinto, adopted resolutions deploring the evil days into which the country had arrived, recommending Houston as the "people's candidate for the presidency," and appealing for support from conservatives in all parties and sections.[35]

Out in Missouri, Edward Bates earnestly desired a nomination on a combined Opposition and Republican ticket. However, a month before the meeting of the Baltimore convention, he confided to his diary that two things were clear—the Crittenden and Bell supporters had resolved that one of them and not he should head the Opposition ticket, and the Democrats were eager that Seward should be nominated by the Republicans rather than either Bates or Bell.[36] He also feared truth of the rumor that John McLean and Bell would be the

[33] Scott to Crittenden, January 6, 27, 1860, *ibid.*, 182, 184.

[34] Laurence to *id.*, January 6, 1860, *ibid.*, 183.

[35] Louis J. Wortham, *A History of Texas* (Fort Worth, 1924), IV, 292–96; W. J. Pendleton to Alexander Robinson Boteler, April 25, 1860, in Alexander Robinson Boteler Papers (Duke University Library).

[36] Howard K. Beale (ed.), *The Diary of Edward Bates, 1859–1860,* American Historical Association, *Annual Report,* 1930, IV, 44, 118.

nominees at Baltimore and would be endorsed by the Republican convention at Chicago.[37]

With Crittenden out of the race, Bell must have felt fairly confident of nomination. Although the popular clamor for Houston was loud, there was little chance that old Whig leaders would support him. During the early months of 1860 Bell and his accomplished wife were busy sounding out opinion and making contacts. Late in January Mrs. Bell and her two daughters were in Washington, stopping at Willard's, receiving both personal and political friends. One Tennessee congressman who called found Mrs. Bell "as agreeable, though as ugly as ever." "She is very shrewd," he remarked, though "Too jealous of the position, and chances of other men for office." [38] Mrs. Bell and her daughters remained in Washington until the middle of March and then left for New Jersey to visit friends.

Shortly after the departure of his family Bell arrived in the capital and began a series of brief conferences; he was off for Tennessee again in less than a week. One friend thought he appeared *"anxious* about his prospects of a nomination at Baltimore." [39] Bell spent the month of April in Nashville, presumably writing letters to many friends, although little of his preconvention correspondence has been preserved.

The Baltimore convention was scheduled for May 9. Bell was in the city by May 7, stopping at the Eutaw House. Houston's friends established headquarters at Barnum's Hotel. Crittenden was also on the scene by May 7, enjoying the

[37] *Ibid.,* 119. Among other persons who were prominently mentioned as possible nominees were Edward Everett, John McLean, William A. Graham, John Minor Botts, William C. Rives, and William L. Sharkey.

[38] "Diary of Robert Hatton," in Drake, *Hatton,* 221, 249. Bell had only two children by his second wife—Jane Erwin (Jennie) and Ann Lorrain (Nannie). After the Civil War they moved to Philadelphia and opened an exclusive girls' school. In 1860 Bell placed in trust for these daughters a portion of his interest in the Cumberland Iron Works. Their half brother, Henry C. Yeatman, was made trustee. See Polk-Yeatman Papers under date of February 26, 1860.

[39] "Diary of Robert Hatton," in Drake, *Hatton,* 256.

hospitality of John P. Kennedy.[40] From its headquarters in the Temperance Temple the executive committee directed the activities of the convention which assembled in the old Presbyterian Church at Fayette and North streets. Delegates came from all the states except "the Pacific and extreme North West." [41]

Although among the delegates were found several prominent leaders of the old Whig and American parties, they were but a remnant of those organizations; most members of those parties had either joined or were preparing to join the Republicans or Democrats. James Gordon Bennett of the New York *Herald* referred to the assembly as a "Great Gathering of Fossil Know Nothings and Southern Americans." [42]

Early reports from newspaper correspondents on the scene noted a "spontaneous movement" for Houston. Edward Everett looked like the best prospect for the vice-presidential nomination. The New York delegation was said to be a unit in favor of this combination. Massachusetts was divided between Houston and Crittenden. Friends of Houston were arguing that his nomination would be a "thunderbolt" to the Republican convention. Some sentiment in favor of John Minor Botts was in evidence. John McLean was the choice of interior Pennsylvania, but the Philadelphia delegates, under the leadership of Henry M. Fuller, were strong for Bell.

By the evening of May 8, Houston was said to be losing ground, although he was still being urged by New York and Kentucky. Mississippi, Virginia, and Maryland were reported in support of Everett, and a ticket composed of Everett and William A. Graham of North Carolina appeared probable. Sentiment for Bell was "coming up," yet it was said that the leaders of the Tennessee delegation preferred Houston. One thing was certain: the Negro question was to have no place on the agenda of the convention. In fact, the rumor

[40] Baltimore *Clipper,* May 7, 8, 1860.   [41] *Ibid.,* May 9, 1860.
[42] New York *Herald,* May 9, 1860.

had spread that any delegate who mentioned the Negro would be ejected from the meeting. In other words, according to a correspondent of the New York *Herald,* "the delegates may sleep with the nigger, eat with the nigger, but don't allow his woolly head to come into the convention." [43]

On the evening of May 8 a number of state delegations went into caucus, and before midnight many shifts were reported. Tennessee, Arkansas, Pennsylvania, Ohio, and Delaware would go for Bell, yet there was "little doubt" that Houston would eventually get the nomination. [44]

On the morning of the ninth, the opening day of the convention, the nomination was still very much in doubt. One observer recorded: "There is one set, and containing no small numbers, that seems determined to galvanize petrified whiggery; another to whitewash embalmed Americanism, and the third to unite hands with the republicans at Chicago; the fourth to harness up a squatter sovereignty team." He feared that the nominee would be "an old rusty whig fossil or an American mummy." [45] Georgia and Alabama, it was said, would support Houston; so would Tennessee, after giving Bell a complimentary vote. The Tennessean was still gaining strength, but his supporters were "not so noisy as those of Houston." [46]

Crittenden called the convention to order, and prayer was offered by the Reverend James D. McCabe, Rector of St. Stephen Episcopal Church of Baltimore. [47] Crittenden then nominated and the convention approved former Governor Washington Hunt of New York as temporary chairman. Later, upon the recommendation of Andrew Jackson Donelson, speaking for the committee on permanent organization, Hunt was made permanent presiding officer. On the first ballot for a nomination for President Bell received 68½ votes and Houston 57. The remaining votes were scattered among

---

[43] *Ibid.,* May 8, 9, 1860.   [44] *Ibid.,* May 9, 1860.   [45] *Ibid.,* May 10, 1860.
[46] *Ibid.*
[47] For complete proceedings, see Baltimore *Clipper,* May 10, 11, 1860,

almost a score of potential nominees. Despite his well-known position, Crittenden received 28 votes.[48]

During the night of May 9–10 there was the usual political jockeying. The Virginia and North Carolina delegations were said to have been particularly active. In a room-to-room canvass, they made a personal appeal for the nomination of an old Whig. Supposedly as a result of such activities, some delegates from New York and New Jersey and the entire Alabama, Georgia, and Florida representation were brought into the Bell camp.[49] Bell later expressed his appreciation to Alexander Robinson Boteler of Virginia for his "steady & efficient friendship, when others (my Tenn. friends, or some of them) wavered, & actually fell away from me, for a time." [50] What part Crittenden played in lining up support for Bell is not certain, but a few days later Bell also thanked the Kentuckian for his course during the convention. It is certain that Crittenden was opposed to Houston.[51] The Hero of San Jacinto was too closely associated with the memory of the Hero of New Orleans to elicit much enthusiasm from the friends of the late Henry Clay.

When balloting was resumed on the second day of the convention, Houston's vote rose to 69, but Bell received 138 and the nomination. One loyal soul refused to take no for an answer and again voted for Crittenden.[52] "The old whigs of the Convention have carried their point," wrote a disappointed onlooker, "and the Young American element will leave with its heads down." [53]

Following Bell's nomination he was eulogized before the convention by Tennessee's "Eagle Orator," Gustavus A. Henry, whose eloquence was sufficient to cause at least one

[48] Horace Greeley and John F. Cleveland, *Political Text-Book for 1860* (New York, 1860), 29.

[49] New York *Herald*, May 11, 1860.

[50] Bell to Boteler, July 2, 1860, in Boteler Papers.

[51] *Id.* to Crittenden, May 29, 1860, in Crittenden Papers (Duke University Library).

[52] Greeley and Cleveland, *Political Text-Book for 1860*, 29.

[53] New York *Herald*, May 11, 1860.

newspaper correspondent to report that he was a grandson of Patrick Henry.[54]

The vice-presidential nomination went to Edward Everett by acclamation. Everett definitely did not desire the nomination. He had tacitly consented to accept the presidential nomination if it were offered, and the Massachusetts delegation had come to Baltimore pledged to vote for Crittenden on the first ballot and then shift to Everett. Upon learning of the Houston and Bell strength, Everett telegraphed his friends to withdraw his name at the proper time.[55] His name was withdrawn after the first ballot, but the friend responsible for the action failed to state that he was acting in accordance with Everett's request. Consequently, the convention, in acclaiming Everett the vice-presidential nominee, was desirous of honoring him.[56] Everett, however, did not take the nomination as a compliment. "It looks like favoring an officer with the command of a sloop-of-war," he wrote his daughter, "after he had magnanimously waived his claim to the flag of the Mediterranean Squadron, in favor of a junior officer." [57]

No list of principles was adopted by the convention, although some Pennsylvania delegates insisted upon a tariff plank; [58] all party issues were declared secondary to the preservation of the Union. The only justification for the formation of a new party was to consolidate the strength of all who placed love for the Union above sectional strife. Accordingly, the Constitutional Union party chose "to recognize no political principle other than the Constitution of the Country, the Union of the States and the Enforcement of the Laws."

Undoubtedly very few delegates to the Baltimore convention confidently expected success for their party. The ambiguous platform which they adopted was subject to as many

[54] Henry's speech was printed in the *Republican Banner and Nashville Whig*, May 16, 1860.
[55] Everett received 25 votes on the first ballot.
[56] Edward Everett to Washington Hunt, May 14, 1860, in Coleman, *Crittenden*, II, 198.
[57] May 14, 1860, quoted in Frothingham, *Edward Everett*, 410.
[58] New York *Herald*, May 10, 1860.

interpretations as there were interpreters. As Edward Bates confided to his diary, "To say only that they go for the Constitution and the enforcement of the laws, is only what every other party says." The only hope for the cause, Bates reasoned, was for another Andrew Jackson to make his appearance and by the force of his own character make a party of his own. This he thought Bell could not do, but he added that Bell was "intrinsically a better man than Jackson."[59]

The Constitutional Union appeal to reason and caution, although commendable, could not have been calculated to generate much enthusiasm. Paradoxically, its strong point was also its weak point. Its refusal to take a stand on the one exciting issue robbed its candidates of all chance of substantial support from more aggressive politicians; few people became excited over a proposal to do nothing. Those who planned the party's strategy based their hope on an expectation that moderate Republicans, sensing defeat for their candidate and having a friendly feeling for Bell, might vote the Constitutional Union ticket in order to prevent a Democratic victory. Furthermore, the division within the ranks of the Democrats, which later resulted in the nomination of both Stephen A. Douglas and John C. Breckinridge, might convince many members of the party that neither candidate could be elected and that they should support Bell and Everett in order to defeat the Republican nominee.[60] If either of these hopes proved well-founded, it would not be too much to expect the contest to be thrown into the House of Representatives for final decision. In other words, the Constitutional Union ticket could win only if used for the purpose of preventing either a Democratic or a Republican victory.

It was with the above ideas in mind that the *National Intelligencer* opened its campaign for Bell and Everett with

[59] Beale (ed.), *Diary of Edward Bates*, 127.
[60] James C. Welling to Bell, May 12, 1860; James Love to *id.*, June 17, 1860, in Polk-Yeatman Papers.

a veiled appeal to the Southern Democrats. Long a supporter of conservatism, the *Intelligencer*, the editorial policy
of which was under the direction of Bell's friend James C.
Welling, undertook a subtle defense of the Constitutional
Union platform. It abandoned no Whig principle, Welling
pointed out, and the only reason the old Whigs had not insisted on the inclusion of a protective tariff and internal improvements in this platform was that in recent years Democrats of the "purest water" had endorsed those principles.[61]
Welling's idea was to suggest to Southern Democrats that by
supporting Bell they would be "voting *worse* in Whig principles than they have already been compelled to take in swallow-
ing the gilded pill of Democracy." [62]

The nomination of Bell was probably an unwise move on
the part of the Constitutional Union party. He had been
too prominent in the congressional struggles during the past
decade. He was hated by many Southern Democrats, and distrusted, if not hated, by the ultra wing of the remnant of the
Southern Whigs. In the North he was admired for his conservatism on the slavery question, but much of this admiration came from supporters of the presidential aspiration of
Douglas. Some of the moderate Republicans also looked with
favor upon him; yet being a large slaveholder, he could not
hope for support from the more radical wing of that party.
Then, Bell was lacking in the qualities required of a popular leader. He was never an idol of the people even of his
home section, although they kept him in office for the greater
portion of thirty years. His speeches exhibited orderliness
and depth of thought, but too much dignity and formality
decreased their effectiveness upon popular assemblies. In
short, he was not a man whose appearance on a political platform would elicit from the audience a wild outburst of
sincere enthusiasm. Furthermore, he was now an elderly man,
reminiscent of the days of Clay and Webster; he had little

61 Washington *National Intelligencer*, May 12, 1860.
62 Welling to Bell, May 12, 1860, in Polk-Yeatman Papers.

appeal for that aggressive younger generation which had reached its maturity during the 1850's. Among his friends he was considered cold and reserved, even to the point of selfishness.[63] Many admired and respected him for his ability and industry; few loved him for his personal qualities.

The nomination of the scholarly Everett added little to the strength of the ticket. His qualities did not complement those of Bell; their positions on public matters had been similar. Both were eminently honorable and capable, yet they lacked color. Everett seriously considered declining the vice-presidential nomination. He had high regard for Bell as a man but not as a leader. Crittenden was his choice for a candidate.[64] John P. Kennedy urged Everett to accept in order to strengthen the ticket. Owing to the division among the Democrats at Charleston, he insisted, it was necessary for the Constitutional Union party to nominate a candidate from the South. Otherwise, events might have taken a different turn at Baltimore. Kennedy expressed little hope for the success of the ticket, but he admitted that almost anything could happen.[65]

Apparently Bell remained at his Baltimore headquarters for the duration of the convention. He was not a member of the Tennessee delegation and later stated that he was not a witness at the convention. A few days after his nomination he was stopping at La Pierre House in Philadelphia; it was while there that he received official notification of his nomination. Along with the notification he was serenaded by a torchlight procession in which an estimated six thousand persons participated. Joseph R. Ingersoll presented him to the crowd as "*the* candidate" and expressed a hope that the "propriety and patriotism" manifested at Baltimore might

[63] Connally F. Trigg to Temple, August 14, 1859, in Temple Papers; William B. Campbell to David Campbell, February 9, 1851, in David Campbell Papers.

[64] Everett to Crittenden, June 2, 1860, in Crittenden Papers (Duke University Library).

[65] John P. Kennedy to Everett, May 23, 1860, in Kennedy Letter Book, John P. Kennedy Papers (Peabody Institute, Baltimore).

convince other parties of the wisdom of concurring in the nomination of Bell and Everett. Bell was "essentially connected and identified with the interests of Pennsylvania," Ingersoll announced. "He understands our wants, our necessity for a tariff, and the wants of iron manufacturers." [66] However, in his brief reply to Ingersoll, Bell had nothing to say on the subject of the tariff!

Bell and his family arrived in Nashville, via the Louisville and Nashville Railroad, on May 18. From the platform of the rear coach of the train he greeted the enthusiastic crowd which had assembled at the station. Former Governor Neil S. Brown and Edwin H. Ewing then ushered him to a waiting carriage drawn by four gray horses, and the procession moved to the City Hotel on the Public Square. In presenting the Union candidate to his Nashville friends, Brown declared Bell's nomination to be "the first time since the days of Washington" that any presidential candidate "had been brought out by a spontaneous movement of the people; who value their country above the behests of party." [67]

Cheers and congratulations over, Bell closeted himself in the City Hotel and began working on his letter of acceptance, which he sent to Washington Hunt on May 21. He enthusiastically endorsed the party's brief platform and expressed the determination that should he be elected he would not depart from his previous conservative course. Sound statesmanship in such critical times, he declared, demanded a spirit of moderation and justice, a steady opposition to all measures which threatened to arouse sectional animosity, and "devotion to the Union, harmony, and prosperity of these States." In his opinion, sectional discord could never be terminated until men of all sections were willing to give due observance to government according to the Constitution, accepting "its restrictions, and requirements, fairly interpreted in accordance with its spirit and objects." Should he be

[66] Philadelphia *North American*, May 12, 1860.
[67] *Republican Banner and Nashville Whig*, May 19, 1860.

elected President, he pledged himself to use all the power
and influence of that office "for the maintenance of the constitution and the Union against all imposing influences and
tendencies." [68]

Bell was well pleased with the nomination, but there is no
evidence that he entertained high hopes of success. He was
profuse in his thanks to Crittenden for the Kentuckian's
"noble and magnanimous course" toward him in the convention, and was especially pleased with Crittenden's refusal to
give "countenance to the insane movement in favor of
Houston." The success of such a movement, Bell insisted,
would "have effectually blighted every hope and prospect of
being able to build up a really conservative Union party."
He expressed surprise at the way some clever men had allowed themselves to be influenced by the idea of "availability." Bell was favorably impressed with the manner in
which his nomination had been received, especially in the
South. This reception he attributed to the "well prepared soil
on which the seed has fallen." [69]

[68] Greeley and Cleveland, *Political Text-Book for 1860*, 213–14.
[69] Bell to Crittenden, May 29, 1860, in Crittenden Papers (Duke University
Library).

Chapter XVIII

FUSION FAILS

PROSLAVERY Democrats severely attacked the Constitutional Unionists for their apparent intention to keep quiet on the slavery question. All that the Bell supporters proposed to do, wrote one prominent Tennessean, was to "fold their arms and ignore." [1] Bell was accused of being oblivious to the fact that the protection of slavery was the protection of Southern rights. The editor of the Richmond *Enquirer* declared that on the question of slavery in the territories "Bell and Lincoln occupy identical positions. Both are pledged to the constitutional power of Congress to abolish slavery in the Territories. Both are pledged to sanction by their official action the exercise of such congressional power." [2] From another Virginia source came a statement that Bell was bankrupt and had lost interest in Southern economic welfare. To this Brownlow replied that no man was "more ready and willing to assert and maintain" the rights of the South than John Bell. Brownlow further claimed that Bell was worth at least $100,000, was the owner of about eighty slaves, and that Mrs. Bell owned an equal number. [3]

Numerous efforts were made to draw from Bell a definite statement of his position on the slavery question. Some inquiries came from friendly seekers after material to be used in combating the Democrats. Other requests for information were of unfriendly origin and designed to destroy whatever strength there was in the noncommittal Constitutional Union

---

[1] W. C. Whitthorne to Johnson, July 24, 1860, in Johnson Papers.

[2] Quoted in Richmond *Whig*, July 23, 1860.

[3] *Brownlow's Knoxville Whig*, September 15, 1860.

platform. Early in the campaign, one John D. Woods of Mississippi, presumably a friend of the party, urgently requested Bell to state his position on the following points: "Are you in favor of restoring the Missouri Compromise of 1820? Are you opposed to Squatter Sovereignty as explained by Mr. Cass & Mr. Douglass? If so, are you willing that a Territory shall only exercise the right to prohibit slavery in her borders when she shall have acquired sufficient population to entitle her to admission in the Union?" [4] Bell's reply to this inquiry has not been preserved; however, later in the campign he stated that since he had been placed in nomination by a convention "which deliberately resolved to adopt no platform, or declaration of principles, other than such as are implied in the pledge to maintain the Constitution, the Union and the Laws, I consider that it would be virtual repudiation of their aim and policy were I to give any new pledges, or to make any new declaration of principles." [5]

Irritated at Bell's refusal to commit himself, the Nashville *Union and American* declared:

> The 'Constitutional Union' Ticket—
> John Bell
>   Nobody's man!
>   Stands on nobody's platform!!
>   Fights nobody!!!
>   Loves nobody!!!!
>   E Pluribus Unum!!!!!

To this the *Republican Banner* replied:

> John Bell
>   A State Senator at 20;
>   Congressman at 30;
>   Speaker of the House at 37;
>   Secretary of War at 44;
>   U.S. Senator at 50;
>   Never defeated before the People! [6]

[4] John D. Woods to Bell, May 23, 1860, in Polk-Yeatman Papers.
[5] Bell to ? , July 23, 1860, in Bell Papers.
[6] *Republican Banner and Nashville Whig*, June 13, 1860.

From the beginning of the campaign, Unionist developments in the eastern states were not such as had been hoped
for. In New York the Buffalo *Commercial* deserted to the
Republican ranks, leaving only one or two "obscure weeklies"
west of the Hudson. In New York City only the *Express* was
left to fight the Union battle. The friends of William H.
Seward, although sorely disappointed over the turn of events
at the Chicago convention, resolved to support Lincoln.[7]

In Massachusetts the outlook was bleak. In general, the
merchants and manufacturers of Boston, greatly desiring
peace and quiet, expressed approval of the Union party's
nominees, but they usually added *"it is of no use."* "If Mr. Bell
could see how difficult it is for us to make even a respectable
opposition to the enthusiasm of the Republicans," wrote
Amos Lawrence to Crittenden, "he would cease to look in this
direction for available support." [8] Some Constitutional Union
men expressed the belief, however, that had Crittenden received the nomination, much of the enthusiasm for "Ole Abe"
would never have made its appearance.[9]

In Pennsylvania Henry M. Fuller, chairman of the state
executive committee of the Constitutional Union party, had
hope but not too much confidence. He thought the party's
potential strength to be considerable but unorganized. However, many who were otherwise kindly inclined toward Bell
deprecated the formation of a new party. In spite of the apparent Lincoln strength in Pennsylvania, Fuller hoped to see
the friends of the Union greatly animated and strengthened
should the division among the Democrats result in a reasonable assurance of a Bell and Everett victory in the South.[10]

Bell was depressed by the discouraging news from the key
states of the East, and before the campaign was a month old,

[7] Washington Hunt to Bell, May 24, 1860, in Bell Papers. James Gordon
Bennett of the New York *Herald* reported on August 2 that Bell had the support of not more than six newspapers and that "they generally [were] of a
local character and limited influence."

[8] Lawrence to Crittenden, May 25, 1860, in Crittenden Papers (Duke University Library).

[9] *Id.* to *id.*, May 26, 1860, *ibid.*

[10] Henry M. Fuller to Bell, June 22, 1860, in Bell Papers.

he confided to Robert Ridgeway of the Richmond *Whig* that in his opinion either Lincoln would be elected by the electoral college, or the election would go to the House of Representatives, where he believed the Union candidate might have a chance of election. Bell advised that special care be exercised not to antagonize the Republicans too much during the campaign. Unless they were needlessly irritated, he had hopes that they would prefer him to either of the Democratic candidates and would support the Union ticket in the House.[11]

As the campaign progressed Bell was ever mindful of the importance of the votes of the large states. It was clear that the tide in Pennsylvania was running heavily in favor of Lincoln. The Philadelphia *North American,* an early advocate of Bell for President, failed to give him the support expected. It vigorously attacked the Democrats, spoke kindly and respectfully of Bell and Everett, and gave most of its space to the defense of the Republicans. Lincoln was a conservative, the editor argued, and had "in no way departed from the old faith, but stands to-day where Mr. Clay stood in the Senate, upholding the same principles, and devoted to the same Constitution and Union." [12]

On July 2, Bell expressed his hopes and fears to the chairman of his national committee, Alexander Robinson Boteler. Assuming that the Democratic party had definitely split, he said, some conclusions might be drawn as to the probable outcome of the campaign. With "proper exertions," the Constitutional Union ticket should "carry in most of the Southern States, even in one or two of the most ultra." But that did not mean election, for all efforts would be "in vain & abortive," unless Lincoln could be defeated. This was the main problem, and he could make only several suggestions for its solution. The details must be left to the friends of the Constitutional Union party. "Pennsylvania must be made to see, if possible, that if she goes for 'Lincoln' she dooms her interests

11 Bell to Ridgeway, May 27, 1860, *ibid.*
12 Philadelphia *North American,* May 30, 1860.

to long years of neglect, if not, to comparative ruin." Bell "had hoped that the enlightened friends of her particular interests (iron & coal) would see that the election of a sectional candidate would be fatal to them." But it seemed that they had become "infatuated from some cause " "I presume it is the passion for novelty in part—for seeing a new power at Washington.—A new dynasty on the throne, & the gratification of seeing the hated Democracy—pretty nearly synonymous with *Southern Oligarchy* (in their vocabulary) overthrown. But whatever may be the cause, the best friends of their interests (such as 'Carey') are infatuated—stone blind." Pennsylvanians should be made to realize that the peace and quiet requisite to their prosperity could be had only as a result of a Union victory. The election of Lincoln would ruin all hope for improvement "in our domestic, commercial, or financial policy." Regardless of "how National, or moderate, or conservative" Lincoln might profess to be, the best that his opposition would permit would be the bare movement of the wheels of government.

The opposition to such an administration *will be the whole South*—yes the whole South, in 30 days after the election of 'Lincoln' would feel his election to be an *insult* to them except the few abolitionists (not emancipationists—they would sympathise with the majority of their fellow citizens) & not a single member of Congress, from the Slave States (St. Louis, Mo. only excepted) whatever may have been his former party associations, but would obey the dictates of his resentments & join in making the most furious & bitter opposition. After one or more caucus meetings, all moderation would cease.—So united & formidable an opposition, it is clear, could and would take an especial interest rather in *punishing those states,* particularly Pennsylvania, which had as the opposition would feel, deliberately delivered the country & Government over to the rule of a sectional party . . . in preference to securing their great material interests by the suppression of sectional strife, when she had the power to do one or the other at her option.

Bell said that he had told Seward several months before that neither the New Yorker nor "any other man of his principles," if elected by a sectional vote, could give the country an efficient administration; for the opposition would "thwart & obstruct" every movement that was calculated to give strength to the Administration.

Returning to the subject of Pennsylvania's probable conduct, Bell further stated:

If Pennsylvania & other states with like interests, cannot be made to see their true policy, & will still incline to 'Lincoln', as I greatly fear she will, then there is no other way in which his election can be defeated but by a fusion of several branches of the opposition in N. Jersey, New York, Connecticut, R. Island, Pennsylvania, Ohio, & Indiana & running but one ticket in these states, against Lincoln. In this way, I can see that the states I have enumerated, or enough of them may be carried against 'Lincoln'; but I will not advise such a fusion or combination, though I confess that, if there is no sacrifice of independence on the part of the voter, each voting his sentiments, & the electoral votes to be apportioned according to the number of votes cast for the respective Presidential tickets, I do not see any violation of *principle* in such an arrangement; but others (our friends) must decide on the policy of such combinations in their respective states. If I should undertake to advise such combinations, I would probably fail to get the vote of the Republican States, in the event the election should go into the House.[13]

In the commercial and manufacturing centers of the East both Democratic and Unionist presses were already picturing the dire results of a sectional victory. James Gordon Bennett of the New York *Herald,* originally a Breckinridge man but later a supporter of Democratic-Unionist fusion, stated the fear explicitly:

The mercantile and manufacturing classes of the North, like the substantial slaveholders of the South, are eminently conservative

---

[13] Bell to Boteler, July 2–30, 1860, in Boteler Papers. This letter was begun on July 2 and completed on July 30.

in their political instincts, habits and opinions. Their interests make them so. These substantial classes of the community are, therefore, as much opposed to the 'irrepressible conflict' of the North against the South as they are to that wild Southern faction which seeks to lead 'the cotton states to revolution,' and a separate Southern confederacy. . . .

The Bell ticket, North and South, at this moment, represents a large portion of the solid wealth of the country.

The Constitutional Union party, he predicted, would grow stronger as the campaign progressed. If the election should go to the House, Bell would be the only one upon whom a compromise could be reached.[14] This same sentiment was expressed by the Richmond *Whig*.[15] And George D. Prentice of the Louisville *Journal* thought that the only hope for the Constitutional Union ticket lay with the House.[16]

The Constitutional Union campaign of 1860 bore a marked resemblance to the Whig campaign of 1840. Colorful demonstrations were the order of the day, especially in the South.[17] Since the platform ignored all public issues, party spokesmen could interpret the platform, and to some extent the motives of the candidates, in accordance with regional desires. On the question of slavery, Bell and Everett were neither abolitionists nor ultra proslavery men; they might be pictured as occupying almost any position between these two extremes. John Minor Botts, a leading Bell supporter in Virginia, declared himself opposed to the extension of slavery into the territories and announced his continued adherence to the "American System." On the other extreme, some prominent Bell supporters in the Lower South, such as Benjamin H. Hill of Georgia, openly advocated congressional protection of

14 New York *Herald,* June 27, 1860.
15 Richmond *Whig,* May 8, 1860.
16 Louisville *Journal,* quoted in Memphis *Enquirer,* June 30, 1860.
17 In Kentucky, a correspondent of the New York *Herald* reported that "Bell ringers" were being used with "terrific effect." At public gatherings men and boys, white and black, instead of cheering, rang bells—cow, tea, dinner, and locomotive. "The plan knocks bonfires and gunpowder to pieces." *Herald,* August 8, 1860.

slavery in the territories. Later in the campaign, however, some of them modified their arguments. In Alabama the Constitutional Unionist convention adopted resolutions advocating protection of slavery in the territories. And one Bell man of the same state received the impression that the candidate himself considered the territories common property in which every citizen was entitled to protection of his own property. But the editor of the Nashville *Republican Banner* was willing to allow the Supreme Court to settle all cases growing out of the slavery controversy. Most Bell-Everett men, it appears, steered clear of the slavery issue while working for the election of their candidates.[18]

Like William Henry Harrison, Bell remained in his home section and made no important statements for publication. It does not appear that he ventured farther from home than Bowling Green, Kentucky, where he went to meet Crittenden and attend the state fair. A special correspondent of the New York *Herald,* traveling through the South interviewing prominent political figures, found Bell and his family residing quietly in the shrub-protected home of his stepson, Henry C. Yeatman, on Summer Street. During Bell's senatorial career he had disposed of his Nashville home on Broad Street and had used the accommodations of the City Hotel when in the city. A temperate man, indulging in "a little wine occasionally," [19] Bell impressed his interviewer with his well-proportioned physique. His "regular and animated" features gave ready expression to his feelings, now a smile and then a frown, depending upon the nature of the conversation.

What was the Constitutional Union candidate's opinion of his opponents? queried the correspondent. All except Douglas were sectional candidates, Bell replied. Then he added an ex-

18 Ollinger Crenshaw, *The Slave States in the Presidential Election of 1860* (Baltimore, 1945), 40–41, 128–29; Dwight L. Dumond, *The Secession Movement, 1860–1861* (New York, 1931), 94–95. *Republican Banner and Nashville Whig,* January 21, 1860.
19 Bell's wine bill for 1856 was $70.50. Daniel Draper to Bell, February 6, March 7, 1856, in Polk-Yeatman Papers.

pression of regret that James Gordon Bennett, editor of the *Herald,* had abandoned his former policy of condemning extremists and had come out in support of Breckinridge, whom Bell considered definitely sectional. Continuing his questioning, the correspondent wanted to know Bell's reaction to the proposed fusion of Democratic and Unionist strength in certain key states for the purpose of defeating the Republicans. This Bell was willing to leave to the discretion of his friends so long as they did not abandon principle. And what course would the Constitutional Union leader take in the case of a Lincoln victory? He would acquiesce, Bell assured his interrogator, and would consider it the duty of his party to help avert any extreme action. He considered Lincoln a "fair, candid, open hearted, common sense man" who would be dangerous only if he came under the influence of men like Seward.[20]

Most of those who were prominently mentioned for the nomination at the Baltimore convention actively supported the nominees. Notable exceptions were Edward Bates, who turned Republican, and the "Texas Warrior," who was not yet ready to give up the fight. One week after the Baltimore convention Houston officially accepted the nomination which had been offered him at the San Jacinto meeting.[21] Apparently he intended to make the race independently, but he could not have been so badly deceived as to believe that he had a chance to be elected. Finally, on August 18, he published a letter to "My Friends in the United States" in which he announced his withdrawal from the race.[22] Three weeks later he confided to a friend that he would never vote for a man who had supported the Nebraska bill; therefore, he could not vote for Douglas or Breckinridge. As for Bell, he thought the Tennessean had allowed himself to be used by "odious men." Besides, he was a "slim chance for a President," and Houston would not "come out in favor of a man who has

[20] New York *Herald,* August 8, 1860.   [21] *Ibid.,* May 30, 1860.
[22] *Ibid.,* September 21, 1860.

no chance of success." [23] Nevertheless, after the lapse of another three weeks, the Texas Governor arose from a sickbed to tell an Austin mass meeting that he would vote a Union ticket.[24]

Crittenden was especially active in the campaign. In addition to touring parts of Kentucky and Tennessee, he journeyed to Missouri, speaking at St. Louis and a few neighboring towns.[25] While in Missouri he conferred with Edward Bates, and according to the latter, stated that he would give all he possessed to see Bates President.[26] (It will be noted, however, that Crittenden had done nothing to bring this about at the Baltimore convention.) Bates was convinced that "designing men" had duped Crittenden into participation in this third party movement.[27] Still, Bates was not at all impressed by Crittenden's St. Louis speech. It was "a poor, *shilly-shally* speech," containing nothing definite except denunciation of Republicans.[28]

Before the campaign was a month old the Constitution Union leaders in New York, despairing of a complete Bell-Everett victory in that state, were considering a coalition with the Douglas men, to form a joint electoral ticket. Early in June, Washington Hunt advised Bell of this possibility. Hunt was almost convinced that such an arrangement was the only method by which Lincoln could be defeated in New York and the election taken to the House of Representatives.[29] Bell apparently gave his approval of the plan, and in a Democratic-Unionist meeting at Syracuse on August 14, agreement was reached on a joint ticket composed of ten Bell men and twenty-five Douglas supporters.[30] Hunt registered some dis-

---

[23] Sam Houston to George Washington Crawford, September 8, 1860, quoted in W. C. Crane, *Life and Select Literary Remains of Sam Houston* (Philadelphia, 1884), 232–33.   [24] Wortham, *History of Texas*, IV, 303 ff.

[25] Crittenden to W. M. Smallwood and John P. Bowman, n.d., in Crittenden Papers (Duke University Library).

[26] Beale (ed.), *Diary of Edward Bates*, 154–55.

[27] *Ibid.*   [28] *Ibid.*

[29] Washington Hunt to Bell, June 7, 1860, in Bell Papers.

[30] New York *Herald*, August 15, 17, 1860.

appointment over his failure to get a larger number of Union men on the ticket, but he was assured by a number of Douglas' friends that should it happen that the vote of the Douglas electors would elect Bell, they would vote for him rather than see the election go to the House. In return for this promise, Hunt assured the Douglas men that should their votes be responsible for the election of Bell, the new President would "not fail to appreciate their patriotism." [31] After further political jockeying, seven Breckinridge supporters were added to the fusionist ticket, replacing a like number of Douglas men. This list of candidates—18 Douglas, 10 Bell, and 7 Breckinridge—was announced before a large anti-Republican mass meeting in New York City on September 17.[32]

Bennett of the New York *Herald* came out strongly in favor of this fusion ticket, urging its support in order to save New York commerce, New Jersey manufacturing, and Pennsylvania mining and manufacturing. Ruin would certainly come "if the fanatical theories that animate the black republican party are allowed to control our national policy." Ships would soon lie idle, for there would be no more Southern trade. The design of the fusionists, he explained, was simply to take the scattered remains of parties and "out of these scattered materials to build up a new and powerful Union party—just as the palaces of the Eternal City were built out of the materials of the Coliseum and other temples of pagan Rome." [33]

There were attempts at fusion in a few other states. Hunt reported that on a trip to New Jersey he had found a perfect understanding between Constitutional Union men and Democrats. The indications were that the state was definitely anti-Lincoln.[34] At a meeting of Democrats and a few old Whigs in Trenton on July 25, a fusion ticket had been proposed.[35] But the straight-out Douglas men, meeting on the same date,

31 Hunt to Bell, August 19, 1860, in Bell Papers.
32 New York *Herald*, August 19, 1860.
33 *Ibid.*, August 29, September 19, 1860.
34 Hunt to Bell, August 19, 1860, in Bell Papers.
35 Newark *Evening Journal*, July 26, 1860.

adopted resolutions opposing fusion with a sectionalist like Breckinridge. The Constitutional Union party discussed fusion but selected a straight electoral ticket.[36] Several weeks later, meeting at the Astor House in New York, representatives of the three parties agreed upon a fusion ticket. After still further revision, this ticket was described by an unfriendly editor as composed of "two original Know Nothings, two Breckinridge-Disunionists, and three converted Douglas-ites." [37] The straight-out Douglas men, persisting in their refusal to join hands with Breckinridge "disunionists," ran a separate ticket composed of the three Douglas men of the union list plus four others. In this action they were carrying out Douglas' suggestion that "we can have no partnership with the bolters." But Douglas had consistently advocated close friendship with the Bell-Everett supporters.[38]

The New Jersey Republicans, fearing the strength of a united opposition, appealed to all good Douglas men to repudiate fusion and remain loyal to their candidate.[39] About the same time, a fusionist editor, in an article headed "Manufacturers, Mechanics, Look to Yourselves," was prophesying a general cessation of business should Lincoln be elected. "Orders will not only cease, but payment for those already ordered will cease." Abram S. Hewitt, the head of large iron interests in Trenton, was quoted as saying that within sixty days after a Republican victory work in his establishments would be terminated. Indeed, the editor insisted, "factories everywhere must suspend work, and thousands of people must be thrown out of bread." [40]

Some Bell supporters in Maryland talked of an agreement with the Democrats, but Henry Winter Davis vigorously denounced such a proposal. Although frequently professing

---

[36] Trenton *True American,* July 26, 1860.

[37] *Ibid.,* September 12, 13, 1860; Trenton *Gazette and Republican,* October 29, 1860.

[38] Stephen A. Douglas to C. H. Lanphier, July 5, 1860, cited in Milton, *Eve of Conflict,* 487.

[39] Trenton *Gazette and Republican,* November 1, 1860.

[40] Trenton *True American,* November 6, 1860.

support of Bell, Davis did not attempt to conceal his admiration for the Republicans, appealing for an "obliteration of the line of demarcation" between Bell and Lincoln men. Republicans, he reasoned, were neither traitors, advocates of servile insurrection, nor destroyers of state institutions. The only way to settle the slavery question, he contended, was to be silent. That is what both Lincoln and Bell would do. Fusion with the Democrats would not benefit Bell, since it would do nothing more than send the election into the House. At the same time it would ruin Bell's chance for Republican support and make him no friends among the Democrats.[41] Instead of fusion with the Democrats, Davis proposed an understanding with the Republicans. Lincoln could not carry Maryland; therefore, there ought not to be a Lincoln ticket in the state. For a similar reason there should be no Bell ticket in Pennsylvania or New Jersey.[42]

In Kentucky an *entente cordiale* was formed among a few Bell and Douglas men,[43] but no joint ticket was arranged. Lincoln observed that Douglas was playing the game with "great adroitness." Douglas was urging his friends in Kentucky to support Bell in order to defeat Breckinridge, while in the North, Bell's friends were being urged to support Douglas in order to defeat Lincoln.[44]

Bell's friends saw no need for fusion in Virginia. There was some hope that Douglas, being a "very sagacious man" and seeing no chance of success, would urge his friends to support Bell. Indeed, might not the Illinois Senator himself, seeing

[41] Bernard C. Steiner, *Life of Henry Winter Davis* (Baltimore, 1916), 162–63, 169–70, quoting from a speech to the constituents of the fourth congressional district of Maryland. The Baltimore *American*, October 1, 1860, pronounced Davis' speech "A Lincoln pronunciamento in Bell clothing, or rather an eccentric Republican sheep with a Union Bell on its neck."

[42] Davis to ? Nicholls, n.d., in Steiner, *Henry Winter Davis*, 191.

[43] August Belmont to Blanton Duncan, August 9, 1860, in Bell Papers; Duncan to Douglas, August 14, 1860, in Stephen A. Douglas Papers (University of Chicago Library).

[44] Abraham Lincoln to Thurlow Weed, August 17, 1860, in John G. Nicolay and John Hay (eds.), *Abraham Lincoln: Complete Works Comprising His Speeches, Letters and State Papers and Miscellaneous Writings* (New York, 1894), I, 648.

the trend, join the Union party and hope for the succession?[45] There was, however, some talk of fusing the Breckinridge and Douglas forces in order to defeat Bell. A hostile statement by Douglas killed a similar attempt to fuse Democrats in North Carolina.[46] From Georgia, Herschel V. Johnson, Douglas' running mate, reported that a plan was being worked out to select an electoral ticket composed of an equal number of Douglas and Bell men. In the electoral college these electors would let conditions be their guide. If their total vote would elect Bell, they would vote for him. If it would elect Douglas, the vote would go for Douglas. In case it would elect neither, the vote would be equally divided. Johnson had no objection to the plan and feared if some such arrangement were not agreed upon Breckinridge would carry the state.[47] Some of Johnson's Georgia friends who also favored fusion reminded him that Douglas and Bell were truly national candidates, while Lincoln and Breckinridge were sectional.[48]

August Belmont of New York, chairman of the Douglas national committee, also approved of fusion in Georgia and suggested that the movement be expanded to include Alabama, Louisiana, Mississippi, and North Carolina. Breckinridge, he calculated, had more than one third of the votes in each of these states and would certainly carry them if three tickets remained in the field. Belmont proposed a fusion with the understanding that the Douglas-Bell electors would vote in the electoral college in proportion to popular vote received. This would necessitate the voters' registering their presidential choice when selecting electors.[49] Belmont had apparently consulted Douglas on this matter, for later in the campaign, Johnson, while on a Northern tour, sent word back to Geor-

[45] A. H. Stuart to Duncan, August 23, 1860, in Bell Papers.

[46] Henry T. Shanks, *The Secession Movement in Virginia* (Richmond, 1934), 110–11; Milton, *Eve of Conflict*, 493.

[47] Johnson to Alexander H. Stephens, July 20, 1860, in Percy S. Flippin, *Herschel V. Johnson of Georgia* (Richmond, 1931), 137.

[48] Hiram Warner to Johnson, July 22, 1860, *ibid*, 138–39.

[49] Belmont to *id.*, n.d., *ibid.*, 140–41.

gia: "It is the wish of Doug., & all our friends North that such union sh'd be formed." [50] The plan was also given strong support by Benjamin H. Hill, the most influential Bell-Everett supporter in Georgia, but the movement collapsed.[51] A similar attempt to fuse Bell and Douglas support was made in Texas, where a ticket composed of two Douglas and two Bell men was announced. All four were pledged to vote for the candidate who could defeat Lincoln.[52]

Rumors of attempts at fusion in several states brought from the editor of the Nashville *Union and American* a warning to all Tennessee Democrats to "beware of the seductive wiles of John Bell. Like the old man of the mountain, let him once mount your shoulders you cannot shake him off. . . ." [53] The fusion movement in Tennessee never advanced beyond the stage of discussion, for Bell men were too confident of victory; there was no Lincoln ticket. In mid-September there was talk of fusing the Douglas-Breckinridge support in order to defeat Bell. Some Breckinridge leaders were favorable but Douglas men, under the leadership of Henry S. Foote, balked.[54] No doubt Foote preferred Bell to Breckinridge; nevertheless, the Memphis *Daily Appeal,* a Douglas paper, insisted that if the supporters of Bell loved their country as much as they professed, they ought to withdraw their candidate in order that a Democrat could defeat Lincoln.[55]

During the campaign there was also some effort on the part of anti-Republicans to persuade Douglas, Breckinridge, and Bell to withdraw in favor of some man who would be "more generally acceptable than either of the three." According to Jefferson Davis, a Breckinridge supporter, Bell "was not am-

[50] Johnson to Stephens, October 1, 1860, *ibid.,* 144.

[51] Benjamin H. Hill, Jr., *Senator Benjamin H. Hill of Georgia* (Atlanta, 1893), 37.

[52] San Antonio *Ledger and Texan,* November 3, 1860, cited in Crenshaw, *The Slave States in the Presidential Election of 1860,* 293.

[53] Nashville *Union and American,* July 26, 1860.

[54] Jack Allen (ed.), "The Diary of Randall William McGavock, 1852–1862" (unpublished Ph.D. thesis, Peabody College, 1941), 390.

[55] Memphis *Daily Appeal,* October 4, 1860.

bitious to the extent of coveting the Presidency," and Breckinridge realized that he was "young enough to wait." Both of these candidates offered to withdraw if a more generally acceptable candidate could be found. However, when Douglas was approached he declared the scheme impracticable. Should he withdraw, he insisted, the Northern Democrats would support Lincoln.[56] A willingness to withdraw from the race is nowhere expressed in Bell's correspondence; consequently, Davis' statement is open to question. Foote later recorded, however, that Bell, "always preferring the happiness of the republic to his personal advancement," would have sustained any "true friend of the Federal Union." [57] During the summer of 1860 when Douglas visited Tennessee, he and Bell met at Foote's Nashville home. Foote reported that during the course of this friendly meeting each of the candidates agreed that should the other be elected the Union would be safe and that "the mad war of sectionalism would be at least held in *suppression* for the coming four years." [58]

On July 30 Bell completed the letter to Boteler, which he had begun on July 2. He had been so overwhelmed with correspondence from all over the country, he explained, that he had been compelled to neglect his friends. These letters had come both from supporters and "concealed enemies," and the great majority of them requested a statement of his views on the leading topics of the day. "They have given me a great deal of trouble & cost me much time in considering of the proper answers," he complained. "I have however uniformly refused to go beyond the 'quasi'-platform adopted at the Baltimore Convention & referring them to my past course on the subject of slavery, extending through a quarter of a century."

During the past month, Bell continued, he had been able to get a little better view of the probable future. He was convinced that he and Everett would "carry all the South or

[56] Jefferson Davis, *Rise and Fall of the Confederate Government* (New York, 1881), I, 52.   [57] Foote, *War of the Rebellion*, 275.
[58] *Ibid.*, 276.

slave holding states, except two or three." And he was further convinced that the party's prospects in the South "should be impressed upon the North by every fair & honorable means." [59] For if the Constitutional Union party could only carry either New York, Pennsylvania, or Ohio, he might be "elected by the Colleges!" And he was "strongly impressed with the belief" that this was the only way he could be elected. "An election by the House," he reluctantly admitted, "I could hardly hope to receive,—the way things go now a days."

Bell had some hope that the fusion movement would meet with success in a few of the states.

Should our friends at the North decide to form a coalition with the Douglas Democrats upon any equal terms, or even though in some of the states, the Douglas electoral ticket should carry, with the aid of our friends, without any stipulation as to a division of the Electoral vote, it can scarcely be doubted, that the entire electoral vote of a state or of the states, so carried, will be given to the Bell & Everett ticket, if when given to Douglas they cannot avail to elect him, but can elect Bell & Everett, when given to them. There is no probability that Douglas can be elected in any contingency likely to happen; nor can Breckinridge get a single vote North.

Bell thought it quite possible that he and Everett would get all free-state electoral votes *"not given to Lincoln."* This possibility gave the ticket "some prospect of an election by the Colleges." And Bell thought this was "the *goal* now to be had in view, and to be won."

During the past month, Bell related,

I have become satisfied from information received from the South that a more wide spread and determined purpose exists in the South, to attempt a separation of the states in the event of the

[59] Three weeks earlier one of Bell's Nashville organs printed a stinging denunciation of William L. Yancey and Jefferson Davis for their alleged efforts to break up the Union. These conspirators, it was asserted, unable to reopen the African slave trade, had next turned their attention to a demand for congressional protection of slavery in the territories. Now they harbored a secret hope of using the election of Lincoln as a pretext for secession and the formation of a slave-holding confederacy. Nashville *Patriot*, July 11, 1860.

election of Lincoln, than I before thought existed. It is now almost certain, that in the event, a secession of three or four States,
if not more, will take place, unless the leaders are foiled in their
designs, or discouraged by the vote—the unexpected strength of
the vote of the Union party cast in those states, in November: and
I am now firmly persuaded that the secession from the Convention at Charleston & again at Baltimore was *instigated,* & finally
passed to consummation by those artful and able instigators, who
said, or believed, that the movement would lead to *the election
of Lincoln.* It was designed that it should. They could not have
supposed, or believed, for a moment, that Breckinridge could get
a single vote in any of the free states; and they must have known
that, weakened as he was sure to be, Douglas could not carry one
state, except perhaps Ill. The conspirators did not dream that
the Union party could rally strength enough to defeat their designs. Hence, I repeat, the Breckinridge movement must have been
made designedly to elect Lincoln. This *design* you will mark, I
impute to the *few* arch leaders, not to the rank & file of the delegates from Va. N.C. Tenn. Ky. & Mo. These latter, are dupes, but
not altogether innocent. The malignancy of some of them, led
them to prefer the election of Lincoln, with all its *possible* evil
consequences, to the election of Douglas.

In view of the fact that the big task before the Constitutional Union party was to defeat Lincoln, Bell suggested the
publication of a pamphlet based upon certain of his own
speeches and the circulation of this pamphlet in the doubtful
states of Pennsylvania and New Jersey. Such a document,
stressing that a Union victory meant peace, might help the
cause, he thought, if circulated in all of the states. A second
pamphlet, pointing out the seriousness of the secession movement, should be distributed throughout the South. Bell
stressed the importance of making these appeals available in
separate form rather than through the party's Washington
organ, the *Union Guard.* And he suggested James C. Welling
of the *National Intelligencer* as the man best fitted for the
preparation of these proposed pamphlets. Therefore, Boteler
would please see Welling and show him this letter. However,

apparently on second thought, Bell decided that, to avert the possibility of his letter's falling into other hands, he should send the letter to Welling and have him hand it to Boteler.[60] Bell made no mention of the slave-insurrection hysteria which swept over the Lower South during 1860 and checked the growth of conservative sentiment. The political value of these greatly exaggerated rumors of plots and conspiracies was evident to the extremists among the supporters of Breckinridge. Those who preached moderation, they exclaimed, were playing into the hands of antislavery agitators and laying the South bare to murder and the torch.[61]

Throughout the slave states from Delaware to the Gulf there was enough encouraging news to give the Bell-Everett supporters some cause for rejoicing. From Dover came assurance that the Constitutional Union ticket would certainly carry Delaware. Lincoln would probably receive several votes, especially in New Castle and Kent counties, but not enough to be dangerous. The informant believed the election must certainly be decided in the House where the Democrats would support Bell "with pleasure." [62]

Through party headquarters in Washington came favorable news from Virginia, Maryland, and Kentucky.[63] Similar reports also came directly from these states. The Douglas and Breckinridge men were "eating each other up" and Kentucky would go for the Union "by an unmistakable majority," reported Thomas L. W. Sawyers.[64] The loyal Union women of Kentucky were even having Bell and Everett printed on their bonnet strings.[65] Maryland was safe by a "decided majority" prophesied a Baltimore business man.[66] A. H. Stuart thought

[60] Bell to Boteler, July 30, 1860, in Boteler Papers.
[61] Crenshaw, *The Slave States in the Presidential Election of 1860*, 89 ff.
[62] Joseph P. Comegys to Bell, July 9, 1860, in Polk-Yeatman Papers.
[63] Jerry Blount [?] to Bell, July 12, 1860; J. C. Welling to *id.*, August 11, 1860, *ibid.* A Constitutional Union newspaper, the *Union Guard*, was published in Washington during the campaign.
[64] Thomas L. W. Sawyers to Temple, July 26, 1860, in Temple Papers.
[65] *Republican Banner and Nashville Whig*, August 10, 1860.
[66] Wilson and Burns to Oliver P. Temple, August 3, 1860, in Temple Papers.

that the Constitutional Union ticket would carry Virginia by
ten to twenty thousand votes. And in a burst of enthusiasm,
he claimed Providential favor and guidance for the actions of
the party.[67]

Even in the states of the Lower South, Bell-Everett men
saw some hope for a very respectable showing. Jere Clemens
wrote encouragingly from Huntsville, Alabama. There was
a chance for Bell if the Douglas men in the southern part of
the state would vote the Union ticket. Alexander H. Stephens,
a Douglas man, saw a chance for a Bell plurality in some of
the Georgia districts. He noted also that some Louisianians
were predicting a Bell victory in that state.[68] As late as July,
Bell himself expected to carry all of the Southern states except
two or three.[69] John P. Kennedy, writing from Maryland on
October 20, still had some hope for the success of the Union
ticket; and he feared the results in case of defeat. Extremists
were driving the country to civil war, he exclaimed, and Bell
and Everett had become "objects of actual derision . . . because they represent peace and lawful rule and right supremacy." Only through their election, however, in his opinion,
could calamity be averted and peace and calm be restored to
the public mind.[70]

What enthusiasm the Constitutional Unionists had been
able to generate was severely chilled by the Republican victory
in the Pennsylvania state election on October 9. "Abraham
Lincoln is already chosen President of the nation," announced
the Philadelphia *North American,* "and the mere formality
of ratification at the ballot box is alone needed to complete
the glorious consummation." [71]

As might have been expected, a vigorous Constitutional

[67] A. H. Stuart to Duncan, August 23, 1860, in Bell Papers.

[68] Clemens to Bell, October 1, 14, 1860, *ibid.;* Stephens to J. Henly Smith,
September 30, 1860, October 13, 1860, in Phillips (ed.), *Correspondence of
Robert Toombs, Alexander H. Stephens, and Howell Cobb,* 500, 502.

[69] Bell to Boteler, July 2–30, 1860, in Boteler Papers.

[70] Kennedy to R. C. Winthrop, October 20, 1860, in Letter Book, Kennedy
Papers.

[71] Philadelphia *North American,* October 10, 1860.

Union campaign was waged in Tennessee, where Bell's loyal
supporters were determined to wipe out the recent humiliation of their hero. "The bare odor of prospective plunder,
and the hope of petty local triumphs over a divided foe,"
complained the Democratic press, "urges them on in their
headlong and most 'wickedly foolish' course." [72] The electoral
ticket was headed by Balie Peyton and included among its
personnel such prominent conservative Whigs as Oliver P.
Temple and Nathaniel G. Taylor. The months of September
and October witnessed one demonstration after another.
Uniformed companies of Bell supporters furnished the color
for celebrations throughout Middle Tennessee. The greatest
of these rallies was held in Nashville on September 25. A few
days previous Bell had gone to Bowling Green to meet Crittenden and to attend the Kentucky state fair. Crittenden
accompanied him back to Nashville on September 24, where
they were greeted with a great ovation. A still greater demonstration had been planned for the following day. The parade
formed on the Public Square and then moved out College
Street to Watkins Park. At the head of the parade rode three
marshals mounted on "steel-grey chargers." Next in the line
of march came five uniformed companies including the
"Union Guards" of Columbia, the "Bell Stars" of Murfreesboro, and the "Bell Ringers" of Franklin. Music was furnished
by Horn's Silver Band. Following the band were a dozen
carriages filled with party notables, including Crittenden and
Bell. Next came a huge furniture van on which was mounted
a two-thousand-pound bell the tones from which could be
heard for miles around. The van was decorated with two large
banners on which was inscribed:

Bell and Everett—Patriots upon whom the whole nation can
look with pride, and say, 'these are our jewels.'

Tennessee gives a free and hearty welcome to John J. Crittenden:
the true son of a Noble State.

[72] Memphis *Daily Appeal,* October 4, 1860.

The remainder of the parade was made up of the members of Bell and Everett clubs, ladies in carriages, and thousands of horsemen and pedestrians.

At the park, addresses were made by Crittenden and Congressman Horace Maynard. The time for partisanship and party ambition had passed, announced Crittenden, and he, for one, was now being guided solely by "unrestricted devotion" to his country. The preservation of the Union was the one great issue before the people. "Can any one who calls himself a freeman sleep sound after having for partizan schemes and party purposes voted with any sectional party whose purpose is destruction of the Union?" Sectionalism, both North and South, was gnawing at the very foundation of the Union. It was the desire to stay that great danger which gave birth to the Constitutional Union party. And that party and its candidates wished to address as "friend" every man who loved the Union more than his section.[73] The speaking was followed by a basket dinner-on-the-ground. "The earth was scattered with white table-cloths, and the clatter of cutlery and crockery prevailed to a considerable extent." [74]

Crittenden was elated over his reception in Nashville, where he was welcomed as though he were "twenty Presidents." He found the Bells to be "all kindness and compliment," and he believed it was *in all sincerity.*" Crittenden felt that he had certainly been *what is called a great man for two whole days.*" [75]

Huge mass meetings and parades were also staged in Memphis and Knoxville. Supporters from all parts of East Tennessee assembled at Knoxville for a two-day rally, delegations arriving by every conceivable means of conveyance. Reminiscent of 1840, one group brought a persimmon tree with a live raccoon in the top of it. According to Brownlow, the celebration exceeded anything seen in Tennessee in twenty years. The principal speaker was Benjamin Hill of Georgia.[76]

[73] *Republican Banner and Nashville Whig,* September 26, 1860.
[74] *Ibid.*
[75] Crittenden to wife, September 24 [25?], 1860, in Coleman, *Crittenden,* II, 218–19.   [76] *Brownlow's Knoxville Whig,* September 29, 1860.

In Memphis a whole week of demonstrations was planned, allowing the people to give full vent to their fondness for parades. From miles around, citizens of the tri-states flocked to the "Charleston of the West" to view the twin spectacles— the mammoth parades and the Fair which was in progress during the same week. The great parade took place on October 8. Hundreds of pedestrians in gala costumes marching to the strains of fife and drum were followed by scores of vehicles of all descriptions. When the Gayoso House was reached the procession was joined by Judge William Sharkey of Mississippi, the most distinguished guest, riding in a four-horse carriage.[77] When night came the demonstrators staged a torchlight procession which was described as probably the largest political demonstration ever witnessed in Memphis. Lights were placed in the windows of homes and public buildings while Court Square was aglow with the rays of torches, candles, and lanterns. The crowd was addressed by Thomas A. R. Nelson and Andrew Jackson Donelson.[78]

The Democrats, especially the Breckinridge wing, also made a vigorous campaign in Tennessee. The Douglas men, led by William Polk and Foote, although encouraged by a visit by Douglas himself, were never able to generate much enthusiasm. In the midst of the campaign, Foote was reputed to have said in a speech at Stanton that, while he was supporting Douglas, he would say that the nation did not contain "a better man, a truer patriot, a purer gentleman, a more trustworthy statesman than John Bell." [79] In another speech, delivered on the Public Square at Nashville, Foote "poured out his vials of wrath copiously" against Breckinridge and his supporters, but, again, he was very respectful when speaking of Bell.[80]

The Breckinridge forces included such prominent Democrats as Governor Isham G. Harris and Senators A. O. P. Nicholson and Andrew Johnson. Although it does not appear

[77] Memphis *Argus,* October 8, 1860.   [78] *Ibid.,* October 9, 1860.
[79] *Brownlow's Knoxville Whig,* September 1, 1860.
[80] Allen (ed.), "Diary of Randall W. McGavock," 391.

that Johnson was especially active, he did participate in a Breckinridge rally at Memphis, where he told his audience that the Douglas ticket should be withdrawn and all Democratic strength centered on Breckinridge, thus defeating Bell.[81] Johnson disapproved of the secessionist sentiments expressed by some Breckinridge supporters and remarked that the whole slavery controversy had "become nauseating to his stomach." [82] In a speech on Broad Street in Nashville, Johnson "gave Jno. Bell the devil and Know Nothingism particular h . . . ," but displeased some Breckinridge men by referring to his own efforts in interest of the Homestead Bill, which measure had been vetoed by President Buchanan.[83]

Alabama's William L. Yancey also included Tennessee in the itinerary of his eastern speaking tour in behalf of Breckinridge. At Knoxville, when his speech was in its third hour, a voice from the audience suddenly yelled "Hurrah for Bell!" In reply, Yancey cried "Hurrah for Greeley, too." "What will you do if Lincoln is elected?" inquired another from the audience. At that point, several prominent East Tennesseans, including Brownlow and Oliver P. Temple, who had passed a note to the speaker, were invited to the platform and questioned as to their politics. They unanimously declared in favor of Bell; however, the loquacious Brownlow further asserted that should Lincoln be elected and the secessionists start for Washington for the purpose of dethroning the new President, he would "seize a bayonet and form an army to resist such an attack." To this threat Yancey retorted that if he found Brownlow blocking his way he would plunge a bayonet through his heart.[84] Here the display was terminated. The quarrelsome "Parson" had given vent to his spleen and the

[81] Memphis *Argus,* October 17, 1860.

[82] *Republican Banner and Nashville Whig,* November 3, 1860.

[83] Allen (ed.), "Diary of Randall W. McGavock," 391.

[84] *Brownlow's Knoxville Whig,* September 22, 1860; John W. DuBose, *Life and Times of William Lowndes Yancey* (Birmingham, 1892), 495–96; William G. Brownlow, *Sketches of the Rise, Progress, and Decline of Secession; with a Narrative of Personal Adventures Among the Rebels* (Philadelphia, 1862), 67.

"fire eating" Yancey had won no votes for Breckinridge in this stronghold of Unionism. Both at Knoxville and at Nashville Yancey treated Bell with "marked respect" and expressed a preference for him over Lincoln.[85]

The election was held on November 6; Bell and Everett carried only three states—Virginia, Kentucky, and Tennessee. Out in Missouri, Edward Bates gleefully recorded in his diary: "Lincoln foremost, Douglas next, Bell next, *cum long intervallo*—and Breckenridge [*sic*] far behind." [86] The fusion ticket in New York, referred to by Greeley as "a hybrid, tesselated, three-legged anti-Republican ticket," [87] lost by more than 50,000 votes even though it polled more than 300,000. Washington Hunt attributed the defeat, in part, to the dissension among the Democrats and to the fact that many Whigs, failing to appreciate the gravity of the situation, refused to cooperate. "But the great and controlling cause," he concluded, "must be found in the fact that a majority of our people in the interior have become thoroughly distempered with an antislavery sectional fanaticism." [88] Horatio Seymour was not so convinced of widespread fanaticism. Many New Yorkers who voted for Lincoln, he explained, "had no partiality for, or confidence in, Republican doctrines"; they did not wish to see the election go to the House of Representatives.[89] August Belmont thought the lack of funds for essential campaign expenses and the influence of Republican victories in the state elections of Pennsylvania, Maine, and Indiana had contributed largely to defeat of the fusion ticket in New York.[90] Regardless of the cause, the failure of the Douglas-Bell-Breckinridge ticket to carry the Empire State clinched the

[85] *Republican Banner and Nashville Whig*, October 28, 1860.
[86] Beale (ed.), *Diary of Edward Bates*, 155.
[87] New York *Tribune*, July 11, 1860.
[88] Hunt to Bell, November 21, 1860, in Bell Papers.
[89] Horatio Seymour to John J. Crittenden, January 18, 1861, in Coleman, *Crittenden*, II, 354 55.
[90] Belmont to John Forsyth, December 19, 1860, in *Letters, Speeches and Addresses of August Belmont* (n.p., 1890), 36–39. For Belmont's unsuccessful effort to raise adequate funds, see Milton, *Eve of Conflict*, 488 ff.

victory for Lincoln. Had the thirty-five votes of that state been divided among the other candidates, the selection would have been made by the House of Representatives. This, however, according to Bell's belief, would not have meant victory for the Constitutional Union party.

One Pennsylvanian, in explaining Lincoln's victory in his state, observed that Bell was really the choice of the Whigs, yet many of them refused to give him their support. They knew that the Constitutional Union ticket had no chance to win before the people, and remembering the recent controversy in the House of Representatives over the election of a Speaker, they hesitated to be a party to any plan to send the election of the President to that body.[91] This might explain the action of some old Whigs, but the real reason for Bell's poor showing—12,776 votes out of a total of 476,422—must be sought elsewhere.

Delaware, "bound hand & foot," had been delivered to the Republicans, reported Joseph P. Comegys. Although Breckinridge would receive the electoral votes, George P. Fisher, a professed friend of Bell, had turned out to be a Republican at heart, and had been elected to Congress by "the whole body of Republicans in Delaware." Henceforth, Delaware's sole member of the House would breathe, politically, at Republican pleasure. Comegys further charged that by assuring the people that the election of Lincoln would not bring the end of the world, such professed Bell supporters as Henry Winter Davis, John Minor Botts, Richard W. Thompson of Indiana, and Emerson Etheridge of Tennessee had indirectly contributed to the Lincoln victory.[92]

In New Jersey the three men whose names were on both the straight-out Douglas and fusion tickets won; the Repub-

91 John Griffen to Johnson, January 7, 1861, in Johnson Papers.
92 Comegys to Bell, November 12, 1860, in Polk-Yeatman Papers. Bell had suspected that Botts's defense of Lincoln's alleged conservatism was damaging the Union cause. Bell to Boteler, July 31, 1860, in Adrian Hoffman Joline Collection (Huntington Library).

licans won the other four places. The Constitutional Union ticket made a respectable showing in every slave state, losing Missouri to the Douglas Democrats by only 429 votes and Maryland to Breckinridge by 722 votes. In neither of the three states carried by Bell and Everett, however, did their vote exceed the combined vote of their opponents.[93]

An analysis of the vote in the slave states fails to support the oft-repeated contention that the election was a referendum on union or secession. All candidates professed strong attachment to the Union. Even though a number of Breckinridge supporters advocated secession in case of defeat, Breckinridge himself was no disunionist; neither was he considered as such by many of his followers, especially in the border states. Bell's support came principally from the sections which had been considered old Whig strongholds, but he was by no means able to unify the elements of that old party; the Toombs faction, like the Seward group in the North, had become too ultra. A number of Douglas men, realizing the weakness of their candidate in the South, also voted for Bell as a second choice.[94]

In Tennessee, owing to the aggressive support of such friends as Temple, Brownlow, Nelson, Taylor, and Maynard, Bell carried the eastern section of the state in spite of Andrew Johnson's support of Breckinridge. Yancey's visit to Knoxville lost votes for Breckinridge; Douglas never had any appreciable strength in that area. Breckinridge was able, however, to carry the traditionally Democratic East Tennessee counties of Greene, Washington, and Sullivan. In Middle Tennessee, where the Jackson and Polk influence was still strong, Breckinridge received a majority, but Nashville, as

[93] Stanwood, *History of the Presidency*, I, 297. Tennessee's vote was Bell 69,274; Breckinridge 64,709; Douglas 11,350.

[94] See Clarence P. Denman, *The Secession Movement in Alabama* (Montgomery, 1933), 82–86; E. Merton Coulter, *The Civil War and Readjustment in Kentucky* (Chapel Hill, 1926), 19 n4; Shanks, *The Secession Movement in Virginia*, 110–11; J. Carlyle Sitterson, *The Secession Movement in North Carolina* (Chapel Hill, 1939), 175.

usual, gave its vote to Bell. He was the only candidate who carried his home county.[95] Bell carried West Tennessee, although, owing probably to the active support of the Memphis *Appeal*, Douglas made some show of strength in the Memphis area.[96]

A few years later one of Bell's ardent East Tennessee supporters, who remained a stanch Union man during the subsequent war, recorded: "Mr. Bell was the only national candidate. His election would have prevented secession. If the North had been as anxious in 1860 to save the Union as it became in 1861, it would have voted for Mr. Bell. . . ." [97] The suggestion is at least worthy of consideration.

[95] James G. Randall, *Lincoln the President, Springfield to Gettysburg* (New York, 1945), I, 195.

[96] *Republican Banner and Nashville Whig*, December 4, 1860. For a more detailed discussion of the Democratic phase of the campaign of 1860 in Tennessee, see Margaret B. Hamer, "The Presidential Campaign of 1860 in Tennessee," in East Tennessee Historical Society's *Publications*, No. 3 (1931), 3–22.

[97] Oliver P. Temple, *East Tennessee and the Civil War* (Cincinnati, 1899), 294.

Chapter XIX

FROM UNIONIST TO REBEL

IT was the consensus of many members of the Constitutional Union party that the public duties and responsibilities of that group and its candidates did not end with the election of Lincoln. Washington Hunt, although not "in the right mood for correspondence," wrote Bell: "Your position is a proud and enviable one. It enables you to render important aid in the work of reconciliation. History will do full justice to you and to the gallant band of union men who rallied under your banner." [1] In a similar vein, August Belmont wrote John C. Bradley of Huntsville, Alabama: "The patriotic men of the country look to the Douglas and Bell party of the South as their only hope in the present crisis." [2]

Before these letters reached their destinations the South Carolina legislature had called for the meeting of a secessionist convention. The Mississippi congressmen had met with Governor John J. Pettus and recommended immediate secession, and a large mass meeting at Jackson had called for open resistance to the incoming Republican Administration.[3] The Mississippi conservatives, however, though greatly outnumbered,[4] were still advocating moderation and delay. A Vicksburg group urgently requested Bell and Douglas to visit the state and use their influence to prevent rash action. Doug-

[1] Hunt to Bell, November 21, 1860, in Bell Papers.

[2] November 28, 1860, in *Letters, Speeches and Addresses of August Belmont*, 28.

[3] Reuben Davis, *Recollections of Mississippi and Mississippians* (New York, 1889), 390–91.

[4] In Mississippi, Bell had polled 25,040 votes against 40,797 for Breckinridge and 3,283 for Douglas.

las was already in the vicinity, making his way up the Mississippi aboard the *James Battle* on his return from a visit to New Orleans and other points south. He stopped at Vicksburg and delivered a stirring Union speech. Bell, on the other hand, had lost none of his caution. No one realized better than he the utter futility of any effort on his part to stay the tide of secession in Mississippi. He declined to visit the state, but he sent a detailed statement of his views relating to the crisis. The election of Lincoln, he stated, seemed to be regular and in accordance with the Constitution. He had long believed, however, that the election of a purely sectional candidate would endanger the Union. The election of Lincoln was certainly "a bold experiment upon the temper and forbearance of the South, and upon the strength of their loyalty to the Union." He would not say that it was "conceived in a spirit of disunion," yet if that was not the case it certainly was made "with a reckless disregard of consequence."

Bell thought the only difference between the Republican party and the abolitionist societies was in the extent to which they were able to inflict "mischiefs" upon the South. But he hastened to add that Abraham Lincoln, if judged by his speeches and past record, was not an extremist. If the President-elect was sincere and possessed the moral courage to stand by his convictions, then the South had no reason to fear extreme measures. Bell believed that Lincoln's policy would be in strict conformity with his expressed sentiments. However, should it be contrary, the new Administration would be "powerless for mischief . . . unless the Southern Senators and Representatives . . . should rashly, and as I think, inexcusably resign their seats or retire from Congress, and thus voluntarily surrender the control in both Houses to the Republican party."

Bell next proceeded to analyze the membership of the Republican party and to explain the election of Lincoln. About one third of those who had voted Republican, he explained, did so because of "strong and inveterate" hostility toward the Democrats. They believed that Lincoln was the only man who could defeat that party. A second third of the Republican voters had joined the new party in retaliation, expressing their resentment of the repeal of the Missouri Compromise and "the attempt to force the Lecompton constitution upon the people of Kansas." These people had no desire to make war on Southern interests. The remaining third Bell classified as dangerous. That group had an intense hatred of slavery and the South, and was either indifferent to the Union or "actually desirous of a separation of the free from the slave States."

After taking into account the seriousness of the problems resulting from the election of a sectional President, Bell still insisted that all real Southern grievances could be satisfactorily adjusted within the Union. Even indignity and insult could be pardoned in the interest of "peace and harmony." Had not the South also contributed liberally to the violent controversy between the sections?

In the closing paragraphs of his letter, Bell got down to the fundamental point—the doctrine of secession. The election had not changed his previously stated position. After due reflection, he had concluded that "secession is but another name for an organized resistance by a State to the laws and constituted authorities of the Union, or, which is the same thing, for *revolution*." He said he had long suspected that certain distinguished men of the South cherished schemes for disunion and were waiting only for a more plausible pretext for putting these schemes into operation.

Should Mississippi attempt secession, Bell concluded, she would

. . . take upon herself the responsibility of doing an act that would expose the peace and security of her sister States of the South to direct and eminent danger, and perhaps decide their destinies for weal or woe forever, without previous consultation with them, and first exhausting every peaceable mode of redress for the grievances of which she complains.

Viewing the subject in every light in which it can be presented, I am constrained to say that by no principle of Public Law, by no code of morals, by no law of Earth or Heaven, would Mississippi or any other State be justified, under existing circumstances, in withdrawing from the Union.

I am resolved to adhere to the Union. I will not say that in *no possible contingency* would I consent to a separation of the States. But I would exhaust every constitutional means for the redress of our grievances, before I would think of dissolving the Union. I am not willing that one State should be withdrawn from the Union—that one star should be stricken from that bright cluster which now emblazons the national flag.[5]

In the meantime, Bell's friend Gustavus A. Henry had been sounding public opinion in parts of Mississippi and Louisiana. He reported to Bell that the people in those states were strongly in favor of secession and were unwilling to listen to plans for compromise or reconciliation. "I fear the old Union is gone forever," Henry lamented. "God knows I have done all I can to prevent it but I fear in vain." The most important question remaining was "ought we to stand idly by & suffer the small fry politicians & Demagogues to run away with every thing & have everything their own way?" Ought not Bell especially throw himself into the current and direct its course? There was no doubt about the cotton states seceding, Henry concluded. The only question was, what would the border states do.[6]

By the time Henry's letter arrived, Bell apparently had conceded the temporary loss of the Lower South. He felt

[5] Bell to A. Burwell, December 6, 1860, in *Republican Banner and Nashville Whig*, December 8, 1860; Burwell to Douglas, November 16, 1860, in Douglas Papers.

[6] Henry to Bell, December 4, 1860, in Bell Papers. This letter was written from New Orleans so could not have reached Nashville prior to Bell's reply to Burwell.

confident though that no state north of Arkansas and Mississippi would ever join with the Gulf States in the formation of a Southern confederacy. He ventured the opinion that even the cotton states would return to the Union after they had experienced a year or two of what they now look forward to as the sweets of a new government of some kind." [7]

Meanwhile, Governor Isham G. Harris had issued a call for the legislature of Tennessee to convene in special session on January 7, 1861. Addressing that body on the opening day of the session, the Governor stated that the representatives of the people had been called together "for the purpose of calm and dispassionate deliberation." The North had climaxed the many outrages against the South, he explained, by elevating to the presidency a man who had "asserted the equality of the *black* and the white races." Attention was called to the poor condition of Tennessee arms resulting from the repeal of the law requiring militia drills and public parades. In the opinion of the Governor a convention should be called for the purpose of considering the problems with which the state was confronted.[8]

In accordance with the Governor's wishes, a bill was introduced in the senate, providing for the organization and equipment of a volunteer corps. The unionists consolidated their forces in opposition. "Allow me to suggest that you . . . dont fail to come out against the proposed army bill, asking for a million of dollars to be put in the hands of the Governor," wrote S. D. Morgan to Bell. "If that bill is passed, and troops are raised, good by [*sic*] to our liberties in Ten— With the patronage it would carry with it any election, or even secession can & will be carried beyond a doubt." [9] Unionist strength was sufficient to block this military measure, and Bell was credited with its defeat. But the legislature did pass a proposal to submit to referendum the question of

[7] Bell to ? , December 10, 1860, in Bell Papers.

[8] Tennessee *Senate Journal*, Extra Session, 1861, pp. 6–19.

[9] S. D. Morgan to Bell, January 22, 1861, in Polk-Yeatman Papers.

the calling of a state convention and set February 9 as the date for voting.[10]

Both secessionists and unionists carried on a vigorous campaign in preparation for the election. On the evening of January 22 Bell spoke before a large audience assembled in the chamber of the House of Representatives, and according to an admirer, held his listeners "spell-bound" for two and one-half hours.[11] He expressed confidence in the new Administration, and criticized Governor Harris for having stated that Lincoln believed in the equality of races. Bell considered the proposed appointment of William H. Seward to the position of Secretary of State encouraging evidence that the policy of Lincoln would be one of conciliation. Apparently he now recognized that Seward was more conservative than he had thought during the recent campaign. There was no immediate danger of the adoption of any coercive measures directed at the South, he insisted. Therefore, he was opposed to the arming of Tennessee. He thought that the Union could never be dissolved, "but if it comes to the worst we can then form a Central Confederacy, which will ultimately be joined by the cotton States." [12]

Proconvention men were vigorous in their denunciation of Bell. Henry S. Foote, who only a few weeks earlier had spoken very kindly of Bell, made a "most terrible dissection" of his speech, stating that Bell had long been an "intimate friend and co-conspirator of Seward" against compromise measures. He prophesied that within a period of two weeks Bell would receive an offer of an appointment from Lincoln and that the offer would arrive under the frank of Seward.[13]

[10] Tennessee *Senate Journal,* Extra Session, 1861, pp. 49, 52, 109, 117; *House Journal,* 217; *Acts,* 16–17. See also summary of Bell's April 23 speech, in *Republican Banner and Nashville Whig,* May 10, 1861.

[11] *Republican Banner and Nashville Whig,* January 23, 1861.

[12] Bell's speech as summarized in Nashville *Union and American,* January 23, 24, 1861.

[13] Memphis *Avalanche,* January 30, 1861. Bell received no offer of an appointment, but Henry J. Raymond of the New York *Times* suggested Bell, Botts, Etheridge, and Henry Winter Davis as wise choices for cabinet positions. *Times,* November 12, 1860.

But disunionist efforts were not sufficient to arouse the voters of Tennessee, and the convention proposal was defeated by a vote of 68,282 to 59,449. The total vote cast was 17,602 less than the vote for President in 1860 and 16,384 less than that for governor in 1859.[14] This rejection of the convention proposal came after South Carolina, Georgia and the Gulf states had adopted ordinances of secession.

The Union men in Tennessee were encouraged. Bell hurried off to Washington to be present at Lincoln's inauguration and to seek conferences with officials of the new Administration in the interest of "a pacific and forbearing policy toward the seceding States." [15] Not much is known of what he did while there or with whom he conferred other than with the President. A correspondent of the Cincinnati *Enquirer* reported Bell's presence in the capital and thought he appeared dejected over the probable effect the inauguration would have on the South. However, on the following day the same reporter telegraphed: "I hear to-day that John Bell has somewhat changed his views in regard to the inaugural, and bases hope on Mr. Lincoln's ambiguous expressions." [16] It is known that Bell conferred with President Lincoln and urged him to proceed with the greatest caution. The Administration should not be deceived by the Tennessee vote of February 9, Bell insisted. That vote was an expression of confidence that the new President would adopt a just and conciliatory policy. Should Lincoln's actions betray this confidence, Tennessee's stand would probably be reversed.

Bell pointed out the importance of averting a collision between Federal troops and those of the seceding states. As insurance against such a clash, he urged the evacuation of the Federal forts within the South. Bell seemed to be cling-

[14] *The War of the Rebellion: A Compilation of the Official Records of the Union and Confederate Armies* (Washington, 1880–1901), Ser. IV, Vol. I, 901 (cited hereafter as *Official Records*); Charles A. Miller, *The Official and Political Manual of the State of Tennessee* (Nashville, 1890), 167, 170.

[15] See summary of Bell's April 23 speech, in *Republican Banner and Nashville Whig*, May 10, 1861.

[16] Cincinnati *Enquirer*, quoted in Memphis *Argus*, March 9, 11, 1861.

ing to the hope that after a cooling-off period the seceding states would voluntarily return to their positions within the Union. Conciliation alone had a chance to succeed, he assured Lincoln; an attempt at coercion through a clash of arms would fail utterly. In case the seceding states rejected conciliation, "the wisest course would be to let them go in peace." [17] Neither Lincoln nor the members of his cabinet made any definite commitments, but when Bell left Washington he was confident that the policy of the new Administration would be pacific.

Secessionists made little progress in the Upper South during the first month of the Republican Administration; they were disarmed by the prevailing hope for compromise and conciliation. Lincoln did not show his hand until early in April, at which time he announced his intention to send supplies to besieged Fort Sumter. The Confederates opened fire on the Fort on April 12, and it capitulated on the following day. Two days later President Lincoln issued his call for 75,000 militia. On April 17 a Virginia convention adopted an ordinance of secession. Governor Harris of Tennessee sent a defiant reply to the Secretary of War, and issued a call for the legislature to meet in special session on April 25. Revived and augmented secession sentiment in Tennessee gave evidence of sweeping all opposition before it. Those who one year earlier had pledged themselves ever to uphold the Constitution and the Union were faced with the necessity for a reappraisal of their loyalty. They must either support the Union government in its policy of coercion or they must join with secessionists in their plans for defense.

In the face of Lincoln's policy, such a man as Bell could not stem the onrushing tide of secession and civil war, and he was aware of the fact. Under the pressure of such times, he was a pathetic figure. Strong in intellect but slow in reach-

[17] Summary of Bell's remarks concerning his conferences in Washington, in *Republican Banner and Nashville Whig*, May 10, 1861. The anonymous author of *The Diary of a Public Man* (New Brunswick, N.J., 1946), 64, commented on how impressed Bell was with Lincoln's conservative tone.

ing decisions, and deliberate and cautious in action, he could never be a leader in a crisis.[18] Mid-April, 1861, found him a sad, disillusioned, and embittered man. His love for the Union had not diminished, yet he had little hope of averting disruption. In his opinion, Lincoln had proved unworthy of the confidence Southern moderates had placed in him, and had left them to be targets of abuse from irate secessionists. Bell was embarrassed by his own words recently spoken in a spirit of conciliation. No one realized better than he that the prosecution of Lincoln's policy would force Tennessee into armed resistance. "Physically, he [Bell] was regarded as a man of courage," wrote a friendly contemporary, "but he seemed to be powerless to resist a counter current of public opinion in times of high excitement." [19] The writer might have added, "especially when resistance seemed futile."

On April 18 Bell took his first step toward rebellion when he and ten other Tennessee conservatives issued a statement to the people. They commended "the wisdom, the justice and the humanity" of Governor Harris' refusal to furnish troops for the coercion of the seceding states. They condemned the policy which had been adopted by Lincoln, but they disapproved of secession "both as a constitutional right and as a remedy for existing evils." Tennessee should neither join with the seceding states nor conform to the military demands of the Union. To do either "would at once terminate her grand mission of peace-maker, between the States of the South and the General Government." The abandonment of neutrality would be the abandonment of hope of reconciliation and would inevitably lead to the shedding of blood on Tennessee soil.

Bell and his associates contended that Tennessee's role in the crisis should be that of defender of the "union and peace of the country against all assailants, whether from the North or South." However, should the General Government be-

---

[18] Temple, *East Tennessee and the Civil War*, 230–37. Temple was a close friend of Bell. [19] *Ibid.*, 231.

gin a war to subjugate the people of the seceding states, "we say unequivocally that it will be the duty of the State to resist at all hazards, at any cost, *and by arms.*" Since there was a strong possibility of an attempt to coerce, Tennessee officials should see that the state was armed sufficiently to meet any emergency. But even when fully prepared for defensive war, Tennessee should continue to devote her best efforts to the preservation of peace. A conference with the border states was urged. "There may yet be time. . . . Let us not despair. The Border Slave States may prevent this civil war." [20] In taking a definite stand against coercion, Bell was not inconsistent with his past record; neither was he out of harmony with the majority of the old Whigs in the other areas of the Upper South. He was definitely identified with the interests of the conservative slaveholders, and civil war would endanger the security of both position and property.

Events crowded upon each other, and John Bell possessed neither the will to stand by the recently expressed policy of the Union nor the power to stem the wave of disunion. By April 23 he was almost persuaded to classify himself as a rebel, if not a secessionist. Speaking before a mass meeting in Nashville, he declared that there was no longer any need to discuss the causes back of the existing crisis. "We must now look to the realities of the present and the contingencies of the future, and make such provisions for both as wisdom and prudence may dictate." A united North apparently was beginning a war of subjugation, he averred, and it must be met by a united South. A well-equipped militia should be organized and placed in readiness. At the same time, Bell advised discretion sufficient "to promote unanimity of feeling, and to secure the hearty co-operation of all our citizens as far as possible, in breasting the storm." He urged complete mobilization of the physical and moral power of the state, and

[20] Washington *National Intelligencer,* April 23, 1861; *Brownlow's Knoxville Whig,* April 27, 1861. The other signers of the statement were Neill S. Brown, Russell Houston, Edwin H. Ewing, Cave Johnson, Return J. Meigs, S. D. Morgan, John S. Brien, Andrew Ewing, John H. Callender, and Balie Peyton.

pointed out that there were thousands who, although opposed to secession, would not hesitate to take up arms in defense of the South. He regretted his part in the defeat of the military bill, and admitted that, in the light of subsequent events, it had been a mistake. But at the time the bill was up for consideration, he still had had confidence in Abraham Lincoln.

Tennessee had strong ties with both the newly organized Confederacy and the states to the north, Bell continued. Under existing circumstances, he could see no sound reason for a change of policy. Of course it was true that Tennessee's refusal to furnish troops for the Union army had placed her in a state of *"quasi* rebellion." However, he could not see the wisdom of assuming a state of "actual rebellion" by adopting an ordinance of secession. Tennessee could co-operate with the Confederate States in defense without joining them in secession. Bell expressed regret that he felt forced to recommend such preparation for defense, but he had been deceived by authorities at Washington and had concluded that "no confident reliance could be placed upon the pacific disposition of the Administration."

Bell showed special concern over the position which Kentucky might take. Regardless of what future developments might bring, he thought that Tennessee and Kentucky ought never to act separately. He recalled that he had once stated that these two states, acting as a bloc, might be able to preserve the Union. Although he did not wish to repeat that statement, he said, he was still hopeful that these states might remain united in purpose. For if war should come, Kentucky and Tennessee would undoubtedly become a battle ground.[21]

A week earlier the *Republican Banner,* probably in pursuance of a suggestion from Bell, had appealed to the border states to "stand firm, and act together, as long as there is a plank of the old ship of State between us and angry waves of

[21] Summary of speech in *Republican Banner and Nashville Whig,* May 10, 1861.

destruction, and until the last beacon light of hope twinkles out in the distance, as we are drifted into an unknown and tempestuous sea." [22]

It is clear that Bell had despaired of any concessions from the Lincoln Administration. And it is equally clear that he had no desire to see Tennessee become a part of a confederacy dominated by the cotton states under the leadership of such men as Jefferson Davis, Robert Toombs, and William L. Yancey. Bell was still clinging to the idea of a border-state bloc which might be able to prevent civil war, and in the event the Union was dissolved, might form the nucleus of a confederacy to which the Lower South might adhere eventually. The friends of the Southern Confederacy were highly pleased with Bell's defection, and not too seriously concerned over the central confederacy idea. "John Bell, Andrew and Ed. Ewing spoke here [Nashville] night before last," wrote William B. Bate. "They are nearly right; so are Bailie Peyton and ex-Governor Campbell.[23] They want to help the South, but not in favor of uniting with it yet. I think I see a dagger behind that smile in the shape of a central republic; but we will grind out the idea; it has no lodgment with the masses." [24] Gideon J. Pillow informed the Confederate Secretary of War that Bell "has at last come out fully for the South. He held back as long as public opinion would tolerate him." [25]

"A more sudden, and utter, and inglorious defection was never suffered by a sacred and imperiled cause," declared George D. Prentice, editor of the Louisville *Journal* and a recent supporter of the Bell-Everett ticket, when he learned of Bell's change of attitude. "It must excite unspeakable mortification, and disgust, and indignation, in the breast of

[22] *Ibid.*, April 16, 1861.
[23] The Ewings, Peyton, and William B. Campbell had been very active in opposition to secession.
[24] William B. Bate to Leroy P. Walker, April 26, 1861, in *Official Records*, Ser. I, Vol. LIX, Pt. II, 74.
[25] Pillow to *id.*, April 30, 1861, *ibid.*, Ser. I, Vol. LII, Pt. II, 69.

every true and enlightened lover of his country. It is a burning scandal to the cause of constitutional liberty." [26] A few days later Horace Greeley, editor of the New York *Tribune,* concluded a denunciation of this erstwhile savior of the Union with the lamentation, "Alas that such should be the ignominious close of the long public life of John Bell!" [27] And John Minor Botts later begged God's forgiveness for voting for Bell and having "labored for his success day and night." He charged that Bell stood firmly on the Union platform as long as there was hope of election, but the moment he was defeated "he knocked the platform from under his feet" and assisted in the attempt to destroy the Union.[28]

Before the Tennessee legislature met in called session on April 25, the seceding states had formed a union. Jefferson Davis, the newly elected president of this Confederacy, sent Henry W. Hilliard of Alabama to Nashville as a commissioner in the interest of secession. Hilliard, a supporter of the Bell-Everett ticket in 1860, had opposed the secession of Alabama, but, following the fall of Fort Sumter, had become an advocate of the Confederacy.[29] His connection with conservative men in Tennessee and his recognized ability as a persuasive speaker made him a logical choice for the mission. Soon after this Confederate ambassador arrived in Nashville, he had a conference with Bell. According to Hilliard's account, Bell confided to him that "Tennessee would certainly become a member of the Confederate States, but that he could not so abruptly change his position as to favor that course im-

---

[26] New York *Tribune,* May 17, 1861. After a few years of meditation, Greeley was even more pronounced in his condemnation of Bell's conduct: "Of the many who weakly, culpably allowed themselves to be beguiled or hurled into complicity in the crime of dividing and destroying their country, there is *no* name whereon will rest a deeper, darker stigma than that of John Bell." Horace Greeley, *The American Conflict,* I, 482.

[27] Louisville *Journal,* quoted in New York *Tribune,* May 3, 1861.

[28] John Minor Botts, *The Great Rebellion* (New York, 1866), 127.

[29] Henry W. Hilliard, *Politics and Pen Pictures at Home and Abroad* (Atlanta, 1892), 309–11, 325–29.

mediately; that it would be more dignified to consider the Constitution before adopting it." [30]

Hilliard addressed the Tennessee legislature on April 30, and on the following day that body authorized the appointment of three commissioners to confer with the Confederate representative. Governor Harris appointed Washington Barrow, Gustavus A. Henry, and Archibald W. O. Totten, and they immediately drew up an agreement with Hilliard, placing Tennessee's military force under the control of President Davis. These three commissioners "were all Bell-wethers," a contemporary later commented, "and tinkled their bells, no doubt, at the said John's bidding." [31] It is true that Henry and Barrow had been prominently associated with the old Whig party, but it is not known whether they consulted Bell during their negotiations with Hilliard. The legislature approved the military agreement and framed an ordinance of secession to be submitted to the people for ratification on June 8.

On June 1, Bell left for East Tennessee, the stronghold of unionism. The exact purpose of his mission is still a question. Neither is it known whether the trip was made on his own volition or as a result of pressure from secessionists. At least some of his East Tennessee friends thought it was the latter.[32] Apparently he went for the purpose of using his influence in the interest of armed resistance, if not secession. He spoke at Athens and Knoxville, but the reports of his speeches are meager and confused. Upon his arrival in Knoxville he apparently was shunned by most of his old Whig friends. On June 6 he spoke at the Knox County courthouse. According to Brownlow, "few union men attended." The East Tennessee unionists "found their old leader in the hands of a set of men who, only last fall, were denouncing him . . . as a d——d old Abolitionist, and traitor to the South! The

[30] Henry W. Hilliard to Toombs, May 1, 1861, in *Official Records,* Ser. I, Vol. LII, Pt. II, 82–83.

[31] C. W. Hall, *Three Score Years and Ten* (Cincinnati, 1884), 140.

[32] Temple, *East Tennessee and the Civil War,* 234.

union men had nobly defended Col. Bell against these slanders, and did not choose to countenance those who perpetrated them, by meeting around the same altar, to worship the false god of Disunion, where John Bell was to be the officiating Priest!"

According to the correspondents of the Knoxville newspapers, Bell was critical of the recent steps taken by the legislature in approving a military agreement with the Confederacy, denouncing its actions as "unconstitutional and tyrannical." However, he expressed great concern over the division of sentiment in East Tennessee. He expressed surprise that any of his friends could suppose "that when this great contest had become, as it had done, a *war between the North and the South,* he could be found occupying any other position than that of *for the South.*" Bell explained that he still considered secession as "heresy" and was opposed to a Southern Confederacy. However, he realized that in his present position he must be classed as a "rebel." [33]

Following his speech, Bell walked across the street to the law office of Oliver P. Temple, where it had been arranged for him to meet with a group of his old Whig friends. "The meeting was embarrassing all around." Bell commented on the fact that none of the group had come to hear him speak. Brownlow then delivered a bitter denunciation of secession. Bell made no attempt to defend either secession or his own actions. And his old friends were careful not to utter "a word of censure or an unkind remark about him personally. All present had too much respect for his dignity, his exalted worth and his greatness, to wound him." [34] In order to relieve the tenseness, Temple proposed that the group walk to his home for "a glass of wine." He later said that during the course of the visit in his home, Bell admitted that had the Union leaders in Middle Tennessee stood firm in their loy-

[33] Knoxville *Register,* quoted in Athens *Post,* June 7, 1861; *Brownlow's Knoxville Whig,* June 15, 1861.

[34] Temple, *East Tennessee and the Civil War,* 234–35.

alty, secession of the state might have been prevented. However, Bell "expressed no regret, made no apology for his own course." Throughout the entire conference, Temple thought Bell appeared "sad and dejected," and spoke with "deep and pathetic sadness." [35] The members of the group parted as friends, but no one had been converted to the cause of resistance.

On June 8 the people of Tennessee ratified the ordinance of secession by a vote of 108,399 to 47,233.[36] The total vote cast in the referendum was 27,901 more than that of February 9. If all of the 69,274 persons who had voted for Bell in 1860 had remained loyal to the Union and voted against the ordinance, the secessionists would have won by a majority of 17,084. Even if Douglas' 11,350 votes had been added to those of Bell, Tennessee still would have seceded from the Union. The slaveholding areas of Middle and West Tennessee cast overwhelming majorities in favor of secession, but mountainous East Tennessee, in which there were comparatively few slaves, cast almost 33,000 of the 47,233 votes recorded against the ordinance. Efforts of the secessionists to win the support of the East Tennesseans had been a failure. One month after the referendum Landon C. Haynes wrote Leroy P. Walker, Confederate Secretary of War, that it would take six regiments to put East Tennessee in line. "Moral power," he said, "can no longer be relied on to crush the rebellion [against the Confederacy]. No man possesses that power. Bell had more than any other man, but he is as helpless as a child." [37] Bell would have been just as helpless had he tried to persuade the slaveholders of the Middle and Western sections to remain loyal to the Union and assist in the coercion of their neighbors to the South.

[35] *Ibid.*   [36] *Official Records,* Ser. IV, Vol. I, 901.
[37] Landon C. Haynes to Walker, July 6, 1861, *ibid.,* Ser. I, Vol. IV, 365.
Haynes had toured East Tennessee in the interest of secession.

Chapter XX

AN ERA ENDS

THE sun had set on John Bell's influence and public service. Sick in body and depressed in spirit, he retired from the active scene and prepared to dispose of his mining interests. On July 19, 1861, he gave M. W. Wetmore the power of attorney for the purpose of selling the Bell Mines in Kentucky. The sale price was set at $150,000.[1] No doubt Bell's belief that Kentucky would soon become a battlefield influenced his decision to dispose of his property there.

The Bell-Yeatman families became ardent supporters of the Confederacy. All of Bell's sons, stepsons, and sons-in-law were connected with the Confederate service at some time during the war. Two days before the Confederate attack upon Fort Sumter, Bell's stepson, Thomas Yeatman, an attorney of New Haven, Connecticut, wrote President Jefferson Davis for permission to raise two companies of troops. All recruits were to be New Haven men upon whom the Confederacy could rely. No financial assistance was desired, Yeatman said, since he himself had an independent fortune. All he wished was assurance that his companies would be received into the Confederate army.[2]

With the fall of Fort Donelson on the Cumberland River, on February 16, 1862, Middle Tennessee was open to invasion by Federal forces. A few miles southeast of the fort and within view of the river was the rolling mill of the Cumber-

[1] Polk Yeatman Papers, under date of July 19, 1861.
[2] Yeatman to Jefferson Davis, April 10, 1861, in *Official Records,* Ser. IV, Vol. I, 216, 225. Yeatman was a graduate of Yale and a veteran of the Mexican War.

land Iron Works. Shells from a Federal gunboat [3] put it out of operation, and Federal control of the river deprived the Confederacy of further use of the iron mines. What disposition was made of approximately four hundred slaves formerly employed in this iron business is not known.

Bell remained in Nashville until the approach of Union forces and then joined his children in Rutherford County. By May, 1862, he was in the vicinity of Huntsville, Alabama, where he and his friend Jere Clemens were discussing plans for terminating the war. From Huntsville, O. M. Mitchell reported to Secretary of War E. M. Stanton: "Unless prohibited, I think the Hon. John Bell and the Hon. Jeremiah Clemens will start for Washington in a few days." The object of the proposed trip was "to learn unofficially in what way the existing controversy might be ended." The trip was not made; Stanton replied that such men could do more good in Alabama than in Washington. [4]

From the Huntsville area, Bell, accompanied by his family and the wife and children of John Bell, Jr., went to Black Creek Falls near the Georgia-Alabama line, thence to Flat Shoals, Georgia, where the group accepted the hospitality of James Freeman. Subsequently they resided for a time at Cedartown. After Sherman's march through Georgia, the Bells moved to Madison, where they apparently remained until the end of the hostilities. [5] What Bell did or thought during the long exile from home is not a matter of record. A La Grange newspaper, recognizing his presence in Georgia, stated that he was very infirm in body. [6]

Following the war Bell returned to Tennessee to become the recipient of protection and courtesy at the hands of his old friend Brownlow, who had been made governor of the

3 Report of Flag-Officer Andrew H. Foote, February 20, 1862, in *Official Records,* Ser. I, Vol. VII, 423.

4 O. M. Mitchell to E. M. Stanton, May 6, 8, 1862, in *Official Records,* Ser. I, Vol. X, Pt. II, 167, 174; P. H. Watson to Mitchell, May 8, 1862, *ibid.,* 175.

5 *Republican Banner and Nashville Whig,* September 11, 1869; statement of John Bell's grandson, Mr. Charles Bell of Murfreesboro.

6 Quoted in Memphis *Bulletin,* March 19, 1865.

BELL HOME IN STEWART COUNTY
In this house, near Bear Spring Furnace, Bell spent his last years.

state. Brownlow, a stanch Union man during the war, had never considered Bell anything but a Union man at heart. His old friend, he insisted, had only yielded to secession "on account of the great pressure, which but few of our Union leaders found themselves able openly to resist." [7] Having no home in Nashville, Bell moved to the site of his property in Stewart County and began an effort to rebuild his rolling mill and reopen his mines. In a plain but substantial brick house located on a slight elevation near the mill and surrounded by the alluvial Cumberland River bottoms he lived out the few remaining years of his life. He died on September 11, 1869. The body was returned to Nashville where it lay in state in the Capitol prior to burial in Mt. Olivet Cemetery.

The passage of years and the finality of death often soften political animosities, and the testimonies of former adversaries may be nearer the truth than the eulogies of close friends. Although he and Bell had opposed each other in politics, remarked Andrew Johnson, he had always found him a courteous, fair, and honorable opponent. Even if at times Bell had "broken a javelin and he had bent a spear," afterward they had met as gentlemen. To these remarks, Henry S. Foote, a former Democratic senator from Mississippi, added that he would remember Bell for "his uniform courteous, dignified and truly Senatorial demeanor, his industry, his ability, his impartiality, his freedom from every thing like chicanery and party trickery; his kind and obliging temper, and his Roman-like integrity and honor." [8]

[7] Brownlow, *Sketches of the Rise, Progress, and Decline of Secession,* 411. Brownlow made these remarks in 1862.
[8] *Republican Banner and Nashville Whig,* September 12, 1869.

CRITICAL ESSAY ON AUTHORITIES

This is not a bibliography of the ante-bellum period of American history. Only those items found helpful in the preparation of this biography are included. A few works from which single bits of information were secured are given in full in the footnotes but are not included in the bibliography.

Manuscripts

No large collection of John Bell papers has been located, and there is no indication that one exists. Bell apparently did not preserve copies of his own letters; therefore, the originals must be sought among the papers of his associates. According to a family story, the finest collection of his letters was preserved by his cousin John Marshall of Franklin, but all were burned during the Civil War. Marshall and Bell were said to have corresponded frequently during a period of thirty years. Bell's descendants apparently have none of his papers, but a small collection, consisting mostly of letters to Bell, was left in the hands of the descendants of the second Mrs. Bell. These letters now make up a portion of the Polk-Yeatman Papers in the Southern Historical Collection of the University of North Carolina. In addition to letters, this collection also contains a number of documents pertaining to Bell's mining interests in Kentucky and Tennessee and his land speculation in Louisiana. Neither this nor any other known collection contains any large number of intimate family letters. A few items relating to Bell genealogy, written many years after John Bell's death, are found in the Tennessee State Library. Other valuable genealogical materials are in the possession of G. E. Bell, Dallas, Texas, and Mrs. W. H. Knox, Nashville.

The John Bell Papers in the Division of Manuscripts of the Library of Congress include a small collection of valuable letters from his political associates in the campaign of 1860.

The David Campbell Papers (Duke University Library), the Thomas A. R. Nelson Papers (Lawson McGhee Library, Knoxville), and the John J. Crittenden Papers (Duke University Library and the Library of Congress) are of great importance. William B. Campbell, a nephew of David Campbell, and Nelson were Whig leaders in Middle and East Tennessee respectively and were closely associated with Bell for many years. Their papers contain many Bell letters and a mass of other correspondence bearing on Tennessee and national politics. The views of Crittenden on national issues were so similar to those of Bell that a rather close personal relationship would be expected. The Crittenden Papers constitute the largest and most important Whig collection relating to Bell's career.

Scattered Bell letters are found in many manuscript collections of his other political associates. There are a few in the Henry Clay Papers (Library of Congress), but the collection as a whole is disappointing. The Daniel Webster Papers (Library of Congress) are valuable for the study of the period, but there are no important Bell letters among them. The same is true of the small collection of John Tyler Papers (Library of Congress) and the large collection of Abraham Lincoln material (Library of Congress). A few Bell letters relating to the Bank controversy are among the Nicholas Biddle correspondence (Library of Congress). And some interesting correspondence pertaining to the cabinet crisis of 1841 is in the Thomas Ewing collection (Library of Congress). Letters touching on the speakership controversy of 1834 are found in the Willie P. Mangum Papers (Library of Congress). There is nothing of importance in the Zachary Taylor manuscripts (Library of Congress), but the Millard Fillmore Papers (Buffalo Historical Society) contain about a half-dozen Bell letters pertaining to the Fillmore Administration. The John P. Kennedy collection (Peabody Institute, Baltimore) and the Alexander Robinson Boteler Papers (Duke University Library) are of value for the campaign of 1860. The latter contains one very valuable Bell letter.

The small Hugh Lawson White collection (Library of Congress) contains no Bell letters and was of little value in the preparation of this study. The Oliver P. Temple Papers (University of Tennessee Library) also contain no Bell letters, but the correspondence of William G. Brownlow and others is filled with references to him. Several Bell items are scattered among the miscellaneous manuscript collections of the Tennessee Historical Society, the Historical Society of Pennsylvania, the Lincoln National Life Foundation, the Henry E. Huntington Library, and the New York Historical Society.

A number of Bell letters are found among the papers of prominent Democratic leaders, but the importance of these collections is in their presentation of the opposition viewpoint. In the early years of his political career Bell corresponded with John Overton of Tennessee, a close friend of Andrew Jackson. A part of this correspondence is preserved in the John Overton Papers (Tennessee Historical Society). Andrew Jackson's papers (Library of Congress and the New York Public Library) are indispensable to a study of the life of any prominent national figure of his day. They are rich in both pro- and anti-Bell material. Of still greater importance for the Democratic viewpoint, however, is the voluminous collection of James K. Polk Papers (Library of Congress). The rivalry between Polk and Bell after 1834 was so intense that neither could discuss politics without condemning the other. In this collection is found the Democratic strategy for blocking the political ambitions of Bell. Of considerable value also are the papers of Alfred O. P. Nicholson (New York Historical Society). The volume is small but the contents are important. Until late in the 1840's Nicholson was a close personal friend of Polk, yet he and Bell corresponded from time to time.

In his earlier years and again late in life Andrew Jackson Donelson was Bell's political and personal friend. His papers (Library of Congress) contain much valuable information but few Bell letters. After the death of Polk, Andrew Johnson became Bell's most bitter political adversary in Tennessee-national politics. Although valuable, his papers (Library of Congress) do not reveal the intensity of feeling found in the Polk manuscripts. Martin Van Buren's papers (Library of Congress) contain little that relates to Bell directly, yet they must be classed among the important collections of the period. Owing principally to his correspondence with Cave Johnson, an active political enemy of Bell, the James Buchanan Papers (Historical Society of Pennsylvania) were of considerable use. The papers of Bell's opponents in the campaign of 1860 contain little that relates to him directly. No John C. Breckinridge papers for this period are among the Breckinridge family collection (Library of Congress). The voluminous Stephen A. Douglas collection (University of Chicago Library) reveals little, though there was considerable co-operation among their friends. If there was any close association between Bell and his running mate in 1860, the Edward Everett Papers (Massachusetts Historical Society) fail to reveal it.

Published Correspondence and Speeches

All writers on the Jackson period are indebted to the late John Spencer Bassett for his *Correspondence of Andrew Jackson,* 6 vols. (Washington, 1926–1935), the most important collection of his private correspondence. The work, however, is far from complete, since it does not include letters already published and since many additional letters have come to light subsequent to its publication. Other important Jackson letters were published in the *American Historical Magazine,* 9 vols. (Nashville, 1896–1904), IV, V (1899, 1900), the New York Public Library *Bulletin,* IV (1900), and in some of the earlier biographies which are mentioned in another section.

William B. Campbell was probably Bell's most intimate friend in public life. A valuable selection of Bell's letters to him, taken from the David Campbell Papers, is found in "Letters of John Bell to William B. Campbell, 1839–1857," in *Tennessee Historical Magazine,* 12 vols. (Nashville, 1915–1937), III (1917), 201–27. In the same volume (pp. 196–200) is found St. George L. Sioussat (ed.), "Correspondence of John Bell and Willie P. Mangum, 1835." These letters were taken from the Mangum papers. Also printed in this volume (pp. 51–73) is Sioussat (ed.), "Letters of James K. Polk to Andrew Jackson Donelson, 1843–1848." Other valuable Polk letters are found in Sioussat (ed.), "Letters of James K. Polk to Cave Johnson," in *Tennessee Historical Magazine,* I (1915), 209–56; Joseph H. Parks (ed.), "Letters from James K. Polk to Alfred O. P. Nicholson, 1835–49," in *Tennessee Historical Quarterly* (Nashville, 1942–), III (1944), 67–80; and *id.,* "Letters from James K. Polk to Samuel H. Laughlin, 1835–1844," in East Tennessee Historical Society's *Publications* (Knoxville, 1929–), No. 18 (1946), 147–67. The Library of Congress has recently acquired the originals of the last group from the Laughlin family. Additional letters relating to Tennessee politics of the period are found in Joseph H. Parks (ed.), "Letters from Aaron V. Brown to Alfred O. P. Nicholson, 1844–1850," and *id.,* "Some Tennessee Letters During the Polk Administration," in *Tennessee Historical Quarterly,* III (1944), 170–79; 275–81, 352–61; and Emma Inman Williams (ed.), "Letters of Adam Huntsman to James K. Polk," in *ibid.,* VI (1947), 337–69.

Valuable correspondence of a number of national figures is found in Ulrich B. Phillips (ed.), *The Correspondence of Robert*

Toombs, Alexander H. Stephens, and Howell Cobb, American Historical Association, *Annual Report,* 1911, II (Washington, 1913); Reginald C. McGrane (ed.), *The Correspondence of Nicholas Biddle Dealing with National Affairs, 1807–1844* (Boston, 1919); J. Franklin Jameson (ed.), *Correspondence of John C. Calhoun,* American Historical Association, *Annual Report,* 1899, II (Washington, 1900); Claude H. Van Tyne (ed.), *Letters of Daniel Webster* (New York, 1902); Fletcher Webster (ed.), *The Private Correspondence of Daniel Webster,* 2 vols. (Boston, 1857); and *Letters, Speeches and Addresses of August Belmont* (n.p., 1890). Of particular importance are the letters published in Mrs. Chapman Coleman, *The Life of John J. Crittenden,* 2 vols. (Philadelphia, 1871); Samuel G. Heiskell, *Andrew Jackson and Early Tennessee History,* 3 vols. (Nashville, 1921); and Nancy Scott, *A Memoir of Hugh Lawson White* (Philadelphia, 1856).

Monumental publications, essential to a study of the period but containing little material relating directly to Bell, are Dunbar Rowland (ed.), *Jefferson Davis, Constitutionalist: His Papers, Letters and Speeches,* 10 vols. (Jackson, 1923); Richard K. Crallé (ed.), *The Works of John C. Calhoun,* 6 vols. (New York, 1851–1859); Calvin Colton (ed.), *The Works of Henry Clay,* 10 vols. (New York, 1904); John Bassett Moore (ed.), *The Works of James Buchanan, Comprising his Speeches, State Papers, and Private Correspondence,* 12 vols. (Philadelphia, 1911); and *Writings and Speeches of Daniel Webster,* 18 vols. (Boston, 1903).

A few of Bell's public addresses were published in pamphlet form: *Speech of the Hon. John Bell delivered at Vauxhall Garden, Nashville, on 23rd of May, 1835* (Nashville, 1835); *An Address Delivered at Nashville, T., October 5th, 1830, Being the First Anniversary of the Alumni Society of the University of Nashville* (Nashville, 1830); *An Address Delivered before the Alumni Society of the University of Nashville, October 3, 1843* (Nashville, 1844).

Diaries, Memoirs, Reminiscences, and Autobiographies

Charles Francis Adams (ed.), *Memoirs of John Quincy Adams,* 12 vols. (Philadelphia, 1874–1877) is a storehouse of information on the period and contains numerous references to Bell. Milo M. Quaife (ed.), *The Diary of James K. Polk During His Presidency, 1845 to 1849,* 4 vols. (Chicago, 1910) is valuable for the years covered and gives the Polk version of the attempted reconciliation between himself and Bell. Allan Nevins (ed.), *The Diary of Philip Hone, 1828–1851,* 2 vols. (New York, 1927) gives an account of the 1837 Whig celebration in New York. "The Diary of Thomas Ewing, August and September, 1841," in *American Historical Review* (New York, 1895–), XVIII (1912), 97–112, contains the best account of the cabinet crisis of 1841. For events centering around the election of 1860, Howard K. Beale (ed.), *The Diary of Edward Bates, 1859–1866*, American Historical Association, *Annual Report*, 1930, IV (Washington, 1933) and Jack Allen (ed.), "The Diary of Randall William McGavock, 1852–1862" (unpublished Ph.D. thesis, Peabody College, 1941) are valuable. There is little pertinent material in Edward G. Bourne (ed.), *Diary and Correspondence of Salmon P. Chase,* American Historical Association, *Annual Report,* 1902, II (Washington, 1903).

Several reminiscences and contemporary accounts of events yield varying amounts of relevant information: Oliver P. Temple, *Notable Men of Tennessee, 1833–1875* (New York, 1912); Josephus C. Guild, *Old Times in Tennessee* (Nashville, 1878); Charles W. March, *Reminiscences of Congress* (New York, 1850); Henry A. Wise, *Seven Decades of the Union* (Philadelphia, 1881); Henry W. Hilliard, *Politics and Pen Pictures at Home and Abroad* (Atlanta, 1892); Ben Perley Poore, *Perley's Reminiscences of Sixty Years in the National Metropolis,* 2 vols. (Philadelphia, 1886); Frederick W. Seward, *Reminiscences of a War-Time Statesman and Diplomat, 1830–1915* (New York, 1916); C. W. Hall, *Three Score Years and Ten* (Cincinnati, 1884); Gaillard Hunt (ed.), *The First Forty Years of Washington Society* (New York, 1906); William G. Brownlow, *Sketches of the Rise, Progress, and Decline of Secession; with a Narrative of Personal Adventures Among the Rebels* (Philadelphia, 1862); Henry S. Foote, *War of the Rebellion; or Scylla and Charybdis* (New York, 1866); Jefferson Davis, *The Rise and Fall of the Confederate Government,* 2 vols. (New York, 1881); Alexander H. Stephens, *A Constitutional View of the Late War Between the States,* 2 vols. (Philadelphia, 1870); and Thomas Hart Benton, *Thirty Years in the United States Senate,* 2 vols. (New York, 1866). Two autobiographies should be mentioned: William Stickney (ed.), *The Autobiography of Amos Kendall* (Boston, 1872) and John C. Fitzpatrick (ed.), *The Autobiography of Martin Van Buren,* American Historical Association, *Annual Report,* 1918, II (Washington, 1920). The latter, though incomplete, is of considerable value. A few significant statements relative to Bell and the secession crisis are found in James G. Blaine, *Twenty Years in Congress,* 2 vols. (Norwich, 1884) and Horace Greeley, *The American Conflict,* 2 vols. (Hartford, 1864–1866).

Biographies

No full-length biography of Bell has heretofore been published. Probably the first biographical sketch of him to be given any extensive circulation was David W. Bartlett, *Presidential Candidates: Containing Sketches, Biographical, Personal and Political, of Prominent Candidates for the Presidency in 1860* (New York, 1859). Bell was listed among twenty-one men who were being prominently mentioned as possible candidates in 1860. The campaign biography published by Rudd and Carleton under the title of *The Life, Speeches, and Public Services of John Bell* (New York, 1860) is short and lacking in objectivity. Joshua W. Caldwell, "John Bell of Tennessee," in *American Historical Review*, IV (1899), 651–64 is a brief objective account of the high points in Bell's career. Sally Fleming Ordway, "John Bell," in *Gulf States Historical Magazine* (Montgomery, 1902–1904), II (1904), 35–44 adds little to the story. In 1930 Mark Sillers Grim wrote an acceptable master's thesis at the University of Tennesee on "The Public Career of John Bell." And in 1942, Norman L. Parks completed an excellent doctoral dissertation at Vanderbilt University on "The Career of John Bell of Tennessee in the United States House of Representatives." An abridgement of this study was published as "The Career of John Bell as Congressman from Tennessee, 1827–1841," in *Tennessee Historical Quarterly*, I (1942), 229–49.

The list of biographies of Bell's contemporaries is almost endless. Only those that were of definite assistance in the preparation of this study will be listed. Men of varying views have written lives of Andrew Jackson. James Parton, *Life of Andrew Jackson*, 3 vols. (Boston, 1866), although written from limited sources, is rich in details. Mention should also be made of William G. Sumner, *Andrew Jackson* (Boston, 1899); Arthur St. Clair Colyar, *Life and Times of Andrew Jackson*, 2 vols. (Nashville, 1904); and Samuel Gordon Heiskell, *Andrew Jackson and Early Tennessee History*, 3 vols. (Nashville, 1921). But the best biographies of Jackson are John Spencer Bassett, *The Life of Andrew Jackson*, 2 vols. (New York, 1911) and two books by Marquis James: *Andrew Jackson, The Border Captain* (Indianapolis, 1933) and *The Portrait of a President* (Indianapolis, 1937).

Two biographies of James K. Polk and Stephen A. Douglas were invaluable in the study of Bell's public life: Eugene I. McCormac, *James K. Polk, A Political Biography* (Berkeley, 1922) and George Fort Milton, *The Eve of Conflict: Stephen A. Douglas and the Needless War* (Boston, 1934). The extensive documentation in these works pointed the way to many pieces of source material.

The biographies of Henry Clay by George D. Prentice and Daniel Mallory were published too early to contain important Bell material. The first of Bernard Mayo's projected three volumes on Clay and his times ends with the War of 1812. The only Clay biographies found useful were Carl Schurz, *Henry Clay,* 2 vols. (Boston, 1887) and Glyndon G. Van Deusen, *The Life of Henry Clay* (Boston, 1937). Both are scholarly works. George Rawlings Poage, *Henry Clay and the Whig Party* (Chapel Hill, 1936) is more than a biography and is excellent for the period covered. Daniel Webster's life is adequately treated in George Ticknor Curtis, *Life of Daniel Webster,* 2 vols. (New York, 1870) and Claude Moore Fuess, *Daniel Webster,* 2 vols. (Boston, 1930). The only John C. Calhoun study found to be of value was William M. Meigs, *The Life of John Caldwell Calhoun,* 2 vols. (New York, 1917).

Other biographies utilized in varying degrees were: Oliver Perry Chitwood, *John Tyler, Champion of the Old South* (New York, 1939); Joseph Howard Parks, *Felix Grundy, Champion of Democracy* (University, La., 1940); Lyon G. Tyler, *The Letters and Times of the Tylers,* 3 vols. (Richmond, 1884–1896); Charles Winslow Elliott, *Winfield Scott, The Soldier and the Man* (New York, 1937); Ulrich B. Phillips, *The Life of Robert Toombs* (New York, 1913); John W. DuBose, *The Life and Times of William Lowndes Yancey* (Birmingham, 1892); Percy Scott Flippin, *Herschel V. Johnson of Georgia, State Rights Unionist* (Richmond, 1931); Paul R. Frothingham, *Edward Everett, Orator and Statesman* (Boston, 1925); Dorothy B. Goebel, *William Henry Harrison: A Political Biography* (Indianapolis, 1926); Glyndon G. Van Deusen, *Thurlow Weed: Wizard of the Lobby* (Boston, 1947); Roy F. Nichols, *Franklin Pierce* (Philadelphia, 1931); Rudolph von Abele, *Alexander H. Stephens* (New York, 1946); Robert M. McElroy, *Jefferson Davis, the Unreal and the Real,* 2 vols. (New York, 1937); Bernard C. Steiner, *The Life of Henry Winter Davis* (Baltimore, 1916); William Ernest Smith, *The Francis Preston Blair Family in Politics,* 2 vols. (New York, 1933); Brainerd Dyer, *Zachary Taylor* (Baton Rouge, 1946); Alexander A. Lawrence, *James Moore Wayne, Southern Unionist* (Chapel Hill, 1943); Theodore D. Jervey, *Robert Y. Hayne and His Times* (New York, 1909); Leland Winfield Meyers, *Life of Colonel Richard M. John-*

son of Kentucky (New York, 1932); W. C. Crane, *Life and Select Literary Remains of Sam Houston* (Philadelphia, 1884); Lloyd Paul Stryker, *Andrew Johnson, A Study in Courage* (New York, 1930); Robert W. Winston, *Andrew Johnson, Plebeian and Patriot* (New York, 1928); Frederic Bancroft, *The Life of William H. Seward*, 2 vols. (New York, 1900); James Vaulx Drake, *Life of General Robert Hatton* (Nashville, 1867); and L. Paul Gresham, "The Public Career of Hugh Lawson White" (Ph.D. dissertation at Vanderbilt University, 1943). The last study appeared in condensed form in the *Tennessee Historical Quarterly*, III (1944), 291–318.

Three collective biographies should also be noted: Henry S. Foote, *The Bench and Bar of the South and Southwest* (St. Louis, 1876); Joshua W. Caldwell, *Sketches of the Bench and Bar of Tennessee* (Knoxville, 1898); and Allan Johnson and Dumas Malone (eds.), *The Dictionary of American Biography*, 20 vols. (New York, 1928–1937).

A few works proved useful for genealogical material: John V. Stephens, *Biographical Sketch of the Late Rev. Claiborn H. Bell* (Lebanon, Tenn., 1909); Richard Beard, *Brief Biographical Sketches of Early Ministers of the Cumberland Presbyterian Church* (Nashville, 1874); and Janie Preston Collop French and Zella Armstrong (comps.), *The Crockett Family and Connecting Lines* (Bristol, Tenn., 1928).

Histories and Monographs

A number of state and local histories of Tennessee are worthy of mention as furnishing background material. W. Woodford Clayton, *History of Davidson County, Tennessee* (Philadelphia, 1880); John Woolridge, *History of Nashville, Tennessee* (Nashville, 1890); Goodspeed Company (Pub.), *History of Tennessee* (Nashville, 1886); James Phelan, *History of Tennessee* (Boston, 1888); Albigence Waldo Putnam, *History of Middle Tennessee or Life and Times of General James Robertson* (Nashville, 1859); John Trotwood Moore and Austin P. Foster, *Tennessee, The Volunteer State*, 4 vols. (Nashville, 1923); Philip M. Hamer, *Tennessee: A History, 1673–1932*, 4 vols. (New York, 1933); Thomas Perkins Abernethy, *From Frontier to Plantation in Tennessee; A Study in Frontier Democracy* (Chapel Hill, 1932); Charles A. Miller, *Official Manual of Tennessee* (Nashville, 1890); Gerald M. Capers, Jr., *The Biography of A River Town, Memphis: Its Heroic Age* (Chapel Hill, 1939); and Emma Inman Williams, *Historic Madison: The Story of Jackson and Madison County, Tennessee* (Jackson, 1946). The last of this group has valuable material in the Appendix.

No attempt will be made to list the general histories covering all or a portion of the ante-bellum period, but special mention should be made of William MacDonald, *Jacksonian Democracy* (New York, 1906); Claude G. Bowers, *Party Battles of the Jackson Period* (Boston, 1928); William O. Lynch, *Fifty Years of Party Warfare* (Indianapolis, 1931); Hugh Russell Fraser, *Democracy in the Making, The Jackson-Tyler Era* (New York, 1938); Frederick Jackson Turner, *The United States, 1830–1850* (New York, 1935); Allan Nevins, *Ordeal of the Union*, 2 vols. (New York, 1947); and Roy F. Nichols, *The Disruption of American Democracy* (New York, 1948).

There is an abundance of monographic studies covering practically every phase of ante-bellum history. Most important for the study of the problems of the Jackson period are E. Malcolm Carroll, *Origins of the Whig Party* (Durham, 1925); Ralph C. H. Catterall, *The Second Bank of the United States* (Chicago, 1903); Edward G. Bourne, *History of the Surplus Revenue of 1837* (New York, 1885); Reginald C. McGrane, *The Panic of 1837: Some Financial Problems of the Jackson Era* (Chicago, 1924); David Kinley, *The Independent Treasury of the United States and Its Relations to the Banks of the Country* (Washington, 1910); Grant Foreman, *Indian Removal; the Emigration of the Five Civilized Tribes of Indians* (Norman, 1932); Roy M. Robbins, *Our Landed Heritage: The Public Domain, 1776–1936* (Princeton, 1942); Benjamin H. Hibbard, *A History of the Public Land Policies* (New York, 1924); Raynor Greenleaf Wellington, *Political and Sectional Influence of the Public Lands, 1828–1842* (Cambridge, 1914); David F. Houston, *A Critical Study of Nullification in South Carolina* (New York, 1896); Chauncey S. Boucher, *The Nullification Controversy in South Carolina* (Chicago, 1916); Frederic Bancroft, *Calhoun and the South Carolina Nullification Movement* (Baltimore, 1928); and Richard R. Stenberg, "The Jefferson Birthday Dinner, 1830," in *Journal of Southern History* (Baton Rouge, 1935–1941; Nashville, 1941–), IV (1938), 334–45.

Articles having a direct bearing upon Tennessee politics during this period are Albert V. Goodpasture, "John Bell's Political Revolt and His Vauxhall Garden Speech," in *Tennessee Historical Magazine,* II (1916), 254–63; Thomas Perkins Abernethy, "Origins of the Whig Party in Tennessee," in *Mississippi Valley His-*

torical Review (Cedar Rapids, 1914–), XII (1925–1926), 502–22; St. George L. Sioussat, "Some Phases of Tennessee Politics in the Jackson Period," in *American Historical Review,* XIV (1908), 51–69; Thomas Perkins Abernethy, "Andrew Jackson and the Rise of Southwestern Democracy," in *ibid.,* XXXIII (1927), 64–77; Powell Moore, "The Political Background of the Revolt Against Jackson in Tennessee," in East Tennessee Historical Society's *Publications,* No. 4 (1932), 45–66; *id.,* "The Revolt Against Jackson in Tennessee, 1835–1836," in *Journal of Southern History,* II (1936), 335–59; *id.,* "James K. Polk and Tennessee Politics, 1839–1841," in East Tennessee Historical Society's *Publications,* No. 9 (1937), 31–52; *id.,* "James K. Polk and the 'Immortal Thirteen,'" in *ibid.,* No. 11 (1939), 20–33; Thomas B. Alexander, "The Presidential Campaign of 1840 in Tennessee," in *Tennessee Historical Quarterly,* I (1942), 21–43.

The national issues of the 1840's and 1850's are dealt with in Dallas Tabor Herndon, "The Nashville Convention of 1850," in Alabama Historical Society's *Transactions* (Montgomery, 1897–1904), V (1904), 203–37; St. George L. Sioussat, "Tennessee, the Compromise of 1850, and the Nashville Convention," in *Mississippi Valley Historical Review,* II (1915), 313–47; *id.,* "Tennessee and National Politics, 1850–1860," in American Historical Association, *Annual Report,* 1914, I (Washington, 1916), 245–58; Ulrich B. Phillips, "The Southern Whigs, 1834–1854," in *Turner Essays in American History* (New York, 1910); William C. Binkley, *The Expansionist Movement in Texas, 1836–1850* (Berkeley, 1925); *id.,* "The Question of Texan Jurisdiction in New Mexico under the United States, 1848–1850," in *Southwestern Historical Quarterly,* XXIV (1920–1921); Frank H. Hodder, "The Authorship of the Compromise of 1850," in *Mississippi Valley Historical Review,* XXII (1935–1936), 525–36; Mrs. Archibald Dixon, *The True History of the Missouri Compromise and Its Repeal* (Cincinnati, 1899); Frank H. Hodder, "Genesis of the Kansas Nebraska Act," *Proceedings* of the Wisconsin Historical Society, 1912, pp. 69–86; *id.,* "The Railroad Background of the Kansas-Nebraska Act," in *Mississippi Valley Historical Review,* XII (1925), 3–22; P. Orman Ray, *The Repeal of the Missouri Compromise: Its Origin and Authorship* (Cleveland, 1909); Joseph H. Parks, "The Tennessee Whigs and the Kansas-Nebraska Bill," in *Journal of Southern History,* X (1944), 308–30; Arthur C. Cole, "The South and the Right of Secession in the Early Fifties," in *Mississippi Valley Historical Review,* I (1914), 376–99; *id., The Whig Party in the South*

(Washington, 1913); Joseph Hodgson, *The Cradle of the Confederacy or the Times of Troup, Quitman and Yancey* (Mobile, 1876).

A number of important studies deal with the campaign of 1860 and the secession which followed: Emerson D. Fite, *The Presidential Campaign of 1860* (New York, 1911); Murat Halstead, *National Political Conventions of the Current Presidential Campaign* (Columbus, 1860); Horace Greeley and John F. Cleveland, *Political Text-Book for 1860* (New York, 1860); Ollinger Crenshaw, *The Slave States in the Presidential Election of 1860* (Baltimore, 1945); *id.*, "Urban and Rural Voting in the Election of 1860," in Eric F. Goldman (ed.), *Historiography and Urbanization: Essays in American History in Honor of W. Stull Holt* (Baltimore, 1941); *id.*, "The Psychological Background of the Election of 1860 in the South," in *North Carolina Historical Review* (Raleigh, 1924–), XIX (1942), 260–79; Margaret B. Hamer, "The Presidential Campaign of 1860 in Tennessee," in East Tennessee Historical Society's *Publications,* No. 3 (1931), 3–22; Charles F. Richardson, "The Constitutional Union Party of 1860," in *Yale Review* (New Haven, 1892–), III (1894); Reinhard H. Luthin, *The First Lincoln Campaign* (Cambridge, 1944); James S. Pike, *First Blows of the Civil War* (New York, 1879); Dwight L. Dumond, *The Secession Movement, 1860–1861* (New York, 1931); James Walter Fertig, *The Secession and Reconstruction of Tennessee* (Chicago, 1898); David Potter, *Lincoln and His Party in the Secession Crisis* (New Haven, 1942); James W. Patton, *Unionism and Reconstruction in Tennessee* (Chapel Hill, 1934); Thomas Humes, *The Loyal Mountaineers of Tennessee* (Knoxville, 1888); Oliver P. Temple, *East Tennessee and the Civil War* (Cincinnati, 1899). In the interest of brevity, special studies on secession in states other than Tennessee are omitted.

Several contemporary pamphlets dealing with Bell's political career should also be noted. *A Looking Glass for the Federal Whig Leaders in Tennessee, or Facts for the People,* as its title implies, is an anti-Whig publication dealing rather severely with Bell and his associates. The title page is missing from the copy located; therefore, the place and exact date of publication are uncertain. It was probably published during the Polk-Cannon campaign of 1839. *John Bell: His 'Past History Connected with the Public Service'* (Nashville, 1860), published by the Breckinridge Democrats, was a violent attack upon Bell's public record from 1827 to 1860. *The Public Record and Past History of John Bell & Edw'd*

Everett (Washington, 1860), brought out by the Breckinridge national committee, carried the attack throughout the Union. *John Bell's Record* (Washington, 1860) was an attempt on the part of Bell's friends to present him in most favorable light.

Contemporary Newspapers

At the time of Bell's entrance into national politics the more prominent Tennessee newspapers were actively supporting Andrew Jackson for the presidency. Most important among the Nashville newspapers were the *National Banner and Nashville Whig* and the Nashville *Republican and State Gazette*. The first of these was both a weekly and a daily publication. In 1832 the daily became the *National Banner and Daily Advertiser*. The *Republican and State Gazette* continued publication until 1837 when it combined with the *Banner* to form the *Republican Banner*. Both of the above-mentioned newspapers passed under the control of Bell and his associates at the time of his break with the Jackson party. The supporters of Van Buren for the presidency then found it necessary to establish a new Democratic organ, the Nashville *Union,* in 1835.

The *Republican Banner,* under varying titles, continued publication until 1875. The *Union* later combined with the Nashville *American* and also continued publication until 1875. Other Nashville newspapers of lesser importance were the *True Whig* (1838–1855), *Daily News* (1857–1860), *Patriot* (1855–1862), and *Politician and Weekly Nashville Whig* (1845–1852). There were many variations in titles.

The files of most other Tennessee newspapers for this period are badly broken. An exception is the Jonesborough *Whig,* edited by William G. Brownlow during the 1840's. After the election of Zachary Taylor, he moved to Knoxville and changed the name of his paper to *Brownlow's Knoxville Whig.* This publication continued until the Civil War and was later resumed under a modified title. The files of the Knoxville *Register* (1816–1863), the Knoxville *Tribune* (1846–1860), and the Knoxville *Post* (1841–1848) are so incomplete as to make them almost valueless. On the other hand, the files of several Memphis newspapers are sufficiently full to be of considerable assistance. Chief among them are the *Eagle* (1842–1861), *Enquirer (1836–1861)*, *Argus* (1859–1866), *Bulletin* (1862–1865), *Avalanche* (1858–1866), and *Appeal* (1849–). The only Chattanooga newspaper used was the *Gazette,* and its broken files yielded little. A few scattered issues of publications

SAY ON AUTHORITIES 421

from other Tennessee towns were found useful: McMinnville *Central Gazette*, Murfreesboro *Central Monitor*, Athens *Post-Athenian*, Randolph *Recorder*, Somerville *Reporter*, Elizabethton *Tennessee Whig*, Franklin *Western Weekly Review*, and Paris *West Tennessean*.

The greatest storehouse of information during the period covered is the files of *Niles' National Register*, 76 vols. (Baltimore, 1811–1849). Hezekiah Niles was an anti-Jackson man in politics, but his paper did not reflect bitter partisanship. By publishing many items from local presses he gave his readers a fair cross section of what was going on throughout the nation. Shortly before Bell entered national politics, Duff Green became the editor of the *United States Telegraph* (1826–1837), a new Jackson organ in Washington. Green and Jackson soon parted company, and Francis P. Blair's Washington *Globe* (1830–1845) became the chief Democratic organ. But Bell and Green remained friends. The *Globe* was the most widely copied Democratic newspaper of its day. After the break between Bell and the Jackson party became complete, the *Globe* was Bell's most aggressive prosecutor; and its attacks were copied in the columns of a host of other Democratic papers.

A more moderate publication, usually supporting the Whig cause but never violent, was the *National Intelligencer* (1813–1869). Its support of Bell over a long period of years was probably the most consistent of any national newspaper. Other Washington publications of importance were the *Evening Star* (1853–1867), *Daily Republican* (1849–1853), *Union* (1845–1859), and *Madisonian* (1837–1845).

The files of a few newspapers of other important cities yielded information on special points. The New York *Daily Express* (1836–1843) and the Boston *Daily Advertiser* (1813–1929) gave accounts of Bell's eastern tour in 1837. The Philadelphia *North American and United States Gazette* (1847–1876) was friendly to Bell for many years but deserted him for the Republican cause in 1860. The New York *Tribune* (1842–1924), *Times* (1851–) and *Herald* (1835–1924) were valuable for the campaign of 1860. The same was true of the Baltimore *Clipper* (1839–1865), Richmond *Whig* (1824–1888), Baltimore *American* (1799–), Newark *Evening Journal* (1857–1895), Trenton *True American* (1849–1913) and *State Gazette* (1829–1913). The *American Whig Review* (New York, 1845–1852) is disappointing. It contains nothing of importance on Bell.

Government Documents: Local, State, and National

Much information on Bell and his family connections is found in the manuscript records of marriages, deeds and inventories, and court minutes of Davidson, Williamson, Rutherford, and Stewart counties, Tennessee, and in the conveyance records of Caddo Parish, Louisiana.

The Tennessee *Journal of the House of Representatives* and *Journal of the Senate* are important for Bell's brief terms in the assembly and for the several legislative fights over presidential nominations and the elections of senators.

The *Register of Debates,* 14 vols. (Washington, 1824–1837) gave verbatim reports of the important debates in both houses of Congress. Beginning with 1833 and continuing through 1873, the debates were also recorded in the *Congressional Globe,* 46 vols. (Washington, 1834–1873). Presidential messages to Congress are found in James D. Richardson (ed.), *A Compilation of the Messages and Papers of the Presidents,* 20 vols. (New York, 1897).

A few references to Bell during the Civil War are found in *The War of the Rebellion: A Compilation of the Official Records of the Union and Confederate Armies,* 128 vols. (Washington, 1880–1901).

INDEX